The Economics of Risk and Insurance

To my family

부모님과 가족에게 바칩니다.

The Economics of Risk and Insurance

S. Hun Seog

A John Wiley & Sons, Ltd., Publication

Registered Office
John Wiley & Sons Ltd, The Atrium, Southern Gate, Chichester, West Sussex, PO19 8SQ, United Kingdom

Editorial Offices
350 Main Street, Malden, MA 02148-5020, USA
9600 Garsington Road, Oxford, OX4 2DQ, UK
The Atrium, Southern Gate, Chichester, West Sussex, PO19 8SQ, UK

For details of our global editorial offices, for customer services, and for information about how to apply for permission to reuse the copyright material in this book please see our website at www.wiley.com/wiley-blackwell.

Library of Congress Cataloging-in-Publication Data

Seog, S. Hun.
  The economics of risk and insurance / S. Hun Seog.
    p. cm.
  Includes bibliographical references and index.
  ISBN 978-1-4051-8552-3 (hardcover : alk. paper) 1. Risk (Insurance)   I. Title.
  HG8054.5.S46 2010
  368–dc22
                                                    2009021976

A catalogue record for this book is available from the British Library.

Set in Times Roman 11/13pt by SPi Publisher Services, Pondicherry, India
Printed and bound in Singapore by Fabulous Printers Pte Ltd

001   2010

Contents

Preface

This book has been written to cover advanced issues in the study of the economics of risk and insurance. While there are several introductory undergraduate textbooks on risk and insurance, it is difficult to find textbooks geared towards higher-level studies. This book has been written to fill this gap.

This book, however, is not intended to cover all risk and insurance issues. Insurance is an interdisciplinary area which encompasses economics, finance, and actuarial science. As such, it is not easy to cover all the relevant issues in a single book. The main focus of this book is on the economic theory of risk and insurance and the industrial organization of insurance markets. I hope it will of interest to researchers in risk and insurance; graduate or doctoral students in risk and insurance, economics, and finance; and undergraduate or MBA students interested in advanced issues in risk and insurance,

This book is based on my lecture notes for the introductory doctoral courses in risk and insurance. In writing this book, I have tried to achieve the following aims:

1　To introduce and summarize important academic results.
2　To make results as comparable as possible. Academic papers derive their results based on different assumptions and notations, which makes it difficult to compare results from different papers. Making results comparable is important in understanding the bigger picture.
3　To enhance understandability. Academic results are often derived using complicated mathematical and statistical techniques. Such complication may hinder a reader from capturing the intuitions and economic rationales behind the results. To enhance understandability, this book reduces

the mathematical complications and includes intuitive explanations and graphical illustrations.

4   To maintain a minimum level of rigor for logical inferences, despite (3).

This book can be used as a textbook or a reference for advanced or graduate courses in risk and insurance. Half of the chapters may be taught in one semester, if the lecturer also uses supplementary readings. For example, Chapters 1–10 can be covered in a course on the economic theory of risk and insurance, while Chapters 11–15 can be covered in a course on the industrial organizations in insurance markets. Alternatively, the entire book may be covered in one semester, possibly with some omissions.

I am indebted to many people. First, I wish to thank those who taught me insurance: Neil Doherty, David Cummins, Sharon Tennyson, and Patricia Danzon, among others. I am also grateful for the help of a number of students at KAIST, Jong-Woon Hong, Hae Won Jung, Chang Mo Kang, Dong-Woo Lee, Kwon Tahk Lee, Sunae Lee, and Sung-won Seo. I would like to thank John Bizjak, Scott Dawson, Scott Marshall, and the School of Business Administration at Portland State University for graciously hosting me during the period in which this book was written. I also thank George Lobell and Laura Stearns for their help in publishing this book with Wiley-Blackwell. Finally, I thank my parents and family for their love.

S. Hun Seog
Graduate School of Business
Seoul National University
Seoul, Korea

Introduction

Uncertainty is an important theme in modern economics. The economics of risk and insurance is focused on the behavior of economic agents facing uncertainty or risks. This book is composed of five parts.

Part I introduces economic tools and principles regarding uncertainty and insurance. A fundamental tool for the analysis of uncertainty is the expected utility theory (Chapter 1). While the expected utility theory is based on strict assumptions on preferences, the main reason for its usefulness is its mathematical tractability. After introducing the theory, we further study risk preference and the riskiness of a project (Chapter 2), including risk premium, the risk aversion measure of Arrow and Pratt, and first-order and second-order stochastic dominance. Even though we develop those concepts based on the expected utility, it is important to note that risk preference and riskiness may be studied without reference to expected utility.

Given that economic agents generally dislike risks, it is natural that society has developed diverse risk sharing institutions. The purpose of insurance is explicitly to implement risk sharing. Insurance is socially desirable since it allows agents to share risks in an efficient way. There are three basic channels through which insurance enhances social welfare: the risk transfer principle, the mutuality principle, and the law of large numbers (Chapter 3). These principles imply that risks need to be pooled and/ or be transferred to less risk averse agents.

After studying economic tools and principles, we move on to specific issues in insurance. Part II focuses on insurance demand and insurance contracts. In the insurance market, insurers assume the risks of insureds in exchange for premiums. An insurance contract is composed of the premium and the benefit payment scheme. Finding optimal insurance contracts is important, since risk sharing is implemented through insurance contracts. Generally, individual insureds purchase insurance because they do not like risks (Chapter 4). As long as insureds dislike risks, it should be optimal to transfer all the risks to the insurers (assumed to be risk neutral). However, if transaction costs should occur in the insurance contract, partial insurance may be optimal. Two important forms of partial insurance are deductible insurance and coinsurance, whose optimality has been intensively studied in literature.

On the other hand, large corporations also purchase insurance (Chapter 5). Since owners of such corporations can easily diversify risks in the financial market, risk aversion does not seem sufficient to justify the demand for insurance. Various rationales for corporate demand for insurance include tax savings, efficient risk sharing, information problems, and strategic concern. Insurance turns out to resolve diverse problems among stakeholders of corporations.

Liability insurance is distinguished from first-party insurance in that it covers third-party loss (Chapter 6). Since liability is determined based on legal rules, understanding liability rules is important. Two basic liability rules are the strict rule and the negligence rule. Moral hazard is an important issue, since, without proper allocation of liability, injurers may not exert enough efforts to prevent injury. A socially desirable liability rule will minimize the moral hazard costs. Since liability insurance aims to cover liability, it is possible that insurance lowers the incentives to exert efforts. Therefore, whether or not insurance enhances efficiency depends on the insurer's controllability of moral hazard.

Part III is devoted to information issues in insurance contracts. An information asymmetry problem occurs when one party to a contract knows information that the other party does not know. Adverse selection and moral hazard are referred to as cases in which the information is about type and about action, respectively. In Rothschild and Stiglitz (1976), contracts are designed to maximize insureds' expected utilities, while minimizing adverse selection costs. However, the result is not satisfactory, since an equilibrium may not exist, or may not be efficient even if it exists. Since Rothschild and Stiglitz, several modified models have been proposed, based on different equilibrium concepts regarding the subsidy between contracts and conjectures of insurers (Chapter 7). The Rothschild and Stiglitz model is further extended to consider diverse cases, such as multi-period models, classification models, information acquisition, and multiple adverse selection models (Chapter 8).

Moral hazard is another important information issue in insurance. Risk transfer lowers the insured's incentives to prevent a loss (Chapter 9). This incentive problem incurs moral hazard costs. An optimally designed contract needs to take into account the tradeoff between moral hazard and risk sharing. Another form of moral hazard is fraud, i.e., reporting false losses (Chapter 10). Fraud is possible because the insurer cannot observe the true loss. Given that the insurer can observe the true loss by incurring some monitoring costs, the issue becomes how to incorporate monitoring into the contract design.

Part IV concerns the supply-side structure of the insurance market. Insurers have diverse organizational forms (Chapter 11). Prominent structures include Lloyd's, stock companies, and mutual companies. Each structure has comparative advantages over other structures in different cases, which explains the coexistence of diverse structures.

Competition in the insurance market is characterized by imperfect information (Chapter 12). Important insurer-sided imperfect information problems include adverse selection and moral hazard, which are studied in Part III. Insureds are also uninformed about insurance contracts. The insured-sided imperfect information also leads to inefficient outcomes in the market. For example, competition does not guarantee the zero profit of a firm, nor maximize the consumer's surplus. As a result, prices and qualities of insurance goods can be dispersed in an equilibrium.

Imperfect information is also related to the insurance cycle (Chapter 13). Under perfect information, insurance prices do not need to fluctuate unless fundamental factors such as discount rate and loss distribution are changed. Due to imperfect information, investors in the financial market may not want to provide capital to insurers, and/or insureds may over- or underestimate risks, following insurance events. These diverse factors contribute to the insurance cycle.

Part V focuses on the management of insurers. Marketing management of insurers is one of the key elements in operation (Chapter 14). Insurance goods are sold directly by insurers, or indirectly through intermediaries. Since insurance goods are exposed to information imperfection as discussed above, it is not surprising that intermediaries play an important role in the market. Intermediaries are information providers and render matching services between insurers and insureds. However, the existence of intermediaries does not completely remove the information problem, simply because information is imperfect. Thus, how to improve efficiency in the intermediary's market becomes another issue.

Determining the right prices is obviously important to market participants (Chapter 15). Difficulty in insurance pricing comes from the fact that true costs are uncertain at the time of sale. A correct price should be determined based on the future distribution of costs. Actuarial science has developed tools to estimate the distribution of costs. On the other hand, discounting is also important because of the time lag between premium reception and loss incurrence. Methodologies to reflect risk and time to pricing and discount factors have been developed in financial asset pricing theories. Understanding both actuarial science and asset pricing will provide useful tools in insurance pricing.

In the Appendix to this book, we briefly outline the techniques for solving the constrained optimization problem, which will be useful in later chapters. Readers who are not familiar with the techniques are referred to the Appendix.

BIBLIOGRAPHY

Rothschild, M. and Stiglitz, J. E. (1976), Equilibrium in competitive insurance markets: an essay on the economics of imperfect information. *Quarterly Journal of Economics*, 90: 629–50.

Part I

Fundamentals of Insurance

Chapter 1

Risk and Expected Utility

Although it is not easy to clearly define risk, it is often defined as uncertainty regarding which outcome will occur. We adopt this definition in general. Economists are mainly concerned with risks that can be described in terms of probability distributions. Given that, risk will be identified with a random variable or its probability distribution throughout this book. This book is concerned with the economic analysis of how risks affect individual, organizational, and social behavior, and vice versa. As a basis for the analysis, we investigate the expected utility theory and the measurement of risks. The expected utility theory provides the basis for most economic and financial analyses of individual decision making under risk. We study the usefulness and weaknesses of the expected utility theory in this chapter. The issues related to risk aversion and the measurement of the riskiness of a project will be studied in the next chapter. We start with utility representation (Section 1.1) and develop the expected utility theory (Section 1.2). Section 1.3 discusses some problems with expected utility.

1.1 Utility Representation

Let us first briefly review the utility theory under certainty. An individual's consumption of goods is determined by his or her preferences. Preferring (consumption of) good A to (consumption of) good B implies that A provides higher satisfaction than B. However, since the notion of preference is rather vague and qualitative in general, it is not easy to work with it directly. Economists have tried to transform preference into more easily manageable measures, one of which is utility. Utility is a mapping

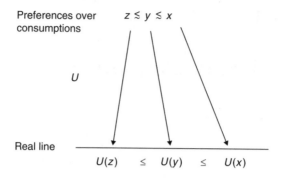

Figure 1.1   Utility representation.

from preferences over consumptions to real numbers which can be math-ematically manipulated (see Figure 1.1). Since preference, in general, does not comply with the operation rules of real numbers, the utility theory can be only applied to a subset of possible preferences. The so-called axio-matic utility theory describes the set of preferences to which the utility theory can be applied.

Let us write $\gtrsim$ for the preference relation of an individual for the consumption set of goods, S. For x, y in S, $x \gtrsim y$ implies that the individual (weakly) prefers x to y. Strict preference and indifference will be denoted by $>$ and $\sim$, respectively. Let us first state the definition of utility representation.

Definition 1.1 (Utility representation).

A function $U(.)$ from S to R (the real numbers) represents the preference relation $\gtrsim$, if $x \gtrsim y \Leftrightarrow U(x) \geq U(y)$.

Now consider the following axioms.

Axiom U1 (Completeness). For all x, y in S, $x \gtrsim y$ or $y \gtrsim x$ (or both).

Axiom U2 (Transitivity). For all x, y, z in S, if $x \gtrsim y$ and $y \gtrsim z$ then $x \gtrsim z$.

Axiom U3 (Continuity). For any sequence of pairs such that $\{(x^n, y^n)\}_{n=1}^{\infty}$ with $x^n \gtrsim y^n$ for all n, and $\lim x^n = x$ and $\lim y^n = y$, we have that $x \gtrsim y$.

Axioms U1 and U2 imply that all goods should be pairwise comparable and can be ranked based on preference. Axiom U3 requires that preference should not suddenly change. The preference is called rational if it satisfies Axioms U1 and U2.

The so-called lexicographic preference exemplifies that Axioms U1 and U2 alone are not enough for utility representation. Lexicographic preference is defined as follows: For $S = R^2$, $x \gtrsim y$ if and only if (i) $x_1 > y_1$, or (ii) $x_2 \geq y_2$

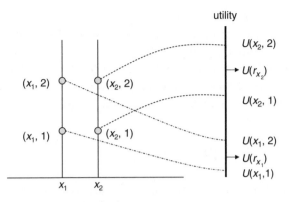

Figure 1.2   Lexicographic preference and utility.

and $x_1 = y_1$. In other words, the first elements have absolute priority in preference. The second elements become important only if the first elements result in a tie. It is easy to see that lexicographic preference satisfies Axioms U1 and U2, thus is rational. However, it cannot be represented by a utility.

Lemma 1.1

(a)   Lexicographic preference does not have a utility representation.
(b)   Lexicographic preference is not continuous.

Proof
(a)   Suppose the contrary. If a utility $U(.)$ exists, then $U(x_1, 2) > U(x_1, 1)$ for any real number x_1. Since the set of rational numbers is dense, there exists a rational number between two different real numbers (see Figure 1.2). Let us take any rational number $r(x_1)$ such that $U(x_1, 2) > r(x_1) > U(x_1, 1)$. Note that for different x_1, a different $r(x_1)$ is allocated. However, one-to-one mapping between real numbers and rational numbers is not possible, since the number of real numbers is uncountable while the number of rational numbers is countable. A contradiction.
(b)   Let $x^n = (1/n, 0)$, $y^n = (0, 1)$. Then $x = \lim x^n = (0, 0)$, $y = \lim y^n = (0, 1)$. For every n, $x^n \succsim y^n$. However, $y \succ x$.   □

Proposition 1.1   (Existence of utility). If a preference satisfies Axioms U1–U3, then there is a continuous utility function that represents the preference.

Proof.   See Mas-Colell, Whinston, and Green (1995).   □

Intuitively, Axioms U1–U3 require preference to behave like real numbers. Note that the real numbers satisfy all the axioms, once $\succsim$ is replaced with $\geq$. Since a utility is a mapping from preference to real numbers, it is not surprising that preference behaving like real numbers will have a utility representation. With the utility function, it is now convenient to analyze the individual's decision making problem. An individual's problem is generally expressed as a utility maximization problem with some constraints, which can be solved by mathematical optimization techniques (see Appendix).

1.2   Expected Utility Theory

We now turn to the utility representation under risk. It is important to note that we are only concerned with risks that can be identified with a random variable or its probability distribution. As in the certainty case, it will be convenient to express an individual's problem under risk as a maximization problem that can be easily manipulated. One convenient way to do so is to apply the average concept to utility. The expected utility theory allows the expected value of utility to represent preference under risk.

While the expected utility is a simple application of statistical concepts to the utility theory, the preference of an individual does not have to comply with the statistical operations. As a result, the application of the expected utility theory can be applied to a subset of preferences.

The expected utility theory can be easily understood by considering preferences over lotteries of a gamble. Suppose that there are n possible payoffs $(x_1, \ldots, x_n)$. A *lottery* L is an ordered n-tuple of probabilities for payoffs, $L = (p_1, \ldots, p_n)$, where p_i is the probability that the payoff x_i is earned and $\Sigma p_i = 1$. Similar to the utility under certainty, the expected utility is a mapping from the preferences over the lotteries to real numbers which can be mathematically manipulated (see Figure 1.3).

Now consider an individual who enters into another gamble in which he earns a lottery of the original gamble. This setting is equivalent to the case in which the individual joins a compound gamble as follows. In this compound gamble, a *compound lottery* is defined as an ordered collection of probabilities of earning lotteries, $L' = (L_1, \ldots, L_K; q_1, \ldots, q_K)$, where L_k is a lottery such that $L_k = (p_1^k, \ldots, p_n^k)$, q_k is the probability that the lottery L_k is earned, and $\Sigma q_k = 1$. It is easy to see that the compound lottery can be expressed as a linear combination of lotteries: $L' = q_1 L_1 + \ldots + q_K L_K$. Thus a compound lottery is equivalent to a lottery $(p_1', \ldots, p_n')$ where $p_i' = \sum_k q_k p_i^k$.

A *basis lottery* L^i is defined as a lottery in which the ith probability is 1 and all others are zero: $L^i = (0, \ldots, p_i = 1, \ldots, 0)$, for $1 \leq i \leq n$. A basis lottery represents a payoff under certainty. Now, any lottery can be expressed as a compound lottery of basis lotteries: $L = (p_1, \ldots, p_n) = p_1 L^1 + \ldots + p_n L^n$.

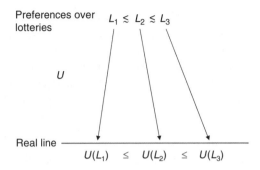

Preferences over lotteries $L_1 \lesssim L_2 \lesssim L_3$

U

Real line

$U(L_1) \quad \le \quad U(L_2) \quad \le \quad U(L_3)$

Figure 1.3   Expected utility representation.

Let us write $\gtrsim$ for the preference relation of an individual on the set of lotteries Λ. For L, L' in Λ, $L \gtrsim L'$ implies that the individual prefers (weakly) L to L'. Strict preference will be denoted by $>$. Like the utility theory under certainty, the expected utility theory requires several restrictions on preference.

Axiom 1 (Completeness). For all L, L' in Λ, $L \gtrsim L'$ or $L' \gtrsim L$.

Axiom 2 (Transitivity). For all L, L', L'' in Λ, if $L \gtrsim L'$ and $L' \gtrsim L''$ then $L \gtrsim L''$.

Axiom 3 (Continuity). For any sequence of pairs, $\{(L^n, L'^n)\}_{n=1}$ with $L^n \gtrsim L'^n$ for all n, $L = \lim L^n$ and $L' = \lim L'^n$, we have $L \gtrsim L'$.

Axiom 4 (Independence). For all L, L', L'' in Λ and $0 < \alpha < 1$, $L \gtrsim L'$ if and only if $\alpha L + (1 - \alpha)L'' \gtrsim \alpha L' + (1 - \alpha)L''$.

Axioms 1–3 are counterparts of Axioms U1–U3 of the utility theory under certainty. In addition, the expected utility theory requires Axiom 4. The independence axiom implies that if the individual prefers L to L', then such a preference should not be changed when each lottery is combined with another lottery. This axiom imposes a strong restriction on preference to prevent some undesirable results of the expected utility.

Definition 1.2 (Expected utility representation). A utility function $U : \Lambda \rightarrow R$ is called an expected utility if there is an n-tuple of real numbers $(u_1, \ldots, u_n)$ such that, for all $L = (p_1, \ldots, p_n)$ in Λ, $U(L) = p_1 u_1 + \ldots + p_n u_n$.

Note that the utility of a basis lottery L^i is u_i: $U(L^i) = u_i$. Since any lottery can be expressed as a linear combination of basis lotteries, the expected utility transforms a linear combination of basis lotteries to a linear combination of utilities of basis lotteries: $U(L) = U(p_1 L^1 + \ldots + p_n L^n) = \Sigma p_i\, U(L^i)$. Note that the expected utility is expressed as an expected value of utilities over outcomes. Indeed, the expected utility is conventionally expressed as $EU(W)$, where W is a random variable, usually representing wealth: $EU(W) = \Sigma p_i U(W_i)$, where $U(.)$ is called a von Neumann–Morgenstern utility. The following lemma shows that a utility is an expected utility if and only if it is linear.

Lemma 1.2 (Linearity). A utility U is an expected utility if and only if it is linear: $U(a_1 L_1 + \ldots + a_K L_K) = a_1 U(L_1) + \ldots + a_K U(L_K)$, where $\Sigma_{k=1}^{K} a_k = 1$, and $a_k \geq 0$ for all k.

Proof. ($\Leftarrow$) Since a lottery can be expressed as a compound lottery of basis lotteries $\{L^i\}$, we may put $L = (p_1, \ldots, p_n) = \Sigma p_i L^i$. Under linearity, $U(L) = \Sigma\, p_i U(L^i) = \Sigma\, p_i u_i$.

($\Rightarrow$) Consider a linear combination of two lotteries L and L', $aL + bL'$, where $a + b = 1$. It suffices to show that $U(aL + bL') = aU(L) + bU(L')$ for an expected utility U. Using basis lotteries, we can express each lottery as a linear combination of basis lotteries: $L = \Sigma p_i L^i$ and $L' = \Sigma q_i L^i$. Therefore, $aL + bL' = \Sigma_i (ap_i + bq_i)L^i$. Then we have $U(aL + bL') = \Sigma_i\, (ap_i + bq_i)u_i = a\Sigma_i p_i\, u_i + b\Sigma_i\, q_i u_i = aU(L) + bU(L')$. ☐

The linearity property of the expected utility is not surprising, once it is observed that the expectation operator is linear, and that the expected utility is expressed as an expected value of utilities. Now, we are ready to show that there is an expected utility for a preference that satisfies Axioms 1–4.

Proposition 1.2 (Existence of expected utility). Suppose that preference $\succsim$ satisfies Axioms 1–4. Then there exists an expected utility $U(.)$ representing the preference. In other words, for $L = (p_1, \ldots, p_n)$ and $L = (p'_1, \ldots, p'_n)$, $L \succsim L'$ if and only if $U(L) \geq U(L')$.

Proof. Let us consider only the bounded case in which there exist lotteries T and D such that $T \succsim L \succsim D$ for every lottery L (see Figure 1.4). Our task is to express the lottery L as $aT + (1 - a)D$, where a is a number. The number a will be assigned as the utility of the lottery. The proof is composed of four steps.

First, note that if $L \succ L'$ and $a \in (0, 1)$, then $L \succ aL + (1 - a)L' \succ L'$. For, from the independence axiom (Axiom 4), $L = aL + (1 - a)L \succ aL + (1 - a)L' \succ aL' + (1 - a)L' = L'$.

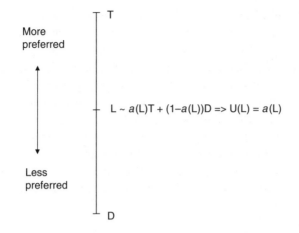

L ~ a(L)T + (1−a(L))D => U(L) = a(L)

Figure 1.4

Second, $bT + (1 - b)D > aT + (1 - a)D$ if and only if $b > a$, for $a, b \in [0, 1]$. For the "if" part ($\Leftarrow$), note that for $b > a$, $bT + (1 - b)D = cT + (1 - c)[aT + (1 - a)D]$, where $c = (b - a)/(1 - a)$. Since $T > aT + (1 - a)D$, $cT + (1 - c)[aT + (1 - a)D] > c[aT + (1 - a)D] + (1 - c)[aT + (1 - a)D] = aT + (1 - a)D$. For the "only if" part ($\Rightarrow$), we need to show that $aT + (1 - a)D \gtrsim bT + (1 - b)D$ for $a \geq b$. If $a = b$, the result holds clearly. If $a > b$, then the result is obtained by exchanging the roles of a and b in the 'if' part of the proof.

Third, for any L, there exists a unique $a(L) \in [0, 1]$ such that $a(L)T + (1 - a(L))D \sim L$ (see Figure 1.4). The existence of such $a(L)$ follows from the second step and the continuity axiom, and the uniqueness from the second step.

Fourth, let us assign $U(L) = a(L)$. Now, it suffices to show this utility is linear, due to Lemma 1.2. For this, note that $L \sim U(L)T + (1 - U(L))D$ and $L' \sim U(L')T + (1 - U(L'))D$. Thus, $aL + (1 - a)L' \sim [aU(L) + (1 - a)U(L')]T + [1 - aU(L) - (1 - a)U(L')]D$. By our definition of U, $U(aL + (1 - a)L') = aU(L) + (1 - a)U(L')$. $\qquad \square$

Even if a preference has a utility representation, it is not unique. In fact, there are infinitely many utilities for the same preference. However, different utilities are related to each other due to the common properties that they share. Note that a utility under certainty only requires a higher number to be assigned to a more preferred consumption. Therefore, two utility functions are compatible if they assign a higher number to a more preferred consumption. This property is called *ordinality*: the order of preference is preserved across utility functions. The ordinality property also implies that the rank of differences in utility values may be changed. For example, for $x \gtrsim y \gtrsim z$, two different utility functions, U and V, can exist such that $U(x) = 1000 > U(y) = 2 > U(z) = 1$; $V(x) = 10 > V(y) = 9 > V(z) = 5$. Note that the order of utility values is preserved in both utilities. However, the rank of differences between utility values is not preserved: $U(x) - U(y) > U(y) - U(z)$, but $V(x) - V(y) < V(y) - V(z)$. It is known that two utilities for a preference have the relation $U(x) = f(V(x))$, where $f(.)$ is an increasing function. The ordinality property can be easily derived from this relation.

On the other hand, the expected utility has the property of *cardinality*, implying that the rank of the utility differences as well as the order is preserved. This cardinality property is obtained from the following relation between expected utilities.

Proposition 1.3 (Cardinality of expected utility). Suppose that U is an expected utility of a preference. Then, another utility V is an expected utility of the preference, if and only if V is an affine transformation of U: $V(L) = sU(L) + t$, $s > 0$ for all L.

Proof. ($\Leftarrow$) For $a + b = 1$, $V(aL + bL') = sU(aL + bL') + t = s[aU(L) + bU(L')] + t = a[sU(L) + t] + b[sU(L') + t] = aV(L) + bV(L')$. Note that the second equality comes from the fact that U is an expected utility. The linearity of V implies that V is an expected utility.

($\Rightarrow$) We will find numbers s and t satisfying the relation. Let T and D be such that $T \gtrsim L \gtrsim D$ for all L. Define a by $U(L) = aU(T) + (1 - a) U(D)$. Thus $a = [U(L) - U(D)]/[U(T) - U(D)]$. Also $V(L) = V(aT + (1 - a)D) = aV(T) + (1 - a)V(D) = a(V(T) - V(D)) + V(D)$.

Now, by substituting a into this equation and defining $s = [V(T) - V(D)]/[U(T) - U(D)] > 0$ and $t = V(D) - U(D)[V(T) - V(D)]/[U(T) - U(D)]$, we have $V(L) = sU(L) + t$. $\square$

Suppose that $L \gtrsim L' \gtrsim L''$. For two expected utilities U and V, $V(L) - V(L') = s[U(L) - U(L')]$. Thus, we should have $V(L) - V(L') > V(L') - V(L'')$ if and only if $U(L) - U(L') > U(L') - U(L'')$. Unlike the utility under certainty, the expected utility preserves the rank of utility differences.

1.3   Problems with the Expected Utility

The expected utility theory allows us to express a utility as an expected value of utilities over possible outcomes. However, this convenience is obtained by restricting the set of preferences to which the theory can be applied. Several problems have been pointed out in literature (see Schoemaker, 1982).

One example is the so-called Allais paradox (Allais and Hagen, 1979). To illustrate, consider the following gamble. The rewards for the first, second, and third prizes are $2,500,000, $500,000, and $0, respectively. Now, consider the lotteries $L_1 = (0, 1, 0)$, $L_1' = (0.10, 0.84, 0.06)$, $L_2 = (0, 0.16, 0.84)$, $L_2' = (0.10, 0, 0.90)$, where each element represents the probability of earning each prize in order. It seems to be acceptable that an individual prefers L_1 to L_1', and L_2' to L_2. However, this preference violates the independence axiom. For this, let us add the lotteries $(0, 0.08, 0.92) - (0, 0.92, 0.08)$ to both sides of $L_1 > L_1'$. If the independent axiom holds, then we will have $(0, 1, 0) + (0, 0.08, 0.92) - (0, 0.92, 0.08) > (0.10, 0.84, 0.06) + (0, 0.08, 0.92) - (0, 0.92, 0.08) \Rightarrow (0, 0.16, 0.84) > (0.10, 0, 0.90) \Rightarrow L_2 > L_2'$. Therefore, $L_1 > L_1'$ and $L_2' > L_2$ violate the independence axiom, which leads to the nonexistence of an expected utility representation. Indeed, if U is an expected utility for this preference, then $L_1 > L_1'$ implies $U(500,000) > 0.10U(2,500,000) + 0.84U(500,000) + 0.06U(0)$. Adding $0.84U(0) - 0.84U(500,000)$ to both sides leads to $0.16U(500,000) + 0.84U(0) > 0.10U(2,500,000) + 0.90U(0)$. This implies $L_2 > L_2'$.

Another problem regarding the expected utility is the treatment of ambiguity, as pointed out by the Ellsberg paradox. Suppose that there are 90 balls in a box. Each ball has one of three colors, red, white, and black. It is known that 30 balls are red, but the proportions of white and black balls are not known. Now, consider the following gambles.

Gamble 1. You choose one color and pick up one ball. You will receive $1m if the colors match, or $0 otherwise.

Gamble 2. You choose two colors and pick up one ball. You will receive $1m if the ball has one of the colors you choose, or $0 otherwise.

It is often the case that people choose red in gamble 1 and choose white and black in gamble 2. This result is interpreted as people disliking the ambiguity, or the uncertainty of probability. The red color has a sure probability of 1/3 in gamble 1, and the white and the black colors have a sure probability of 2/3 in gamble 2. However, this preference cannot be captured by the expected utility, since it is linear in probability. Since the rational expected value of the probability of white (or black) is 1/3 as for red, choosing any color(s) should provide the same expected utility. Dislike of ambiguity may be important in the insurance context when people have little or no information regarding risks. Examples of such risks will include new types of catastrophe risks or terrorism risks. Incorporating this ambiguity into utility may require nonlinearity in the probability. Diverse nonexpected utility models have been suggested. A general form of utility is the one which transforms both probabilities and wealth. For example, general utility can be expressed as $\Sigma\pi_i V(W_i)$, where π_i is the transformation obtained from the distribution function of wealth (see Quiggin, 1982). In Yaari's dual theory, $V(W_i) = W_i$ (Yaari, 1987). In the prospect theory, $V(W_i) = W_i - R_i$, where R_i is a reference point (Kahneman and Tversky, 1979). In general, the function is nonlinear in the probability due to the transformation of distribution π_i. Interested readers are referred to Machina (1987, 2000) and Gollier (2000). Given the problems with the expected utility, we should be cautious in interpreting the results of analyses with the expected utility. Nevertheless, the expected utility is the most widely accepted analytic tool in the insurance and finance areas.

Our discussions in this book will also be based on the expected utility framework. In this book, utilities under risk are von Neumann–Morgenstern utilities, unless stated otherwise. In addition, utility is usually expressed as a function of wealth in literature, which is also adopted throughout this book. Since higher wealth is preferred to lower wealth, $U(W)$ is increasing in W.

1.4   Conclusion

Risk is generally identified with uncertainty of outcomes. Expected utility is an important tool in dealing with decision making under risk. Expected utility is a natural extension of utility under risk. Expected utility, however, is based on strict assumptions regarding preference. Therefore, it is possible that some decision making is not explained by the expected utility, if the preference violates the assumptions. The violation of the assumptions of the expected utility theory is often described as irrational. Diverse non-expected utility theories such as the prospect theory have been developed to explain such irrational behavior, which forms the basis for behavioral economics.

Risk is generally described by the probability distribution in economics. However, some risks (for example, catastrophe risks) may not have a well-established probability distribution. The probability distribution itself may be exposed to uncertainty, in that the realized probability distribution is not known (Knight, 1921). Under the expected utility theory, uncertainty in the probability distribution is not a problem, since it does not affect the expected utility due to linearity. However, if the probabilities are transformed in the calculation of utility as in nonexpected utility theories, then the uncertainty in probability will affect the utility. The uncertainty in the probability distribution will then become important in understanding decision making under uncertainty. Moreover, in highly uncertain cases even the probability distribution may not be known (see Gomory, 1995). These cases will be difficult to analyze, since proper analytic tools have not yet been developed.

BIBLIOGRAPHY

Allais, M. and O. Hagen (1979) *Expected Utility Hypotheses and the Allais Paradox*. Dordrecht: D. Reidel.

Gollier, C. (2000) Optimal Insurance design: what can we do with and without expected utility. In G. Dionne (ed.), *Handbook of Insurance*. Boston: Kluwer Academic Publishers.

Gomory, R. E. (1995) The known, the unknown, and the unknowable. *Scientific American*, 272: 120.

Kahneman, D. and A. Tversky (1979) Prospect theory: an analysis of decision under risk. *Econometrica*, 47: 263–91.

Knight, F. H. (1921) *Risk, Uncertainty and Profit*. Chicago: Chicago University Press.

Machina, M. J. (1987) Choice under uncertainty: problems solved and unsolved. *Journal of Economic Perspectives*, 1: 121–54.

Machina, M. J. (2000) Non-expected utility and the robustness of the classical insurance paradigm. In G. Dionne (ed.), *Handbook of Insurance*. Boston: Kluwer Academic.

Mas-Colell, A., M. D. Whinston, and J. R. Green (1995) *Microeconomic Theory*. New York: Oxford University Press.

Quiggin, J. (1982) A theory of anticipated utility. *Journal of Economic Behavior and Organization*, 3: 323–43.

Schoemaker, P. J. H. (1982) The expected utility model: its variants, purposes, evidence and limitations. *Journal of Economic Literature*, 20: 529–63.

Yaari, M. E. (1987) The dual theory of choice under risk. *Econometrica*, 55: 95–116.

Chapter 2

Risk Aversion and Riskiness

The important issues related to preference under risk are attitudes toward risks and the riskiness of projects. In most of the cases in this book, individuals are assumed to dislike risk. That is, individuals are risk averters. In the first four sections of this chapter, we study the measures of risk aversion and the relation between utility and risk aversion. We will study the risk premium, the Arrow and Pratt measure of risk aversion, and prudence (Sections 2.1–2.3). Utilities often used in the literature are listed in Section 2.4. Risk aversion based on expected utility is referred to as second-order risk aversion. In Section 2.5, this is contrasted with first-order risk aversion. While risk aversion measures provide us with information about whether or not an individual prefers one project to another project, it does not directly measure the riskiness of the two projects. Thus, another interesting concern is when we can state that one project is more risky than another project. This concern leads to the measurement of riskiness (Section 2.6). For this, we study the first- and second-order stochastic dominances and the mean preserving spreads.

2.1 Risk Aversion

It is commonly accepted that the attitude of a normal individual towards a risk can best be described in terms of risk aversion. For this, let us first define an *actuarially fair gamble* as a gamble in which a participant earns a zero expected payoff: $E(z) = 0$, where z denotes a random payoff from the gamble.

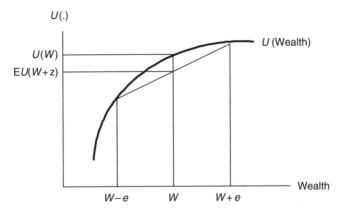

Figure 2.1   Risk aversion and utility.

Definition 2.1   An individual is said to be risk averse at a wealth level W if he dislikes any actuarially fair gamble at the wealth level W; or formally, if $U(W) \geq EU(W + z)$, where z is the random payoff from the actuarially fair gamble. When he is risk averse at every wealth level, then he is simply said to be risk averse.

In general, the attitude towards a risk may be described as being risk neutral, or risk loving. An individual is risk loving if $U(W) \leq EU(W + z)$, or risk neutral if $U(W) = EU(W + z)$. Note that the definition can be extended to the case of a gamble with a nonzero expected payoff, since any gamble can be decomposed into $z = E(z) + \varepsilon$, where ε is a random variable with a zero mean. Thus, the same logic can be applied to the wealth level $W + E(z)$. In this application, we should interpret the risk aversion as the case in which the individual prefers receiving the sure expected payoff to accepting the gamble.

Different attitudes toward a risk are associated with different graphical shapes of utilities. The utility of a risk averse individual is concave, while that of a risk loving individual is convex. The risk neutral individual's utility is linear. The concave utility of a risk averse individual is depicted in Figure 2.1. The actuarially fair gamble is described by $z = +e$ or $-e$, each with probability ½. Since $EU(W + z)$ is a linear combination of $U(W - \varepsilon)$ and $U(W + \varepsilon)$ with equal weights, $U(W)$ is higher than $EU(W + z)$ if the utility is concave. By applying a similar reasoning to a convex utility, we are able to show that $U(W)$ is lower than $EU(W + z)$. Formally, this result is obtained by the application of Jensen's inequality. Jensen's inequality implies that for any concave function $f(.)$, $E(f(x)) \leq f(E(x))$, where x is a random variable. Therefore, the risk aversion can be understood in terms

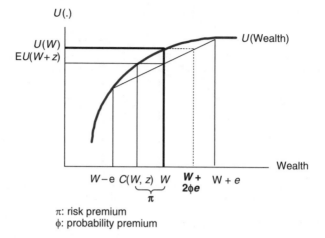

Figure 2.2　Risk premium and probability premium.

of Jensen's inequality, with the interpretation of $f(.)$ as a utility. Since a convex function $g(x)$ can be expressed as $-(-g(x))$, where $-g(x)$ is a concave function, we have $E(g(x)) \geq g(E(x))$.

Since a risk averter will require a premium in bearing a risk, risk aversion is also closely related to risk premiums. For this, let us first define the *certainty equivalent* (CE) of a gamble as the sure wealth level that provides the individual with the same utility as the expected utility with the gamble. Formally, $C(W, z)$ is defined as the CE for a utility U and an actuarially fair gamble z at W, if $U(C) = EU(W + z)$. The *risk premium*, $\pi(W, z)$, is defined as $W - C(W, z)$. It is easy to see that when the individual is risk averse, we have $C(W, z) \leq W$, thus $\pi \geq 0$. Another related measure is the *probability premium* $\phi(W, z')$ which is defined as follows: $U(W) = (\frac{1}{2} + \phi) U(W + e) + (\frac{1}{2} - \phi)U(W - e)$, for $e > 0$, where $z' = +e$ or $-e$, each with probability $\frac{1}{2}$. In other words, the probability premium is the additional probability attached to the positive payoff of a binary symmetric gamble z' (i.e., a gamble with two equally probable opposite payoffs) to make the individual indifferent between staying out of the gamble and taking on the gamble. Obviously, the probability premium is different for different values of the payoff e. Risk premium and probability premium are depicted in Figure 2.2.

As illustrated in Figure 2.2, risk aversion can be equivalently expressed using different notions as follows.

Proposition 2.1　The following statements are equivalent:

(a)　$U(.)$ exhibits risk aversion.
(b)　$U(.)$ is concave.

(c) $\pi(W, z) \geq 0$ for any W and any actuarially fair gamble z.
(d) $\phi(W, z') \geq 0$ for any W and any binary symmetric gamble z'.

Proof Omitted.   □

Since the concavity of a utility is a key element of risk aversion, it seems to be reasonable to conjecture that a higher degree of risk aversion is related to higher concavity. The *absolute risk aversion* (ARA) measure of Arrow and Pratt relates concavity to risk aversion as follows (Arrow, 1971; Pratt, 1964).

Definition 2.2 The absolute risk aversion measure of Arrow and Pratt at wealth W, ARA(W), is defined by $-U''(W)/U'(W)$.

ARA measures the concavity of a utility normalized by the marginal utility. Since risk aversion implies $U'' \leq 0$, ARA(W) ≥ 0 for all W if and only if $U(.)$ exhibits risk aversion. Note that ARA is invariant across different forms of expected utility for a given preference. To see this, recall that two different expected utilities are related by $V(W) = sU(W) + t$, for $s > 0$. Thus, $-V(W)''/V(W)' = -U''(W)/U(W)$. It is also important to note that ARA is defined using derivatives of the utility. This implies that ARA is considering a small risk, not a large risk. Simply put, ARA measures risk aversion (concavity) when wealth changes by 1 dollar. Finally, ARA is the risk aversion measure that is most widely used, due to its convenience.

There is a close relationship between ARA and risk premium for a small risk. From the definition of risk premium, we have

$$U(W - \pi) = EU(W + z).$$

Taylor expansions of both sides at W lead to

$$U(W) - U'(W)\pi \approx E[U(W) + U'(W)z + \tfrac{1}{2}U''(W)z^2]$$
$$\Rightarrow -U'(W)\pi \approx \tfrac{1}{2}U''(W)E(z)^2$$
$$\Rightarrow \pi \approx \tfrac{1}{2}\text{ARA}(W)\sigma_z^2,$$

where σ_z^2 denotes the variance of the gamble payoff z. Therefore, given a small risk, the risk premium at W is approximately equal to one half of ARA multiplied by the variance of the risk.

On the other hand, the inverse of absolute risk aversion also plays an important role in the analysis of risk taking behavior.

Definition 2.3 An absolute risk tolerance (RT) measure at wealth W is defined by $1/\text{ARA}(W)$.

Since RT is calculated as the inverse of ARA, an individual with higher RT tolerates a risk more than an individual with lower RT. When ARA(W) takes the form $1/(a + bW)$, RT(W) becomes linear, RT(W) = $a + bW$, where a and b are constants. A utility function with linear RT is called *hyperbolic absolute risk aversion* (HARA) utility; most forms of utility widely used in insurance and finance are HARA utilities (Merton, 1971).[1]

While ARA is concerned with the risk aversion when the wealth changes by 1 dollar, the *relative risk aversion* (RRA) measure is concerned with the risk aversion when the wealth changes by 1%. RRA is defined as follows.

Definition 2.4 A relative risk aversion measure at wealth W is defined by $-WU''(W)/U'(W)$.

RRA(W) is obtained by multiplying ARA(W) by the current wealth W. RRA can be considered the elasticity of the marginal utility with respect to wealth, since the elasticity is

$$-\frac{dU'(W)/U'(W)}{dW/W} = -\frac{WU''(W)}{U'(W)}$$

Thus, RRA measures the rate of change of the marginal utility with respect to the rate of change of wealth. Another way of interpreting RRA is to consider the utility as a function of the proportion of wealth change $V(t) = U(W + tW)$, given W. Note that $V'(t) = WU'(W + tW)$ and $V''(t) = W^2U''(W + tW)$. Therefore, the ARA of $V(t)$ at $t = 0$ becomes $-V''(0)/V'(0) = -WU''(W)/U'(W)$.

If we consider a gamble whose payoffs are expressed as proportions of wealth, then the risk premium π satisfies $U(W - \pi) = EU(W(1 + z))$, where z denotes a proportional risk. Letting $\pi' = \pi/W$, we have $U(W(1 - \pi')) = EU(W(1 + z))$. To distinguish between π' and π, let us call π' a relative risk premium. Similar to the case of ARA, there is a close relationship between the RRA and the relative risk premium for a small risk. By applying the Taylor expansion to both sides of the equation $U(W - \pi) = EU(W(1 + z))$, we can show that $\pi \approx \frac{1}{2}[-U''(W)/U'(W)]W^2\sigma_z^2$, where σ_z^2 denotes the variance of the proportional risk z. Note that W^2 appears on the right-hand side, since the payoff of the gamble is zW, not z. Dividing both sides by W gives the following relationship between RRA and the relative risk premium.

$$\pi' \approx \frac{1}{2}\text{RRA}(W)\,\sigma_z^2.$$

---

[1]   See Section 2.4 for examples of utilities.

Therefore, given a small risk, the relative risk premium at W is approximately equal to one half of RRA multiplied by the variance of the proportional risk.

2.2   Comparison of Risk Aversion

The above-mentioned measures of risk aversion can be used in comparing risk aversion between different individuals or between different wealth levels of an individual. Let us first compare absolute risk aversion between different individuals. For this purpose, we denote two individuals by subscripts 1 and 2.

Proposition 2.2 The following statements are equivalent:

(a) $\text{ARA}_2(W) \geq \text{ARA}_1(W)$ for all W.
(b) $U_2(W) = f(U_1(W))$ for a concave increasing function $f(.)$.
(c) $\pi_2(W, z) \geq \pi_1(W, z)$ for any W and any actuarially fair gamble z.
(d) $\phi_2(W, z') \geq \phi_1(W, z')$ for any W and any binary symmetric gamble z'.

Proof For (a) $\Leftrightarrow$ (b), note first that $f(.)$ should be increasing for U_2 to be a utility. Note that

$$U_2'(W) = f'(U_1(W))\, U_i'(W)$$

and

$$U_2''(W) = f'(U_1(W))\, U_1''(W) + f''(U_1(W))\, U_1'(W)^2.$$

Thus,

$$\text{ARA}_2(W) = -U_2''(W)/U_2'(W)$$

$$= -U_1''(W)/U_1'(W) - f''(U_1(W)) \cdot U_1'(W)/f'(U_1(W))$$

$$= \text{ARA}_1(W) - f''(U_1(W))\, U_1'(W)/f'(U_1(W)).$$

Therefore, $\text{ARA}_2(W) \geq \text{ARA}_1(W)$ is equivalent to the concavity of $f(.)$. (c) $\Rightarrow$ (a) is obtained by Taylor expansion.

For (b) $\Rightarrow$ (c), note that $U_2(W - \pi_2) = EU_2(W + z) = Ef(U_1(W + z))$. Applying Jensen's inequality to $f(.)$, $Ef(U_1(W + z)) \leq f(EU_1(W + z))$. Since $U_1(W - \pi_1) = EU_1(W + z)$, $f(EU_1(W + z)) = f(U_1(W - \pi_1)) = U_2(W - \pi_1)$. Thus, we have that $U_2(W - \pi_2) \leq U_2(W - \pi_1)$, implying $\pi_2 \geq \pi_1$.

For (b) $\Rightarrow$ (d), by the definition of the probability premium and (b), we have that

$$U_2(W) = (\tfrac{1}{2} + \phi_2)U_2(W + e) + (\tfrac{1}{2} - \phi_2)U_2(W - e)$$
$$= (\tfrac{1}{2} + \phi_2)f(U_1(W + e)) + (\tfrac{1}{2} - \phi_2)f(U_1(W - e))$$
$$\leq f[(\tfrac{1}{2} + \phi_2)U_1(W + e) + (\tfrac{1}{2} - \phi_2)U_1(W - e)].$$

The inequality is obtained from Jensen's inequality. If $\phi_2 < \phi_1$, then

$$f[(\tfrac{1}{2} + \phi_2)U_1(W + e) + (\tfrac{1}{2} - \phi_2)U_1(W - e)] < f[(\tfrac{1}{2} + \phi_1)U_1(W + e)$$
$$+ (\tfrac{1}{2} - \phi_1)U_1(W - e)] = f(U_1(W)) = U_2(W),$$

leading to a contradiction: $U_2(W) < U_2(W)$. Therefore, $\phi_2 \geq \phi_1$.

We prove (d) $\Rightarrow$ (b) by contraposition. Suppose that $f(.)$ is strictly convex at W. Then, for some e,

$$U_2(W) = (\tfrac{1}{2} + \phi_2)f(U_1(W + e)) + (\tfrac{1}{2} - \phi_2)f(U_1(W - e))$$
$$> f[(\tfrac{1}{2} + \phi_2)U_1(W + e) + (\tfrac{1}{2} - \phi_2)U_1(W - e)].$$

If $\phi_2 \geq \phi_1$, then

$$f[(\tfrac{1}{2} + \phi_2)U_1(W + e) + (\tfrac{1}{2} - \phi_2)U_1(W - e)] \geq f[(\tfrac{1}{2} + \phi_1)U_1(W + e)$$
$$+ (\tfrac{1}{2} - \phi_1)U_1(W - e)] = f(U_1(W)) = U_2(W),$$

leading to a contradiction: $U_2(W) > U_2(W)$. Therefore, $\phi_2 < \phi_1$. $\square$

This proposition is intuitive and shows that diverse risk aversion measures are indeed consistent in measuring risk aversion. A more risk averse individual has a higher ARA, a more concave utility, a higher risk premium, and a higher probability premium.

2.3   Risk Aversion, Wealth, and Prudence

The risk aversion of an individual can change when his wealth changes. As the wealth increases, changes in ARA and RRA are often of concern. Decreasing ARA (DARA) refers to the case in which ARA is decreasing in wealth. Constant ARA (CARA) and increasing ARA (IARA) refer to the cases where ARA is constant and increasing in wealth, respectively. Similarly, DRRA, CRRA, and IRRA refer to the cases where RRA is decreasing, constant, and increasing in wealth, respectively.

One may think that a rich individual is more willing to join a gamble with a given dollar risk than a poor one. For example, consider a gamble with a gain or loss of $1,000 with equal probabilities. An individual with total wealth of $1 million will feel more comfortable with the gamble than an individual with total wealth of $10,000. Under this conjecture, DARA can be considered a normal case. For DARA, we should have:

$$\frac{d\text{ARA}(W)}{dW} = \frac{-U'''(W)U'(W) + U''(W)^2}{U'(W)^2}$$

$$= -\frac{U''(W)}{U'(W)}\left[\frac{U''(W)}{U'(W)} + \frac{U'''(W)}{U''(W)}\right] \le 0.$$

This inequality can be rearranged as

$$\text{ARA}(W)[\text{ARA}(W) - \text{AP}(W)] \le 0,$$

where $\text{AP}(W)$ is defined as $-U'''(W)/U''(W)$, which is called the *absolute prudence measure* at W. Therefore, DARA holds if and only if $\text{AP}(W) \ge \text{ARA}(W)$ for all W. Note that DARA requires $\text{AP}(W) \ge 0$, thus $U'''(W) \ge 0$. When $\text{AP}(W) \ge 0$, the individual is said to exhibit *prudence*. Since positive $\text{AP}(W)$ can be less than $\text{ARA}(W)$, DARA implies prudence, while prudence does not necessarily imply DARA. In Chapter 4, we will show that prudence is related to precautionary savings, i.e. savings against an uncertain future. The following proposition states equivalent relations among risk aversion measures.

Proposition 2.3 The following statements are equivalent:

(a)   DARA.
(b)   For $W_1 < W_2$, $U(W)$ is a concave transformation of $V(W) = U(W + \Delta)$, where $\Delta = W_2 - W_1$.
(c)   For any gamble z, $\pi(W, z)$ is decreasing in W.
(d)   For any binary symmetric gamble z', $\phi(W, z')$ is decreasing in W.

Proof. For any $W_1 < W_2$, with the definitions of V and U in (b), we can rewrite (a) ~ (d) as follows: (a) $\text{ARA}_U(W) \ge \text{ARA}_V(W)$ for all W. (b) $U(W) = f(V(W))$ for a concave increasing function $f(.)$. (c) $\pi_U(W, z) \ge \pi_V(W, z)$ for any W and any actuarially fair gamble z. (d) $\phi_U(W, z') \ge \phi_V(W, z')$ for any W and any binary symmetric gamble z'. This proposition now follows from Proposition 2.2. $\square$

Notice that utilities of different wealth levels can be expressed as if they are two different utilities at a wealth level. From this viewpoint, Proposition 2.3 is equivalent to Proposition 2.2. If an individual becomes less risk averse as his wealth increases, then a higher wealth level is associated with a lower ARA, a less concave utility, a lower risk premium, and a lower probability premium.

While DARA is considered a normal case, it is hard to say which relationship between RRA and wealth is normal, since RRA is related to gambles with a proportion of wealth, not with absolute dollars. For example, consider a gamble with gain or loss of 10% of wealth with equal probabilities. Under this gamble, an individual with total wealth of $1 million will face a risk of gain or loss of $100,000, while an individual with total wealth of $10,000 will face a risk of gain or loss of $1,000. It is not clear whether or not the rich individual will feel more comfortable with the gamble than the poor one. Similarly to the ARA case, we have the following result.

Proposition 2.4 The following statements are equivalent:

(a) DRRA.
(b) For $W_1 < W_2$, $u(t) = U(tW_1)$ is a concave transformation of $v(t) = U(tW_2)$.
(c) For any risk z proportional to wealth, $\pi'(W, z)$ is decreasing in W, where $\pi'(W, z)$ satisfies $U(W(1 - \pi'(W, z))) = EU(W(1 + z))$.

Proof Omitted.   □

2.4   Examples of Utility

The following utilities are widely used in literature.

1 $U(W) = -\exp(-\gamma W)$, $\gamma > 0$: a negative exponential utility. This utility exhibits CARA and IRRA: $ARA(W) = \gamma$, $RRA(W) = \gamma W$, and $RT(W) = 1/\gamma$.
2 $U(W) = W^{1-\gamma}/(1 - \gamma)$, for $W > 0$, $\gamma > 0$, $\gamma \neq 1$: a power utility. This utility exhibits DARA and CRRA: $ARA(W) = \gamma/W$, $RRA(W) = \gamma$, and $RT(W) = W/\gamma$.
3 $U(W) = \log(W)$: a (natural) logarithmic utility. This utility exhibits DARA and CRRA: $ARA(W) = 1/W$, $RRA(W) = 1$, and $RT(W) = W$. The logarithmic utility can be considered a limiting case of a power utility as γ tends to 1.[2]

---

[2] Note that the power utility is not defined at $\gamma = 1$. However, due to the cardinality of expected utility, the following affine transformation of the power utility also represents the same preference: $(W^{1-\gamma} - 1)/(1 - \gamma)$. Now, using l'Hopital's rule, we have the following result:

$$\lim_{\gamma \to 1} \frac{W^{1-\gamma} - 1}{1 - \gamma} = \lim_{\gamma \to 1} \frac{[d(W^{1-\gamma} - 1)/d(1 - \gamma)][d(1 - \gamma)/d\gamma]}{d(1 - \gamma)/d\gamma}$$

$$= \lim_{\gamma \to 1} \frac{W^{1-\gamma} \log(W)(-1)}{-1} = \log(W).$$

4   $U(W) = \sqrt{W}$. This utility exhibits DARA and CRRA: $ARA(W) = 1/(2W)$, $RRA(W) = \frac{1}{2}$, and $RT(W) = 2W$. This utility is a special case of the power utility when $\gamma = \frac{1}{2}$.

Note that all of the above utilities are HARA utility functions exhibiting linear risk tolerance. In general, a HARA utility function with $RT(W) = a + bW$ can be expressed as

$$U(W) = \begin{cases} -a\exp(-W/a) & \text{for } b = 0 \\ \log(W + a) & \text{for } b = 1 \\ \dfrac{(a + bW)^{(b-1)/b}}{b - 1} & \text{otherwise.}^3 \end{cases}$$

Note that a HARA utility exhibits DARA if $b > 0$, and CARA if $b = 0$. It also exhibits DRRA if $a < 0$, and CRRA if $a = 0$.

2.5   First-Order and Second-Order Risk Aversion

The above discussion of risk aversion is based on expected utility. As pointed out in Chapter 1, the expected utility is built on strict assumptions. Due to these strict assumptions, the risk aversion based on expected utility sometimes exhibits restricted characteristics. Consider the expected utility under the actuarially fair binary gamble

$$EU = 0.5U(W - z) + 0.5U(W + z).$$

The marginal expected utility with respect to the gamble size z is

$$\partial EU/\partial z = 0.5U'(W - z) + 0.5U'(W + z).$$

Therefore, $\partial EU/\partial z|_{z=0} = 0$.

This implies that a small risk does not affect the utility level. In other words, when the risk is very small, a risk averse individual behaves like a risk neutral one. However, this result cannot explain the finding that individuals often appear to be more averse to a small risk than to a large risk (see Kandel and Stambaugh, 1991). For example, individuals often purchase expensive insurance against a small risk.

---

³   For $\log(W + a)$ to be well defined, $W > -a$. For $\dfrac{(a + bW)^{(b-1)}}{b - 1}$, $W > -\dfrac{a}{b}$ if $b > 0$, and $W < -\dfrac{a}{b}$ if $b < 0$.

Segal and Spivak (1990) distinguish between first-order risk aversion and second-order risk aversion. For a simple exposition, let us follow Schlesinger (1997). First, define $\pi(t)$ as the risk premium for actuarially fair gamble tz, where $t > 0$. That is, $0 \sim tz + \pi(t)$. Note that we directly work with preference, since we are not assuming expected utility. When t goes to zero, we know that $\pi(t)$ also goes to zero. The orders of risk aversion are distinguished based on the speed of $\pi(t)$ near zero. Now, let $\pi'(0) = \lim_{t \to 0} \pi'(t)$. If $\pi'(0) > 0$, then risk aversion is of first order. If $\pi'(0) = 0$, then risk aversion is of the second order. It is easy to see that risk aversion under expected utility is of second order. Obviously, the degree of risk aversion to a small risk is higher under first-order risk aversion than under second-order risk aversion. It is known that, under first-order risk aversion, the indifference curve in the state space is kinked along the 45° line, which has an important implication for insurance demand (see Chapter 4).

2.6   Measures of Riskiness

While risk aversion measures are concerned with "who dislikes a risk more," measures of risk are directly concerned with "which risk is more risky?" One conceivable answer to this question is that risk A is more risky than risk B if all risk averse individuals prefer B to A. This condition is called the second-order stochastic dominance. Another approach is that risk A is more risky than risk B if A is made by adding a noise to B. It is shown that these two approaches are in fact equivalent. Let us start with the first-order stochastic dominance between two risks.

Definition 2.5 (First-order stochastic dominance). For two probability distributions $F(.)$ and $G(.)$, $F(.)$ first-order stochastically (FS-) dominates $G(.)$ if $\int U(W)dF(W) \geq \int U(W)dG(W)$ for every increasing function $U: R_+ \to R$.

Note that both sides of the inequality are forms of expected utility. In this regard, first-order stochastic dominance can be rephrased as follows: $F(.)$ FS-dominates $G(.)$ if all individuals with increasing utilities prefer $F(.)$ to $G(.)$. The following result shows that first-order stochastic dominance can be understood by comparing the two probability distributions.

Proposition 2.5 $F(.)$ FS-dominates $G(.)$ if and only if $F(W) \leq G(W)$ for every W.

Proof (<=) Let $H(W) = F(W) - G(W)$. Consider an increasing function $U(.)$. We want to show that $\int U(W)dH(W) \geq 0$, if $H(W) \leq 0$ for all W.

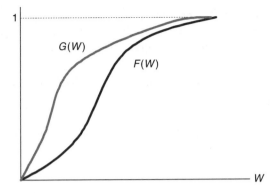

Figure 2.3   First-order stochastic dominance.

Integrating by parts yields $\int U(W)dH(W) = U(W)H(W)|_0^\infty -$ $\int U'(W)H(W)dW$. We have $U(W)H(W)|_0^\infty = 0$, since $H(0) = 0$ and $H(W) = 0$ for sufficiently large W, given scarce resources. Now $\int U(W)dH(W) = -\int U'(W)H(W)dW \geq 0$ since $U'(W) \geq 0$ and $H(W) \leq 0$ for all W.

($\Rightarrow$) Consider an increasing function $U(W) = 0$ for $W \leq M$, and $U(W) = 1$ for $W > M$. First-order stochastic dominance implies

$$\int_0^M 0 \bullet dF(W) + 1(1 - F(M)) \geq \int_0^M 0 \bullet dG(W) + 1(1 - G(M)).$$

Thus, $F(M) \leq G(M)$. The result follows, since M is arbitrary.   □

Note that the condition that $F(W) \leq G(W)$, for all W, can be rewritten as $\Pr(w \leq W; F) \leq \Pr(w \leq W; G)$, or equivalently $\Pr(w > W; F) \geq \Pr(w > W; G)$, for all W. In other words, the probability that wealth is higher than W under $F(.)$ is higher than the probability that wealth is higher than W under $G(.)$ for all W. Therefore, any individual who prefers more rather than less will prefer $F(.)$ to $G(.)$. Figure 2.3 depicts the proposition.

Definition 2.6 (Second-order stochastic dominance). For two probability distributions $F(.)$ and $G(.)$ with the same mean, $F(.)$ second-order stochastically (SS-) dominates $G(.)$ if $\int U(W)dF(W) \geq \int U(W)dG(W)$, for every increasing concave function $U: R_+ \to R$.

Note that the function U is required to be concave as well as increasing. Thus, second-order stochastic dominance can be rephrased as follows:

$F(.)$ SS-dominates $G(.)$ if all risk averse individuals prefer $F(.)$ to $G(.)$. The following result shows that second-order stochastic dominance can be understood by comparing two integrated distribution values.

Proposition 2.6 $F(.)$ SS-dominates $G(.)$ if and only if $\displaystyle\int^{W} F(t)dt \le \int^{W} G(t)dt$ for every W.

Proof. ($\Leftarrow$) Let $H(x) = F(W) - G(W)$. The assumption implies $K(W) = \int^{W} H(t)dt \le 0$. Integrating by parts gives

$$\int U(W)dH(W) = U(W)H(W)\big|_{0}^{\infty} - \int U'(W)H(W)dW$$
$$= -\int U'(W)dK(W),$$

since $H(0) = H(\infty) = 0$. Applying integration by parts again, we have

$$\int U'(W)dK(W) = U'(W)K(W)\big|_{0}^{\infty} - \int K(W)dU'(W).$$

Here, we have $U'(W)K(W)\big|_{0}^{\infty} = 0$, since $K(0) = 0$ (assuming $U'(0) < \infty$), and

$$K(\infty) = \int H(t)dt = H(t)t\big|_{0}^{\infty} - \int tdH(t)dt = -\int tdH(t)dt = 0,$$

since $H(0) = H(W) = 0$ for sufficiently large W under resource scarcity. The last equality follows from the assumption of the equal mean. Thus, $\int U(W)dH(W) = \int K(W)dU'(W) \ge 0$, since $K(W) \le 0$ and $dU'(W) = U''(W)\, dW \le 0$.

($\Rightarrow$) Consider a concave utility of the form $U(W) = \min(W, M)$ for any M. Second-order stochastic dominance implies that

$$\int^{M} U(W)dF(W) + M(1 - F(M)) \ge \int^{M} U(W)dG(W) + M(1 - G(M)).$$

With $U'(W) = 1$ for $W < M$, integration by parts shows that

$$\int^{M} F(W)dW \ge \int^{M} G(W)dW.$$

$\square$

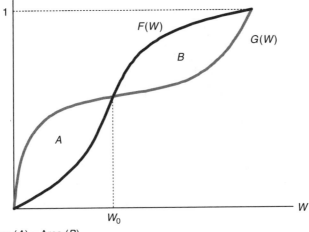

Area (A) = Area (B)

Figure 2.4   Second-order stochastic dominance.

The condition that $\int^{W} F(t)dt \leq \int^{W} G(t)dt$ is depicted in Figure 2.4, where $F(.)$ and $G(.)$ are assumed to cross each other only once. The cumulative area between 0 and W is larger under $G(.)$ than under $F(.)$ for all W. Since $F(.)$ and $G(.)$ have the same mean, we should have $\int F(t)dt = \int G(t)dt$. In other words, the cumulative difference of the distribution should go to zero as W increases. Therefore, $G(.)$ should be greater than $F(.)$ for small W; and $F(.)$ should be greater than $G(.)$ for large W.

Another way of interpreting this condition is to construct $G(.)$ from $F(.)$ by adding some risk. For this, it is convenient to consider the probability density functions $f(.)$ and $g(.)$ of $F(.)$ and $G(.)$ as depicted in Figure 2.5. From $f(.)$, $g(.)$ is constructed by moving some parts in the middle interval I towards the ends, resulting in a higher dispersion of the distribution. By so doing, the risk is increased, while the mean is preserved. As a result, a risk averse individual will prefer $F(.)$ to $G(.)$. The approach depicted in Figure 2.5 is known as a *mean preserving spread*.

Definition 2.7 (Mean preserving spread).[4] $G(.)$ is a mean preserving spread of $F(.)$ if (a) they have the same mean; and (b) there is an internal I such that $g(W) \leq f(W)$ for all W in I and $g(W) \geq f(W)$ for all W outside I, where $f(.)$ and $g(.)$ are the probability density functions for $F(.)$ and $G(.)$, respectively.

---

[4]   This definition is from Eeckhoudt, Gollier, and Schlesinger (2005). The original definition can be found in Rothschild and Stiglitz (1970).

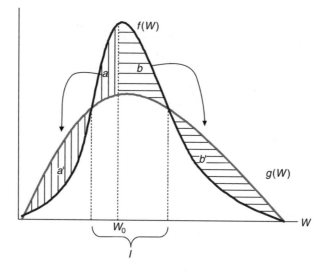

Figure 2.5   Mean preserving spread.

As depicted in Figures 2.4 and 2.5, it turns out that second-order sto-chastic dominance is equivalently described by an iterated application of mean preserving spread (Rothschild and Stiglitz, 1970). It is also known that the application of mean preserving spread is equivalent to adding a noise. If we make a new random variable by adding a noise to an original random variable, then one may think that the new random variable should be riskier than the original. Indeed, the concepts of second-order stochas-tic dominance, mean preserving spread, and adding a noise are proved to be equivalent in Rothschild and Stiglitz (1970). Let us summarize these results as follows.

Proposition 2.7 The following statements are equivalent:

(a) $F(.)$ SS-dominates $G(.)$.
(b) $G(.)$ can be constructed from $F(.)$ by a sequence of mean preserv-ing spreads.
(c) $G(.)$ can be obtained by adding to $F(.)$ a noise with a zero mean. Formally, let W_F and W_G be random variables under $F(.)$ and $G(.)$, respectively. W_G has the same distribution as $W_F + \varepsilon$, where ε is a noise with $E(\varepsilon \mid W_F = W) = 0$ for all W.

Proof Omitted.   □

2.7 Conclusion

In insurance economics, risk aversion is a fundamental assumption regarding individuals' risk attitudes. Absolute and relative risk aversion are widely used measures. Absolute aversion is closely related to risk premium and probability premium. A more risk averse individual has a higher ARA, a more concave utility, a higher risk premium, and a higher probability premium.

Absolute risk aversion requires the first- and second-order differentiations of utility. A full description of a utility, however, will require higher degrees of differentiations, even if it is differentiable. For example, DARA, a commonly accepted assumption, is obtained when the third-order differentiation is positive. While the positive sign of the third-order differentiation is interpreted as prudence, the interpretation of the signs of higher-order differentiations is far from straightforward.

There exist approaches to directly measure the riskiness of a project. When project A second-order stochastically dominates project B, project A is said to be more risky than project B because all risk averse individuals prefer A to B. It is also shown that the second-order stochastic dominance is equivalent to the mean preserving spread and is also equivalent to adding a noise.

BIBLIOGRAPHY

Arrow, K. J. (1971) *Essays in the Theory of Risk Bearing*. Chicago: Markham Publishing Co.

Eeckhoudt, L., C. Gollier, and H. Schlesinger (2005) *Economic and Financial Decisions under Risk*. Princeton, NJ: Princeton University Press.

Hadar, J. and W. R. Russell (1969) Rules for ordering uncertain prospects. *American Economic Review*, 59: 25–34.

Hanoch, G. and H. Levy (1969) Efficiency analysis of choices involving risk. *Review of Economic Studies*, 36: 335–46.

Kandel, S. and R. F. Stambaugh (1991) Asset returns and intertemporal preferences. *Journal of Monetary Economics*, 27: 39–71.

Kimball, M. S. (1990) Precautionary saving in the small and in the large. *Econometrica*, 58: 53–73.

Mas-Colell, A., M. D. Whinston, and J. R. Green (1995), *Microeconomic Theory* New York, NY: Oxford University Press.

Merton, R. C. (1971) Optimum consumption and portfolio rules in a continuous-time model. *Journal of Economic Theory* 3: 373–413.

Pratt, J. W. (1964) Risk aversion in the small and in the large. *Econometrica*, 32: 122–36.

Rothschild, M. and J. E. Stiglitz (1970), Increasing risk I. A definition. *Journal of Economic Theory*, 2: 225–43.

Schlesinger, H. (1997), Insurance demand without the expected-utility paradigm. *Journal of Risk and Insurance*, 64: 19–39.

Segal, U. and A. Spivak (1990) First order versus second order risk aversion, *Journal of Economic Theory*, 51: 111–25.

Chapter 3

Principles of Insurance

Economic institutions and mechanisms can survive in the long run only if they contribute to society. As insurance has been playing an important role in society, there is no doubt that insurance must provide a function to increase social welfare. In this chapter, we discuss how insurance can contribute to society. Based on the Pareto efficiency (Section 3.1), we formally present two basic mechanisms by which insurance increases social welfare. One mechanism is a risk transfer to risk neutral insurers (Section 3.2), and the other is a mutualization of risks among risk averse insureds (Section 3.3). In addition, we investigate the law of large numbers that allows risk averse insurers to eventually behave as if they are risk neutral (Section 3.4).

3.1 Pareto Efficiency

Consider a pool of n individuals. Let us write $(c_1,...,c_n)$ for an allocation of (risky) wealth to n individuals, where c_i is allocated to individual i. Note that the realized value of c_i can vary across the states of nature. There is a resource constraint that the sum of allocated wealth cannot exceed the total resources of the pool in each state. A *feasible allocation* is defined as an allocation that satisfies the resource constraint. Note that a feasible allocation should satisfy the resource constraint at every state of nature, since the total resources may vary under uncertainty. It is assumed that no costs are incurred in allocating risks. One of the main concerns of economists is "what is the best allocation for the pool among feasible allocations?" While it is not easy to define the best allocation since there are many individuals with different tastes, Pareto efficiency is one criterion most widely used by economists. A *Pareto efficient* (or *Pareto optimal*) allocation can be defined as an allocation such that any change to the allocation cannot increase an individual's utility without hurting other(s), given the resource constraint.

Definition 3.1 A feasible allocation $Y = (c_1,...,c_n)$ is Pareto efficient if there is no other feasible allocation $Y' = (c_1',...,c_n')$ such that $EU_i(c_i') \geq EU_i(c_i)$ for all i, and $EU_i(c_i') > EU_i(c_i)$ for some i, where EU_i is the expected utility of individual i.

For simplicity, we will often suppress the term "Pareto" in "Pareto efficient." If an allocation Y is not (Pareto) efficient, then, by definition, there is another feasible allocation Y'' that can increase some individual's utility without reducing others' utilities. In other words, no individuals become less happy, while someone becomes happier. This new allocation Y'' is said to improve (Pareto) efficiency over allocation Y.

When there are two individuals, an efficient allocation can be formulated as a solution to the following program.

$$\max_{\{Y\}} EU_1(c_1) \tag{3.1}$$

$$\text{s.t. } EU_2(c_2) \geq K$$

$$c_1(s) + c_2(s) \leq Z(s) \text{ for every state } s,$$

where $Z(s)$ is the total resources at state s, and $c_i(s)$ is the realized allocation at state s.

This program also has an obvious intuition. A solution to this program, say Y^*, maximizes individual 1's utility, given individual 2's utility as K. Therefore, if another allocation, say Y', is to increase one individual's utility, then it should lower the other's utility, since, if not, Y^* should not be a solution. By changing K, we can find all efficient allocations.

This result can be generalized to the n-individual case. In the n-individual case, an efficient allocation is a solution to the following program.

$$\max_i EU_i(c_i) \tag{3.2}$$

$$\text{s.t. } EU_j(c_j) \geq K_j, \text{ for all } j \neq i,$$

$$c_1 + c_2 + .. + c_n \leq Z, \text{ for every state,}$$

where Z is the total resources.

Note that we suppress argument s in $c_i(s)$ and $Z(s)$ for expository simplicity.

It is also known that an allocation Y is efficient if it can be obtained by solving the following program with a set of positive constant weights $\{w_i\}$:

$$\max_{\{Y\}} \; w_1 EU_1(c_1) + w_2 EU_2(c_2) + \ldots + w_n EU_n(c_n) \tag{3.3}$$

s.t. $c_1 + c_2 + \ldots + c_n \leq Z$, for every state.

The solution to this program is obviously an efficient allocation. There is no way to improve one individual's utility without hurting another, since, if so, the allocation would not be a solution. The converse can be obtained by interpreting w_j as a Lagrange multiplier associated with the constraint for individual j in program (3.2). By changing the weights $\{w_i\}$, we can find all efficient allocations.

By solving program (3.3), we can further characterize the efficient allocation. The Lagrangian becomes

$$L = w_1 EU_1(c_1) + w_2 EU_2(c_2) + \ldots + w_n EU_n(c_n) + \Sigma_s \lambda^0(s)(Z(s) \\ - c_1(s) - c_2(s) - \ldots - c_n(s)),$$

where $\lambda^0(s)$ is the Lagrange multiplier associated with the constraint for state s. At each state s, the first-order conditions are

$$L_i = w_i p_s U_i'(c_i(s)) - \lambda^0(s) = 0, \quad \text{for all } i, \text{ where } p_s \text{ is the probability}$$
of state s.

Thus,

$$w_i U_i'(c_i(s)) = \lambda(s), \quad \text{for all } i \text{ and all } s, \text{ where } \lambda(s) = \lambda^0(s)/p_s. \tag{3.4}$$

From this, we have that, for any two individuals i and j,

$$\frac{U_i'(c_i(s))}{U_i'(c_i(s'))} = \frac{U_j'(c_j(s))}{U_j'(c_j(s'))} = \frac{\lambda(s)}{\lambda(s')} \quad \text{for any states } s \text{ and } s'. \tag{3.5}$$

Since $U_i'(c_i(s))/U_i'(c_i(s'))$ measures the marginal rate of substitution between states s and s', (3.5) can be restated to say that the marginal rate of substitution between states is equalized across all individuals. Let us summarize this result as follows.

Lemma 3.1 Under a Pareto efficient allocation $Y = (c_1, \ldots, c_n)$, the marginal rate of substitution between any two states is equalized across all individuals:

$$\frac{U_i'(c_i(s))}{U_i'(c_i(s'))} = \frac{U_j'(c_j(s))}{U_j'(c_j(s'))}, \text{ for any individuals } i \text{ and } j, \text{ and for any states}$$

s and s'.

By rearranging (3.5), we also have

$$\frac{U_i'(c_i(s))}{U_j'(c_j(s))} = \frac{U_i'(c_i(s'))}{U_j'(c_j(s'))} \quad \text{for any states } s \text{ and } s'. \tag{3.6}$$

That is, the ratio of marginal utilities between two individuals is equalized across all states.

3.1.1   Insurance context

In the insurance context, it is often convenient to work directly with losses, instead of wealth. Individual i is endowed with an initial wealth level of W_i, and faces an initial risk of a loss x_i. In state s, his wealth becomes $W_i - x_i(s)$. An allocation of risk $Y = (y_1, \ldots, y_n)$ is a redistribution of the initial risks, $X = (x_1, \ldots, x_n)$. A feasible allocation should satisfy $\sum_i y_i(s) = \sum_i x_i(s)$, for all s. An allocation Y changes $W_i - x_i(s)$ to $W_i - y_i(s)$ for each i. Now, notice that $W_i - y_i(s)$ is no other than $c_i(s)$ in the above discussion. Finally, let us define $z(s)$ as the total loss of the pool in state s, i.e. $z(s) = x_1(s) + \ldots + x_n(s)$.

Figure 3.1 depicts Pareto efficient allocations given two individuals and two states of nature. The origin of individual 1 is O_1, and the origin of individual 2 is O_2. Individual i's endowment is $(W_i - x_i(1), W_i - x_i(2))$. Point E denotes the endowments of two individuals. The length of the horizontal (vertical) line segment is the sum of the endowments of two individuals in state 1 (state 2). At E, the expected utility of individual i is denoted by $EU_i(E)$. A Pareto efficient allocation of risk is depicted as P. At P, the expected utility of individual i is $EU_i(P)$, which is greater than $EU_i(E)$, for both $i = 1, 2$. Note that P is one of the Pareto efficient allocations. Curve O_1O_2 denotes the contour of all Pareto efficient allocations. While curve O_1O_2 represents all possible Pareto efficient allocations, individuals are willing to accept the new allocation only if it provides higher expected utilities than the endowment. The allocations

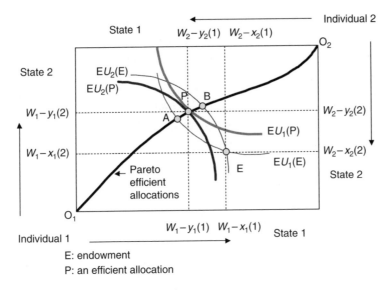

Figure 3.1   Pareto efficient allocation.

that individuals are willing to accept are depicted by the curve segment AB in Figure 3.1.

3.1.2   First best and second best efficiency

The literature often distinguishes between two efficiency concepts: first best and second best. We will consider the information asymmetry problems in later chapters. Researchers have tried to figure out the effect of information asymmetry on efficiency. In general, information asymmetry lowers the efficiency level, since it distorts resource allocation. Technically, information asymmetry adds one or more constraints to the programs for Pareto efficiency (3.2) or (3.3), which lowers efficiency. An allocation is *first best efficient* if it is Pareto efficient without the information asymmetry constraints. In contrast, an allocation is *second best efficient* if it is Pareto efficient given the information asymmetry constraints. First best efficiency is investigated in this chapter.

3.2   Risk Transfer Principle

One may conjecture that when an individual is risk neutral, it will be efficient for him to play the role of an insurer by taking all others' risks. This is because a risk neutral individual is not hurt by taking risks, while risk averse individuals become happier by removing their risks. The following discussion formally shows that this conjecture is correct. Therefore, it improves efficiency in risk allocation for a risk neutral insurer to provide insurance to risk averse insureds.

Let us consider a pool of two individuals 1 and 2, where 1 is risk neutral and 2 is strictly risk averse. Our task is to find a Pareto efficient allocation of risk between these two individuals. A Pareto efficient allocation $Y = (y_1, y_2)$ will solve the following program for some K:

$$\max_{\{Y\}} EU_1(W_1 - y_1) \tag{3.7}$$
$$\text{s.t. } EU_2(W_2 - y_2) \geq K$$
$$y_1 + y_2 = z, \text{ for each realized } (x_1, x_2), \text{ where } z = x_1 + x_2.$$

By plugging the second constraint into the first constraint, the program can be simplified into:

$$\max_{\{Y\}} EU_1(W_1 - y_1) \tag{3.8}$$
$$\text{s.t. } EU_2(W_2 - z + y_1) \geq K$$

The Lagrangian is

$$L = EU_1(W_1 - y_1) + \lambda[EU_2(W_2 - z + y_1) - K],$$

where λ is the Lagrange muliplier for the constraint.
Given each realized state of nature, the efficient allocation should satisfy the following.

$$L_{y1} = 0 \Rightarrow -U_1'(W_1 - y_1) + \lambda U_2'(W_2 - z + y_1) = 0$$
$$\Rightarrow U_1'(W_1 - y_1) / U_2'(W_2 - z + y_1) = \lambda \text{ for each } (x_1, x_2). \tag{3.9}$$

Note that this relationship can be directly obtained by Lemma 3.1. Since individual 1 is risk neutral, we may set $U_1'(W_1 - y_1) = 1$, for every (x_1, x_2). Then, (9) implies that the marginal utility of individual 2 is constant in all states: $U_2'(W_2 - z + y_1) = 1/\lambda$, for every (x_1, x_2). This implies that the wealth is the same across all possible (x_1, x_2), since individual 2 is risk averse. Therefore, individual 2 should face no risk under a Pareto efficient allocation. Since the total loss z is risky, all risk is assumed by individual 1. This result is intuitive, since by imposing all risk on the risk neutral individual, the risk averse individual can increase utility, without hurting the risk neutral

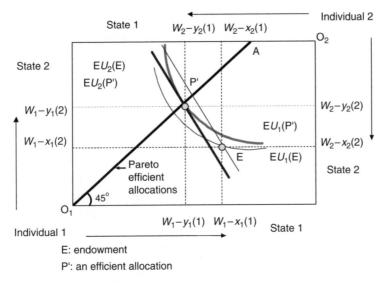

State 1 $W_2-y_2(1)$ $W_2-x_2(1)$ Individual 2

O_2

State 2 $EU_2(E)$
$EU_2(P')$

A

P'

$W_1-y_1(2)$ $W_2-y_2(2)$

$EU_1(P')$

$W_1-x_1(2)$ $W_2-x_2(2)$

E $EU_1(E)$ State 2

Pareto
efficient
allocations

$45°$

O_1

$W_1-y_1(1)$ $W_1-x_1(1)$ State 1

Individual 1

E: endowment
P': an efficient allocation

Figure 3.2   Risk transfer principle.

individual. In the terminology of insurance, under a Pareto efficient allocation, individual 1 becomes an insurer who fully insures the risk of individual 2 who becomes an insured.

The absolute level of wealth will be determined by the utility level K.
Given full insurance, the constraint can be rewritten as $EU_2(W_2 - z + y_1) = U_2(W_2 - z + y_1) = K$. Therefore, $W_2 - z + y_1 = U_2^{-1}(K)$, for all z. The result
can be easily generalized to the case of many individuals, since any risk
averse individual can increase utility by removing his risk, while a risk
neutral individual is not hurt by taking risks.

Proposition 3.1 (Risk transfer principle). Suppose that a pool is composed of n individuals among whom one individual is risk neutral and
others are risk averse. Then it is Pareto efficient that the risk neutral
individual takes all risks of the pool.

Proof Let individual i be the risk neutral one. By the risk neutrality of
individual i and Lemma 1,

$$1 = U_i'(W_i - y_i(s))/U_i'(W_i - y_i(s')) = U_j'(W_j - y_j(s))/U_j'(W_j - y_j(s')).$$

Thus, $U_j'(W_j - y_j(s)) = U_j'(W_j - y_j(s'))$ for all s, and s', implying full
insurance for every individual $j \neq i$.   □

The risk transfer principle is depicted by Figure 3.2, given two individuals
and two states of nature. Figure 3.2 is basically identical to Figure 3.1,

except that individual 2 is assumed to be risk neutral. Line O_1A with a slope of 45° represents the Pareto efficient allocations. An efficient allocation is depicted by P' which is located on O_1A. At P', individual 1 is not exposed to any risk and individual 2 assumes the risk.

3.3   Mutuality Principle

If all individuals are strictly risk averse in the above structure, then no one may want to take all the risks of others. Our next issue discusses the efficient allocation in such a case. It will be shown that an efficient allocation is such that an individual's wealth depends only on the total wealth level of the pool; this is called the *mutuality principle* (Borch, 1962). That is, wealth is allocated to each individual based only on the total wealth of the pool. For a simple example, consider two individuals, each of whom has the initial wealth level of 100 and faces a risk of loss of 40 with probability ½. However, suppose that one individual has wealth of 100, whenever the other has 60 (i.e., the correlation of the risk is −1). In this case, even if each individual faces a risk, the pool is not exposed to a risk. The total wealth is always 160. The mutuality principle implies that an efficient allocation should allocate equal wealth to each individual for all states: for example, 70 to individual 1, 90 to individual 2 in each state.

Proposition 3.2 (Mutuality principle). Consider a pool of n individuals. Suppose that $z(s) = z(s')$ for states s and s'. Then, in a Pareto efficient allocation, $y_i(s) = y_i(s')$ for all individual i.

Proof. It suffices to show that allocation $y_i(s)$ depends only on the total loss $z(s)$, not on the distribution of individual losses. From Lemma 3.1 (or equation (3.6)), we know that, for all i, $U_i'(W_i - y_i(s)) = \mu_i U_1'(W_1 - y_1(s))$, where μ_i is a constant and $\mu_1 = 1$. Noting that a realized state can be replaced by a realized value of $X = (x_1, ..., x_n)$, we can regard y_i as a function of X. By differentiating both sides with respect to x_j, we have $U_i''(W_i - y_i(X))\partial y_i/\partial x_j = \mu_i U_1''(W_1 - y_1(X)) \partial y_1/\partial x_j$. Dividing both sides by $U_i''(W_i - y_i(X))$ and summing over all i, we have

$$\sum_{i=1}^{n} \frac{\partial y_i}{\partial x_j} = U_1''(W_1 - y_1(X))\frac{\partial y_1}{\partial x_j} \sum_{i=1}^{n} \frac{\mu_i}{U_i''(W_i - y_i(X))}. \tag{3.10}$$

Note that the left-hand side of (3.10) is 1 since $\sum_i y_i = \sum_i x_i$, for a feasible allocation. Thus,

$$\frac{\partial y_1}{\partial x_j} = \frac{\dfrac{1}{U_1''(W_1 - y_1(X))}}{\displaystyle\sum_{i=1}^{n} \dfrac{\mu_i}{U_i''(W_i - y_i(X))}} \qquad (3.11)$$

Since the right-hand side of (3.11) does not depend on j, we should have that $\partial y_1/\partial x_j = \partial y_1/\partial x_k$, for any j and k. This implies that y_1 is a function of $z = \sum_i x_i$. Since individual 1 is arbitrarily chosen, the result implies that all y_k are a function of z. That is,

$$\frac{\partial y_k}{\partial x_1} = \frac{\partial y_k}{\partial x_2} = \ldots = \frac{\partial y_k}{\partial x_n} = \frac{\partial y_k}{\partial z},$$

which proves the proposition. Specifically,

$$\frac{\partial y_k}{\partial z} = \frac{\dfrac{\mu_k}{U_k''(W_k - y_k(X))}}{\displaystyle\sum_{i=1}^{n} \dfrac{\mu_i}{U_i''(W_i - y_i(X))}}. \qquad (3.12)$$

$\square$

The mutuality principle can be intuitively understood as follows. Note that the risk of a pool, in general, is less than the sum of individual risks. This is because some risks are offset by other risks unless all risk correlations are unity. Therefore, risk averse individuals can reduce risks by allocating risks based on the pooled risks. Notice the similarity between the mutuality principle and the portfolio theory of finance. In the portfolio theory, the market compensates only for the systematic part of the risk of an asset return. The nonsystematic part of the risk is not important, since it can be removed by diversification. With these finance terminologies, the mutuality principle can be restated to say that, in an efficient allocation, risks are allocated based on the systematic risk of the pool.

The mutuality principle is depicted in Figure 3.3, given two risk averse individuals. Figure 3.3 is basically identical to Figure 3.1 except that the wealth levels are assumed to be the same in the two states of nature. The mutuality principle implies that each individual's final wealth is a function of the total wealth levels of states under a Pareto efficient allocation. Therefore, the wealth levels should be the same across two states of nature as depicted in Figure 3.3. Such an allocation is depicted by P″. Line O_1O_2 with a slope of 45° represents the contour of the Pareto efficient allocation.

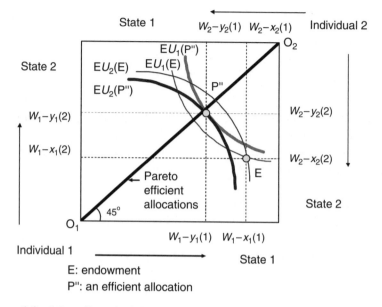

State 1 $W_2-y_2(1)$ $W_2-x_2(1)$ Individual 2

O_2

$EU_1(P'')$

State 2 $EU_2(E)$ $EU_1(E)$

$EU_2(P'')$

P''

$W_1-y_1(2)$

$W_2-y_2(2)$

$W_1-x_1(2)$

$W_2-x_2(2)$

Pareto efficient allocations

E

State 2

$45°$

O_1

$W_1-y_1(1)$ $W_1-x_1(1)$

Individual 1

State 1

E: endowment
P'': an efficient allocation

Figure 3.3   Mutuality principle.

Example 3.1 (Demange and Laroque, 2006). Suppose that all individuals have CARA utilities, $U_i(c_i) = -\exp(-a_i c_i)$, where $c_i(s) = W_i - y_i(s)$. From (3.4),

$$w_i a_i \exp(-a_i c_i(s)) = \lambda(s), \text{ for all } i. \tag{3.13}$$

In order to find the sum of wealth $Z(s) = \Sigma_i c_i(s)$, let us first take logs of (3.13):

$$\log(w_i a_i) - a_i c_i(s) = \log \lambda(s). \tag{3.14}$$

Rearranging for $c_i(s)$,

$$c_i(s) = \frac{\log(w_i a_i)}{a_i} - \frac{\log \lambda(s)}{a_i}, \tag{3.15}$$

Thus,

$$Z(s) = \sum_{j=1}^{n} \frac{\log(w_j a_j)}{a_j} - \log \lambda(s) \bullet \sum_{j=1}^{n} \frac{1}{a_j}, \tag{3.16}$$

From (3.15) and (3.16),

$$c_i(s) = \frac{\log w_i a_i}{a_i} + \frac{1}{a_i \sum_{j=1}^{n} (1/a_j)} \left\{ Z(s) - \sum_{i=1}^{n} \frac{\log w_i a_i}{a_i} \right\}.$$

Noting that $c_i(s) = W_i - y_i(s)$, and $z(s) = \sum_i x_i = \sum_i y_i$,

$$y_i(s) = W_i - \left[\frac{\log w_i a_i}{a_i} + \frac{1}{a_i \sum_{j=1}^{n} (1/a_j)} \left\{ \sum_{i=1}^{n} W_i - z(s) - \sum_{i=1}^{n} \frac{\log w_i a_i}{a_i} \right\} \right].$$

This result shows that the allocation of risk depends on the sum of losses $z(s)$, not on individual losses $x_i(s)$, as stated by the mutuality principle. Furthermore, it shows that the risk aversion of individuals is also important in determining the allocation.

3.4 Law of Large Numbers

The *law of large numbers* is a statistical result which provides the basis for insurance. Roughly speaking, the law of large numbers, under some conditions, allows a risk averse insurer to behave as if she is risk neutral, when the number of insureds is very large. Let us first state the law of large numbers.

Lemma 3.2 (Law of large numbers). Let $\{X_1, ..., X_n\}$, be random samples of size n independently selected from any population with mean μ and variance σ^2. Then, the sample mean $y_n = \sum_{i=1}^{n} X_i / n$ converges in probability to the population mean μ, as n tends to infinity. That is, $\lim_{n \to \infty} \Pr(|y_n - \mu| < e) = 1$ for all $e > 0$.

Proof. Omitted. □

The law of large numbers is depicted in Figure 3.4. Note that the variance of y_n is σ^2/n. Therefore, this variance goes to zero as n tends to infinity. The law of large numbers states that the mean of samples eventually becomes certain as the sample size increases, even if the population is exposed to uncertainty. For its implication for insurance, let us consider a pool of risk averse individuals. As seen above, the mutuality principle states that an efficient allocation of risks should be based on the risk of the pool. In this case, there is no distinction between an insurer and an insured.

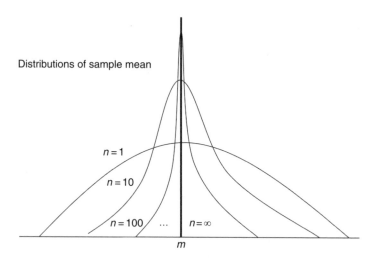

Figure 3.4   Law of large numbers.

All individuals share the risks. The law of large numbers provides another way of allocating risks, when the number of individuals becomes large. Suppose that individual 1 plays the role of an insurer, by assuming all others' risks. This is not efficient, since individual 1 is risk averse. However, the law of large numbers implies that individual 1 may face no risk per insured when the pool size becomes infinity. A risk averse individual may play the role of an insurer as if she is risk neutral.

It is important that the law of large numbers requires that risks be independent. When risks are not independent, there is no guarantee that the risk per individual becomes zero, even if the pool size tends to infinity. For example, if all risks are perfectly correlated, then the average risk does not decrease with the pool size. This issue is particularly important for some insurance lines such as catastrophe insurance. The dependence among risks is often cited as the reason for the lack of catastrophe insurance.

It is also important to note that the law of large numbers is about the average risk (sample mean), not about the total risk. The sample sum is $\sum_{i=1}^{n} X_i$. The variance of the sample sum is $n\sigma^2$, which goes to infinity as n tends to infinity. Therefore, the law of large numbers does not say that the total risk of the pool eventually becomes zero. It simply says that the average risk per individual becomes zero.

The law of large numbers can be understood in a slightly different setting as follows. Suppose that an insurer sells insurance to n individuals with independent and identical risks. Since the total risk does not get smaller as the pool size increases, it is possible for the total loss to exceed the expected total loss. If the insurer wants to cover such risks, she may need some surplus, or a buffer fund, beyond the expected total loss. The level of the buffer fund will be determined by the desired extent of the insurer's coverage. Given the extent of coverage, the law of large numbers implies that the buffer fund per individual becomes zero as the pool size tends to infinity. In a market economy, the insurance premium will include a charge for the buffer fund as well as the expected loss. Therefore, the law of large numbers provides a rationale for the economies of scale, since the portion of the buffer fund in a premium decreases with the number of insureds.

3.5 Conclusion

Three important principles found in insurance economics are presented: the risk transfer principle, the mutuality principle, and the law of large numbers. The risk transfer principle focuses on the risk sharing between a risk averse individual and a risk neutral individual. It is an efficient outcome that a risk neutral individual assumes all the risk of the risk averse individual.

The mutuality principle and the law of large numbers are concerned with pooling of risks. Pooling of risks reduces the risk per individual, if risks are not perfectly correlated. This outcome is reminiscent of the portfolio theory of finance in which diversification reduces the risk of the portfolio. One important difference between portfolio diversification and risk pooling is that pooling does not reduce the total risk of the pool, while diversification reduces the total portfolio risk. Since pooling is adding up risks, the total risk does not decrease. However, if risks are not perfectly correlated, some risks are offset by other risks. As risks are pooled, the total risk of the pool does not increase proportionately to the pool size. Thus, the risk per individual, i.e. average risk, is reduced. On the other hand, the portfolio risk does not decrease, since diversification does not add up risks.

The law of large numbers addresses the statistical result of a special case of pooling. When risks are independent, the average risk can eventually be reduced to zero as the pool size tends to infinity. On the other hand, the mutuality principle addresses the allocation of risks among risk averse individuals. The mutuality principle implies that risks should be pooled in the first place, then be allocated based on the total risk of the pool. This result is intuitive once we understand that the risk per individual decreases in the pool size.

These principles provide justification for the existence of the insurance industry, since the role of the insurance industry is basically the transfer of risks and/or the pooling and redistribution of risks. These principles can also justify the existence of diverse insurer organizations, as will be seen in Chapter 10.

BIBLIOGRAPHY

Borch, K. H. (1962) Equilibrium in a reinsurance market. *Econometrica*, 30: 424–44.

Cummins, J. D. (1991) Statistical and financial models of insurance pricing and the insurance firm. *Journal of Risk and Insurance*, 58: 261–302.

Demange, G. and G. Laroque (2006) *Finance and the Economics of Uncertainty.* Malden, MA: Blackwell Publishing Co.

Eeckhoudt, L., C. Gollier, and H. Schlesinger (2005) *Economic and Financial Decisions under Risk.* Princeton, NJ: Princeton University Press.

Hogg, R. V., A. Craig, and J. W. McKean (2004) *Introduction to Mathematical Statistics.* Upper Saddle River, NJ: Prentice Hall.

Mas-Colell, A., M. D. Whinston, and J. R. Green (1995) *Microeconomic Theory.* New York: Oxford University Press.

Part II

Demand for Insurance and Insurance Contract

Chapter 4

Risk Aversion and the Demand for Insurance

In this chapter, we focus on the insurance contracts between an insurer and an insured. We investigate how risk aversion and insurance costs are related to the design of insurance contracts. Sections 4.1 and 4.2 focus on the optimal level of insurance, given specific forms of insurance: coinsurance and deductible insurance. Then in Section 4.3 we discuss what an optimal contract form looks like. In Section 4.4, we investigate the simultaneous choice of insurance and investments in loss reduction and prevention. Section 4.5 briefly discusses several related issues including the effects of riskiness of a loss on the insurance demand, precautionary savings, state dependent utilities, background risks, and first-order risk aversion.

4.1 Coinsurance

The following discussion is based on Mossin (1968). Let us consider an insured who has initial wealth W at time 0 and faces a random loss x at time 1. The distribution function and density function of x are denoted by $F(x)$ and $f(x)$, respectively. The insured is considering purchasing insurance with proportional coverage α (i.e., coinsurance). That is, the insurer pays the insured the indemnity $I(x) = \alpha x$, given loss x, in exchange for the insurance premium $Q = \alpha Q^F$, where Q^F is the insurance premium for full insurance such that $Q^F = (1 + \lambda)E(x)$, where λ is a nonnegative loading factor. Q is actuarially fair (unfavorable) if $\lambda = 0$ ($\lambda > 0$). Throughout this book, negative insurance and over-insurance are not allowed, unless stated otherwise, which implies $0 \leq \alpha \leq 1$. In a competitive market, Q will be determined so as to make the insurer earn a zero profit. Given coverage α, the wealth at time 1 becomes $W_1 = W - x + \alpha x - \alpha Q^F$. The problem is to find an optimal coverage α which will solve the following program.

$$\max_{\alpha} EU(W_1)$$
$$\text{s.t. } 0 \leq \alpha \leq 1. \tag{4.1}$$

For an interior solution, we have the first-order condition (FOC)

$$\partial EU/\partial \alpha = E[U'(W_1)(x - Q^F)] = 0, \tag{4.2a}$$

and the second-order condition (SOC)

$$\partial^2 EU/\partial \alpha^2 = E[U''(W_1)(x - Q^F)^2] < 0. \tag{4.2b}$$

Since the SOC is satisfied, the solution to the FOC is indeed the optimal coverage. The next proposition presents an optimal coverage and its comparative statics.

Proposition 4.1 (A coinsurance case).

(a)   Partial insurance ($\alpha < 1$) is optimal if and only if the insurance premium is actuarially unfavorable.
(b)   Under DARA (IARA), the coverage decreases (increases) as the initial wealth increases. Under CARA, the coverage does not change as the initial wealth increases.
(c)   Under CARA and IARA, the coverage decreases as the premium becomes more expensive.
(d)   A more risk averse individual purchases higher coverage.

Proof
(a)   For full insurance to be optimal, the following should hold.

$$\partial EU/\partial \alpha|_{\alpha=1} = U'(W - Q^F)(E(x) - Q^F) \geq 0.$$

Therefore, full insurance is optimal if and only if $E(x) - Q^F \geq 0$; that is, the premium is acturially fair or favorable. In other words, partial insurance is optimal if and only if $E(x) - Q^F < 0$, or the premium is actuarially unfavorable.
(b)   Differentiate the FOC with respect to W:

$$E[U''(W_1)(x - Q^F)(1 + (x - Q^F)(\partial \alpha/\partial W))] = 0,$$

leading to

$$\frac{\partial \alpha}{\partial W} = -\frac{E[U''(W_1)(x-Q^F)]}{E[U''(W_1)(x-Q^F)^2]}.$$

The sign of $\partial \alpha / \partial W$ is the same as the sign of $E[U''(W_1)(x-Q^F)]$. We need to show that $\partial \alpha / \partial W \leq 0$ under DARA.

Note that $W_1 \leq (>) W - Q^F$, where $x \geq (<) Q^F$. Thus, under DARA, we have

$$ARA(W_1) \geq ARA(W - Q^F), \text{ where } x \geq Q^F,$$

$$ARA(W_1) < ARA(W - Q^F), \text{ where } x < Q^F.$$

Multiplying both inequalities by $U'(W_1)(x-Q^F)$, we have

$$ARA(W_1)U'(W_1)(x-Q^F) \geq ARA(W-Q^F)\, U'(W_1)(x-Q^F)$$

for both cases. Taking expectations, we have

$$E[ARA(W_1)\, U'(W_1)(x-Q^F)] \geq ARA(W-Q^F)E[U'(W_1)(x-Q^F)] = 0,$$

where the equality sign follows from the FOC.

Since $E[ARA(W_1)U'(W_1)(x-Q^F)] = -E[U''(W_1)(x-Q^F)]$, we have $\partial \alpha / \partial W \leq 0$. The same logic applies to the IARA case, except for the reversed inequality sign. The same logic also applies to the CARA case, with inequality signs replaced by equality signs.

(c)   Differentiating the FOC with respect to λ gives

$$E[U''(W_1)(x-Q^F)\{-\alpha E(x) + (x-Q^F)\partial \alpha / \partial \lambda\} - U'(W_1)E(x)] = 0,$$

leading to

$$\frac{\partial \alpha}{\partial \lambda} = \frac{E(x)[\alpha E\{U''(W_1)(x-Q^F)\} + EU'(W_1)]}{E[U''(W_1)(x-Q^F)^2]}.$$

Since the denominator is negative, the sign of $\partial \alpha / \partial \lambda$ is the opposite of that of the numerator. From the proof of (b), we know that, under CARA or IARA, $E[U''(W_1)(x-Q^F)] \geq 0$, implying that the numerator is positive. Therefore, $\partial \alpha / \partial \lambda \leq 0$ under CARA and IARA.

(d) Suppose that utility V exhibits higher risk aversion than utility U. Then, $V(W) = f(U(W))$, where $f(.)$ is an increasing concave function. The left-hand side of the FOC with utility V can be stated as $E[f' \cdot U'(W_1)(x-Q^F)]$. It suffices to show that $E[f' \cdot U'(W_1)(x-Q^F)] \geq 0$

when we evaluate this expression at the optimal α for utility U such that $E[U'(W_1)(x - Q^F)] = 0$. Now, $E[f' \cdot U'(W_1)(x - Q^F)] \geq 0$ is obtained, since the concavity of $f(.)$ puts higher weights $f'(.)$ on a lower value of W_1 (thus a higher value of $U'(W_1)$) and a higher value of x. (Alternatively, one may formally show this by applying the logic in the proof of (b).)   □

The results are intuitive. When the insurance premium is expensive (actuarially unfavorable), the individual will assume some risks, instead of purchasing full insurance (a). For (b), note that, with a higher wealth level, the individual becomes less risk averse under DARA. Therefore, he will purchase less coverage when he becomes wealthier. Therefore, insurance is an *inferior good*, when the individual exhibits DARA. However, note that full insurance ($\alpha = 1$) is optimal if the premium is actuarially fair, or $Q^F = E(x)$.

It seems natural to conjecture that a higher price leads to lower demand. However, (c) implies that that is true only for CARA or IARA. Under DARA, the coverage may increase as the premium becomes more expensive. In this case, insurance is a *Giffen good*; that is, the demand for insurance decreases when the price decreases. A necessary and sufficient condition for insurance to be a Giffen good is that ARA decreases sufficiently rapidly (Briys, Dionne, and Eeckhoudt, 1989). To see this, note that the price decrease can be translated to a wealth increase (wealth effect). If this wealth effect lowers ARA rapidly, then the individual may purchase less insurance, even though the price decreases. Finally, (d) is also an intuitive result.

Figure 4.1 depicts (a) in a binary case in which x is fixed and the loss probability is p. Note that zero profit lines (or fair odds lines) satisfy $Q = (1 + \lambda)pI$. Wealth in the no-loss state is $W_{10} = W - Q$, and in the loss state is $W_{11} = W - x + I - Q$. From these relationships, we have the zero profit expression on the (W_{10}, W_{11}) plane as $W_{11} = (1 - 1/[(1 + \lambda)p])W_{10} - x + W/(1 + \lambda)p$.[1] Figure 4.1 shows that full (partial) insurance is optimal when the premium is actuarially fair (unfavorable).

4.2   Deductible Insurance

Let us consider the same case as above, except that the insured is now considering purchasing insurance with a deductible $D \geq 0$: $I(x) = \max[0, x - D]$. The insurance premium is denoted by $Q = (1 + \lambda)E(I(x))$, where

---

[1]   From the relationships, we have $Q = W - W_{10}$; and $I = W_{11} - W_{10} + x$. Thus, the zero profit line for insurers on the (W_{10}, W_{11}) plane should satisfy $W - W_{10} - (1 + \lambda)p(W_{11} - W_{10} + x) = 0$.

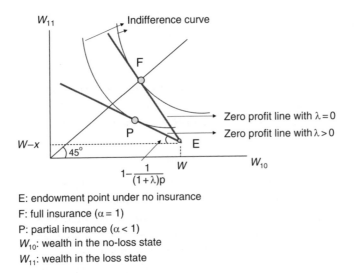

E: endowment point under no insurance
F: full insurance ($\alpha = 1$)
P: partial insurance ($\alpha < 1$)
W_{10}: wealth in the no-loss state
W_{11}: wealth in the loss state

Figure 4.1   Cost and demand for insurance.

λ is a nonnegative loading factor. Given deductible D, the wealth at time 1 becomes $W_1 = W - x + I(x) - Q$. We have

$$EU(W_1) = \int_0^D U(W - Q - x)f(x)dx + U(W - Q - D)(1 - F(D)), \qquad (4.3)$$

$$Q = (1 + \lambda)\int_D^\infty (x - D)f(x)dx.$$

Now the problem is to find an optimal deductible. An optimal deductible D will solve the following program.

$$\max_D EU(W_1) \qquad (4.4)$$

s.t. $0 \leq D$.

For an interior solution, we have the FOC

$$\partial EU/\partial D = (1 - F(D))[(1 + \lambda)\int_0^D U'(W - Q - x)f(x)dx \qquad (4.5)$$

$$- U'(W - Q - D)\{1 - (1 + \lambda)(1 - F(D))\}] = 0.$$

For this result, we have used Leibniz's rule, according to which, for

$$G(t) = \int_{a(t)}^{b(t)} k(x,t)dx$$

$$\frac{dG(t)}{dt} = b'(t)k(b,t) - a'(t)k(a,t) + \int_a^b \frac{\partial k(x,t)}{\partial t} dx,$$

and the fact that $\partial Q/\partial D = -(1+\lambda)(1 - F(D))$. We assume that the SOC is satisfied, while it does not have be satisified in general. The following proposition presents an opitmal deductible level and its comparative statics.

Proposition 4.2 (A deductible case).

(a)   A positive deductible ($D > 0$) is optimal if and only if the insurance premium is actuarially unfavorable.
(b)   Under DARA (IARA), the deductible level increases (decreases) as the initial wealth increases. Under CARA, the deductible level does not change as the initial wealth increases.
(c)   Under CARA and IARA, the deductible level increases as the premium becomes more expensive.
(d)   A more risk averse individual purchases a lower deductible.

Proof

(a)   Assuming that the SOC is satisfied, we have

$$\partial EU/\partial D|_{D=0} = \lambda U'(W - Q) > 0 \text{ if and only if } \lambda > 0.$$

Thus, an optimal deductible D is positive if and only if the loading factor is positive, or the premium is actuarially unfavorable.

(b)   By differentiating the FOC with respect to W, we have

$$\frac{\partial^2 EU}{\partial D^2}\frac{\partial D}{\partial W} + \frac{\partial^2 EU}{\partial D \partial W} = 0.$$

Thus, we have

$$\frac{\partial D}{\partial W} = -\frac{\partial^2 EU/\partial D \partial W}{\partial^2 EU/\partial D^2}.$$

Given that the SOC is satisfied at the solution, the sign of $\partial D/\partial W$ equals the sign of

$$\partial^2 EU/\partial D \partial W = (1 - F(D))[(1+\lambda)\int_0^D U''(W - Q - x)f(x)dx$$

$$- U''(W - Q - D)\{1 - (1+\lambda)(1 - F(D))\}]. \tag{4.6}$$

Let $W(x) = W - Q - x$. For $x \leq D$, we have $W(x) \geq W(D)$, thus $\text{ARA}(W(x))) \leq \text{ARA}(W(D))$ under DARA. Thus,

$$U''(W(x)) \geq -\text{ARA}(W(D))U'(W(x)).$$

Multiplying by $(1 + \lambda)$ and integrating both sides between 0 and D, we have

$$(1+\lambda)\int_0^D U''(W(x))f(x)dx \geq -\text{ARA}(W(D))$$

$$\times (1+\lambda)\int_0^D U'(W(x))f(x)dx.$$

Subtracting $U''(W(D))\{1 - (1+\lambda)(1-F(D))\}$ gives

$$(1+\lambda)\int_0^D U''(W(x))f(x)dx - U''(W(D))\{1-(1+\lambda)(1-F(D))\}$$

$$\geq -\text{ARA}(W(D))(1+\lambda)\int_0^D U'(W(x))f(x)dx - U''(W(D))$$

$$\times \{1-(1+\lambda)(1-F(D))\}$$

$$= -\text{ARA}(W(D))[(1+\lambda)\int_0^D U'(W(x))f(x)dx$$

$$-U'(W(D))\{1-(1+\lambda)(1-F(D))\}] = 0.$$

The last equality is from the FOC. Therefore, $\partial^2 EU/\partial D dW \geq 0$, implying $\partial D/\partial W \geq 0$. The same logic applies to the IARA case, except for the reversed inequality sign; and to the CARA case, with inequality signs replaced by equality signs.

(c) Differentiating the FOC with respect to λ gives

$$\frac{\partial^2 EU}{\partial D^2}\frac{\partial D}{\partial \lambda} + \frac{\partial^2 EU}{\partial D \partial \lambda} = 0.$$

Thus, we have

$$\frac{\partial D}{\partial \lambda} = -\frac{\partial^2 EU/\partial D \partial \lambda}{\partial^2 EU/\partial D^2}.$$

The sign of $\partial D/\partial \lambda$ is equal to the sign of $\partial^2 EU/\partial D \partial \lambda$. $\partial^2 EU/\partial D \partial \lambda$ is calculated as $(1 - F(D))$ multiplied by

$$EU'(W_1) - E(I(x))[(1+\lambda)\int_0^D U''(W(x))f(x)dx$$

$$-U''(W(D))\{1-(1+\lambda)(1-F(D))\}].$$

(4.7)

The expression in the brackets in (4.7) is nonpositive under CARA or IARA as shown in (b). Thus, $\partial D/\partial \lambda \geq 0$ under CARA and IARA.

(d) Suppose that utility V exhibits higher risk aversion than utility U. Then, $V(W) = f(U(W))$, where $f(.)$ is an increasing concave function. The FOC for utility $V(.)$ is the same as (4.5) except that U' is replaced with $f' \cdot U'$. Now, the resulting expression is negative when evaluated at the optimal D for utility U, since the concavity of $f(.)$ puts higher weights $f'(.)$ on a higher value of $U'(W - Q - x)$.

□

The intuition of the results is similar to the coinsurance case. When the insurance premium is expensive (actuarially unfavorable), the individual will assume some risks instead of purchasing full insurance, resulting in a positive deductible (a). Under DARA, he will purchase less insurance when he becomes wealthier, resulting in (b). However, note that full insurance ($D = 0$) is optimal, if the premium is actuarially fair. Part (c) also shows that a price increase lowers the demand only for the CARA and IARA cases. Under DARA, the demand may increase as the premium becomes more expensive, which is similar to the coinsurance case. Part (d) is an intuitive result.

4.3   Optimal Insurance Form

While the above analysis presents optimal insurance demands, given insurance contract forms, it is known that deductible insurance is the most favored form of contract in many cases. The optimality of deductible insurance can be proved by observing that other types of insurance can be considered as a mean preserving spread of deductible insurance. As a result, risk averse insureds will prefer deductible insurance to other types of insurance. The following proposition presents the optimality of insurance with a straight deductible (Arrow, 1974).

Proposition 4.3 (Optimality of a straight deductible). Suppose that an insurance premium is determined as the sum of the expected indemnity and the proportional loading, $Q = (1 + \lambda)E(I(x))$, where $I(x)$ denotes the indemnity for loss x such that $0 \leq I(x) \leq x$, and λ is a nonnegative loading

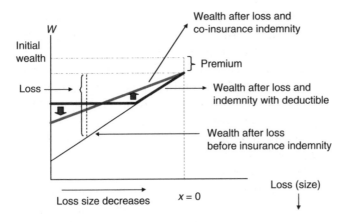

Figure 4.2   Optimality of deductible.

factor. Then, a straight deductible insurance is optimal; that is, $I(x) = \max(0, x - D)$, for some $D \geq 0$.

Proof. We will show that, given Q, any other insurance contract can be considered a mean preserving spread of the straight deductible insurance. Given the deductible insurance, $I(x) = \max(0, x - D)$, the wealth of the insured is $W - x$ for $x \leq D$, and $W - D$ for $x > D$. Given a fixed premium, an indemnity change implies that an increase of wealth in some range of x should be accompanied by a decrease of wealth in some other range of x. First, note that the insured has no risk in the range of $x > D$. Therefore, if the change is made only in the range of $x > D$, it will simply increase the risk, and thus lower the utility. Now, let us consider a change in the range of $x \leq D$. For $x \leq D$, the wealth is $W - x$. Thus, it is not possible to lower $W - x$, since it would require a negative indemnity. Therefore, a change of indemnity scheme will require a decrease of wealth in some range in $x > D$, and an increase of wealth in some range in $x \leq D$. This change increases a risk in the sense of the mean preserving spread, since a high wealth level becomes higher and a low wealth level becomes lower. □

Figure 4.2 depicts the optimality of deductible insurance. A coinsurance contract can be considered a mean preserving spread of the deductible insurance by making a high wealth level higher and a low wealth level lower.

We note the importance of the underlying assumptions of the above result. First, the cost (loading) is assumed to be proportional to the indemnity. In general, the cost can be nonlinear. Under a nonlinear cost, a change of indemnity schedule may also change the total cost even if the expected indemnity is the same. In this case, a straight deductible may not be optimal. Second, note that the insurer is not explicitly considered. We have considered the premium scheme only. However, this corresponds to the assumption of a risk neutral insurer. In a competitive market, the premium is determined to make the insurer earn a zero profit. As long as her expected profit is nonnegative, the insurer is willing to take all the risk beyond a deductible. However, if the insurer is risk averse, then risk sharing between two parties will be desirable.

Raviv (1979) investigates the optimality of deductible insurance in a more general setting in which the insurer can be risk averse and costs may not be proportional. It is shown that an optimal insurance design involves coinsurance beyond a deductible. The intuition for coinsurance is as follows. While straight deductible insurance makes the insurer assume all the risk above the deductible, coinsurance allows both parties to share the risks. When both parties are risk averse, coinsurance may be more efficient than straight deductible. On the other hand, if the cost is nonlinearly increasing in the size of indemnity, coinsurance may also be more efficient than a straight deductible, since it can save on the cost. A straight deductible can be optimal in a special case in the Raviv's model.

For a formal analysis, let us denote the insurer's utility by $V(.)$; we have $V' > 0$, $V'' \leq 0$. The insured's utility is denoted by $U(.)$; we have $U' > 0$, $U'' < 0$. Note that the insurer can be risk averse or risk neutral. W_r and W denote the initial wealth of the insurer and insured, respectively. The random loss x is incurred by the insured. The insurance contract dictates the indemnity schedule $I(x)$ for each realized x, in exchange for the insurance premium Q. We assume that $0 \leq I(x) \leq x$. The insurance premium can be actuarially unfavorable, so that $c(I)$ is the cost following indemnity I such that $c(0) \geq 0$, $c' \geq 0$, and $c'' \geq 0$.

An efficient insurance contract can be found by solving the following program for some K.

$$\max_{\{I(x)\}} EU(W - Q - x + I(x)) \tag{4.8}$$
$$\text{s.t. } EV(W_r + Q - I(x) - c(I(x))) \geq K,$$
$$0 \leq I(x) \leq x.$$

Ignoring the second constraint, the Lagrangian becomes

$$L = EU + \lambda[EV - K]$$

For an interior solution given x, we have the FOC

$$L_I(I,\ x) = \{U'(W^l) - \lambda V'(W_r^l)(1 + c'(I(x)))\} f(x) = 0, \tag{4.9}$$

where $W^l = W - Q - x + I(x)$, and $W_r^l = W_r + Q - I(x) - c(I(x))$.

The following proposition presents general results.

Proposition 4.4
(a) An efficient insurance contract is characterized by a deductible and coinsurance above the deductible.
(b) A straight deductible is efficient if the cost is proportional to the indemnity and the insurer is risk neutral.

Proof. (a) From the FOC, the solution becomes

(i) $I = 0$, if $L_I (I = 0, x) = U'(W - Q - x)$
$- \lambda V'(W_r + Q - c(0))(1 + c'(0)) \le 0$;

(ii) $0 < I < x$, if $L_I (I, x) = U'(W - Q)$
$- \lambda V'(W_r + Q - I - c(I))(1 + c'(I)) = 0$; or

(iii) $I = x$, if $L_I (I = x, x) = U'(W - Q)$
$- \lambda V'(W_r + Q - x - c(x))(1 + c'(x)) \ge 0$.

Note that, with $I(x) = 0$, $L_I (I = 0, x)$ is continuous and increasing in x, and that, with $I(x) = x$, $L_I (I = x, x)$ is continuous and decreasing in x. If $L_I (I = 0, x = 0) \ge 0$, then $L_I (I = 0, x) > 0$ for all $x > 0$. Thus, $I(x) > 0$ for all $x > 0$. If $L_I (I = 0, x = 0) \le 0$, then $L_I (I = x, x) < 0$ for all $x > 0$. Thus, $I(x) < x$ for all $x > 0$. This also implies that we should observe either (i) or (iii), not both. In other words, the solution satisfies either (i) and (ii), or (ii) and (iii).
  Now define x_1 and x_2 by

$$L_I (I = 0, x_1) = U'(W - Q - x_1) - \lambda V'(W_r + Q - c(0))(1 + c'(0)) = 0;$$
$$L_I (I = x_2, x_2) = U'(W - Q) - \lambda V'(W_r + Q - x_2 - c(x_2))(1 + c'(x_2)) = 0.$$

Thus, the solution should be of either of the following two types (see Figure 4.3).

(Type 1) Deductible: $I(x) = 0$ for $x \le x_1$, and $0 < I(x) < x$ for $x > x_1$.
(Type 2) Upper limit: $I(x) = x$ for $x \le x_2$, and $0 < I(x) < x$ for $x > x_2$.

This result implies that we have interior solutions for $x > x_i$, in each type of solution. In such an interior solution, differentiating the FOC with respect to x gives

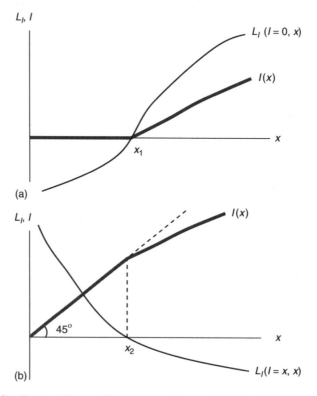

Figure 4.3   Optimal form of insurance: (a) type 1, deductible case; (b) type 2, upper limit case.

$$U''(W^1)(I'(x) - 1) + \lambda V''(W_r^1)(1 + c'(I(x)))^2 I'(x)$$
$$- \lambda V'(W_r^1)c''(I(c))I'(x) = 0,$$

Substituting λ from the FOC, we have

$$I'(x) = \frac{ARA_U(W^1)}{ARA_U(W^1) + ARA_V(W_r^1)(1 + c') + c''/(1 + c')}, \quad \text{for } 0 < I(x) < x,$$

$$(4.10)$$

where $ARA_i(.)$ is the absolute risk aversion measure for the insurer ($i = V$) and the insured ($i = U$). From (4.10), we have $0 < I'(x) < 1$, which implies coinsurance, if the insurer is risk averse or the cost is convex, or both. Finally, using a similar logic as in Proposition 4.3, it can be shown that solution type 2 is, in fact, second-order stochastically dominated by solution type 1, since the risk is reduced under solution type 1 (see Raviv, 1979). As a result, the solution is characterized by a deductible and possible coinsurance above the deductible.

(b) From (4.10), $I'(x) = 1$ if and only if $ARA_V = 0$ and $c(I) = bI$, for a constant $b > 0$. $\qquad\qquad\qquad\qquad\qquad\qquad\qquad\qquad\qquad\qquad$ □

4.4   Insurance and Investment in Loss Reduction and Prevention

4.4.1   Insurance and loss reduction

We now consider investment in loss reduction, i.e. loss severity reduction. Our discussion is based on Ehrlich and Becker (1972). Let us write $x(c)$ for the loss when the individual makes a loss reduction investment of c. We assume that $x'(c) \le 0$. Let q be the unit premium, i.e., $q = (1+\lambda)p$, where λ is a loading factor. The individual solves the following program.

$$\max_{c,I} (1-p)U(W - c - qI) + pU(W - x(c) - c - qI + I) \qquad (4.11)$$

with FOCs

$$-(1-p)U'(W_0) + pU'(W_1)(-x' - 1) = 0 \qquad (4.12)$$

$$-(1-p)U'(W_0)q + pU'(W_1)(1-q) = 0 \qquad (4.13)$$

where $W_0 = W - c - qI$ and $W_1 = W - x(c) - c - qI + I$.
Rearranging the FOCs, we have

$$x'(c) + 1 = -(1-p)U'(W_0)/pU'(W_1) \qquad (4.14)$$

$$(1-q)/q = (1-p)U'(W_0)/pU'(W_1) \qquad (4.15)$$

For (4.14), note that a positive investment requires $x'(c) < -1$. Condition (4.14) requires that the marginal transformation of the loss reduction investment (MRT) equal the marginal rate of substitution (MRS). To see this, consider the loss reduction investment on $(W_1, W_0) \Rightarrow (W_0, W_1)$ plane. Ignoring insurance, the investment of c in the technology will result in $W_0 = W - c$ and $W_1 = W - c - x(c)$. Differentiating W_0 and W_1 with respect to c will give $dW_1/dc = -1 - x'$, and $dW_0/dc = -1$. On the $(W_1, W_0) \Rightarrow (W_0, W_1)$ plane, the slope of the loss reduction technology function is $dW_0/dW_1 = 1/(x'(c) + 1)$ $dW_1/dW_0 = x'(c) + 1$, which is the left-hand side of (4.14).

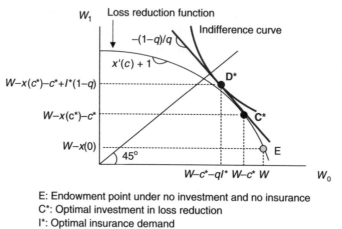

E: Endowment point under no investment and no insurance
C*: Optimal investment in loss reduction
I*: Optimal insurance demand
D*: Final wealth pair

Figure 4.4   Insurance and the investment in loss reduction.

The right-hand side of (4.14) is none other than the slope of the indifference curve on the $(W_1, W_0) \Rightarrow (W_0, W_1)$ plane, representing the MRS. Therefore, (4.14) requires that the slope of the technology function should equal the slope of the indifference curve. On the other hand, (4.15) is the usual condition for the optimal level of insurance. The individual will purchase full insurance if the premium is actuarially fair ($q = p$). Combining (4.14) and (4.15) results in

$$1/(x'(c)+1) = -q/(1-q) \Rightarrow x'(c)+1 = -(1-q)/q \qquad (4.16)$$

This result is depicted in Figure 4.4. The optimal loss reduction investment is described by point C*, and the subsequent demand for insurance is described by point D*. Note that the investment level is independent of the risk attitude of the individual (i.e., the shape of the indifference curve). Graphically, the investment point is determined at the tangent point between the insurance price line (with slope $-(1-q)/q$) and the loss reduction technology curve. Given price q, regardless of the risk attitude, the investment level is determined to satisfy (4.16), which will maximize the wealth level after the investment. Then, the insurance demand is determined based on the risk attitude. Graphically, the insurance demand is determined at the tangent point between the insurance price line and the indifference curve. This result is reminiscent of Fisher's separation in finance, in which individuals select production levels regardless of their risk attitudes, and then select consumptions based on their risk attitudes.

4.4.2   Insurance and loss prevention

We now consider the investment in loss prevention, that is, loss frequency reduction. Let us write $p(r)$ for the probability of a loss occurrence given the loss prevention investment r. We assume that $p'(r) \leq 0$. Let q be the unit premium, $q = (1+\lambda)p$, where λ is a loading factor. The problem can be stated as follows.

$$\max_{r, I}(1 - p(r))U(W - r - qI) + p(r)U(W - x - r - qI + I) \qquad (4.17)$$

with first-order conditions

$$-p'U(W_0) - (1 - p)U'(W_0)(1 + (1+\lambda)p'I) \\ + p'U(W_1) - pU'(W_1)(1 + (1+\lambda)p'I) = 0 \qquad (4.18)$$

$$-(1 - p)U'(W_0)q + pU'(W_1)(1 - q) = 0 \qquad (4.19)$$

where $W_0 = W - r - qI$, and $W_1 = W - x - r - qI + I$.
Rearranging the FOCs, we have

$$-p'[U(W_0) - U(W_1)] - [(1 - p)U'(W_0) + pU'(W_1)](1 + \lambda)p'I \\ = (1 - p)U'(W_0) + pU'(W_1) \qquad (4.20)$$

$$q/(1 - q) = pU'(W_1)/[(1 - p)U'(W_0)] \qquad (4.21)$$

Let us assume that the SOC is satisfied. It is well known that the SOC is not necessarily satisfied even with $p'' > 0$. In (4.20), the left-hand side is the marginal benefit of the loss prevention investment and the right-hand side is the marginal cost of the investment. Therefore, (4.20) states that the optimal investment is determined by balancing its marginal benefit and its marginal cost. Again, (4.21) is the usual condition for the insurance demand. Unlike in the loss reduction case, the investment in loss prevention is not independent of the risk attitude. This is because the investment in loss prevention changes the risk itself. Note also that the risk change affects the unit price of insurance. Therefore, risk attitudes interact with the investment in loss prevention and the insurance demand.

On the other hand, as long as the insurance premium is actuarially fair, an individual purchases full insurance regardless of his risk attitude. In this case, we may observe the separation between the risk attitude and the investment as in the loss reduction case. To see this, when the premium is

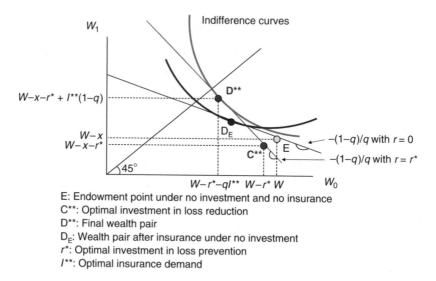

E: Endowment point under no investment and no insurance
C**: Optimal investment in loss reduction
D**: Final wealth pair
D_E: Wealth pair after insurance under no investment
r^*: Optimal investment in loss prevention
I^{**}: Optimal insurance demand

Figure 4.5   Insurance and the investment in loss prevention.

actuarially fair, by (4.21), we have full insurance ($I = x$), implying that $U(W_1) = U(W_0)$. From (4.20), we should have $-p'x = 1$, or $p' = -1/x$. To interpret this result, note that the expected income under full insurance is $W - px - r$. Therefore, $p' = -1/x$ maximizes the expected income without considering the risk. This result is intuitive, since the individual does not care about risk when he can be fully insured.

Figure 4.5 depicts the loss prevention investment and insurance demand. The optimal loss prevention investment is described by point C**, and the subsequent demand for insurance is described by point D**. D_E is the wealth pair when the individual purchases insurance with no investment in loss prevention. As the individual increases the investment level, the probability of loss is reduced, which is depicted by the steeper-sloped price line. The insurance demand is determined at the tangent point between the insurance price line and the indifference curve. In the figure, D** provides a higher utility than D_E.

4.5   Related Issues

4.5.1   Riskiness and insurance

We have studied the effects of risk aversion on insurance demand. A more risk averse individual will purchase more insurance, *ceteris paribus*.

Another related question concerns the effect of the riskiness of a loss on the insurance demand. Even though it seems reasonable that an increase in risk will increase insurance demand, it is not true, in general. From Chapter 2, we know that a mean preserving spread of a risk makes a risk averse individual worse off. However, this does not necessarily mean that the individual will purchase more insurance. For example, if the individual becomes less risk averse as a result of a change in wealth which follows a change of loss distribution, then he may reduce the demand for insurance. Gollier (1995, 1997) proposes a necessary and sufficient condition, called "central dominance," for riskiness to induce a higher demand. A distribution $G(x)$ dominates a distribution $F(x)$ in the sense of central dominance, if there is a positive real number M, such that

$$\int\limits^{y} x dG(x) \le M \bullet \int\limits^{y} x dF(x) \text{ for all } y.$$

It turns out that the second-order stochastic dominance is not necessary or sufficient for central dominance.

4.5.2 Precautionary savings

Consider the following two-date savings problem (see Eeckhoudt, Gollier, and Schlesinger, 2005). At time 0, the individual has wealth W_0. However, his income at time 1, W_1, is random. Letting S and r denote savings and the interest rate, respectively, the problem for savings can be stated as

$$\max_S U_0(W_0 - S) + EU_1(W_1 + (1+r)S) \qquad (4.22)$$

The optimal savings S^* will solve the FOC

$$-U_0'(W_0 - S) + (1+r)EU_1'(W_1 + (1+r)S) = 0. \qquad (4.23)$$

Our question concerns the effect of the income risk on the savings. For this, let us consider the following problem with the certain income at time 1.

$$\max_S U_0(W_0 - S) + U_1(EW_1 + (1+r)S) \qquad (4.24)$$

The optimal savings S' will solve the FOC

$$-U_0'(W_0 - S) + (1+r)U_1'(EW_1 + (1+r)S) = 0 \qquad (4.25)$$

If $S^* > S'$, we can conclude that the risk of the income provides an individual with an incentive to save more. The increased savings due to the risk are referred to as "precautionary savings." To check for precautionary savings, let us evaluate the left-hand side of (4.23) at $S = S'$. If this value is positive, then we can conclude that $S^* \geq S'$:

$$-U_0'(W_0 - S') + (1 + r)EU_1'(W_1 + (1 + r)S')$$

$$= -U_0'(W_0 - S') + (1 + r)U_1'(EW_1 + (1 + r)S') - (1 + r)U_1'(EW_1 + (1 + r)S') + (1 + r)EU_1'(W_1 + (1 + r)S')$$

$$= -(1 + r)[U_1'(EW_1 + (1 + r)S') - EU_1'(W_1 + (1 + r)S')].$$

The last equality is obtained by (4.25). Therefore, $S^* \geq S'$ if and only if U_1' $(EW_1 + (1 + r)S') \leq EU_1'(W_1 + (1 + r)S')$. If U_1' is convex, then this relationship will hold by Jensen's inequality. The convexity of U_1' implies $U'''(W) \geq 0$ (i.e., $AP(W) = -U'''(W)/U''(W) \geq 0$), which is interpreted as "prudent." Recall that DARA implies prudence. Thus, under DARA, the precautionary saving is positive.

4.5.3   State-dependent utility

Consider the following simplified coinsurance problem under the binary risk case. A loss of L can occur with probability p, or 0 with probability $1 - p$. Insurance premium Q^F is $(1+\lambda)pL$ for full insurance. The insured needs to select an optimal coverage α. His expected utility with α is given by

$$EU(\alpha) = (1 - p)U(W_0) + pU(W_1),$$

where $W_1 = W - \alpha Q^F - L + \alpha L$ and $W_0 = W - \alpha Q^F$. Now the optimal α will satisfy the FOC

$$U'(W_1)/U'(W_0) = (1 - p)(1 + \lambda)/[1 - (1 + \lambda)p)].$$

For $\lambda = 0$, $U'(W_1)/U'(W_0) = 1$; full insurance is optimal. For $\lambda > 0$, $U'(W_1)/U'(W_0) > 1$; partial insurance is optimal.

Now suppose that the utility function itself changes when a loss occurs. For example, when a loss involves losing health, or pain and suffering, an individual may be less happy even after being fully compensated for any lost income and expenses for medical treatment. Reflecting this observation, let us introduce a state-dependent utility (Cook and Graham, 1977). The utility is denoted by U_0 in the no-loss state, and U_1 in the loss state. It may be reasonable to assume that $U_1(W) < U_0(W)$. For simplicity, let us assume that there is a positive constant R such that $U_1(W) = U_0(W - R)$. Note that this implies that $U_1'(W_1) = U_0'(W_0)$ if $W_0 = W_1 - R$.

The optimal coverage will be determined by the FOC

$$U_1'(W_1)/U_0'(W_0) = (1-p)(1+\lambda)/[1-(1+\lambda)p)] \qquad (4.26)$$

As before, for $\lambda = 0$, $U_1'(W_1)/U_0'(W_0) = 1$. However, this implies that $W_1 > W_0 = W_1 - R$. In other words, the individual wants to be overinsured when the premium is actuarially fair. Similarly, even for $\lambda > 0$, $U_1'(W_1)/U_0'(W_0) > 1$, we may still have $W_1 > W_0$. Therefore, the individual may still want to be over-insured, even if the premium is actuarially unfavorable. The intuition is simple. Since the individual cannot fully recover the disutility even with the full monetary indemnity, he is willing to be overinsured.

4.5.4   Background risk

We have focused on the case of a single risk, and have assumed that there are no other risks. In reality, however, the insurance decision is not the only one that an individual should make. It generally interacts with other considerations. Such considerations include portfolio investments, risky income flows, and other risk management. In such cases, the results of this chapter do not necessarily hold (Mayers and Smith, 1983; Doherty and Schlesinger, 1983). The effect of the background risk on risk taking behavior has been intensively studied in the literature (see, for example, Eeckhoudt, Gollier, and Schlesinger, 1996; Eeckhoudt and Kimball, 1992; Kimball, 1993).

As a simple illustration, we focus on the case in which there is a background risk as well as an insurable risk. A background risk is exogenous to an insurance decision. For example, income flow risk is background risk when the individual makes a decision to purchase insurance. Our simple model shows that the interaction between an insurance decision and other factors (the background risk here) should not be ignored.

Recall the coinsurance problem:

$$\max_\alpha \ EU(W - x - \alpha Q^F + \alpha x), \text{ where } Q^F = (1+\lambda)E(x).$$

Note that W was assumed to be fixed. Now, let us introduce a background risk by assuming that W is random. Since the insurance decision should be made before the resolutions of the background risk and the insurable risk, we need double expectations across W and x. Therefore, the coinsurance problem becomes as follows:

$$\max_{\alpha} E_W E_{x|W} U(W - x - \alpha Q^F + \alpha x) \qquad (4.27)$$

with FOC

$$L_{\alpha} = E_W E_{x|W} [U'(W_1)(-Q^F + x)] = 0 \qquad (4.28)$$

Let us evaluate L_{α} at $\alpha = 1$. Note that with $\alpha = 1$, $W_1 = W - Q^F$ is independent of x. We have

$$L_{\alpha}|_{\alpha=1} = E_W\{U'(W_1)[-Q^F + E_{x|W}(x)]\}$$

$$= \text{cov}\{U'(W_1), -Q^F + E_{x|W}(x)\} + E_W\{U'(W_1)\}(-\lambda E_x(x)), \qquad (4.29)$$

where we have used the fact that $-Q^F + E_W(E_{x|W}(x)) = -Q^F + E_x(x) = -\lambda E_x(x)$.
If W and x are independent, then $E_{x|W}(x) = E_x(x)$, which means that $\text{cov}\{U'(W_1), -Q^F + E_{x|W}(x)\} = 0$, leading to

$$L_{\alpha}|_{\alpha=1} = E_W\{U'(W_1)\}(-\lambda E_x(x)).$$

Therefore, $\alpha = 1$ is optimal if and only if the premium is actuarially fair or favorable ($\lambda \leq 0$, or $Q^F \leq E_x(x)$), which coincides with the no background risk case.

It is a different story, however, if W and x are not independent. Suppose that W and x are negatively correlated. Then, as W gets larger (smaller), $U'(W - Q^F)$ and $E_{x|W}(x)$ get smaller (larger). Thus, $\text{cov}\{U'(W_1), -Q + E_{x|W}(x)\}$ becomes positive. As a result, the individual may purchase full insurance even if the premium is actuarially unfavorable, as long as $-\lambda E_x(x)$ is small enough to make

$$L_{\alpha}|_{\alpha=1} = \text{cov}\{U'(W_1), -Q + E_{x|W}(x)\} + E_W\{U'(W_1)\}(-\lambda E_x(x)) \geq 0.$$

That is, the individual is willing to be overinsured even if the premium is actuarially unfavorable.

On the other hand, if W and x are positively correlated, then $\text{cov}\{U'(W_1), -Q + E_{x|W}(x)\}$ is negative. Thus, we may have $L_{\alpha}|_{\alpha=1} < 0$, even if the premium is actuarially favorable. That is, the individual may not want to purchase full insurance under an actuarially favorable premium.

For an intuitive explanation, note that a positive correlation between W and x implies that the background wealth plays the role of a homemade hedge to the insurable loss: a high (low) income is earned when a loss is high (low). In such a case, the incentive for purchasing insurance will be reduced. On the other hand, when W and x are negatively correlated, a high (low) loss is associated with a low (high) background income. Therefore, the risk of total wealth is augmented. In such a case, the individual will wish to hedge the total risk by being overinsured.

4.5.5   First-order risk aversion and insurance demand

Recall that risk aversion based on expected utility is of second order (see Section 2.5). Since first-order risk aversion implies more risk aversion to a small risk, we may expect an insured to purchase more insurance, at least against a small risk, under first-order risk aversion than under second-order risk aversion. Consider coinsurance of the binary case depicted in Figure 4.1. If risk aversion is of first order, it is known that the indifference curve is kinked along the 45° line, as depicted in Figure 4.6(a) (Schlesinger, 1997).

If insurance is actuarially fair, then the insured will purchase full insurance (F) as in the expected utility case (see Figure 4.1). The difference can be found when insurance is actuarially unfavorable. Figure 4.6(b) shows that, under first-order risk aversion, the insured may still purchase full insurance, for example, F′, even if insurance is actuarially unfavorable. The insured will purchase no insurance (E), if the premium becomes more expensive than a critical level. This example shows that, under first-order risk aversion, the insured purchases full insurance or no insurance. The insured never purchases partial insurance. This demand pattern is called "bang-bang" demand for insurance, which is sometimes observed in practice. Notice that this demand pattern cannot be easily explained under expected utility.

4.6   Conclusion

Risk aversion is the main rationale for an individual's demand for insurance. In this chapter, we have studied the efficient insurance contract between a risk averse insured and an insurer. The insured purchases full insurance under an actuarially fair premium. However, if the premium is unfavorable, the insured purchases partial insurance. When the insurer is risk neutral and the insurance cost (loading) is linear, an efficient insurance contract is a straight deductible. In general, however, an efficient

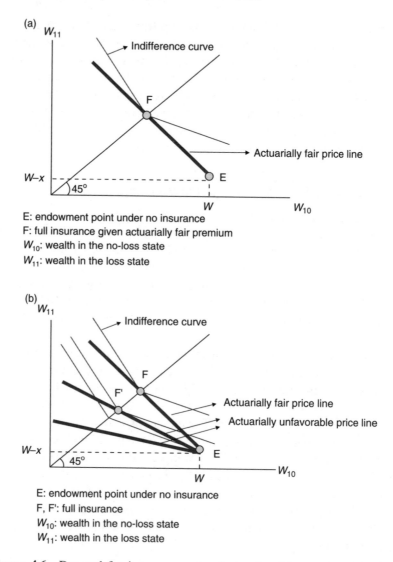

(a)

E: endowment point under no insurance
F: full insurance given actuarially fair premium
W_{10}: wealth in the no-loss state
W_{11}: wealth in the loss state

(b)

E: endowment point under no insurance
F, F': full insurance
W_{10}: wealth in the no-loss state
W_{11}: wealth in the loss state

Figure 4.6 Demand for insurance under first-order risk aversion: (a) kinked indifference curve; (b) bang-bang demand.

contract is characterized by a deductible and coinsurance above the deductible. We also investigated the interaction between insurance and investments in loss reduction and loss prevention. Finally, we discussed several related issues including the effects of riskiness of a loss on the insurance demand, precautionary savings, state dependent utilities, background risks, and the bang-bang demand for insurance under first-order risk aversion.

Other important issues for insurance contracts are information problems such as adverse selection and moral hazard. This chapter has ignored information issues in order to focus on risk aversion. Information problems will be discussed in detail in Chapters 7–10.

BIBLIOGRAPHY

Arrow, K. J. (1974) Optimal insurance and generalized deductibles. *Scandinavian Actuarial Journal*, 1: 1–42.

Briys, E., G. Dionne, and L. Eeckhoudt (1989), More on insurance as a Giffen good. *Journal of Risk and Uncertainty*, 2: 415–20.

Cook, P. J. and D. Graham (1977) The demand for insurance and protection: the case of irreplaceable commodities. *Quarterly Journal of Economics*, 91: 143–56.

Doherty, N. A., and H. Schlesinger (1983) Optimal insurance in incomplete markets. *Journal of Political Economy*, 91: 1045–54.

Eeckhoudt, L., C. Gollier and H. Schlesinger (1996) Changes in background risk and risk taking behavior. *Econometrica*, 64: 683–9.

Eeckhoudt, L. and M. S. Kimball (1992) Background risk, prudence, and the demand for insurance. In G. Dionne (ed.), *Contributions to Insurance Economics* (pp. 239–54). Boston: Kluwer Academic Publishers.

Eeckhoudt, L., C. Gollier, and H. Schlesinger (2005). *Economic and Financial Decisions under Risk*. Princeton, NJ: Princeton University Press.

Ehrlich, I. and G. Becker (1972) Market insurance, self-insurance and self-protection. *Journal of Political Economy*, 80: 623–648.

Gollier, C. (1995) The comparative statics of changes in risk revisited. *Journal of Economic Theory*, 66: 522–36.

Gollier, C. (1997) A note on portfolio dominance. *Review of Economic Studies*, 64: 147–50.

Gollier, C. and J. W. Pratt (1996) Risk vulnerability and the tempering effect of background risk. *Econometrica*, 64: 1109–23.

Gollier, C. and H. Schlesinger (1996) Arrow's theorem on the optimality of deductibles: a stochastic dominance approach. *Economic Theory*, 7: 359–63.

Kimball, M. S. (1990) Precautionary saving in the small and in the large. *Econometrica*, 58, 53–73.

Kimball, M. S. (1993) Standard risk aversion. *Econometrica*, 61: 589–611.

Mayers, D. and C. W. Smith, Jr. (1983) The interdependence of individual portfolio decisions and the demand for insurance. *Journal of Political Economy*, 91: 304–11.

Mossin, J. (1968) Aspects of rational insurance purchasing. *Journal of Political Economy*, 76: 533–68.

Raviv, A. (1979) The design of an optimal insurance policy. *American Economic Review*, 69: 84–96.

Schlesinger, H. (1997) Insurance demand without the expected-utility paradigm. *Journal of Risk and Insurance*, 64: 19–39.

Chapter 5

Corporate Insurance and Risk Management

In the perfect market considered in Modigliani and Miller (1958), corporate financial strategy is irrelevant to the firm's value, given operational strategy. This implies that financial risk management including insurance is also irrelevant. Therefore, risk management can be meaningful only when the market is imperfect, and thus transaction costs are incurred. In general, different financial strategies result in different transaction costs, which, in turn, affect the firm's value. Such transaction costs include taxes and regulation (Section 5.1), inefficiency in real service (Section 5.2), bankruptcy costs (Section 5.3), market incompleteness (Section 5.4), and information costs (Sections 5.5 and 5.6), among others. In addition, financial strategies may interact with the operational strategies which affect the firm's value (Section 5.7). In this chapter, we investigate the rationales for corporate risk management. We also briefly address the risk management of insurers (Section 5.8). While our discussion is focused on insurance, it also has implications for general risk management.

5.1 Tax and Regulation

In most countries, the tax schedules exhibit convexity because taxes are effective only for the positive profit, and are often progressive. (Even though the loss-carry provision may mitigate the tax convexity, it does not fully offset the convexity.) This tax schedule makes insurance valuable. For example, suppose that the tax rate is 35%. Consider a firm whose profit may be $200 or −$100, with equal probability. When the firm's profit is $200, it will pay $70 in taxes. However, the firm will not pay −$35 (i.e., does not receive a subsidy of $35), when its profit is −$100. Thus, the firm's expected tax cost is $35. Now suppose that the firm purchases insurance so that the firm's profit profile is changed to $50 with no risk. The firm will pay $17.50 in taxes. On average, the tax saving from insurance is $17.50.

Regulation may affect the demand for insurance. Suppose that a firm's pricing needs to be approved by the government. Suppose further that product warranties are important costs to the firm. Note, however, that the warranty costs will be incurred in the future, not now. In this case, the firm may have difficulty in justifying the costs for pricing. If the firm can purchase liability insurance for the warranties, then the premium payment will become observable. Now the firm can justify the warranty costs more easily. The key issue here is the communication costs. When parties to a contract are not perfectly informed, communication may incur costs. Hard (soft) information refers to information that can (not) be easily verified. Insurance purchase transforms soft information to hard information.

Proposition 5.1 Firms may purchase insurance as a result of tax and regulation concerns.

5.2   Real Services

Firms are exposed to the risk of lawsuits. A firm's customers may sue the firm for product failures. In such a case, the firm needs to incur costs in defending itself. If the firm purchases liability insurance, it can reduce the legal costs, since insurers have, as experts, comparative advantages in processing lawsuit claims. In addition, insurers may also provide consulting services in the risk management of hazardous facilities. These cases exemplify that insurance purchases enable firms to lower costs where insurers have comparative advantages. Note that the real service provision is not obtained by internal risk management. In this aspect, external risk management has advantage over internal risk management. In other cases, however, external risk management can be costly. For example, the firm may not have incentives to lower risks, since the risk is transferred outside of the firm under the external risk management.

Proposition 5.2 Corporate insurance can increase the firm's value through the valuable services provided by insurers.

5.3   Bankruptcy Costs

When a firm goes bankrupt, the remaining assets are distributed to stake-holders, including creditors and shareholders. If the distribution does not incur any costs, then there are no bankruptcy costs. In general, however, determination of the firm's value and distribution among stakeholders incur costs. For example, the firm may have to sell its assets at prices lower than market prices. The firm may have to consult accounting firms and law firms in determining the value and distribution rules. Conflicts among stakeholders regarding distribution rules will also incur costs. These bankruptcy costs can be saved if the firm does not go bankrupt. Since insurance reduces the probabilities of losses and the loss sizes, it can reduce the possibility of bankruptcy. Therefore, insurance can help save the bankruptcy costs.

Proposition 5.3 Corporate insurance can lower the expected bankruptcy costs.

5.4   Market Incompleteness

A financial market is called "complete" if any payoff structure can be obtained by the portfolio of existing assets (see Chapter 15 for more details). For example, suppose that tomorrow's uncertainty is described by three states of nature, G, M, and B. Suppose further that there are three assets X, Y, and Z. The payoff of each asset in dollars is as follows: $X = (1, 1, 1)$, $Y = (1, 1, 0)$, and $Z = (1, 0, 0)$. Now, consider a payoff structure of ($3 in G, $2 in M, $1 in B). The payoff $(3, 2, 1)$ can be obtained by the portfolio of $X + Y + Z$. As a matter of fact, any payoff (a, b, c) can be obtained by $cX + (b - c)Y + (a - b)Z$. Thus, the market is complete. However, if there are only Y and Z in the market, then the payoff $(3, 2, 1)$ cannot be obtained by any portfolio of Y and Z. In this case, the market is incomplete.

When the market is incomplete, a firm cannot attain a desirable payoff structure. Insurance may improve the situation in two ways. First, insurance may become an additional asset to help complete the market. (This rationale can be applied to individuals as well as firms.) For example, suppose that the firm value is $(3, 5, 5)$. Even if the firm prefers $(4, 4, 4)$ to $(3, 5, 5)$, $(4, 4, 4)$ cannot be achieved using the existing assets, when there are only Y and Z in the market. Insurance can be considered an asset with payoff $(1, -1, -1)$, where the negative payoff is the insurance premium.

With Y, Z and insurance, the market becomes complete. By purchasing one unit of insurance, the payoff of the firm becomes (4, 4, 4), as desired.

Second, insurance may improve efficiency by implementing efficient risk sharing. A firm can be considered a nexus of contracts among diverse stakeholders. The stakeholders may have different risk attitudes. Therefore, it may be in the stakeholders' interests to allocate risks among themselves. If the market is complete, however, the risk allocation among the stakeholders does not matter, as long as assets are fairly priced. This is because each stakeholder can trade assets for their own interests. In such a case, risk allocation among stakeholders does not affect the firm's value.

However, if the market is incomplete, stakeholders may not attain the payoff structure they prefer. Now, the risk allocation becomes important to stakeholders. It will be efficient to allocate risks to those who have a comparative advantage in risk bearing. For example, capitalists (creditors and equityholders) can be considered less risk averse than consumers. Then, shifting risk from consumers to capitalists may be desirable. Equityholders can also be considered less risk averse than creditors. In such a case, shifting risk from creditors to equityholders will improve efficiency. However, it may not be efficient to leave all the risk to equityholders, since they are risk averse individuals. As long as outside insurers have a comparative advantage in risk bearing, shifting risk to those insurers can improve efficiency. In general, the voluntary insurance contract effectively transfers the firm's risk to the insurer that can bear the risk more efficiently. In this way, insurance can improve the efficiency in risk sharing.

Proposition 5.4 Corporate insurance can improve the efficiency in risk sharing when the market is incomplete.

5.5   Moral Hazard

Conflicts of interest among stakeholders of a firm may incur costs. Important conflicts between the owners and the creditors include the debt overhang problem and the asset substitution problem. The debt overhang problem refers to the case in which the owners may forgo an investment with positive net present value (NPV) due to the debt. When the NPV of a project is positive, the firm's value will increase if the project is taken on. However, if the firm does not have cash enough to pay back the maturing debt, then a large part of its payoff may have to be distributed to the creditors. Anticipating this result, the owners will prefer not to invest in the project in the first place. Therefore, the debt overhang problem leads to underinvestment. The loss of the NPV is the cost to the firm. Since proper risk management can lower the possibility of cash deficiency, it can lower the costs due to debt overhang.

The asset substitution problem occurs when the owners substitute riskier assets for safer assets. Note that the ownership value can be considered a call option to the firm's value and that a call option value increases in risk. Therefore, the asset substitution increases the ownership value at the expense of creditors. Note that this problem becomes serious when the firm does not have enough cash to pay back the debt. For example, suppose that the firm is sure to become bankrupt if it does not invest. Now, assume that there is a project with a negative NPV. Normally, the firm should not invest in the project. However, the owners may want to invest in a high-risk project if, with luck, they can earn profits. Even if the project payoff is low, the owners will lose nothing because, without investment, the firm will go bankrupt. Therefore, the asset substitution problem may lead to overinvestment. The negative NPV of the project is the cost to the firm. Since proper risk management can lower the possibility of bankruptcy, it can lower the costs due to asset substitution.

Interest conflicts between a manager and owners may also exist. Incentive compensation for the manager is often used to control the conflicts. While the incentive compensation scheme aligns the interests of the manager with those of the owners, it may expose the manager to excessive risks. Since the manager is risk averse, the manager should be compensated for bearing such risks. Therefore, lowering risks in compensation may improve the efficiency. For example, if the risk is not relevant to the manager's ability, removing the risk can lower the costs, without affecting the interest alignment. Thus, risk management can improve efficiency in the incentive compensation scheme. Now, let us investigate formal models for moral hazard.

5.5.1   Debt overhang problem

The debt overhang problem refers to the case in which the owners of a firm may forgo an investment opportunity with positive NPV, when the debt level is high compared to the firm's value. The owners will do so since the increased value will be reaped by the creditors, not by themselves. The following example (see also Mayers and Smith, 1987) shows how insurance can increase the firm's value by providing the owners with the incentives to take the investment.

Let us consider a firm with the debt face value F at time 0 (see Figure 5.1 for the timeline). The debt matures at time 1. For simplicity, assume that the debt pays a zero interest rate. The firm value will be V at time 1 where $F < V$, when no loss occurs and no further investment is taken. A zero

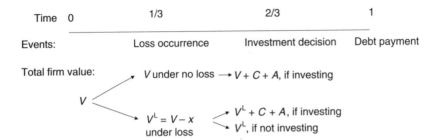

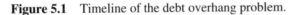

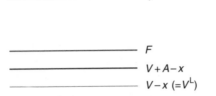

Figure 5.1   Timeline of the debt overhang problem.

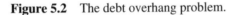

Figure 5.2   The debt overhang problem.

discount rate is assumed. At time $\frac{1}{3}$, a loss of x may occur with probability p, reducing the firm value to $V^L = V - x$, where $V^L < F$. On the other hand, the firm has a risk-free investment opportunity with the positive NPV of A, where $V^L + A < F$ at time $\frac{2}{3}$ (see Figure 5.2). The investment requires a cost of C that should be raised from investors. We simplify the analysis by assuming that the investment cost will be financed from the existing owner, if possible.

If no loss occurs at time $\frac{1}{3}$, the owner will be willing to fund the investment, since the owner's value (net of the investment cost) after debt payment increases from $V - F$ to $V + A - F$. However, if the loss occurs, the situation is changed. After the loss, the firm's value becomes V^L. If the owner funds the investment, then she will lose money since the total firm value net of debt payment is less than the cost: $V^L + C + A - F < C$. Thus, the owner will refuse to fund the investment opportunity. The ex ante firm value (net of the investment cost) at time 0 will be $(1 - p)(V + A) + p(V - x) = V + (1 - p)A - px$. If the firm has no debt, the owner will take on the investment regardless of the loss occurrence. In this case, the firm's ex ante value will be $V + A - px$. The conflict between the creditor and the owner results in a reduction in the firm's ex ante value by pA.

This case exhibits an underinvestment problem, since the firm forgoes a good investment opportunity. This example illustrates how debt may incur costs to the firm. From another point of view, this problem may be

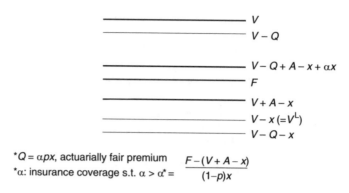

$^*Q = \alpha px$, actuarially fair premium

$^*\alpha$: insurance coverage s.t. $\alpha > \alpha^* = \dfrac{F-(V+A-x)}{(1-p)x}$

Figure 5.3   Insurance as a solution to the debt overhang problem.

considered one in which risk management fails so that the firm's value is reduced too much. If the firm purchases insurance to cover the loss, then the firm's value will not be so reduced after a loss. Now, let us show how risk management or insurance can allow the firm to avoid this underinvestment problem.

Suppose that the firm purchases insurance at time 0. Let α be the insurance coverage. Assume that the insurance premium Q is actuarially fair: $Q = \alpha px$. With no loss, the firm's total value will be $V - Q + C + A$, assuming that the firm will invest. With a loss, the total firm value will be $V - Q + C + A - x + \alpha x$, if the owner is willing to fund the investment cost. The owner will fund the investment if and only if $V - Q + C + A - x + \alpha x - F \geq C$. Since $Q = \alpha px$, this inequality will hold if

$$\alpha \geq \alpha^* = \frac{F-(V+A-x)}{(1-p)x}.$$

With $\alpha \geq \alpha^*$, the firm's ex ante value at time 0 become $V + A - px$, since the firm will always undertake the investment. Figure 5.3 depicts the case of $\alpha > \alpha^*$. Insurance increases the firm's ex ante value by pA. This example shows that proper risk management can increase the firm value by resolving incentive conflicts between creditors and owners.

5.5.2   Asset substitution

Let us reconsider the example of the debt overhang problem. Recall that at time $\frac{1}{3}$, a loss of x may occur with probability p, reducing the firm's value to $V^L = V - x$, where $V^L < F$. Let us now suppose that the firm has an investment opportunity with NPV of $-B$ at time $\frac{2}{3}$. The investment incurs a cost of C. Let us assume that the investment cost is funded from the firm's existing assets, say cash. On the other hand, the investment is risky, such that the payoff of the investment is K or 0, each with probability ½. Note that NPV $= K/2 - C = -B$. When the payoff is K, the firm's ex post value is assumed to be greater than the debt payment: $V^L - C + K > F$.

Normally, the firm should not undertake the investment, since it has a negative NPV. However, the self-interested owner will invest, since the payoff to her is higher if she does so. If the owner does not undertake the investment, the firm will go bankrupt since $V^L < F$. Thus, the owner gets nothing. If the owner invests, then she may get $V^L - C + K - F > 0$ with probability ½. When the payoff from the investment is zero, the firm goes bankrupt as in the case of no investment. As a result, undertaking the investment is in the interest of the owner. Since the NPV is negative, the firm value is lowered. Even though the investment has a negative NPV, the owner has incentives to substitute cash with the risky project, since the risk of the project provides the owner with the chance to make money. This asset substitution problem leads to overinvestment. Given this behavior of the owner, the firm's ex ante value at time 0 becomes $(1 - p)V + p(V - x - B) = V - px - pB$. If the firm has no debt, the owner will not take the investment regardless of the loss occurrence. In this case, the firm's ex ante value will be $V - px$. The conflict between the creditor and the owner results in a loss of the firm's ex ante value by pB.

Let us now show that insurance can resolve this overinvestment problem. Suppose that the firm purchases insurance at time 0. Let α be the insurance coverage. The insurance premium Q is actuarially fair. With no loss, the firm's value will be $V - Q$. We assume that $V - Q$ is high enough to not undertake the investment. After a loss occurs, the firm's value will be $V - Q - x + \alpha x$. If the firm does not undertake the investment, the payoff to the owner becomes $E^N = V - Q - x + \alpha x - F$.[1] If the firm invests and the payoff from the investment is K, then the payoff to the owner becomea $E^G = V - Q - x + \alpha x + K - C - F$. If the payoff from the investment is 0, then the payoff to the owner becomes $E^B = \max[V - Q - x + \alpha x - C - F, 0]$.

The firm (the owner) will not invest if $E^N \geq (E^G + E^B)/2$. Suppose that $V - Q - x + \alpha x - C - F \geq 0$, or

$$\alpha \geq \alpha^{**} = \frac{-(V - x - C - F)}{(1 - p)x}.$$

---

[1] We are assuming that E^N is greater than zero, which will be the case with the relevant range of coverage, as shown below.

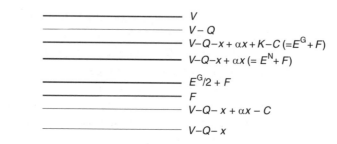

$$V$$
$$V - Q$$
$$V - Q - x + \alpha x + K - C \, (= E^G + F)$$
$$V - Q - x + \alpha x \, (= E^N + F)$$
$$E^G/2 + F$$
$$F$$
$$V - Q - x + \alpha x - C$$
$$V - Q - x$$

$^*Q = \alpha px$, actuarially fair premium
$^*\alpha$: insurance coverage s.t.

$$\alpha^{**} = \frac{-(V - x - C - F)}{(1-p)x} > \alpha > \frac{-(V - x - F) + K - C}{(1-p)x} = \alpha^{***}$$

Figure 5.4   Insurance as a solution to the asset substitution problem.

Then, $E^B = V - Q - x + \alpha x - C - F$, so that $(E^G + E^B)/2 = V - Q - x + \alpha x - B - F$. In this case, $E^N \ge (E^G + E^B)/2$ holds. Now, suppose that $V - Q - x + \alpha x - C - F < 0$, so that $E^B = 0$. Then, $(E^G + E^B)/2 = E^G/2$. For $E^N \ge E^G/2$,

$$\alpha \ge \alpha^{***} = \frac{-(V - x - F) + K - C}{(1-p)x}.$$

Since NPV $= K/2 - C < 0$, $\alpha^{**} \ge \alpha^{***}$. Therefore, if $\alpha \ge \alpha^{***}$, then the firm will not undertake the investment. Finally, it can be confirmed that $E^N > 0$ for $\alpha \ge \alpha^{***}$. This situation is depicted in Figure 5.4 where $\alpha^{**} > \alpha > \alpha^{***}$. Insurance prevents the firm from losing pB. This and previous examples show that proper risk management can increase the firm's value by resolving incentive conflicts between creditors and owners.

Proposition 5.5 Corporate insurance can increase the firm's value by resolving the incentive conflicts between creditors and owners.

5.5.3 Managerial compensation

Insurance can be used to resolve conflicts between the owners and the manager of a firm (Han, 1996). Suppose that a risk averse manager of a firm and a risk neutral owner enter into an incentive contract. The utility of the manager is denoted by U. The manager can affect the firm value by selecting two types of efforts: operating effort, e_1, and risk management effort, e_2. Efforts incur private costs $C_1(e_1)$ and $C_2(e_2)$, respectively. We assume that $C_i' > 0$ and $C_i'' > 0$, $i = 1, 2$. Effort levels are private information.

The gross operating value V can be V^H or V^L, where $V^H \geq V^L$. The operating effort determines $p(e_1)$, the probability that $V = V^H$. We assume that $p' \geq 0$ and $p'' \leq 0$. The operating value, however, can be reduced by a loss occurrence. A loss D can be either x or 0, where $x > 0$. The risk management effort determines $q(e_2)$, the probability that $D = x$. We assume that $q' \leq 0$, and $q'' \geq 0$. There are four states of nature: state 1 for $(V = V^H, D = 0)$, state 2 for $(V = V^H, D = x)$, state 3 for $(V = V^L, D = 0)$, state 4 for $(V = V^L, D = x)$. The firm's ex post gross value $W = V - D$. Potentially, W can have four realized values depending on states: $W_1 = V^H$, $W_2 = V^H - x$, $W_3 = V^L$, $W_4 = V^L - x$.

The payment from the owner to the manager, R, is contingent on states: $R = R_i$ for state i. The owner will solve the following program to find an optimal payment scheme.[2]

$$\max pV^H + (1-p)V^L - qx - [p(1-q)R_1 + pqR_2$$
$$+ (1-p)(1-q)R_3 + (1-p)qR_4]$$
$$\text{s.t. } p(1-q)U(R_1) + pqU(R_2) + (1-p)(1-q)U(R_3)$$
$$+ (1-p)qU(R_4) - C_1(e_1) - C_2(e_2) \geq \bar{U}, \tag{5.1}$$

$$e_1 \in \arg\max_{e_1'} \; p(1-q)U(R_1) + pqU(R_2) + (1-p)(1-q)U(R_3)$$
$$+ (1-p)q\bar{U}(R_4) - C_1(e_1') - C_2(e_2),$$

$$e_2 \in \arg\max_{e_2'} \; p(1-q)U(R_1) + pqU(R_2) + (1-p)(1-q)U(R_3)$$
$$+ (1-p)q\bar{U}(R_4) - C_1(e_1) - C_2(e_2').$$

The first constraint is the participation condition for the manager, where $\bar{U}$ is the reservation utility. The second and third constraints denote agency problems in selecting operating and risk management efforts, respectively. Provided that e_1 and e_2 are interior solutions satisfying their own FOCs, the second and third constraints are replaced by the FOCs

$$p'[(1-q)U(R_1) + qU(R_2) - (1-q)U(R_3) - qU(R_4)] - C_1'(e_1) = 0$$
$$-q'[pU(R_1) - pU(R_2) + (1-p)U(R_3) - (1-p)U(R_4)] - C_2'(e_2) = 0 \tag{5.2}$$

Let us write λ, μ, and δ for the Lagrange multipliers for three constraints, respectively.

Now, we obtain the following FOCs to the program:

---

[2] Moral hazard problems will be studied in detail in Chapters 9 and 10. Readers who are not familiar with the program formulation are referred to those chapters.

$$L_{R1} = -p(1-q) + \lambda p(1-q)U_1' + \mu p'(1-q)U_1' - \delta q' p U_1' = 0$$

$$L_{R2} = -pq + \lambda pq U_2' + \mu p' q U_2' + \delta q' p U_2' = 0$$

$$L_{R3} = -(1-p)(1-q) + \lambda(1-p)(1-q)U_3' - \mu p'(1-q)U_3'$$
$$\quad - \delta q'(1-p)U_3' = 0$$

$$L_{R4} = -(1-p)q + \lambda(1-p)q U_4' - \mu p' q U_4' + \delta q'(1-p)U_4' = 0$$

$$L_{e1} = p'[V^H - V^L - (1-q)R_1 - qR_2 + (1-q)R_3 + qR_4]$$
$$\quad + \lambda[p'\{(1-q)U_1 + qU_2 - (1-q)U_3 - qU_4\} - C_1']$$
$$\quad + \mu[p''\{(1-q)U_1 + qU_2 - (1-q)U_3 - qU_4\} - C_1'']$$
$$\quad + \delta p'q'[-U_1 + U_2 + U_3 - U_4] = 0$$

$$L_{e2} = q'[-x + pR_1 - pR_2 + (1-p)R_3 - (1-p)R_4]$$
$$\quad + \lambda[q'\{-pU_1 + pU_2 - (1-p)U_3 + (1-p)U_4\} - C_2']$$
$$\quad + \mu p'q'[-U_1 + U_2 + U_3 - U_4] + \delta[q''\{-pU_1 + pU_2$$
$$\quad - (1-p)U_3 + (1-p)U_4\} - C_2''] = 0$$

$$(5.3)$$

where $U_i = U(R_i)$.
Rearranging the FOCs, we have

$$U_1' = \frac{p}{\lambda p + \mu p' - \delta q' p / (1-q)}$$

$$U_2' = \frac{p}{\lambda p + \mu p' + \delta q' p / q}$$

$$U_3' = \frac{1-p}{\lambda(1-p) - \mu p' - \delta q'(1-p)/(1-q)}$$

$$U_4' = \frac{1-p}{\lambda(1-p) - \mu p' + \delta q'(1-p)/q}$$

$$(5.4)$$

Comparing these values, we have $U_4' \geq U_2'$, $U_3' \geq U_1'$. That is, $R_1 \geq R_2$, $R_3 \geq R_4$. The result that $R_1 \geq R_2$ and $R_3 \geq R_4$ comes from the negative marginal risk management effort ($q' \leq 0$). The result that $R_1 \geq R_3$ and $R_2 \geq R_4$ comes from the positive marginal operating effort ($p' \geq 0$). Even if the manager is risk averse, fully removing the manager's risk is not optimal, due to the moral hazard problem. In order to induce him to make proper efforts, risks should be imposed on him.

If the risk management effort is not relevant in reducing risks, or $q' = 0$, then we have $e_2 = 0$. In this case we obtain $R_1 = R_2$ and $R_3 = R_4$. In other words, the manager is fully protected from the risk of loss. This result can be easily understood by noting that removing the risk of the risk averse manager is optimal, since his risk management effort is not responsible for the risk. Similarly, if the operating effort does not contribute to the operating value, or $p' = 0$, then we have $e_1 = 0$. In this case, we obtain $R_1 = R_3$ and $R_2 = R_4$. The manager is fully protected from the operating value risk for which his effort is not responsible.

While we assumed that the owner is risk neutral so that she can directly insure the manager, this insurance function can be equivalently performed by corporate insurance as well. The risk neutral owner is indifferent between purchasing actuarially fair insurance and self-insurance. If the owner is risk averse, the compensation scheme will have to additionally incorporate the risk aversion of the owner. Technically, the left-hand sides of expressions (5.4) should be now divided by the marginal utilities of the owner at her wealth in each state. Note that (5.4) is obtained under the assumption of the risk neutral owner, since her marginal utility is 1.

When the owner is risk averse, (5.4) can be considered FOCs under the assumption that she can purchase corporate insurance to fully protect against the risk of the remaining value $W_i - R_i$. In this case, the owner can behave as if she is risk neutral, since the remaining risk will be optimally transferred to an insurer. Now, corporate insurance is strictly preferred to self-insurance. Even though full insurance against the firm risk may not be available, the owner can still benefit from purchasing partial insurance, which is analogous to the case of the individual demand for insurance. In any case, an optimally determined insurance level improves the efficiency in the compensation scheme. The result is summarized as follows.

Proposition 5.6 Corporate insurance can improve the efficiency in managerial compensation by reducing risks of the manager and/or the owner.[3]

Let us now suppose that the compensation scheme does not distinguish between results from risk management and from operating management. It is often the case that the compensation is based on aggregated performance measures such as accounting profit or stock price. In this case, the information that can be obtained from segregated measures is ignored.

---

[3] However, it is possible that insurance may be purchased as a result of the conflicts, not as a solution for the conflicts. For example, as a risk averter, the manager may want to purchase excessive corporate insurance, sacrificing firm value (Core, 1997).

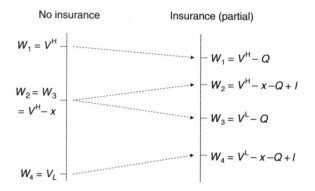

Figure 5.5 Separation between cash flows from operations and from risk management.

To address this issue, let us suppose that $x = V^H - V^L$, so that by observing the firm's value, the owner cannot distinguish between state 2 and state 3 (see Figure 5.5). This program can be solved by adding a constraint $R_2 = R_3$ to the above program. The additional constraint will decrease the utility of the owner.

Corporate insurance may enhance efficiency by allowing the owner to differentiate the firm values between state 2 and state 3.[4] Now, suppose that the firm purchases insurance against the loss x. Coverage α is such that $0 < \alpha < 1$. Given the actuarially fair premium, the owner does not become worse off by purchasing insurance. In addition, the insurance scheme can play the role of separating states. The firm's values become

$$W_1 = V^H - Q, \ W_2 = V^H - x - Q + I, \ W_3 = V^L - Q, \ W_4 = V^L - x - Q + I.$$

When $x = V^H - V^L$, recall that $W_2 = W_3 = V^L$ before purchasing insurance. With insurance, $W_2 = V^L - Q + I > V^L - Q = W_3$. As a result, insurance allows the owner to separate states, which can provide useful information (see Figure 5.5). Thus, the owner may have incentives to purchase insurance. Since the premium is actuarially fair, any positive coverage can successfully separate states 2 and 3. However, if $\alpha = 1$, then $W_1 = W_2$ and $W_3 = W_4$. Note that this result will be obtained as optimal when the

[4] Alternatively, we may assume that insurers have superior abilities in identifying the (insurable) loss. While we focus on the differentiation of the firm's value in the simple model, our logic can be applied as long as insurance can help separate cash flows from risk management and those from operating management.

distinctions between states 1 and 2 and between states 3 and 4 are not important. For example, this case may be observable when the risk management effort is beyond the manager's control. In general, however, the optimal coverage should be partial; $0 < \alpha < 1$.

The main implication of this simple example is that corporate insurance may be purchased to separate cash flows from operating management and those from risk management. Separation allows the owner to offer a more efficient contract to the manager. The role of corporate insurance is reminiscent of the role of completing the market discussed in Section 5.4. Insurance allows the owner to identify states by changing firm values in states. Now, the owner can design a compensation scheme contingent on the realized states, which will improve efficiency.

Proposition 5.7 Corporate insurance can improve the efficiency in managerial compensation by separating cash flows from operating management and those from risk management.

5.6 Adverse Selection

Myers and Majluf (1984) show that information asymmetry may lead a firm to forgo good investment opportunities, unless the firm has sufficient internal capital. This possibility occurs since outside investors, without knowing the true value of the firm, may take a high-value firm for a low-value firm if it seeks external financing. If the loss of value due to this wrong belief is greater than the benefit of undertaking the new investment, then the firm may forgo the good investment opportunity. The lost value from the investment is the cost of external financing. Let us briefly review the Myers and Majluf model.

Consider a firm that has an asset in place A and an investment opportunity with NPV $V > 0$. The initial cost for the investment is I. There are two states of nature (denoted by S): the state can be good ($S = G$) with probability p, or bad ($S = B$) with probability $1 - p$. In state S, $A = A_S$ and $V = V_S$, where $A_G > A_B$ and $V_G > V_B$. Write $\bar{A}$ and $\bar{V}$ for the ex ante values of A and V: $\bar{A} = pA_G + (1 - p)A_B$ and $\bar{V} = pV_G + (1 - p)V_B$.

Let us set up the model in a signaling game over two periods. In the first period, the (existing) owner of the firm observes the realized state of nature and determines whether or not she seeks external financing through issuing stocks. The funding size is denoted by E. Let us assume that $E = I$ or 0. Assume that the capital market is competitive and the fair return is zero, so that the investor will provide funds as long as she expects to earn nonnegative profit. The expected profit of the outside investor will be

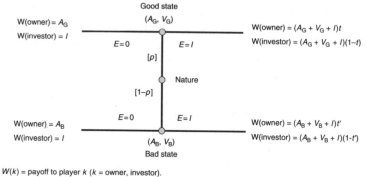

Figure 5.6   External financing game under information asymmetry.

calculated based on her belief regarding the states which, in turn, depends on the interpretation of the funding behavior of the firm. In an equilibrium, the belief should be fulfilled, and neither the owner of the insurer nor the investor should have incentives to deviate from the equilibrium. The signaling game structure is depicted in Figure 5.6. At the end of each node, the payoffs to players are noted.

When the firm does not raise capital (at the left nodes), the payoff to the investor is simply I. When the firm raises capital (at the right nodes), the payoffs to the owner and the investor will depend on the firm's value which is determined in the market based on the investor's beliefs. In the second period, the information asymmetry problem resolves. The firm's value is distributed to the existing owner and the new owner (i.e., the investor) if the capital is raised.

Lemma 5.1 (External financing under adverse selection). There are two equilibria:

(a)   a pooling equilibrium in which the firm in both states raises capital, if

$$A_G \leq \frac{\overline{A} + \overline{V}}{\overline{A} + \overline{V} + I}(A_G + V_G + I);$$

(b)   a separating equilibrium in which only the firm in the bad state raises capital, if

$$A_G \geq \frac{A_B + V_B}{A_B + V_B + I}(A_G + V_G + I);$$

Proof. (a) Since the firm in both states raises capital, the outside investor cannot distinguish between two states. Therefore, the firm's value is calculated based on the ex ante values in the market. The ownership proportions for the investor and the owner become $I/(\bar{A} + \bar{V} + I)$ and $(\bar{A} + \bar{V})/(\bar{A} + \bar{V} + I)$, respectively. In the good state, the total firm value is $A_G + V_G + I$. Thus, the payoff distributed to the owner is

$$\frac{\bar{A} + \bar{V}}{\bar{A} + \bar{V} + I}(A_G + V_G + I)$$

in the good state. On the other hand, the owner in the good state will have A_G without raising capital. Comparing the two payoffs, the firm in the good state will not deviate to $E = 0$, if

$$A_G \leq \frac{\bar{A} + \bar{V}}{\bar{A} + \bar{V} + I}(A_G + V_G + I).$$

It is easy to see that the firm in the bad state will not deviate from the equilibrium.

(b) Since only the firm in the bad state raises capital, outside investors can tell that the firm is in the bad state if it raises capital. Therefore, the ownership proportions for the investor and the owner become $I/(A_B + V_B + I)$ and $(A_B + V_B)/(A_B + V_B + I)$, respectively. In the bad state, the firm's total value is $A_B + V_B + I$. Thus, the payoff distributed to the owner is $A_B + V_B$ in the bad state. Obviously, the firm in the bad state has no incentive to deviate from the equilibrium. It remains to check the possibility of deviation of the firm in the good state. The owner in the good state will have A_G without raising capital. If the firm in the good state raises capital, the ownership proportion for the owner will be $(A_B + V_B)/(A_B + V_B + I)$, since the outside investor's conjecture that it is in the bad state. Therefore, the firm value to distribute to the owner in the good state is

$$\frac{A_B + V_B}{A_B + V_B + I}(A_G + V_G + I).$$

Comparing this payoff with $A_{G'}$ we obtain the result.

Finally, let us show that no other types of equilibrium exist. Potentially, there can be two more types of equilibrium: a pooling equilibrium in which the firm in both states raises no capital, and a separating equilibrium in which only the firm in the good state raises capital. It is easy to see that these equilibria cannot exist, since the firm in the bad state always has incentives to raise capital.   □

When the firm in the good state does not take up the investment as in (b), the firm fails to raise the firm's value by the NPV of the investment. This lost NPV is the cost of the external financing under adverse selection. Note that this cost is due to the adverse selection and the lack of sufficient internal capital. If the firm has enough internal capital, then the firm will take up the investment regardless of adverse selection.

An important message of Myers and Majluf is that in order to avoid the costs of external financing, the firm needs to have sufficient internal capital. A failure of proper risk management, however, may cause there to be insufficient internal capital. Since insufficient internal capital exposes the firm to costly external financing, proper risk management can enhance firm value by providing the firm with stable internal capital (Froot, Scharfstein, and Stein, 1993).

Grace and Rebello (1993) suggest another case in which corporate insurance may help resolve adverse selection, when insurance purchase conveys information regarding the firm value. For this, suppose that investors in the capital market have no information regarding operating cash flows of the firm. If the higher insurance risk is accompanied by higher operating cash flow, the firm's high demand for insurance may signal high cash flow. In this case, corporate insurance can be used in resolving information asymmetry between investors and the firm.

Proposition 5.8 Corporate insurance can reduce adverse selection costs.

5.7   Strategic Demand for Insurance

Firms may purchase insurance for strategic purposes (Ashby and Diacon, 1998; Seog, 2006), even if they are risk neutral. Since insurance may allow firms to transfer risks to third parties, firms may become more aggressive in the output market competition. This effect of insurance on competitiveness leads risk neutral firms to purchase even actuarially unfavorable insurance. For this, let us consider the Cournot–Nash duopoly model of Seog (2006).

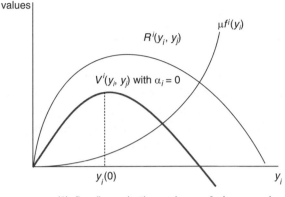

$y_i(0)$: firm i's production under $\alpha_j = 0$ given y_j and α_j

Figure 5.7 Functions for firm i under $\alpha_i = 0$, given y_j and α_j.

Let us denote two risk neutral firms by i or $j = 1, 2$. Firms determine insurance coverage in period 1 and then production levels in period 2. An insurable loss may occur in period 2. The discount rate is zero. Firm i's insurance coverage is denoted by α_i, where $0 \leq \alpha_i \leq 1$. The premium loading factor is denoted by $\lambda \geq 0$. Firm i's production level in period 2 is denoted by y_i. The operating profit of firm i is $R^i(y_i, y_j)$ when production levels are y_i and y_j. We assume that $R^i_i \ (= \partial R^i(y_i, y_j)/\partial y_i) < 0$, $R^i_{ii} \ (= \partial^2 R^i(y_i, y_j)/\partial y_i^2) < 0$, $R^i_i(0, y_j) = \infty$, and $R^i_i(\infty, y_j) = -\infty$. We focus on the case of substitute goods, $R^j_{ij} < 0$. On the other hand, the loss size is denoted by $z_i f^i(y_i)$, a multiplication of random factor z_i and the nonrandom "loss base" $f^i(y_i)$. A loss base may be interpreted as a potential maximum loss. We assume that $\partial f^i(y_i)/\partial y_i = f^i_i > 0$, $f^i_{ii} \geq 0$; and that $E(z_1) = E(z_2) = \mu$.

Now, the (net) profit of firm i in period 2 is the operating profit net of the loss not covered by insurance: $R^i(y_i, y_j) - z_i(1 - \alpha_i)f^i(y_i)$. Given α_i and α_j, let $V^i(y_i, y_j)$ be the expected profit of firm i in period 2. Then

$$V^i(y_i, y_j) = E\{R^i(y_i, y_j) - z_i(1 - \alpha_i)f^i(y_i)\}$$
$$= R^i(y_i, y_j) - (1 - \alpha_i)\mu f^i(y_i). \tag{5.5}$$

Figure 5.7 illustrates R^i, μf^i, and V^i as functions of y_i under no insurance ($\alpha_i = 0$), given y_j and α_j.

Now, let us consider the insurance decision in period 1. Define $W^i(\alpha_i, \alpha_j)$ as the ex ante expected profit of firm i, given α_i and α_j in period 1. Then,

$$W^i(\alpha_i, \alpha_j) = V^i(y_i, y_j) - (1+\lambda)\alpha_i \mu f^i(y_i)$$
$$= R^i(y_i, y_j) - (1+\lambda\alpha_i)\, \mu f^i(y_i). \tag{5.6}$$

Each firm will simultaneously determine the insurance coverage in period 1. In period 2, each firm will also simultaneously determine the production level. We formulate the production decision in period 2 as the usual Cournot–Nash duopoly game. We assume the following stability condition for the Cournot–Nash equilibrium in period 2:[5]

$$V^i_{ij} = R^i_{ij} < 0, \tag{5.7}$$

$$S \equiv V^i_{ii} V^j_{jj} - V^i_{ij} V^j_{ji} = R^i_{ii} R^j_{jj} - R^i_{ij} R^j_{ji} > 0. \tag{5.8}$$

In an equilibrium of the overall game, each firm should not have any incentives to change its insurance coverage and production level, given its competitor's insurance coverage and production level. Working backwards, let us start with the production level decision problem in period 2. The firm i solves the following program, given y_j, α_i and α_j:

$$\text{Max}_{yi}\ V^i(y_i, y_j) = R^i(y_i, y_j) - (1-\alpha_i)\mu\, f^i(y_i, x_i). \tag{5.9}$$

The FOC to this problem is

$$R^i_i - (1-\alpha_i)\mu f^i_i = 0, \tag{5.10}$$

The SOC is satisfied: $\partial^2 V^i / \partial y^2_i = R^i_{ii} - (1-\alpha_i)f^i_{ii} < 0$, where $0 \le \alpha_i \le 1$.

By simultaneously solving two FOCs for firms 1 and 2, we can find the Cournot–Nash outcome (y^*_1, y^*_2). From the comparative statics we obtain the following results.

Lemma 5.2.

(a) In a Cournot–Nash equilibrium in period 2, an increase in insurance coverage of a firm will increase its production level, but lower the production level of its competitor.

(b) In the symmetric case in which $\alpha_i = \alpha_j = \alpha$, and $y_i = y_j = y$, an increase in insurance coverage increases the production level in a Cournot–Nash equilibrium.

---

[5] By (5.7), the reaction curves have downward slopes. By (5.8), the slope of the reaction curve of firm j is steeper than that of firm i in (y_j, y_i) space.

Proof.

(a)   Let us differentiate FOCs (5.10) for i and j with respect to α_i:

$$\{R_{ii}^i - (1-\alpha_i)\mu f_{ii}^i\}dy_i + R_{ij}^i dy_j = -\mu f_i^i d\alpha_i$$

$$R_{ji}^j dy_i + \{R_{jj}^j - (1-\alpha_j)\mu f_{jj}^j\}dy_j = 0.$$

Using Cramer's rule,

$$dy_i/d\alpha_i = -\mu f_i^i \{R_{jj}^j - (1-\alpha_j)\mu f_{jj}^j\}/S > 0,$$

$$dy_j/d\alpha_i = \mu f_i^i R_{ji}^j/S < 0$$

where S is defined by (10.8).

(b)   For the symmetry case, the FOCs become

$$R_i^i - (1-\alpha)\mu f_i^i = 0,$$

where $\alpha_i = \alpha_j = \alpha$ and $y_i = y_j = y$. Differentiate the FOC with respect to α:

$$\{R_{ii}^i + R_{ij}^i - (1-\alpha)\mu f_{ii}^i\}dy = -\mu f_i^i d\alpha,$$

$$dy/d\alpha = -\mu f_i^i/\{R_{ii}^i + R_{ij}^i - (1-\alpha)\mu f_{ii}^i\} > 0. \qquad \square$$

Lemma 5.2 (a) comes from the fact that a firm produces more with higher insurance coverage. An increase in the production level has two offsetting effects on the profit: the increase in the operation profit and the increase in loss sizes. However, the adverse effect of the loss size increase can be mitigated if the insurance coverage is higher. Therefore, the firm will increase its production level more aggressively. As the firm becomes more aggressive, the competitor will lower the production level, since its marginal profit is lowered ($R_{ij}^j < 0$). In the symmetric case, both firms will increase their production levels, when the insurance coverage simultaneously increases (Lemma 5.2(b)).

In period 1, firms will select insurance coverage considering its effect on the production level in period 2. Firm i solves the following program:

$$\max_{\alpha i} W^i(\alpha_i, \alpha_j) = R^i(y_i, y_j) - (1+\lambda\alpha_i)\mu f^i(y_i, x_i). \qquad (5.11)$$

The FOC becomes

$$\partial W^i(\alpha_i, \alpha_j)/\partial \alpha_i = -(1+\lambda)\alpha_i \mu f_i^i(dy_i/d\alpha_i)$$
$$+ R_j^i dy_j/d\alpha_i - \lambda\mu f^i = 0.^6 \qquad (5.12)$$

---

6   We use the fact that $R_i^i - (1-\alpha_i)\mu f_i^i = 0$ from the FOC in period 2.

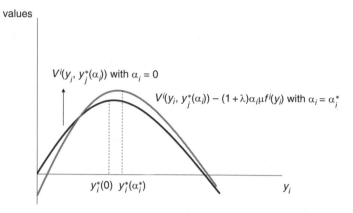

$y_j^*(\alpha_i)$: firm i's production under the insurance coverage α_i and α_j^*
$y_j^*(\alpha_i)$: firm j's production under the insurance coverage α_i and α_j^*

Figure 5.8   Strategic demand for insurance.

Assuming that the SOC is satisfied, we have the following results.

Proposition 5.9 In an equilibrium of the overall game, the insurance coverage of firm i is positive if and only if $R_j^i dy_j/d\alpha_i > \lambda\mu f^i$ at $\alpha_i = 0$.

Proof With $\alpha_i = 0$, the left-hand side of FOC (5.12) becomes $R_j^i dy_j/d\alpha_i - \lambda\mu f^i$. Thus, we have $\alpha_i > 0$ if and only if $R_j^i \, dy_j/d\alpha_i - \lambda\mu f^i > 0$ at $\alpha_i = 0$.   □

$R_j^i \, dy_j/d\alpha_i$ can be interpreted as the "strategic effect" of the coverage increase, since it reflects the change in the operating profit through the effect of coverage on the competitor's production level. On the other hand, $\lambda\mu f^i$ measures the "premium loading effect" of the coverage increase. Proposition 5.8 implies that a risk neutral firm may purchase insurance when the strategic effect is greater than the premium loading effect of insurance. Firms purchase insurance based on strategic purposes. As long as the strategic effect is larger than the premium loading effect, a risk neutral firm will purchase insurance even if the premium is actuarially unfair.

Figure 5.8 illustrates a positive coverage case. In Figure 5.8, functions are depicted as functions of y_i, given $y_j^* (\alpha_i)$, α_i^* and α_j^*, where α_i^* and α_j^* are evaluated at an equilibrium, and $y^*(\alpha_i)$ is firm j's equilibrium production level determined in period 2, given α_i and α_j^*. In Figure 5.8, the optimal production level and the firm's value are higher under a positive coverage ($\alpha_j^* > 0$) than under no insurance.

5.8   Risk Management of Insurers

The aforementioned rationales for corporate risk management are generally applied to insurers. What may distinguish insurers and financial firms from manufacturing firms is the focus on financial risk management. Since, like other financial firms, a large portion of the assets of insurers is typically composed of financial assets, it is not surprising that financial risk management is more often used by insurers than by manufacturing firms. Compared to real assets, financial assets are often characterized by high liquidity and low transaction costs. High liquidity and low transaction costs enable financial firms to utilize sophisticated risk management tools using financial markets including asset liability management, value at risk, risk hedging with options and futures, and alternative risk transfer, among others.

On the other hand, the liability of insurers is nothing more than a pool of risks, which is a direct result of their business. Since the business of insurers is taking insureds' risks, the business itself exposes insurers to risks. Therefore, as going concerns, insurers have strong incentives to manage liability risks. Liability risk is not a problem as long as the asset values move together with liability values. However, the liability risks are generated by insurance risks and are different from the risk factors affecting financial assets such as stocks and bonds. Desirable risk management by insurers should use a holistic enterprise-level approach with respect to both assets and liabilities. With the developments of financial theory and information technology, holistic risk management, or enterprise risk management, is more readily available than ever before.

Risk management is also directly related to the competitive strength of an insurer, since it is particularly important for insureds to make sure that their insurer is solvent when they experience losses. As a result, efficient risk management is essential for an insurer to survive and prosper. In this regard, it is not surprising that diverse risk management techniques have been developed, especially in the area of catastrophe (CAT) risk. Catastrophic events do not occur frequently, but have a large impact on firm values once they occur. Therefore, CAT risk dramatically points to the importance of risk management.

One of the important recent developments regarding CAT risk management is that it now makes use of the capital from financial markets.

CAT risks are traditionally considered noninsurable due to their lack of reliable data and violation of the law of large numbers. With the recent developments in financial and information techniques, insurers now seek diverse innovative ways to utilize financial markets for insuring them (see Doherty, 1997, 2000).

Among the innovations are CAT securities such as CAT options, CAT bonds, and CAT equity puts. A CAT option is an option whose underlying assets are CAT losses or CAT loss-related indexes. When the loss or index is above a prespecified level, an insurer with a long position in CAT options can receive payoffs corresponding to the difference. Insurers may raise capital in advance by issuing CAT bonds. CAT bonds are similar to ordinary corporate bonds, except for an additional clause regarding CAT events. When a prespecified CAT event does not occur, then the insurer should make interest and face value payments as promised. However, part or all of such payments may be forgiven if the loss level due to the CAT event exceeds prespecified trigger levels. As a result, CAT bonds can provide insurers with the funds they need when they face large loss claims following a CAT event. The loss level can be measured by an actual loss size or an index.

CAT equity puts are one means of securing financing after a loss occurs. In the CAT equity put contract, the insurer obtains the right to sell its stocks at the prespecified exercise price after a CAT event occurs. The counterparty has the obligation to buy the stocks at the exercise price. This contract alleviates the insurer's financial burden in raising capital after a loss occurrence. Other financial innovations, such as CAT risk swap, sidecars, and industry loss warranties, have also been developed.

In many cases, the payoff structures of CAT securities are based on two types of triggers: indemnity and index. Under indemnity triggers, the payoffs to investors are based on the actual loss of the insurer. Under index triggers, the payoffs to investors are based on prespecified indexes such as industry losses or parametric values such as of earthquake activity magnitudes. Since transferring all risks to financial markets, if possible, is optimal to the insurer, the insurer will prefer indemnity triggers, *ceteris paribus*. The use of index triggers, however, is becoming popular for several reasons, and the theoretical background for using index triggers has been developed in the insurance literature.

Under the systematic risk approach, a CAT risk is considered a mixture of systematic (or undiversifiable) risk and nonsystematic (or diversifiable) risk (Doherty and Richter, 2002; Doherty and

Schlesinger, 2002; Mahul, 2002). The systematic risk portion is hedged by index-triggered securities, and the remaining nonsystematic risk is hedged through indemnity-triggered vehicles, including traditional insurance.

The moral hazard approach focuses on the fact that the loss size of an insurer is exposed to a moral hazard problem. In this case, index triggers can be preferred to indemnity triggers, since indexing can protect insurers from the loss without incurring a moral hazard problem. A good index should be highly correlated with the individual insurer's loss, without being manipulated by the insurer (Doherty, 1997; Doherty and Mahul, 2001; Froot 1999).

The downside risk approach focuses on the size of loss (Seog and Kang, 2008). For insurers facing a large CAT risk, downside risk seems to be extremely important. Insurers may go bankrupt after a CAT loss. Even if they survive, they may have to incur large costs to finance and recover from the loss. Such insurers are worried about the downside effect of a CAT loss, rather than about variation itself. In the case of downside risk aversion, indexing is optimal, since indexing can remove downside risk, without incurring costs for upside risk. The trigger level is determined by comparing financing costs and risk costs, where risk costs are referred to as the costs incurred when financing after a loss.

Obviously, the observability of a loss is a key factor for indexing (Seog and Kang, 2008). Observing the size of a CAT loss is difficult for following reasons. First, identifying the CAT loss may well be inherently difficult. In particular, for an insurer, its CAT loss is the sum of the policyholders' losses. The determination of the eventual sum of policyholders' losses may well take several years. Second, unlike the default of ordinary bonds, a CAT event does not allow investors to take over the insurer. With such weak rights to protect their claim values, CAT bondholders, for example, will incur higher costs in identifying the CAT loss of the insurer. In addition, the effects of a CAT event on cash flows of a firm are not easily separable from the effects of other operations. The nonseparability of cash flows leads the firm to inflate the reported loss by transferring costs from other operations to the CAT loss. As a result, indexing is a cost saving tool when the actual loss is not easily observable.

However, indexing exposes the security issuer to the basis risk, since the index is not necessarily consistent with the actual loss. While indexing may help control the aforementioned problems, the basis risk will be the costs to indexing.

5.9   Conclusion

Like individuals, firms purchase insurance. However, risk aversion is not enough to explain the firm's (especially a large firm's) demand for insurance, since owners can reduce risks by diversifying their portfolios. The rationales for corporate insurance and risk management are related to transaction costs and market imperfection. Firms may purchase insurance based on the considerations of taxes and regulation, efficiency in real service, bankruptcy costs, market incompleteness, moral hazard, and adverse selection. Firms may also purchase insurance based on strategic purposes.

Since most insurers are also firms, the aforementioned rationales for risk management are applied to insurers. On the other hand, diverse financial innovations, including alternative risk transfer, have been and will be developed in order to manage insurers' risks and to extend the capital pool for the insurance market. These financial innovations make the conventional borderline between insurance markets and capital markets less clear.

BIBLIOGRAPHY

Ashby, S. G. and S. R. Diacon (1998) The corporate demand for insurance: a strategic perspective. *Geneva Papers on Risk and Insurance*, 23: 34–51.
Campbell, T. S. and W. A. Kracaw (1990) Corporate risk management and the incentive effects of debt, *Journal of Finance*, 45: 1673–86.
Core, J. E. (1997) On the corporate demand for directors' and officers' insurance. *Journal of Risk and Insurance*, 64: 63–87.
Davidson, W. N., M. L. Cross and J. H. Thornton (1992) Corporate demand for insurance: some empirical and theoretical results. *Journal of Financial Services Research*, 6: 61–72.
DeAngelo, H. and R. W. Masulis (1980) Optimal capital structure under corporate and personal taxation. *Journal of Financial Economics*, 8: 3–27.
Doherty, N. A. (1997) Innovations in managing catastrophe risk. *Journal of Risk and Insurance*, 64: 713–18.
Doherty, N. A. (2000) Innovation in corporate risk management: the case of catastrophe risk. In G. Dionne (ed.), *Handbook of Insurance* Boston: Kluwer Academic Publishers.
Doherty, N. A. and O. Mahul (2001) Mickey mouse and moral hazard: uninformative but correlated triggers. Working paper, The Wharton School, University of Pennsylvania.
Doherty, N. A. and A. Richter (2002) Moral hazard, basis risk, and gap insurance. *Journal of Risk and Insurance*, 69(1): 9–24.

Doherty, N. A. and H. Schlesinger (2002) Insurance contracts and securitization. *Journal of Risk and Insurance*, 69(1): 45–62.

Froot, K. A. (1999) The evolving market for catastrophic event risk. *Risk management and Insurance Review*, 2(3): 1–28.

Froot, K. A., D. S. Scharfstein, and J. C. Stein (1993) Risk management: coordinating corporate investment and financing policies. *Journal of Finance*, 48: 1629–58.

Garven, J. R. and R. D. MacMinn (1993) The underinvestment problem, bond covenants and insurance. *Journal of Risk and Insurance*, 60: 635–46.

Grace, M. F. and M. J. Rebello (1993) Financing and the demand for corporate insurance. *Geneva Papers on Risk and Insurance Theory*, 18: 147–72.

Han, L.-M. (1996) Managerial compensation and corporate demand for insurance. *Journal of Risk and Insurance*, 63: 381–404.

Hirshleifer, J. (1965) Investment decision under uncertainty: choice-theoretic approaches. *Quarterly Journal of Economics*, 89: 509–36.

Jaffee, D. M. and T. Russell (1997) Catastrophe insurance, capital markets, and uninsurable risks. *Journal of Risk and Insurance*, 64: 205–30.

Jensen, M. and W. Meckling (1976) Theory of the firm: managerial behavior, agency costs and ownership structure. *Journal of Financial Economics*, 3: 305–60.

Leland, H. (1972) Theory of the firm facing uncertain demand. *American Economic Review*, 62: 278–91.

MacMinn, R. D. (1987) Insurance and corporate risk management. *Journal of Risk and Insurance*, 54: 658–77.

MacMinn, R. D. and P. L. Brockett (1995) Corporate spin-offs as a value enhancing technique when faced with legal liability. *Insurance: Mathematics and Economics*, 16: 63–8.

MacMinn, R. D., and L.-M. Han (1990) Limited liability, corporate value, and the demand for liability insurance. *Journal of Risk and Insurance*, 57: 581–607.

Mahul, O. (2002) Coping with catastrophic risk: the role of (non)-participating contracts. Paper presented at the 29th Seminar of the European Group of Risk and Insurance Economists, Nottingham.

Mayers, D. and C. W. Smith, Jr. (1982) On the corporate demand for insurance. *Journal of Business*, 55: 281–96.

Mayers, D. and C. W. Smith, Jr. (1987) Corporate insurance and the underinvestment problem. *Journal of Risk and Insurance*, 54: 45–54.

Mayers, D. and C. W. Smith, Jr. (1990) On the corporate demand for insurance: evidence from the reinsurance market. *Journal of Business*, 63: 19–40.

Modigliani, F. and M. H. Miller (1958) The cost of capital, corporation finance and the theory of investment. *American Economic Review*, 48: 261–97.

Myers, S. C. (1977) The determinants of corporate borrowing. *Journal of Financial Economics*, 5: 147–75.

Myers, S. C. and N. S. Majluf (1984) Corporate financing and investment decisions when firms have information that investors do not have. *Journal of Financial Economics*, 13: 187–221.

Seog, S. H. (2006) Strategic demand for insurance. *Journal of Risk and Insurance*, 73: 277–93.

Seog, S. H. and J. Kang (2008), Indexing catastrophe securities. KAIST Business School Working Paper, KBS-WP-2008-003,. http://ssrn.com/abstract=1083854.

Smith, C. W. and R. M. Stulz (1985) The determinants of firms' hedging policies. *Journal of Financial and Quantitative Analysis*, 20: 391–405.

Chapter 6

Liability and Insurance

In a liability case, there are three key elements: injurer, injured (victim), and injury (loss). When an injurer causes an injury to an injured, the injurer is potentially liable for the injury. In general, liability rules describe whether or not and how much the injurer is liable to pay for the injury. Liability insurance aims to cover the liability of the injurer to the injured. Liability insurance is distinguished from first-party insurance in that the latter directly covers the loss to the insured, while the former covers the loss to the third party. The injured may cover, through first-party insurance, the loss that is not covered by the injurer. Important types of liability insurance include auto liability insurance, workers' compensation insurance, and commercial general liability insurance. The increased focus on responsible management and a more complex business environment exposes the business to a higher risk of liability. Such examples include product liability, environment-related liability, directors' and officers' liability, and professional liability. The insurance for these liabilities is becoming more important than ever before.

Since the size of the liability is eventually determined by the legal liability, we first consider the legal liability rules (Section 6.1). Then we discuss the effects of liability rules and liability insurance on the precautions of the injurer and the injured. We distinguish between the unilateral precaution case (Section 6.2) and the bilateral precaution case (Section 6.3). Only the injurer can affect the loss probability in the unilateral precaution case, while both the injurer and the injured can affect the loss probability in the bilateral precaution case. In these sections, we see how liability insurance may improve efficiency. Section 6.4 briefly discusses the caveats for such efficiency outcomes. While the liability rules are designed to make the injurer responsible for the injury, it is sometimes the case that the wealth of the injurer is too low to pay for the liability, which is called the judgment proof problem. We discuss the relationship between the judgment proof problem and the efficiency of the liability rules and insurance (Section 6.5). Finally, we address the demand for liability insurance under the negligence rule (Section 6.6).

6.1   Liability Rules

In general, an injury is affected by the levels of care of the injurer and the injured. Given an injury, liability rules distribute the obligation for the payment for the injury to the injurer and the injured based on diverse standards of due care (Brown, 1973; Cooter and Ulen, 2004). The standard of due care is eventually determined by the courts or by law. Let us write C_N and C_D for the standards of due care of the injurer and of the injured, respectively, where $C_N \geq 0$ and $C_D \geq 0$. A failure in exercising due care will expose the party to the risk of bearing the loss.

Under a *no-liability rule*, the injurer is not liable for the loss. This case corresponds to the case where $C_N = 0$ and $C_D = \infty$ (see Table 6.1). The *(simple) strict liability rule* and *(simple) negligence rule* are two benchmark liability rules. A strict liability rule is the case in which $C_N = \infty$ and $C_D = 0$, the opposite of the no-liability rule. Under a strict liability rule, the injurer is liable for the loss as long as she causes an injury, regardless of her level of care. On the other hand, a (simple) negligence rule is the case in which $0 < C_N < \infty$, and $C_D = 0$. Under the negligence rule, the injurer is liable for the loss if her actual level of care is below C_N, regardless of the injured's actual level of care.

Under *the rule of negligence with a defense of contributory negligence*, the injurer is liable for the loss if her actual level of care is below C_N and

Table 6.1   Liability rule and standard of due care

Liability rule	C_N	C_D
No liability rule	0	∞
Simple strict liability rule	∞	0
Simple negligence rule	+	0
Rule of negligence with a defense of contributory negligence	+	+
Rule of comparative negligence	+	+
Rule of strict liability with a defense of contributory negligence	∞	+

the injured's actual level of care is above C_D, where $0 < C_N < \infty$ and $0 < C_D < \infty$. In other words, the injurer is not liable if she exercises due care, or if the injured fails to exercise due care. Under *the rule of comparative negligence*, the injurer is liable for the loss if her actual level of care is below C_N and the injured's actual level of care is above C_D, where $0 < C_N < \infty$ and $0 < C_D < \infty$, as under the rule of negligence with a defense of contributory negligence. The difference is that when both parties fail to exercise due care, the obligations are distributed in proportion to the degree of negligence. Note that the injurer is not liable in this case under the rule of negligence with a defense of contributory negligence. Under *the rule of strict liability with a defense of contributory negligence*, the injurer is liable for the loss if the injured's actual level of care is above C_D, where $C_N = \infty$ and $0 < C_D < \infty$. In many countries, negligence rules are widely adopted for personal and professional liability. The strict liability rule is also adopted in workers' compensation and product liability.

6.2 The Unilateral Precaution Case: Liability Rules, Insurance, and Efficiency

Strict liability and negligence rules are two benchmark liability rules. Under a simple negligence rule, the (positive) standard due care is defined. An injurer is liable if she causes an injury to an injured, and her level of care is below that of due care. Under a simple strict liability rule, the injurer is liable if she causes an injury, regardless of her level of care.

While there are many variations between the simple strict liability rule and the simple negligence rule, we will focus on these two benchmark rules. Our concern with the liability rules is under which rules the injury probability is efficiently controlled. Our description is based on Shavell (1982).

We consider a case in which a potential insured (consumer) purchases a product from a potential injurer (producer) in a competitive product market. Let us assume that the production cost is zero. The product price R will be competitively determined to make the expected utility of the injurer a minimum (at the reservation utility level). The consumption of the product provides the (potential) injured with the benefit corresponding to wealth W_d^e. The initial wealth of the (potential) injurer is assumed to be W_r^e.

A product failure, or an accident, may occur with probability p that is a function of a level of care of the injurer. The level of care is denoted by its costs c. We assume that $p'(c) < 0$, and $p''(c) > 0$. The loss to the injured caused by the accident is denoted by x. We assume that $x < W_r^e$, so that the insurer has wealth high enough to pay for the loss. Let y be the payment from the injurer to the injured.

Let us write U and V for the utilities of the potential injurer and the potential injured, respectively. We denote the states of nature as subscripts 0 and 1. W_{i0} and W_{i1} denote the wealth of individual i ($= r$ for the injurer, d for the injured) in the no accident state and accident state, respectively. Note that we have the following identities:

$$W_{r0} = W_r^e + R - c$$
$$W_{r1} = W_r^e + R - c - y$$
$$W_{d0} = W_d^e - R \qquad (6.1)$$
$$W_{d1} = W_d^e - R - x + y.$$

As a benchmark case, let us find a first best solution that will be obtained by a benevolent dictator with perfect information.[1] In what follows, we add a star (*) for the first best solution. The first best solution will solve the following program.

$$\max_{\{c,y,R\}} EV = (1 - p(c))V(W_{d0}) + p(c)V(W_{d1})$$
$$\text{s.t. } EU = (1 - p(c))U(W_{r0}) + p(c)U(W_{r1}) = \bar{U}, \qquad (6.2)$$
$$(1 - p(c))(W_{d0} + W_{r0}) + p(c)(W_{d1} + W_{r1} + x) + c = W_d^e + W_r^e.$$

The first constraint is the participation constraint for the injurer, where $\bar{U}$ is the reservation utility and the second constraint is the resource constraint.

Using the fact that an efficient solution removes risks, we can suppose that $W_{i0} = W_{i1} = W_i$. Then, the program can be restated as:

$$\max_{\{c, y, R\}} V(W_d)$$
$$\text{s.t. } U(W_r) = \bar{U}, \qquad (6.3)$$
$$W_d + W_r + p(c)x + c = W_d^e + W_r^e.$$

Proposition 6.1 (A first best outcome). A first best level of care minimizes the expected total costs which are the expected loss plus the care costs.

Proof. From the first constraint of program (6.3), $W_r^* = U^{-1}(\bar{U})$. Plugging this into the second constraint of (6.3), we have $W_d^* = W_d^e + W_r^e - (U^{-1}(\bar{U}) + p(c^*)x + c^*)$. Since $W_d^e + W_r^e - U^{-1}(\bar{U})$ are fixed, maximizing $V(W_d)$ is equal to minimizing $p(c)x + c$. The optimal level of care c^* satisfies $p'(c^*)x + 1 = 0$.   □

The proposition is intuitive. Since all risks are hedged, there is no cost involved in the risk bearing. Thus, the remaining cost comes from the real costs. An efficient outcome should minimize those costs.

Now, we consider the case of a decentralized decision, where the level of care is determined by the injurer. The efficient outcome under this situation is called a second-best outcome. Under either liability rule, the program for the second-best outcome can be stated as follows. (This is a typical moral hazard program; see Chapter 9 for the discussion of this formulation.)

$$\max_{\{c,y,R\}} EV = (1 - p(c))V(W_{d0}) + p(c)V(W_{d1})$$

$$\text{s.t. } EU = (1 - p(c))U(W_{r0}) + p(c)U(W_{r1}) = \bar{U} \tag{6.4}$$

$$c \in \arg\max EU \text{ given } y \text{ and } R.$$

We assume that the second constraint can be replaced by the first-order condition for an interior solution:[2]

$$\partial EU/\partial c = 0$$

or

$$-p'[U(W_{r0}) - U(W_{r1})] - (1 - p)U'(W_{r0}) - pU'(W_{r1}) = 0.$$

6.2.1   Strict liability rule under no insurance

The standard of the injurer's due care under a strict liability rule is denoted by $C_N = \infty$. Since the injured's level of care is irrelevant, we can set $C_D = 0$. As a result, we are focused on the simple strict liability rule. The outcome may depend on the risk aversion of the insurer.

Let us first consider the case in which the injurer is risk neutral. In this case, since the injurer is risk neutral and is solely responsible for care, it should be optimal for her to take all the risks. Note also that the second constraint of (6.4) can be replaced by $p'y + 1 = 0$, since the expected wealth of the injurer is $W_r^e + R - c - py$. Thus, it is easy to see that the first best outcome is obtained by letting $y = x$. The optimal solutions are $c = c^*$, $y = x$, $R = \bar{U} - W_r^e + p(c^*)x + c^*$, where c^* is the first best level of care. In this case, the expected utility of the injurer becomes $EU = W_r^e + R - c^* - p(c^*)x = \bar{U}$.

However, when the injurer is risk averse, the first best outcome may not be obtained. Since the injurer is risk averse, it is not efficient for her to bear the full risk. Thus, the efficient outcome will require $y < x$ (see

---

[2]   For the discussion of this formulation, see Chapter 9.

Proposition 6.2). Since the injurer is not fully responsible for the injury, the care does not minimize the total costs. As a result, a first best outcome is not achieved.

Proposition 6.2 (Strict liability rule with no insurance). When the injurer is risk neutral, a first best outcome is obtained. However, when the injurer is risk averse, a first best outcome is not obtained.

Proof. For the risk neutral case, see the text above. For the risk averse case, we show that $y < x$. For this, it suffices to show that EV is decreasing in y at x, with the constraints satisfied. We write $EV(y)$ for EV as a function of y, where $c = c(y)$ and $R = R(y)$ are determined according to y, satisfying the constraints:

$$EV(y) = (1 - p(c))V(W_d^e - R) + p(c)V(W_d^e - R - x + y).$$

Differentiation with respect to y leads to

$$EV'(y) = - p'c'[V(W_d^e - R) - V(W_d^e - R - x + y)]$$
$$+ pV'(W_d^e - R - x + y) - R'[(1 - p)V'(W_d^e - R)$$
$$+ pV'(W_d^e - R - x + y)]$$

At $y = x$, $EV'(y) = (p - R')V'(W_d^e - R)$. Therefore, $EV'(y) < 0$ if and only if $R' > p$. By totally differentiating the first constraint of (6.4) with respect to y, we have

$$\partial EU/\partial y + (\partial EU/\partial c)c' + (\partial EU/\partial R)R' = 0.$$

Since $\partial EU/\partial c = 0$ from the second constraint, we have

$$R' = -\frac{\partial EU / \partial y}{\partial EU / \partial R}$$
$$= \frac{pU'(W_{r1})}{(1 - p)U'(W_{r0}) + pU'(W_{r1})}$$
$$= \frac{p}{(1 - p)U'(W_{r0}) / U'(W_{r1}) + p}.$$

Since $U'(W_{r0}) < U'(W_{r1})$ for $y > 0$, we have $R' > p$ at $y = x$. Thus, $EV'(y) < 0$ at $y = x$. ☐

6.2.2   Negligence rule under no insurance

The standard of the injurer's due care under a negligence rule is $C_N > 0$. By setting $C_D = 0$, we are focused on the simple negligence rule. Now the efficiency of the outcome depends on the risk aversion of the insured. When the injured is risk neutral, setting the standard of due care $C_N = c^*$ with the payment $y = x$ will achieve the first best outcome. For this, note that the injurer will be liable if her level of care is less than C_N. If $c < C_N$, then

$$EU = (1 - p(c))U(W_r^e + R - c) + p(c)U(W_r^e + R - c - x)$$

$$\leq U(W_r^e + R - c - p(c)x) \leq U(W_r^e + R - c^* - p(c^*)x)$$

$$< U(W_r^e + R - c^*).$$

The first inequality is obtained since U is concave, and the second inequality is obtained since c^* is the cost-minimizing level of care given payment x. Therefore, the injurer will prefer to take due care, which completely removes the risk of the injurer. Since the injured is risk neutral, bearing the full risk does not incur costs. Therefore, the result is a first best outcome.

When the injured is risk averse, however, we predict that it is not efficient for the risk averse injured to take the full risk, similar to the strict liability case. The following proposition shows that this prediction is correct.

Proposition 6.3 (Negligence rule with no insurance). When the injured is risk neutral, a first best outcome is obtained. However, when the injured is risk averse, a first best outcome is not obtained.

Proof. For the risk neutral case, see the text above. For the risk averse case, note that given C_N, the injurer will not be liable for the loss when exercising level of care C_N. Thus, we have

$$EV = (1 - p(C_N))V(W_d^e - R) + p(C_N)V(W_d^e - R - x),$$

$$EU = U(W_r^e + R - C_N).$$

Now, program (6.4) can be replaced by the following program:

$$\text{Max}_{\{C_N, R\}} \ EV = (1 - p(C_N))V(W_d^e - R) + p(C_N)V(W_d^e - R - x) \tag{6.5}$$

$$\text{s.t. } EU = U(W_r^e + R - C_N) = \bar{U}.$$

If a first best outcome is to be obtained, the solution to this program should be $C_N = c^*$. Note that R is determined by $C_N + K$, where $K = -W_r^e + U^{-1}(\bar{U})$, a constant. Thus, this program can be restated as

$$\text{Max}_{C_N} \ EV = (1 - p(C_N))V(W_d^e - C_N - K)$$

$$+ p(C_N)V(W_d^e - C_N - K - x). \tag{6.6}$$

with FOC

$$-p'[V(W_d^e - C_N - K) - V(W_d^e - C_N - K - x)]$$
$$- (1 - p)V'(W_d^e - C_N - K) - pV'(W_d^e - C_N - K - x) = 0.$$

If the injured is risk neutral so that $V(W) = W$ and $V'(W) = 1$, this FOC becomes $-p'x - 1 = 0$, achieving a first best outcome c^*. However, when V is concave, this solution will be different from c^* in general. $\square$

When the injured is risk averse, we may expect that the standard level of due care is higher than c^*, so that the injured's risk is reduced. However, it is also possible that the standard level of due care becomes lower than the first best level c^*. This possibility comes from the fact that the price should be increased when the level of care increases. Then, the expected utility may decrease with the increase in level of care, when the decrease in wealth makes the injured more risk averse.

6.2.3 Liability rule and insurance

The above analysis assumes that there is no insurance. When insurance is available, it may affect the efficiency of the outcomes. We assume that the insurance market is competitive, so that the insurance premium is actuarially fair. We also assume that the level of care is observable by the insurer.

Let us first consider the strict liability rule. When the injurer purchases liability insurance, a first best outcome can be obtained. When the injurer is risk neutral, we already know that a first best outcome is obtained. In fact, she does not need to purchase liability insurance. Recall from the previous section that, when the injurer is risk averse, the main reason for the failure to achieve a first best outcome is the excessive risk taking of the injurer. If liability insurance is available, the risk can be transferred to the insurer, with an actuarially fair premium. Since a first best level of care minimizes the total costs, it is optimal for the injurer to take the first best level of care. Therefore, a first best outcome is now obtained.

Now, let us consider the negligence rule. When the injured is risk neutral, a first best outcome is obtained without insurance. When the injured is risk averse, the main reason for the failure to achieve a first best outcome is the excess risk taking of the injured. If first party insurance is available, the risk can be transferred to an insurer with an actuarially fair premium. Therefore, with $C_N = c^*$, both the injurer and the injured face no risks, and the injurer takes the first best level of care, leading to a first best outcome.

Proposition 6.4 (Liability rule and insurance). Suppose that the insurance premium is actuarially fair and that insurers can observe the level of care.[3]

---

[3] In fact, the observability of the level of care is not needed in the case of the negligence rule.

(a)   Under a strict liability rule, a first best outcome is obtained, regardless of the risk attitude of the injurer. A risk averse injurer purchases full liability insurance.

(b)   Under a negligence rule, a first best outcome is obtained, regardless of the risk attitude of the injured. A risk averse injured purchases full first-party insurance.

6.3   The Bilateral Precaution Case: Liability Rules, Insurance, and Efficiency

Let us change some of the assumptions of the previous section to reflect bilateral precaution as follows. A product failure may occur with probability p that is a function of the level of care of the injurer and the injured that are denoted by care costs c and d, respectively. We assume that $\partial p/\partial k = p_k(c,d) < 0$ and $\partial^2 p/\partial k^2 = p_{kk}(c,d) > 0$, where $k = c,d$. The loss to the injured caused by the accident is denoted by x. Now we have the following wealth positions;

$$W_{r0} = W_r^e + R - c$$
$$W_{r1} = W_r^e + R - c - y$$
$$W_{d0} = W_d^e - R - d \qquad\qquad (6.7)$$
$$W_{d1} = W_d^e - R - d - x + y.$$

As a benchmark case, let us find a first best solution that will be obtained by a benevolent dictator with perfect information. Double star (**) will denote the first best soultions. The first best solution will solve the following program:

$$\max_{\{c,d,y,R\}} EV = (1-p)V(W_{d0}) + pV(W_{d1}) \qquad\qquad (6.8)$$
$$\text{s.t. } EU = (1-p)U(W_{r0}) + pU(W_{r1}) = \bar{U},$$
$$(1-p)(W_{d0} + W_{r0}) + p(W_{d1} + W_{r1} + x) + c + d = W_d^e + W_r^e,$$

Using the fact that an efficient solution removes risks, we can suppose that $W_{i0} = W_{i1} = W_i$. Then, the program can be restated as:

$$\max_{\{c,d,y,R\}} V(W_d) \qquad\qquad (6.9)$$
$$\text{s.t. } U(W_r) = \bar{U},$$
$$W_d + W_r + px + c + d = W_d^e + W_r^e.$$

Proposition 6.5 (A first best outcome in the bilateral case). A first best level of care minimizes the expected total costs which are the expected loss plus the care costs. The level of care c^{**} satisfies $p_c x + 1 = 0$, and d^{**} satisfies $p_d x + 1 = 0$.

Proof. From the first constraint of program (6.9), $W_r^{**} = U^{-1}(\bar{U})$. Plugging this into the second constraint of (6.9), we have $W_d^{**} = W_d^e + W_r^e - (U^{-1}(\bar{U}) + p^{**}x + c^{**} + d^{**})$, where $p^{**} = p(c^{**}, d^{**})$. Since $W_d^e + W_r^e - U^{-1}(\bar{U})$ are fixed, maximizing $V(W_d)$ is equal to minimizing $px + c + d$. The optimal level of care c^{**} satisfies $p_c x + 1 = 0$, and d^{**} satisfies $p_d x + 1 = 0$. $\qquad\square$

The proposition has the same intuition as Proposition 6.1.

We now consider a second-best outcome. Under either liability rule, the program for the second-best outcome can be stated as follows:

$$\max_{\{c,d,y,R\}} EV = (1-p)V(W_{d0}) + pV(W_{d1}) \qquad (6.10)$$

$$\text{s.t. } EU = (1-p)U(W_{r0}) + pU(W_{r1}) = \bar{U}$$

$$-p_c[U(W_{r0}) - U(W_{r1})] - (1-p)U'(W_{r0}) - pU'(W_{r1}) = 0.$$

$$-p_d[V(W_{d0}) - U(W_{d1})] - (1-p)V'(W_{d0}) - pV'(W_{d1}) = 0.$$

Here, the second and third constraints are the FOCs for interior solutions regarding c and d, respectively.

6.3.1   Strict liability rule under no insurance

Under the strict liability rule, the injurer is liable for the loss. In general, the outcome is not efficient. To see this, let us suppose that the injurer is risk neutral. Recall that we had an efficient outcome in the unilateral precaution case. The second constraint of (6.10) becomes $p_c y + 1 = 0$. By setting $y = x$, we can make the injurer exercise the first best level of care c^{**}. However, this will distort the incentives for the injured to exercise the first best level of care. For this, consider the case of the risk neutral injured. The third constraint of (6.10) becomes $-p_d(x - y) - 1 = 0$. When $y = x$, the left-hand side of this expression becomes -1. The best choice of the injured's level of care is 0. Since the injurer will bear all the risk, the injured's incentive to exercise care is minimized. In general, it is efficient to make the injured take positive care, implying that $y < x$. This example shows that even if both parties are risk neutral, we cannot achieve the first best outcome under the strict liability rule.

On the other hand, under the rule of strict liability with a defense of contributory negligence, we can obtain similar results as in the unilateral case. By setting $C_D = d^{**}$, the injured will exercise due care d^{**}. Then, when the injurer is risk neutral, she will select her level of care at c^{**}, since it minimizes costs. Thus, the first best outcome is achieved. However, when the injurer is risk averse, , by a similar logic as in the unilateral case the first best outcome is not achieved.

Proposition 6.6 (Strict liability rule with no insurance in the bilateral case).

(a)   Under a strict liability rule, a first best outcome is not obtained, regardless of the risk attitudes of the injurer and the injured.
(b)   Under the rule of strict liability with a defense of contributory negligence, a first best outcome is obtained when the injurer is risk neutral. However, when the injurer is risk averse, a first best outcome is not obtained.

6.3.2   Negligence rule under no insurance

Suppose that the injured is risk neutral. Then the third constraint of (6.10) becomes $-p_d(x - y) - 1 = 0$. Let $C_N = c^{**}$ and suppose that the injurer selects c^{**}. Now, she will not be liable for the loss; that is, $y = 0$. The third constraint then becomes $-p_d x - 1 = 0$, implying that the injured selects d^{**}. Given that the injured selects d^{**}, the injurer indeed selects c^{**} since, if $c < C_N$, then

$$EU = (1 - p)U(W_r^e + R - c) + pU(W_r^e + R - c - x)$$
$$\leq U(W_r^e + R - c - px) \leq U(W_r^e + R - c^{**} - p^{**} x)$$
$$< U(W_r^e + R - c^{**}).$$

As a result, we achieve a first best outcome when the injured is risk neutral, as in the unilateral case. When the injured is risk averse, however, it is not efficient for the risk averse injured to take the full risk, similar to the unilateral case. Under the variants of the negligence rule, we have the same results if the levels of due care are set as $C_N = c^{**}$ and $C_D = d^{**}$. The following proposition summarizes the result.

Proposition 6.7 (Negligence rule with no insurance in the bilateral case). Under a negligence rule and its variants, a first best outcome is obtained, when the injured is risk neutral. However, when the injured is risk averse, a first best outcome is not obtained.

6.3.3   Liability rule and insurance

As in the unilateral case, we assume that the insurance market is competitive, so that the insurance premium is actuarially fair. We also assume that the level of care is observable by the insurer.

Let us first consider the strict liability rule. Insurance can improve the efficiency of the outcome since it can remove the risk. Unlike in the unilateral case, however, it fails to achieve a first best outcome, since the injured will not exercise the first best care. Note that the injured does not need insurance, since the injurer will pay for the loss. Therefore, the existence of insurance does not affect the injured's level of care, which prohibits achieving a first best outcome.

However, under the rule of strict liability with a defense of contributory negligence, we can achieve a first best outcome by setting $C_D = d^{**}$. In this case, the actual levels of care are c^{**} and d^{**}, and the injurer purchases full liability insurance. Both the injurer and the injured face no risk. As a result, a first best outcome is achieved.

Now let us consider the negligence rule. When the injured is risk neutral, we know that a first best outcome is obtained without insurance. When the injured is risk averse, the main reason for the failure to achieve a first best outcome is the excess risk taking of the injured. If first-party insurance is available, the risk can be transferred to an insurer with an actuarially fair premium. Therefore, with $C_N = c^{**}$, the actual levels of care are c^{**} and d^{**}, and both the injurer and the injured face no risks, leading to a first best outcome. It is not difficult to see that the same results are obtained under the variants of the negligence rule.

Proposition 6.8 (Liability rule and insurance in the bilateral case). Suppose that the insurance premium is actuarially fair and that insurers can observe the level of care.[4]

(a)   Under a strict liability rule, a first best outcome is not obtained. Under the rule of strict liability with a defense of contributory negligence, a first best outcome is obtained, regardless of the risk attitude of the injurer. A risk averse injurer purchases full liability insurance.
(b)   Under a negligence rule and its variants, a first best outcome is obtained, regardless of the risk attitude of the injured. A risk averse injured purchases full first-party insurance.

6.4   Caveats

In the previous sections, we found that the existence of insurance markets can improve the efficiency of the liability rule. A first best outcome is achieved, except in the bilateral precaution case under the strict liability

---

[4]   As in the unilateral case, the observability of the injurer's level of care is not needed in case of the negligence rule.

rule, when insurance is available. As long as first best outcomes are achieved with insurance, liability rules are irrelevant.

However, it is important to note that achieving a first best outcome is possible only if the insurer can observe the level of care of the insured. In general, insurers may not observe the level of care, leading to a moral hazard case (see Chapter 9). In this case, a first best outcome is not obtained even with insurance.

Our discussion in the case of a negligence rule is also based on the assumption that the court can observe the level of care to judge whether or not the injurer is negligent. If the court cannot observe the level of care, or, in general, the court's decision regarding the level of care is uncertain, then the injurer and the injured will be exposed to additional risk. Without insurance, such a risk will negatively affect the expected utilities, compared with the first best outcome. This risk may lead an injurer to purchase liability insurance, even when she exercises due care.

Finally, note also that insurance is assumed to be actuarially fair. If insurance is actuarially unfair, then purchasing insurance incurs costs, lowering the efficiency of the outcome. Recall that full insurance is not optimal when the premium is not actuarially fair.

6.5   Judgment Proof Problem

A complication may occur if the injurer does not have enough wealth to pay for the loss, which is referred to as a judgment proof case (see Shavell, 1986). To see how the judgment proof problem leads to inefficiency, let us reconsider the liability rules under no liability insurance. Let us assume that the wealth cannot be less than zero.

First suppose that the strict liability rule is applied under the unilateral precaution case. For simplicity, let us assume that the injurer's wealth is so low that it cannot fully pay for the loss x at a reasonable price R: $W_{r0} = W_r^e + R - c < x$. Thus, under the strict liability rule, we have

$$EU = (1 - p(c))U(W_r^e + R - c) + p(c)U(0).$$

Recall that a first best outcome is obtained if the injurer is risk neutral when she has enough wealth. For comparison, let us assume that she is risk neutral. Then

$$EU = (1 - p(c))(W_r^e + R - c)$$
$$\partial EU/\partial c = -p'W_{r0} - (1 - p) = 0.$$

This can be rewritten as

$$\partial EU/\partial c = -p'(x - x + W_{r0}) - (1 - p) = -p'x - 1 + p'(x - W_{r0}) + p = 0.$$

Note that at $c = c^*$, $-p'x - 1 = 0$. Thus, at $c = c^*$,

$$\partial EU/\partial c|_{c=c^*} = p(c^*)'(x - W_{r0}^*) + p(c^*) = W_{r0}^*/x - (1 - p),$$

where W_{r0}^* is the wealth achieved with c^*. This value can be greater than or less than zero. When W_{r0}^* is sufficiently low compared with x, then $\partial EU/\partial c|_{c=c^*} < 0$. In this case, the injurer will take less care than the efficient level c^*. When the wealth level is very low, the wealth effect of the care cost will dominate the loss reduction effect, so that the level of care will be lowered. However, the level of care can be greater than c^*, if $\partial EU/\partial c|_{c=c^*} > 0$ which can be obtained, for example, when W_{r0}^* is close to x. Excessive care is possible since the utility in the bad state is not affected by the increase in the care cost. If the injurer had high wealth so that no judgment proof problem occurs, then the increased care cost would decrease utilities in both states. However, with low wealth, the increase in the care cost only reduces the wealth in the good state, leading to under-internalization of the care cost.

Now, consider the negligence rule. Even if the standard of due care is set at a first best level, $C_N = c^*$, it is possible that the injurer exercises lower care than c^* when the wealth of the injurer is very low.

Let us show that an injurer may have an incentive to deviate from exercising c^*, when the due care (c^*) and the price (R^*) are determined as in the first best case. With care cost $c < c^*$, the injurer will be liable for the loss. To reflect the judgment proof problem, let us suppose that $W_r^e + R^* - c$ is lower than x. Then, the expected utility of the injurer is expressed as

$$EU = (1 - p(c))U(W_r^e + R^* - c) + p(c)U(0).$$

Assuming a risk neutral injurer,

$$EU = (1 - p(c))(W_r^e + R^* - c).$$

Now, the injurer may exercise lower care than c^*, if

$$(1 - p(c))(W_r^e + R^* - c) > W_r^e + R^* - c^*, \text{ or}$$

$$p(c)(W_r^e + R^* - c) < c^* - c.$$

These simple examples show that the judgment proof problem makes the liability rules inefficient, even though they are efficient when no judgment problem exists. The main reason for the inefficiency is that the judgment proof problem allows the injurer to not bear the full cost for which she is responsible. A part of the cost is transferred to the injured. That is, the judgment proof problem creates an externality cost, which causes inefficiency.

The judgment proof problem may also hinder the efficiency results when insurance is available. Recall that, under the strict liability rule, the existence of liability insurance leads to a first best outcome even if the injurer is risk averse. Note that the insurance premium will fully reflect the expected loss. With low wealth, however, the injurer does not have to fully pay for the loss. For example, if the injurer's wealth is near zero, then she will pay almost zero for the loss. In this case, the insurance premium based on the full loss payment may be too high compared with the expected payment under no insurance. Although insurance provides the benefit of risk reduction, the injurer may have no incentive to purchase actuarially fair insurance, if the benefit is outweighed by the excessive premium.

A similar rationale is applied to the case of the negligence rule. Note that the aforementioned example shows that the injurer may prefer a level of care lower than first best. The existence of liability insurance does not change this result, since the premium will be zero if the injurer exercises the first best care. The existence of first-party insurance does not induce the injurer to exercise a first best level of care, although it may help the injured to reduce risks.

The injurer is not willing to purchase insurance, since the insurance premium internalizes the full costs that the injurer does not have to bear without insurance. On the other hand, the first best outcome will be achieved, insofar as the injurer bears the full cost. This observation implies that compulsory liability insurance may help achieve the first best outcome when the judgment proof problem exists (Shavell, 1986). When the premium is actuarially fair, the injurer will minimize the expected loss in order to minimize the premium.[5] The first best outcome is achieved similarly as in Proposition 6.4.[6] It is, however, important that the achievement of the first best outcome depends on the observability of the level of care as discussed in Section 6.4. Let us summarize the discussion of this section.

Proposition 6.9 (Judgment proof problem).

(a)   When the judgment proof problem exists, a first best outcome is possibly not achieved, regardless of the existence of insurance.

---

[5]   We assume that the injurer has wealth enough to pay the premium.

[6]   Under the negligence rule, the premium will be zero when the injurer exercises the standard due care.

(b)   When the judgment proof problem exists, a first best outcome is possibly achieved by compulsory liability insurance.

6.6   Demand for Liability Insurance under the Negligence Rule

An interesting theoretical issue is whether or not an injurer purchases liability insurance under the negligence rule. When the court can observe the level of care, the injurer is not exposed to risk as long as she takes the standard due care. However, it is often the case that injurers purchase liability insurance under the negligence rule.[7] One obvious reason is that the court decision can be uncertain (Doherty, 1991). For example, the court may not observe the actual level of care. In another example, the standard of due care may change. When the changed standard of due care is applied, an injurer who would not have been liable based on the old standard might be liable for the loss. In sum, when an injurer is exposed to uncertainty through the court decision, she has an incentive to remove the uncertainty by purchasing liability insurance, although she exercises the standard due care.

Another interesting case can be found where the demand for liability insurance is based on strategic considerations. Seog (2006) argues that injurers may strategically purchase liability insurance, even if they are not legally liable for losses. Moreover, risk neutral injurers may have incentives to purchase insurance. Let us briefly consider Seog's model.

In a competitive product market, there are many consumers, each of whom has initial wealth of W^e and purchases one unit of the product from firms. There are two states of nature: a good state and a bad state. The bad state will be realized with probability p. A consumer enjoys the (monetary) consumption benefit of b. A consumer experiences fixed loss x in the bad state, and no loss in the good state.

Each firm produces only one product with a zero production cost. Each firm has two strategies, price and warranty. Given other firms' strategies, each firm selects price and warranty to maximize its expected profit. With the warranty, the firm is liable for the losses. Let us denote the warranty level by G.

---

[7]   If the standard of due care is not properly determined, then it is clear that the injurer may have incentives to purchase liability insurance, instead of exercising the standard due care. For example, when injurers have different characteristics, one standard of due care does not fit all injurers, leading to the demand for liability insurance (Bajtelsmit and Thistle, 2008).

We consider a consumer who purchases a product with price q and the warranty level G with loss probability p. The consumer's expected utility can be expressed as follows:

$$EU(q, G, p) = (1 - p)U(W - q) + pU(W - q - x + G)$$

where $W = W^e + b$. Let us define $W_0 = W - q$ and $W_1 = W - q - x + G$.

The profit of a firm that sells a product at price q with warranty G is $\pi = (1 - p)q + p(q - G)$. For $\pi = 0$, $q = pG$. In an equilibrium, firms maximize expected profits and consumers maximize their expected utilities given their information on others; no firms or consumers want to change their behaviors.

In this case, it is easy to see that in an equilibrium, each firm will offer a full warranty so as to remove the consumer's risk. Competition will lead to a zero profit. That is, $G = x$, and $q = px$. Note that this result is also a first best outcome.

Now, assume that there are two types of firms, depending on their asset values. Some firms (say H-firms) have asset values high enough to pay the entire loss x, while others (L-firms) do not. More specifically, the asset value of an L-firm is denoted by A, where $px < A < x$.

If consumers can observe the firm types, L-firms can provide warranties up to A. In this case, the consumer's expected utility becomes

$$EU(q, G = A, p) = (1 - p)U(W - q) + pU(W - q - x + A), \text{ where } q = pA.$$

Since H-firms can still offer a full warranty, consumers will be better off if they purchase from H-firms. In an equilibrium, only H-firms may survive. This situation is depicted in Figure 6.1.

Now suppose that actuarially fair liability insurance is available and that insurers can observe the types of firms. Obviously, L-firms have incentives to purchase liability insurance. The full insurance premium is $Q = px$. In this case, L-firms can also provide a full warranty $G = x$ with the product price $q = Q$. Consumers are indifferent between purchasing from L-firms and H-firms. In an equilibrium, L-firms have incentives to purchase liability insurance, while H-firms do not necessarily purchase insurance. Both types of firms offer full warranties.

A more interesting result can be obtained if consumers cannot observe the firm types. In this case, the H-firm now has to purchase liability insurance in an equilibrium. For, if not, an L-firm will have a strong incentive to mimic an H-firm, by offering a warranty without purchasing insurance. By doing so, the L-firm will default on its warranty and make a positive profit.

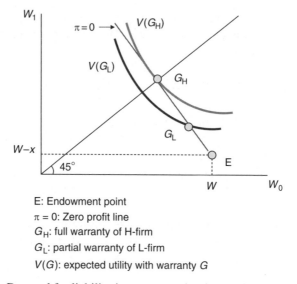

E: Endowment point
$\pi = 0$: Zero profit line
G_H: full warranty of H-firm
G_L: partial warranty of L-firm
$V(G)$: expected utility with warranty G

Figure 6.1   Demand for liability insurance under the negligence rule.

To prevent such opportunistic L-firm behavior, H-firms have to purchase liability insurance. L-firms also have to purchase insurance, since, otherwise, consumers will not purchase products from them. Therefore, in an equilibrium, both types of firms will purchase liability insurance and offer full warranties.

Note that both the warranty offer and the purchase of liability insurance are voluntary, regardless of the liability rule. Firms do so for strategic purposes, not from the legal liability. That is, even if a firm exercises the standard due care under the negligence rule, the firm will still have an incentive to offer a full warranty and purchase liability insurance.

Proposition 6.10 An injurer may purchase liability insurance, even if she exercises the standard due care under the negligence rule. The reasons include (i) the uncertainty in the court decision and (ii) strategic purposes.

6.7   Conclusion

While the basic logics for insurance can still be applied to liability insurance, a separate discussion is useful to understand it. Unlike in first-party insurance, the loss is incurred by the third party in liability insurance. As a result, the moral hazard problem is a key issue since the injurer does not have to bear the full loss. Since liability is determined by the courts and by law, investigation of the liability rules and their interaction with insurance is necessary. On the other hand, the liability size may be greater than the wealth that the injurer can dispose of. This judgment proof problem makes the issues of liability insurance more complicated than first-party insurance. Although we find that liability insurance may increase efficiency, it depends on the observability of levels of care by the insurers. If the insurers cannot observe the levels of care, then there is no guarantee that liability insurance improves efficiency.

BIBLIOGRAPHY

Abraham, K. S. (1988) Environmental liability and the limits of insurance. *Columbia Law Review*, 88: 942–88.

Bajtelsmit, V. and P. D. Thistle (2008) The reasonable person negligence standard and liability insurance. *Journal of Risk and Insurance*, 75: 815–23.

Berger, L. A. and J. D. Cummins (1992) Adverse selection and equilibrium in liability insurance markets. *Journal of Risk and Uncertainty*, 5: 253–72.

Born, P. and W. K. Viscusi (1994) Insurance market responses to the 1980s liability reforms: an analysis of firm level data. *Journal of Risk and Insurance*, 61: 194–218.

Brown, J. P. (1973) Toward an economic theory of liability. *Journal of Legal Studies*, 2: 323–50.

Cooter, R. and T. Ulen (2004) *Law and Economics*, 4th edition. Boston, MA: Pearson.

Danzon, P. M. (1984) Tort reform and the role of government in private insurance markets. *Journal of Legal Studies*, 13: 517–49.

Danzon, P. M. (1985) Liability and liability insurance for medical malpractice. *Journal of Health Economics*, 4: 309–31.

Doherty, N. A. (1991) The design of insurance contracts when liability insurance rules are unstable. *Journal of Risk and Insurance*, 58: 227–46.

Easterbrook, F. H. and D. R. Fischel (1985) Limited liability and the corporation. *University of Chicago Law Review*, 52: 89–117.

Seog, S. H. (2006) The strategic role of insurance: the warranty case. *Journal of Insurance Issues*, 29: 33–50.

Shavell, S. (1980) Strict liability versus negligence. *Journal of Legal Studies*, 9: 1–25.

Shavell, S. (1982) On liability and insurance. *Bell Journal of Economics*, 13: 120–32.

Shavell, S. (1986) The judgment proof problem. *International Review of Law and Economics*, 6: 45–58.

Part III

Information and Insurance Contract

Chapter 7

Basic Adverse Selection Models

An adverse selection or information asymmetry problem occurs when one party to a contract cannot observe the other party's characteristics. In the insurance context, the characteristics include risk types of insureds, the degree of risk aversion, and the solvency risks of insurers, among others. Much of the literature considers the adverse selection problem regarding risk types of insureds, in which insurers cannot observe the risk types of insureds (i.e., the risk type is private information of insureds). The focus is on equilibrium contract designs and the efficiency and existence of equilibrium.

Without information problems, market competition leads to efficient outcomes that maximize social welfare. Insurers will offer full insurance to each insured. Given the adverse selection problem in risk types, however, insurers will experience a loss if they offer the same contracts as under perfect information, since high-risk insureds will have incentives to select the contracts for low-risk insureds. Insurers can avoid losses by redesigning the contracts or by screening the risk types. One possible way is to offer the same (i.e., pooling) contracts for different risk types. If the pooling contracts are offered at an equilibrium, the equilibrium is called a "pooling equilibrium." However, such a pooling contract often provides the opportunity for competitors to offer other contracts that fit specific risk types. As a result, the insurer offering a pooling contract may well make a loss. In this case, a pooling equilibrium fails to exist.

Alternatively, insurers may offer several contracts each of which attracts different risk types. An equilibrium in which different types of insureds select different contracts is called a "separating equilibrium." Since insurers cannot observe the risk types, the contracts need to be designed to prevent insureds from selecting contracts for other types. Due to this additional restriction, the efficiency level under a separating equilibrium is lower than that in the case of no adverse selection.

In this chapter, we investigate the existence and characteristics of equilibrium in basic models. Rothschild and Stiglitz (1976) adopt the self-selection idea for insurance contracts (Section 7.2). They seek a Nash equilibrium where each contract needs to break even and each insurer determines contracts under the conjecture that other insurers will not change contracts (referred to as the Rothschild and Stiglitz conjecture). They find that a (pure strategy) equilibrium possibly does not exist. If an equilibrium exists, it is a separating one. While nonexistence of an equilibrium is bad news to economists, an equilibrium can be shown to exist if the Rothschild and Stiglitz assumptions are changed (Sections 7.3 and 7.4). In particular, an equilibrium exists if the insurers' conjecture is more sophisticated than the Rothschild and Stiglitz conjecture and if a cross-subsidy is allowed (Wilson, 1977; Miyazaki, 1977; Spence, 1978). In the next chapter, we further study advanced issues related to adverse selection, such as multi-period models, information acquisition, risk classification, and multi-dimensional adverse selection.

7.1   Description of the Basic Adverse Selection Models

There are two risk types of insureds, high-risk (H) and low-risk (L). The population proportion of high-risk insureds is denoted by θ. A type i insured faces a fixed loss x with probability p_i, where $p_H > p_L$. The ex ante (average) probability of a loss is $p_U = \theta p_H + (1 - \theta)p_L$. Insureds are assumed to be identical except for the risk types. An insurance contract C_i is a set consisting of a premium and an indemnity $\{Q_i, I_i\}$. The market is competitive. All information except for the risk types is public information and is well understood by all insurers and insureds.[1] Our concern is with the equilibrium outcomes under information asymmetry regarding the risk types of the insureds.

Given contract C_i, the wealth of the type i insured can be expressed as $W_{i_0} = W - Q_i$ in the no-loss state, $W_{i_1} = W - x + I_i - Q_i$ in the loss state. From these relationships, we have $Q_i = W - W_{i_0}$ and $I_i = W_{i_1} - W_{i_0} + x$. Note that the profit of an insurer is $\pi(C_i) = Q_i - p_i I_i$. Thus, the zero profit line (or fair odds line) for insurers on the (W_0, W_1) plane should satisfy the relationship.

---

[1]   In game theory terminology, it is common knowledge.

$$W - W_{i0} - p_i(W_{i1} - W_{i0} + x) = 0$$

or

$$W_{i_1} = -\frac{1-p_i}{p_i}W_{i_0} - x + \frac{W}{p_i}. \tag{7.1}$$

Since $(1 - p_L)/p_L > (1 - p_H)/p_H$, the slope of the zero profit line for low risks is steeper than that for high risks (see Figure 7.1). Note that both zero profit lines should pass through the endowment point (no insurance) since no insurance also makes zero profits.

Now consider an indifference curve of type i passing the wealth pair of (W_0, W_1). Since an indifference curve of type i is defined by $(1 - p_i)U(W_0) + p_iU(W_1) = K$, for given K, total differentiation provides the slopes of indifference curves

$$(1 - p_i)U_0'dW_0 + p_iU_1'dW_1 = 0,$$

that is,

$$dW_1/dW_0 = -(1 - p_i)U_0' / p_iU_1' . \tag{7.2}$$

Note that indifference curves have negative slopes on the (W_0, W_1) plane. At a given point (W_0, W_1), the slope of the indifference curve for low risk is steeper than that for high risk, since $p_L < p_H$ (see Figure 7.1). It is important to note that this result depends on the assumption that both types have the same utility functions. If two types have different utility functions, so that U_0'/U_1' are different for different risks, then the result does not necessarily hold.

In a more general setting, one important standard assumption regarding indifference curves is the so-called *single crossing property* which implies that indifference curves of two risks cross each other only once. Our model satisfies this property since the slope of the indifference curve for low risk is steeper than that for high risk. While the single crossing property simplifies the analysis, diverse characteristics of insureds may lead to the violation of the single crossing property. For example, different risk aversion of insureds will make indifference curves cross more than once, which will be addressed in the next chapter.

As a benchmark, let us first investigate the no adverse selection case in which insurers can observe the risk types of insureds (i.e., risk types are public information). In a competitive market, insurers maximize the insured's expected utility, given their expected profits are nonnegative. For notational simplicity, $V_i(C)$ is defined as the expected utility of the type i insured given contract C.

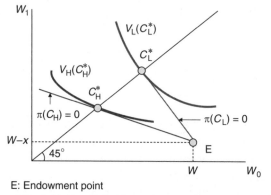

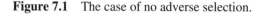

E: Endowment point

$\pi(C) = 0$: Zero profit line for an insurer offering contract C

Figure 7.1   The case of no adverse selection.

Program 7.1 (No adverse selection). For type i insured:

$$\max_{\{I_i, Q_i\}} V_i(C_i) = (1 - p_i)U(W - Q_i) + p_i U(W - x + I_i - Q_i) \qquad (7.3)$$

$$s.t.\ Q_i - p_i I_i = 0,$$

The Lagrangian is

$$L = (1 - p_i)U(W - Q_i) + p_i U(W - x + I_i - Q_i) + \lambda[Q_i - p_i I_i].$$

The two first-order conditions (FOCs) are

$$\partial L / \partial I_i = p_i U_1' - \lambda p_i = 0$$
$$\partial L / \partial Q_i = -(1 - p_i)U_0' - p_i U_1' + \lambda = 0. \qquad (7.4)$$

Combining these two FOCs, we have

$$(1 - p_i)[U_1' - U_0'] = 0$$
$$U_1' = U_0' \Rightarrow W_{i1} = W_{i0} \Rightarrow I_i = x, Q_i = p_i x. \qquad (7.5)$$

We obtain an efficient equilibrium in which insureds are fully insured. The equilibrium contracts are depicted as C_H^* and C_L^*. Note that each contract is located on the zero profit line.

7.2   Rothschild and Stiglitz Model

The full insurance outcome in the no adverse selection case is not obtainable if risk types are private information. To see why, let us consider Figure 7.1.

The high-risk insured will be happier with C_L^* than with C_H^*. However, he was not able to select C_L^* under information symmetry, since the insurer would not sell the contract to him. If the risk type is not observed by the insurer, the insured may purchase C_L^*, pretending to be of low risk. In that case, the insurer offering C_L^* will lose money. Anticipating this loss, the insurer will not offer C_L^* in the first place.

Rothschild and Stiglitz (1976) investigate the competitive equilibrium outcome under information asymmetry. Rothschild and Stiglitz (henceforth RS) consider the following equilibrium conditions. An equilibrium satisfying these conditions will be called an RS equilibrium throughout this book.

RS equilibrium conditions. At an RS equilibrium, (i) insurers should make a nonnegative profit from each contract; and (ii) insurers should have no incentives to offer other contracts, taking other insurers' contracts as given.

Note that condition (i) can be replaced by the zero profit from each contract, since the market is competitive.[2] Note that condition (i) is stronger than the usual zero profit condition for a competitive equilibrium, since it rules out the cross-subsidy between contracts. Condition (ii) also needs further explanation. An insurer will have no incentive to offer other contracts if she conjectures that doing so is not profitable. Since the profit of a contract depends on other contracts offered by competing insurers, how the insurer conjectures regarding other insurers' contracts becomes crucial. In RS, the insurer conjectures that other insurers do not change contracts after new contracts are offered. This conjecture will be called the RS conjecture in this book (in the literature it is often referred to as the Cournot–Nash conjecture). These equilibrium conditions are crucial to the RS equilibrium outcome and are also exposed to a criticism. It is important to note that modification of these conditions will lead to different equilibrium outcomes. As will be seen later, a Wilson–Miyazaki–Spence equilibrium requires zero profits of insurers (not of each contract) and a more sophisticated conjecture.

Equilibria are classified into two categories. A pooling equilibrium is an equilibrium in which both types of insureds select the same contracts. A separating equilibrium is an equilibrium in which different types of insureds select different contracts. At a separating equilibrium, an insured's risk type is identified according to his selection of contracts.

It is easy to see that no pooling equilibrium can exist. In Figure 7.2, a candidate contract for an equilibrium is depicted as C_p on the zero profit line for

---

[2] However, when the single crossing property does not hold, an insurer may earn a positive profit at an RS equilibrium (see the next chapter).

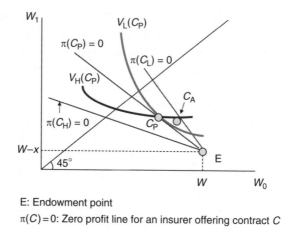

E: Endowment point

$\pi(C) = 0$: Zero profit line for an insurer offering contract C

Figure 7.2   No pooling equilibrium in the RS model.

the risk pool. Note that the slope of the zero profit line is $-(1 - p_U)/p_U$, where p_U is the ex ante probability of loss. At C_P, the slope of the indifference curve of a high-risk insured is steeper than that of a low-risk insured. Therefore we can always find another contract like C_A as in Figure 7.2 which is located between two indifference curves. Now, suppose that an insurer offers C_A. Note that C_A attracts only low risks, since high risks will prefer C_P to C_A. Therefore, the insurer offering C_A will make a positive profit, which violates the equilibrium conditions.[3] As a result, a pooling equilibrium is not possible.

In a separating equilibrium, different risk types will select different contracts. Since insurers do not directly observe the risk types, it is possible that an insured attempts to deceive insurers in reporting his risk type. This possibility makes the problem complicated to analyze. The complication, however, can be greatly reduced by the *revelation principle* (Myerson, 1979), which states that any contract is weakly dominated by a truth-telling contract.[4] Therefore, an equilibrium outcome will be found even if we focus on the truth-telling cases. However, the revelation principle does not imply that an insured always tells the truth. We need to impose constraints to make sure that the insured tells the truth. These constraints are called *self-selection* or *incentive compatibility* (IC) constraints.

In our context, the IC constraints make sure that one risk type does not want to select the contract for the other risk type. Recall that $V_i(C_k)$ is the expected utility of type i when purchasing C_k:

---

[3]   Note that a contract for a risk type is profitable if it is below the zero profit line for the risk type in the (W_0, W_1) plane.

[4]   For an intuitive proof, consider the case in which the insured's report strategy is $y(t)$ when the true type is t. Suppose that the insurer's strategy is given by $I(y)$. This insurer's strategy is equivalent to another strategy $I^*(t) = I(y(t))$, with truth-telling $y^*(t) = t$.

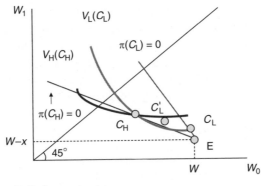

E: Endowment point

$\pi(C) = 0$: Zero profit line for an insurer offering contract C

Figure 7.3 Incentive compatibility for low risk is not binding in an RS equilibrium.

$$V_i(C_k) = (1 - p_i)U(W - Q_k) + p_i U(W - x + I_k - Q_k).$$

Then IC can be expressed as

$$V_i(C_i) \geq V_i(C_j), \quad \text{for } j \neq i. \tag{7.6}$$

In detail,

$$(1 - p_L)U(W - Q_L) + p_L U(W - x + I_L - Q_L) \tag{7.7a}$$
$$\geq (1 - p_L)U(W - Q_H) + p_L U(W - x + I_H - Q_H),$$

$$(1 - p_H)U(W - Q_H) + p_H U(W - x + I_H - Q_H) \tag{7.7b}$$
$$\geq (1 - p_H)U(W - Q_L) + p_H U(W - x + I_L - Q_L).$$

The following lemma shows that only the second IC is binding.

Lemma 7.1 At an RS equilibrium, the IC for high risks (inequality (7.7b)) is binding and the IC for low risks (inequality (7.7a)) is not.

Proof Since the indifference curve for low risk is steeper than that for high risk, two risk types cannot simultaneously be indifferent between two points. Therefore, two incentive constraints cannot be binding simultaneously. Now, suppose that (7.7a) is binding and (7.7b) is not. Such a situation is obtained with contracts C_H and C_L in Figure 7.3. This case, however, cannot hold at an equilibrium, since we can always find another contract, say C_L', for low risks such that C_L' will attract low risks without violating other constraints. Similarly, it does not hold that neither IC is binding. Therefore, at an equilibrium, (7.7b) is binding and (7.7a) is not. □

By Lemma 7.1, we can ignore IC constraint (7.7a) and replace the inequality sign in (7.7b) with the equality sign. Finally, we can formulate the problem as the maximization problem of expected utility for low risk, since once we find solutions, the expected utility for high risk is also maximized given constraints. Based on the above observations, the equilibrium can be found by solving the following program.

Program 7.2 (RS equilibrium).

$$
\begin{aligned}
\max_{\{Q_L, Q_H, I_L, I_H\}} V_L(C_L) &= (1 - p_L)U(W - Q_L) \\
&+ p_L U(W - x + I_L - Q_L) \\
\text{s.t.} (1 - p_H)U(W - Q_H) &+ p_H U(W - x + I_H - Q_H) \\
&= (1 - p_H)U(W - Q_L) + p_H U(W - x + I_L - Q_L) \\
Q_i - p_i I_i &= 0, \quad \text{for } i = \text{H, L.}
\end{aligned}
\tag{7.8}
$$

The Lagrangian becomes

$$
\begin{aligned}
L &= (1 - p_L)U(W - Q_L) + p_L U(W - x + I_L - Q_L) \\
&+ \lambda[(1 - p_H)U(W - Q_H) + p_H U(W - x + I_H - Q_H) \\
&- (1 - p_H)U(W - Q_L) - p_H U(W - x + I_L - Q_L)] \\
&+ \phi[Q_H - p_H I_H] + \delta[Q_L - p_L I_L].
\end{aligned}
$$

Proposition 7.1 (Rothschild and Stiglitz equilibrium). At a separating RS equilibrium, the high-risk insured is fully insured, while the low-risk insured is partially insured.

Proof. From the Lagrangian, the following FOCs are obtained:

$$
\begin{aligned}
L_{Q_L} &= -(1 - p_L)U'_{L0} - p_L U'_{L1} + \lambda[(1 - p_H)U'_{L0} + p_H U'_{L1}] + \delta = 0, \\
L_{Q_H} &= -\lambda[(1 - p_H)U'_{H0} + p_H U'_{H1}] + \phi = 0, \\
L_{I_L} &= p_L U'_{L1} - \lambda p_H U'_{L1} - \delta p_L = 0, \\
L_{I_H} &= \lambda p_H U'_{H1} - \phi p_H = 0.
\end{aligned}
\tag{7.9}
$$

Rearranging the FOCs leads to

$$
L_{I_H} = 0 \Rightarrow \lambda U'_{H1} = \phi.
$$

Replacing ϕ with this expression in $L_{Q_H} = 0$, we have

$$
U'_{H1} = U'_{H0} \Rightarrow W_{H1} = W_{H0}.
$$

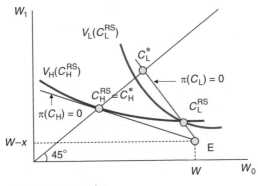

E: Endowment point

$\pi(C) = 0$: Zero profit line for an insurer offering contract C

Figure 7.4   RS separating equilibrium.

This result implies full insurance such that $I_H = x$, and $Q_H = p_H x$. Also, we have

$$L_{I_L} = 0 \Rightarrow U'_{L1} = \delta p_L / [p_L - \lambda p_H] \qquad (7.10)$$

Plugging this expression for U'_{L_1} into $L_{Q_L} = 0$ leads to

$$L_{Q_L} = -(1 - p_L)U'_{L0} + \lambda(1 - p_H)U'_{L0} + \delta(1 - p_L) = 0,$$

that is, $U'_{L0} = \delta(1 - p_L) / [(1 - p_L) - \lambda(1 - p_H)]$. \qquad (7.11)

Comparing between U'_{L1} and U'_{L0}, we have that $U'_{L1} > U'_{L0} \Rightarrow W_{L1} < W_{L0}$. This result implies partial insurance such that $I_L < x$, $Q_L = p_L I_L$. $\qquad \square$

A separating RS equilibrium is depicted in Figure 7.4. Equilibrium contracts are denoted by C_H^{RS} and C_L^{RS}. The high-risk insured is indifferent between the two contracts, while the low-risk insured strictly prefers C_L^{RS} to C_H^{RS}. Contracts C_H^* and C_L^*; are equilibrium contracts under information symmetry. Note that C_H^{RS} is none other than C_H^*. Therefore, the high-risk insured is no worse off. However, the low-risk insured is worse off with C_L^{RS} than with C_L^*. The utility loss of the low-risk insured represents the efficiency loss due to an adverse selection problem.

One important issue is whether or not an RS equilibrium always exists. Rothschild and Stiglitz show that an RS equilibrium may not exist if the population proportion of high risks is not high enough. In other words, an RS equilibrium exists if and only if $\theta \geq \theta^{RS}$ for some θ^{RS}. Consider Figure 7.5. Notice that the zero profit line for the risk pool is close to the zero

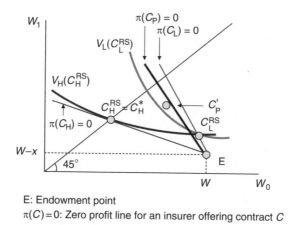

E: Endowment point

$\pi(C) = 0$: Zero profit line for an insurer offering contract C

Figure 7.5   Nonexistence of RS equilibrium.

profit line for low risks. In this case, we can find a contract like C'_P such that both risks prefer C'_P to RS contracts. Moreover, C'_P is profitable, when both types purchase it. Therefore, contracts C_H^{RS} and C_L^{RS} cannot constitute an equilibrium. Since no pooling equilibrium is possible, no equilibrium exists in this case. Note that contracts like C'_P cannot be found if the population proportion of high risks is high enough, so that the zero profit line for the risk pool is far away from the zero profit line for low risks. Therefore, there is a threshold θ^{RS} such that an RS equilibrium exists for $\theta \geq \theta^{RS}$. Threshold θ^{RS} is determined so that the zero profit line for the risk pool meets tangentially the indifference curve for low risk passing through C_L^{RS}.

Another important issue is whether or not the RS equilibrium is second best efficient. It is well known that the RS equilibrium is not second best efficient, in general. As we will show later, the Wilson–Miyazaki–Spence equilibrium is second best efficient. Therefore, the RS equilibrium is not second best efficient, unless two equilibria coincide with each other. This result can be explained by the fact that the second set of constraints to (7.8) (Program 7.2) is different from the resource constraint. An RS equilibrium imposes the resource constraint per contract, while the second best outcome will impose the resource constraint for the whole market. The discussion is summarized as follows.

Proposition 7.2   (Rothschild and Stiglitz equilibrium).

(a)   An RS equilibrium may not exist, if the population proportion of high-risk insureds is low enough.

(b)   An RS equilibrium is not second best, in general.

Proof

(a) See the text above.
(b) See the text above and the next section.   □

7.3   Wilson Model

The results of Rothschild and Stiglitz are not very satisfactory since an equilibrium may not exist and is not second best even if it exists. Subsequent studies extend RS in several ways. Among others, Wilson, Miyazaki, and Spence modify the nonnegative profit condition for each contract and the RS conjecture. Under the RS conjecture, an insurer conjectures that other insurers will not respond even if the insurer introduces a new contract. A criticism is that insurers may be too naïve under the RS conjecture. Insurers will actively respond to a competitor's introduction of a new contract, especially if it lowers the profits of their contracts. A more sophisticated conjecture is suggested by Wilson (1977). Under the Wilson conjecture, an insurer makes the decision to introduce a contract under the conjecture that other insurers will withdraw their contracts that become unprofitable as a result of the introduction of the contract. At an equilibrium, (i) contracts should make nonnegative profits; and (ii) there should be no other contracts profitable under the Wilson conjecture. This equilibrium is called a Wilson (or anticipatory) equilibrium.

Note that the Wilson conjecture provides an insurer with lower incentives to offer a new contract than the RS conjecture. This implies that a separating Wilson equilibrium corresponds to a separating RS equilibrium if the RS equilibrium exists. Unlike the RS equilibrium, however, a pooling Wilson equilibrium may exist. At the pooling Wilson equilibrium, a pooling contract maximizes the low risk's expected utility (see the following proposition). Unlike in RS, a pooling contract can constitute an equilibrium, since a new contract attracting only low risks is not profitable under the Wilson conjecture. These results are summarized as follows.

Proposition 7.3 (Wilson equilibrium).

(a) A Wilson equilibrium always exists.
(b) If an RS separating equilibrium exists, then the equilibrium is a Wilson separating equilibrium.
(c) If no RS equilibrium exists, a Wilson equilibrium is a pooling equilibrium at which the expected utility of the low risk is maximized.

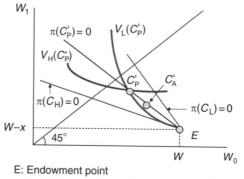

E: Endowment point

$\pi(C) = 0$: Zero profit line for an insurer offering contract C

Figure 7.6 C_P' fails to maximize the expected utility of low risk.

Proof

(a)   The existence of a Wilson equilibrium comes from (b) and (c).

(b)   This comes from the observation that the Wilson conjecture provides an insurer with lower incentives to offer a new contract than the RS conjecture.

(c)   Now let us show that a pooling Wilson equilibrium exists when no RS equilibrium exists. Consider Figure 7.2. Let us show that the pooling contract C_P constitutes a Wilson equilibrium. Recall that C_P cannot constitute an RS equilibrium, since there is a new profitable contract offer, C_A, attracting low risks only. However, this logic fails to apply here since offering C_A makes the existing contract C_P unprofitable. Once contract C_P is withdrawn, contract C_A cannot be profitable since high risks will also select it. Anticipating this loss, an insurer will not introduce contract C_A. Note that the zero profit line passing C_P meets tangentially the indifference curve of the low risk at C_P in Figure 7.2, so that the expected utility of the low-risk insured is maximized. It should be so because, if not, a profitable contract can be found. This case is depicted in Figure 7.6. Contract C_P' cannot constitute a Wilson equilibrium, since it fails to maximize the expected utility of a low-risk insured. In this case, for example, contract C_A' is profitable even if C_P' is withdrawn.   □

7.4   Wilson–Miyazaki–Spence Model

Another interesting extension to the RS equilibrium is to allow cross-subsidy between contracts. Under the cross-subsidy, the total profit of an insurer is required to be nonnegative. Individual contracts may lose money or make a positive profit. A Wilson–Miyazaki–Spence (WMS) equilibrium is one in which (i) insurers should make nonnegative total profits; and (ii) insurers should have no incentive to offer other contracts under the Wilson conjecture. To find a WMS equilibrium, let us consider the following program.

Program 7.3 (WMS equilibrium).

$$\max_{\{Q_L, Q_H, I_L, I_H\}} (1-p_L)U(W-Q_L) + p_L U(W-x+I_L-Q_L) \tag{7.12}$$

s.t.

$$(1-p_H)U(W-Q_H) + p_H U(W-x+I_H-Q_H)$$
$$= (1-p_H)U(W-Q_L) + p_H U(W-x+I_L-Q_L),$$
$$\theta(Q_H - p_H I_H) + (1-\theta)(Q_L - p_L I_L) = 0,$$
$$Q_H - p_H I_H \leq 0.$$

The first constraint is the IC constraint as in the RS case. Unlike in the RS case, however, we require zero total profit of an insurer (the second constraint); and nonpositive profit from the contract for the high risk (the third constraint). The nonpositive profit of the contract for the high risk comes from the observation that the subsidy should be made from low risks to high risks. At an equilibrium, the subsidy from the high risks to the low risks is not possible, since it opens an opportunity for an insurer to offer a profitable contract for the high risk.

The Lagrangian is

$$\begin{aligned} L = {} & (1-p_L)U(W-Q_L) + p_L U(W-x+I_L-Q_L) \\ & + \lambda[(1-p_H)U(W-Q_H) + p_H U(W-x+I_H-Q_H) \\ & - (1-p_H)U(W-Q_L) - p_H U(W-x+I_L-Q_L) \\ & + \phi[\theta(Q_H - p_H I_H) + (1-\theta)(Q_L - p_L I_L)] + \delta[p_H I_H - Q_H] \end{aligned} \tag{7.13}$$

The FOCs are

$$\begin{aligned} L_{Q_L} = {} & -(1-p_L)U'_{L0} - p_L U'_{L1} + \lambda[(1-p_H)U'_{L0} + p_H U'_{L1}] \\ & + \phi(1-\theta) = 0, \\ L_{Q_H} = {} & -\lambda\left[(1-p_H)U'_{H0} + p_H U'_{H1}\right] + \phi\theta - \delta = 0, \\ L_{I_L} = {} & p_L U'_{L1} - \lambda p_H U'_{L1} - \phi(1-\theta)p_L = 0, \\ L_{I_H} = {} & \lambda p_H U'_{H1} - \phi\theta p_H + \delta p_H = 0. \end{aligned} \tag{7.14}$$

Lemma 7.2 (WMS equilibrium). At a WMS equilibrium, the high-risk insured is fully insured and the low-risk insured is partially insured.

Proof. From the FOCs,

$$L_{I_H} = 0 \Rightarrow \lambda U'_{H1} = \phi\theta - \delta.$$

Using this result,

$$L_{Q_H} = 0 \Rightarrow U'_{H1} = U'_{H0} \Rightarrow W_{H1} = W_{H0}.$$

Thus, the high risk is fully insured.
Now,

$$L_{I_L} = 0 \Rightarrow U'_{L1} = \phi\,(1-\theta)p_L/[p_L - \lambda p_H].$$

Using this result,

$$L_{Q_L} = -(1-p_L)U'_{L0} + \lambda(1-p_H)U'_{L0} + \phi\,(1-\theta)(1-p_L) = 0$$

$$\Rightarrow U'_{L0} = \phi\,(1-\theta)(1-p_L)/[(1-p_L) - \lambda(1-p_H)].$$

Comparing U'_{L0} with U'_{L1}, we have that

$$U'_{L1} > U'_{L0} \Rightarrow W_{L1} < W_{L0}.$$

Thus, the low risk is partially insured.   □

If the third constraint is binding, then no subsidy is made, implying that the solutions correspond to RS separating contracts. If the third constraint is not binding, the solution is different from RS separating contracts. In such a case, the expected utility of the high risk will be higher than that under RS contracts, since the high risk is subsidized by the low risk. However, this does not mean that the expected utility of the low risk is lower than that under the RS contracts. On the contrary, the expected utility of the low risk should be higher than that under the RS contracts, since Program 7.3 maximizes the expected utility of low risks with more flexible constraints than under the RS contract case. To see this, note that the low risk is partially insured under the RS contracts. Since reducing risks increases the expected utility, the low-risk insured is willing to subsidize the high-risk insured in exchange for a higher level of insurance. As a result, the low-risk insured can be happier even if he subsidizes the high-risk insured.

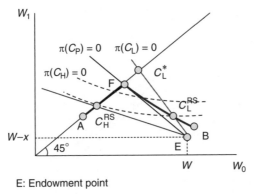

E: Endowment point

$\pi(C) = 0$: Zero profit line for an insurer offering contract C

Figure 7.7   Locus of contacts for zero total profit.

It is helpful in understanding the WMS equilibrium to see where the contract for the low risk may be located on the (W_0, W_1) plane. For this purpose, let us first find the locus of contracts for the low risk along with the subsidy to the high-risk insured, given zero total profit. Let us ignore the third constraint for now. Since the high-risk insured is fully insured at any level of subsidy, the locus of the contracts for the high risk includes the $45°$ line segment AF in Figure 7.7, where F is the pooling contract with full insurance. As the contract for a high risk moves from A to F along the AF line segment, the contract for the low risk is determined so as to make the zero total profit. The locus of the contract for the low risk is depicted by curve BF. Note that the high-risk insured subsidizes (is subsidized by) the low-risk insured for the line segment AC_H^{RS} ($C_H^{RS}F$, respectively). As the high risk is more subsidized, his contract points move toward F along the AF line segment, while the contract points of the low risk move toward F along the BF curve. Note also that when the high risk is offered C_H^{RS}, the corresponding contract for the low risk is C_L^{RS}. Therefore, the RS equilibrium outcome is one of the potential outcomes in WMS.

For an analytic expression for BF, note that the zero total profit $\theta(Q_H - p_H I_H) + (1 - \theta)(Q_L - p_L I_L) = 0$ can be rewritten using W_0 and W_1 as follows:

$$\theta[W - W_{H0} - p_H x] + (1 - \theta)[W - (1 - p_L)W_{L0} - p_L(W_{L1} + x)].$$

Therefore, the IC constraint and the zero total profit constraint become

$$U(W_{H0}) = (1 - p_H)U(W_{L0}) + p_H U(W_{L1}),$$
$$\theta[W - W_{H0} - p_H x] + (1 - \theta)[W - (1 - p_L)W_{L0} - p_L(W_{L1} + x)] = 0.$$

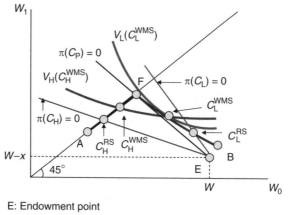

E: Endowment point
$\pi(C) = 0$: Zero profit line for an insurer offering contract C

Figure 7.8   WMS equilibrium.

Totally differentiating both equations with respect to W_{L0} gives

$$U'(W_{H0})dW_{H0}/dW_{L0} = (1 - p_H)U'(W_{L0}) + p_H U'(W_{L1})dW_{L1}/dW_{L0}, (7.15)$$

$$-\theta dW_{H0}/dW_{L0} + (1-\theta)[-(1-p_L) - p_L dW_{L1}/dW_{L0}] = 0 \qquad (7.16)$$

Solving for dW_{H0}/dW_{L0} from (7.16) and plugging it into (7.15), we have

$$dW_{L1}/dW_{L0} = -[\theta(1 - p_H)U'(W_{L0})$$
$$+ (1-\theta)(1-p_L)U'(W_{H0})]/[\theta p_H U'(W_{L1}) \qquad (7.17)$$
$$+ (1-\theta)p_L U'(W_{H0})].$$

This is the slope of the BF curve. This locus will pass through the RS contract for the low risk (C_L^{RS}) and ends at the full insurance contract on the zero profit line for the risk pool.

Since the solution to Program 7.3 should maximize the expected utility of the low risk, the optimal contract for the low risk will be determined by the tangent point where the indifference curve of the low risk meets the locus curve. Thus,

$$\frac{(1-p_L)U'(W_{L0})}{p_L U'(W_{L1})} = \frac{[\theta(1-p_H)U'(W_{L0}) + (1-\theta)(1-p_L)U'(W_{H0})]}{[\theta p_H U'(W_{L1}) + (1-\theta)p_L U'(W_{H0})]}. \qquad (7.18)$$

The contract for the low risk satisfying (7.18) is depicted as C_L^{WMS} in Figure 7.8. The corresponding contract for the high risk is C_H^{WMS}. In Figure 7.8,

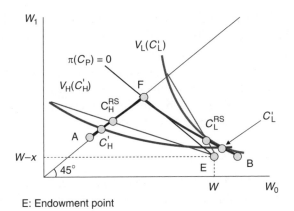

E: Endowment point

Figure 7.9   The RS equilibrium may coincide with the WMS equilibrium.

$\{C_H^{WMS}, C_L^{WMS}\}$ is depicted so as to satisfy the third constraint to Program 7.3. That is, the third constraint is not binding. Therefore, as depicted in Figure 7.8, $\{C_H^{WMS}, C_L^{WMS}\}$ is the set of the WMS equilibrium contracts that solves Program 7.3.

In general, however, the solution to (7.18) does not have to satisfy the third constraint. In such a case, the RS separating contracts becomes the solutions to Program 7.3, where the third constraint is binding. Graphically, such a case will occur when the solution to (7.18) for the low risk is located above the zero profit line for the low risk, which implies that a subsidy should be made from the high risk to the low risk, violating the third constraint. This case is depicted in Figure 7.9. The solution to (7.18) for low risk is denoted by C_L', which is above the zero profit line for low risks. C_H' denotes for the corresponding contract for the high risks. Since C_H' and C_L' do not satisfy the third constraint, they are not the WMS equilibrium contracts. Since expected utility of the low risk is lowered as his contract points move toward F along the $C_L'F$ curve, the best contract for him is the RS contract C_L^{RS} at which the third constraint becomes just binding. In this case, the RS equilibrium coincides with the WMS equilibrium.

As the population proportion of high risks, θ, is higher, subsidizing high risks becomes more costly. Therefore, the solution to (7.18) for low risk is likely to be located above the zero profit line for low risks, so that no subsidy is made from the low risk to the high risk. Therefore, for large θ, the solutions to Program 7.3 correspond to the RS equilibrium contracts. However, even if an RS equilibrium exists (i.e., $\theta \geq \theta^{RS}$), the solutions to Program 7.3 may be different from the RS contracts, as depicted in Figure 7.8. In Figure 7.8, C_H^{RS} and C_L^{RS} are RS equilibrium contracts, which are different from C_H^{WMS} and C_L^{WMS}. This observation implies that the solution to Program 7.3 corresponds to the RS equilibrium for $\theta \geq \theta^{WMS}$, where $\theta^{WMS} \geq \theta^{RS}$. For θ such that $\theta^{WMS} > \theta \geq \theta^{RS}$, an RS equilibrium exists but is different from the WMS equilibrium.

Finally, note that the solution to Program 7.3 always constitutes an equilibrium. It is not difficult to see that any deviation from the solution to Program 7.3 is not profitable under the Wilson conjecture. The following proposition summarizes the discussion above.

Proposition 7.4 (WMS equilibrium).

(a)   A WMS equilibrium always exists and is separating.
(b)   A WMS equilibrium corresponds to the RS equilibrium if the population proportion of high risks is high enough, i.e., if $\theta \geq \theta^{WMS}$ for some θ^{WMS} where $\theta^{WMS} \geq \theta^{RS}$. For $\theta < \theta^{WMS}$, a WMS equilibrium exhibits a subsidy from the contract for the low risk to the contract for the high risk.
(c)   A WMS equilibrium is second best efficient.

Proof For (a) and (b), see text above.

(c) Note that the second constraint to Program 7.3 can be considered the resource constraint and that the third constraint can be interpreted as the requirement for the minimum expected utility of high risks, $EU_H \geq \bar{U}$, where $\bar{U} = EU_H(C_H^{RS})$. The first constraint takes into account the information asymmetry problem. Therefore, Program 7.3 is none other than the program for Pareto efficiency under information asymmetry.   □

7.5   Conclusion

The problems of adverse selection or information asymmetry are important issues in insurance and information economics. In general, adverse selection problems lower efficiency of the market. In the insurance context, the inefficiency comes from the fact that the low-risk insured is offered partial insurance at an equilibrium. Moreover, as seen in the Rothschild and Stiglitz model, an equilibrium may not even exist.

Adverse selection consideration provides another rationale for partial insurance. Recall from Chapter 4 that partial insurance can be an outcome when insurance is costly and/or when both parties to the insurance contract are risk averse. In the presence of adverse selection problems, partial insurance can still be an outcome even if the insurer is risk neutral and the insurance premium is actuarially fair.

In the literature, approaches to the adverse selection problems are often classified into signaling models and screening models. In signaling contexts, the informed move first. The informed try to signal information to the uninformed. For example, new workers may try to signal their abilities to recruiters in the job market. In the capital market, firms may try to signal their growth opportunities in order to lower capital raising costs. On the other hand, in screening contexts, the uninformed move first. The uninformed try to screen the information given by the informed. The models considered in this chapter are screening models in which insurers try to screen the insureds by offering different contracts.

Note also that we are focused on the contract design. With some costs, the insurer may try to directly observe the information of the insured. To the extent that the insurer observes the information, the differences in contracts for different risks may not be as obvious as anticipated by the aforementioned models. In addition, diverse factors may affect the contract designs, such as moral hazard, risk aversion, wealth levels, reputation, and experience rating. It is often difficult to separate these factors from adverse selection in contract designs in practice.

BIBLIOGRAPHY

Dionne, G. and N. A. Doherty (1992) Adverse selection in insurance markets: a selective survey. In G. Dionne (ed.), *Contributions to Insurance Economics*. Boston: Kluwer Academic Publishers.

Dionne, G., N. A. Doherty, and N. Fombaron (2000) Adverse selection in insurance markets. In G. Dionne (ed.), *Handbook of Insurance*. Boston: Kluwer Academic Publishers.

Miyazaki, H. (1977) The rate race and internal labour markets. *Bell Journal of Economics*, 8: 394–418.

Myerson, R. B. (1979) Incentive compatibility and the bargaining problem. *Econometrica*, 47: 61–74.

Riley, J. G. (1979) Informational equilibrium. *Econometrica*, 47: 331–59.

Rothschild, M. and J. E. Stiglitz (1976) Equilibrium in competitive insurance markets: an essay on the economics of imperfect information. *Quarterly Journal of Economics*, 90: 629–50.

Rothschild, M. and J. E. Stiglitz (1997) Competition and insurance twenty years later. *Geneva Papers on Risk and Insurance Theory*, 22: 73–9.

Spence, M. (1973) Job market signaling. *Quarterly Journal of Economics*, 87: 355–74.

Spence, M. (1978) Product differentiation and performance in insurance markets. *Journal of Public Economics*, 10: 427–47.

Stiglitz, J. E. (1977) Monopoly, nonlinear pricing, and imperfect information: the insurance market. *Review of Economic Studies*, 44: 407–30.

Wilson, C. (1977) A model of insurance markets with incomplete information. *Journal of Economic Theory*, 16: 167–207.

Chapter 8

Advanced Topics in Adverse Selection

In this chapter, we study multi-period extensions to the Rothschild and Stiglitz model, the information acquisition issue, the classification of risks, and the effects of multi-dimensional characteristics on the equilibrium outcomes. The basic models studied in the previous chapter are one-period models. Multi-period models will provide additional intuitions on the insurance contract, since the contract is often renewable or a long-term contract in practice (Section 8.1). The information acquisition issue is related to whether or not acquiring information is valuable (Section 8.2). Unlike in the case of a single decision maker, an insured may experience a utility loss when he obtains information, if the insurer strategically changes the contract offered. This issue is interesting since an insured may not want to be informed, whereas the basic models simply assume that the insured is informed.

Uninformed insurers may want to classify the insureds' risks. We will see that such a classification of risks may or may not improve efficiency (Section 8.3). While basic models assume one source of adverse selection, diverse factors may interact with the adverse selection problem (Section 8.4). Insurers may have superior information regarding the risk. Severity risk or risk aversion may affect the adverse selection problem in the loss probability, or frequency risk.

8.1 Multi-period Models

In the previous chapter, one-period models were studied. Now, let us consider two-period models. One obvious difference between a one-period model and a two-period model is that long-term contracts as well as one-period (i.e., short-term) contracts are possible in the two-period model.

Therefore, the solutions to the two-period models are potentially more complicated.

Another important difference is that insurers can use the information of a loss occurrence in the first period in determining the second-period contract, which is called *experience rating* in practice. Note that experience rating does not rule out the case in which insurers ignore the information. As a result, the equilibrium outcome with experience rating will improve efficiency over the repetition of the one-period contract. One related issue is who can observe the loss experience. It is natural to assume that the insurer can observe the experience of her policyholders. However, whether or not other insurers can observe the experience is not clear. Some information, such as car accident records, can be shared among insurers. We follow, unless stated otherwise, the conventional assumption that the loss experience of an insured can be observed only by his insurer, not by other insurers.

The third difference is that commitment becomes an issue in the two-period model. Even though both the insurer and the insured agree on the long-term contracts, it is possible that one or both cannot commit to fulfill the contracts. As we will see later, the equilibrium outcomes are affected by the availability of information and the possibility of commitment.

8.1.1   Commitment case

The following discussion is based on Cooper and Hayes (1987). Let us first introduce some notation and definitions. There are two time periods, $t = 1$ and 2. Insurance markets are similar to the RS setting, except that there are two periods, instead of one. The insurer's conjecture regarding other competitor's reactions is the RS conjecture.

Let C_i^1 be the short-term (one-period) contract for the type i insured at $t = 1$, where $i =$ H (high risk) or L (low risk). At the end of period 1, insureds will experience a loss of x or no loss. Insurers can use the information on the loss experience in determining the period 2 contract. Let us define state A as the loss state and state N as the no-loss state at $t = 1$. Then, C_{is}^2 is the short-term contract for the type i insured at state s at period 2, where i is the risk type and state s is the state regarding loss occurrence of the insured ($s =$ A or N).

A long-term contract, denoted by C^T, which is available in period 1 can be considered as a collection of two short-term contracts.[1] That is,

---

[1]   The distinction between a long-term contract and two short-term contracts may be important when the subsidy between contracts becomes an issue. For example, even under the RS approach, a subsidy may be allowed between short-term contracts constituting one long-term contract. This issue may be important when parties to the contract can renegotiate in period 2 based on the information revealed in period 1 (see Section 8.1.3).

$C_i^{\mathrm{T}} = \{Q_i^1, I_i^1; Q_{iA}^2, I_{iA}^2; Q_{iN}^2, I_{iN}^2\}$, where Q and I denote the premium and indemnity, respectively. Succinctly, $C_i^{\mathrm{T}} = \{C_i^1, C_{is}^2\}_{s=\mathrm{A,N}}$.

Now, define $V_i(C)$ as the expected utility of the type i insured given contract C. For short-term contract C,

$$V_i(C) = (1 - p_i)U(W - Q) + p_i U(W - x - Q + I). \tag{8.1}$$

With some abuse of notation, $V_i(C^{\mathrm{T}})$ is defined as the ex ante expected utility of the type i insured for two periods over the long term C^{T} (see below). It is assumed that the discount rate for period 2 is zero, so that the ex ante expected utility for two periods is the simple summation of expected utilities for period 1 and for period 2.

Now let us first consider the commitment case in which both the insurer and the insured should commit to the fulfillment of the contract. In general, the equilibrium outcome under commitment improves Pareto efficiency over the equilibrium outcome under no commitment, since both parties can always commit to the equilibrium contracts under no commitment. The problem can be formulated as follows.

Program 8.1 (Two-period model under commitment)

$$\max_{\{C_{\mathrm{H}}^{\mathrm{T}}, C_{\mathrm{L}}^{\mathrm{T}}\}} V_{\mathrm{L}}(C_{\mathrm{L}}^{\mathrm{T}}) \tag{8.2}$$

s.t.

$$V_{\mathrm{H}}(C_{\mathrm{H}}^{\mathrm{T}}) \geq V_{\mathrm{H}}(C_{\mathrm{L}}^{\mathrm{T}}),$$

$$V_{\mathrm{L}}(C_{\mathrm{L}}^{\mathrm{T}}) \geq V_{\mathrm{L}}(C_{\mathrm{H}}^{\mathrm{T}}),$$

$$\pi(C_{\mathrm{H}}^{\mathrm{T}}) = 0,$$

$$\pi(C_{\mathrm{L}}^{\mathrm{T}}) = 0,$$

where

$$\begin{aligned} V_i(C_j^{\mathrm{T}}) = (1 - p_i)[U(W - Q_j^1) + \{(1 - p_i)U(W - Q_{jN}^2) \\ + p_i U(W - x - Q_{jN}^2 + I_{jN}^2)\}] + p_i [U(W - x - Q_j^1 + I_j^1) \\ + \{(1 - p_i)U(W - Q_{jA}^2) + p_i U(W - x - Q_{jA}^2 + I_{jA}^2)\}], \end{aligned} \tag{8.3}$$

$$\pi(C_i^{\mathrm{T}}) = Q_i^1 - p_i I_i^1 + \{(1 - p_i)(Q_{iN}^2 - p_i I_{iN}^2) + p_i(Q_{iA}^2 - p_i I_{iA}^2)\}. \tag{8.4}$$

This program can be solved by the Kuhn–Tucker optimization technique. Let us summarize the characteristics of the solution.

Proposition 8.1 (Two-period model under commitment).

(a) The high-risk insured is offered the RS contract in each period. That is, the high-risk insured is fully insured in each period, and is not experience rated:

$$Q_H^1 = Q_{HA}^2 = Q_{HN}^2 = p_H x,$$

$$I_H^1 = I_{HA}^2 = I_{HN}^2 = x.$$

(b) The low-risk insured is partially insured in each period; and is experience rated:

$$Q_{LA}^2 > Q_L^1 > Q_{LN}^2,$$

$$I_{LA}^2 < I_L^1 < I_{LN}^2.$$

Proof (Sketch.) The second constraint is not binding as in the one-period model. Therefore, we can ignore the second constraint. Then, finding the Lagrangian and solving first-order conditions with respect to 12 variables ($\{Q_i^1, Q_{iA}^2, Q_{iN}^2; I_i^1, I_{iA}^2, I_{iN}^2\}_{i=H, L}$) will produce the result. $\qquad\square$

For an intuitive explanation, note first that the RS contract for high risk is full insurance and is efficient. Therefore, it is efficient to repeat the RS contract, which explains part (a). On the other hand, recall that the RS contract for low risk is partial insurance and is not efficient. Since the efficiency loss comes from the possibility of mimicry of the low risk by the high risk, the efficiency improvement can be achieved by making it more difficult for the high risk to mimic the low risk. Since the low risk has a lower probability of loss occurrence, experience rating will lower the incentives for the high risk to mimic the low risk. This observation explains part (b).

8.1.2   Semi-commitment case

In the semi-commitment case, the insurer should commit to the long-term contract while the insured may switch insurers in period 2. This situation seems to be more realistic than the commitment case. In the semi-commitment case, the insurer should design long-term contracts so that the insured has no incentive to switch insurers in period 2. Let us first find the no-switching condition in period 2. Given the assumption that the loss experience of an insured can be observed only by his insurer, insurers in period 2 can offer the RS contracts to insureds who were not their policyholders in period 1. Therefore, in period 2, a long-term contract should provide a type i insured with expected utility greater than or equal to $V_i(C_i^{RS})$. We can also use the fact from the commitment case that offering the high-risk insured the RS contract in each period is efficient. That is, $C_H^T = \{C_H^{RS}, C_H^{RS}\}$. Therefore, the insurer will solve the following program.

Program 8.2 (Two-period model under semi-commitment)

$$\max_{\{C_L^T, C_H^T\}} V_L(C_L^T) \tag{8.5}$$

s.t.

$$2V_H(C_H^{RS}) \geq V_H(C_L^1) + p_H \max[V_H(C_{LA}^2), V_H(C_H^{RS})] \tag{8.5a}$$
$$+ (1 - p_H) \max[V_H(C_{LN}^2), V_H(C_H^{RS})],$$

$$V_L(C_L^T) \geq V_L(C_H^{RS}) + V_L(C_L^{RS}), \tag{8.5b}$$

$$V_L(C_{LA}^2) \geq V_L(C_L^{RS}), \tag{8.5c}$$

$$V_L(C_{LN}^2) \geq V_L(C_L^{RS}), \tag{8.5d}$$

$$\pi(C_L^T) = Q_L^1 - p_L I_L^1 + \{(1 - p_L)(Q_{LN}^2 - p_L I_{LN}^2) \atop + p_L(Q_{LA}^2 - p_L I_{LA}^2)\} = 0. \tag{8.5e}$$

The first two constraints are incentive constraints (ICs). The third and the fourth constraints are no switching constraints in period 2. The final constraint is the zero profit condition for the long-term contract for low risks C_L^T. Note that the zero profit condition for high risk is omitted, since the profit is zero with $C_H^T = \{C_H^{RS}, C_H^{RS}\}$.

Solving this program, we have the following equilibrium outcomes.

Proposition 8.2 (CH equilibrium: two-period model under semi-commitment). In the two-period model under semi-commitment, the following holds at an equilibrium (called a CH equilibrium).

(a) The high-risk insured is offered the RS contract in each period. That is, the high-risk insured is fully insured in each period, and is not experience rated:

$$Q_H^1 = Q_{HA}^2 = Q_{HN}^2 = p_H x,$$

$$I_H^1 = I_{HA}^2 = I_{HN}^2 = x.$$

(b)   The low-risk insured is partially insured in each period, and is experience rated:

$$Q_L^1 > Q_{LN}^2 \text{ and } I_L^1 < I_{LN}^2,$$

$$V_L(C_{LN}^2) > V_L(C_{LA}^2) > V_L(C_L^1).$$

(c)   The contracts for the low-risk insured exhibit *highballing*: the first-period profit is positive, and the second-period profit is negative. However, the profit from the second period contract for the low-risk insured with a loss experience is positive: $\pi(C_L^1) > 0$, $\pi(C_{LA}^2) > 0$, and $\pi(C_{LN}^2) < 0$.

Proof (Sketch.) For (a) it is efficient to repeat the RS contract, since the RS contract for high risk is full insurance and is efficient. The rest of this sketch proof is concerned with (b) and (c).

(i)   Note that (8.5a) should be binding, since, if not, a slight change of C_L^T toward full insurance will be preferred to C_L^T by the low-risk insurer without violating any constraint. This contradicts the optimality of C_L^T. We need to have $V_L(C_{LA}^2) \le V_L(C_{LN}^2)$, i.e., a loss experience is punished, in order to prevent the high risk from mimicking the low risk. In addition, (8.5c) should be binding. If not, the outcome would be the same as the commitment case, implying that the switching option is useless (see below). Now, we guess that (8.5d) is not binding, since $V_L(C_{LA}^2) \le V_L(C_{LN}^2)$. We also guess that (8.5b) is not binding, since typically, only one of two ICs is binding. In sum, we solve the program, ignoring (8.5b) and (8.5d). Then, we check whether or not the solutions satisfy (8.5b) and (8.5d).

(ii) In (8.5a), the relevant maximands are $V_H(C_{LA}^2)$ and $V_H(C_{LN}^2)$. For the first maximand, suppose on the contrary that $V_H(C_{LA}^2) < V_H(C_H^{RS})$. If so, a slight change of C_{LA}^2 toward full insurance, without violating any constraint, will be preferred to C_{LA}^2, which is contradictory to the optimality of C_{LA}^2. Similarly, we should have $V_H(C_{LN}^2) \ge V_H(C_H^{RS})$.

(iii) Experience rating for low risks is obtained. For experience rating will make it more difficult for the high risk to mimic the low risk, since the high-risk insured has a high probability of a loss occurrence. This will lead to a reward for no loss experience and a penalty against a loss experience. Thus, $Q_L^1 > Q_{LN}^2$ and $I_L^1 < I_{LN}^2$ as in the commitment case.

(iv) However, unlike in the commitment case, the penalty against a loss experience cannot be severe, since the insured may switch insurers. Due to the switching possibility, we cannot have $Q_{LA}^2 > Q_L^1$

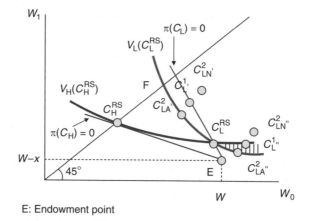

Figure 8.1   Design of CH equilibrium contracts.

and $I_{LA}^2 < I_L^1$, unlike in the commitment case. (This is why (8.5c) is binding.) To see this, suppose, to the contrary, that $Q_{LA}^2 > Q_L^1$ and $I_{LA}^2 < I_L^1$. Since $V_L(C_{LA}^2) \geq V_L(C_L^{RS})$ from (8.5c), $\{C_{LA}^2, C_L^1, C_{LN}^2\}$ are located as $\{C_{LA}^{2'}, C_L^{1'}, C_{LN}^{2'}\}$ or as $\{C_{LA}^{2''}, C_L^{1''}, C_{LN}^{2''}\}$ in Figure 8.1. The former case violates IC for high-risk insureds and the latter case violates the zero profit condition.

(v) $V_L(C_{LA}^2) > V_L(C_L^1)$. Suppose, to the contrary, that $V_L(C_{LA}^2) \leq V_L(C_L^1)$. The IC for the high risk (and (ii)) implies that C_L^1 should not be preferred to C_H^{RS} by the high risk. This implies that C_L^1 should be located in the shaded region in Figure 8.1, and make a negative profit. Thus, $Q_{LA}^2 > Q_L^1$. Note that C_{LN}^2 should also make a negative profit. However, this result along with the optimality condition would require that $Q_{LA}^2 > Q_L^1$ and $I_{LA}^2 < I_L^1$, which is a contradiction, as seen above. Therefore, C_L^1 should make a positive profit; and we should have $V_L(C_{LA}^2) > V_L(C_L^1)$. This result implies highballing. It also points to the usual observation that an insurer with commitment makes a positive profit in period 1.

(vi)   Let us confirm that constraints (8.5b) and (8.5d) are not binding. We have $V_L(C_L^T) > V_L(C_H^{RS}) + V_L(C_L^{RS})$, since $V_L(C_L^T) \geq V_L(C_L^{RS}) + V_L(C_H^{RS}) > V_L(C_H^{RS}) + V_L(C_L^{RS})$. We should also have that $V_L(C_{LN}^2) > V_L(C_L^{RS})$. For, if not, then $V_L(C_{LN}^2) = V_L(C_L^{RS}) = V_L(C_{LA}^2)$. Then, offering C_L^{RS} regardless of loss occurrence is preferred, since it increases profits without changing low risk's expected utility or violating constraints. This is a contradiction. In summary, $\square$
$$V_L(C_{LN}^2) > V_L(C_L^{RS}) = V_L(C_{LA}^2) > V_L(C_L^1)$$

A CH equilibrium is depicted in Figure 8.2. The semi-commitment case is different from the commitment case because the insurer cannot severely

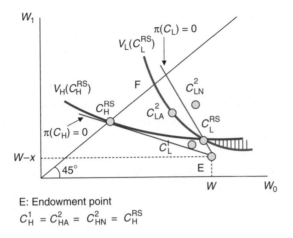

Figure 8.2   CH equilibrium.

penalize the loss experience due to the possibility of switching. The costs following this constraint are eventually imposed on the low-risk insured. Note that the profit of the insurer is zero and the expected utility of the high risk is the same in both cases.

Highballing is commonly observed where insurers commit to the contracts. In period 1, the expected utility of low-risk insureds is lower with C_L^1 than with C_L^{RS}. Under commitment, the loss of expected utility in period 1 is compensated by the gain of expected utility in period 2. The profit of the insurer in period 1 is offset by the loss in period 2. Without commitment, however, the insurer will not offer the period 2 contracts which are nonprofitable. Anticipating this opportunistic behavior of the insurer without commitment, the low-risk insured is not willing to buy C_L^1 in period 1. When the insurer does not commit to the contracts, the profit pattern commonly exhibits *lowballing*, implying that the profit of the insurer is negative in period 1 and positive in period 2 (Nilssen, 2000; Dionne, Doherty, and Fombaron, 2000).

8.1.3   Semi-commitment with renegotiation

The previous subsection ignores the possibility that the insurer and the insured may renegotiate the long-term contract in period 2. Note that risks are separated in period 1 at a CH equilibrium. Then, in period 2, it is optimal for the insurer to renegotiate the contract terms and provide full insurance for the low risk. In other words, the CH equilibrium contracts of Proposition 8.6 are not optimal in period 2. Once renegotiation is allowed, the CH equilibrium fails to be an equilibrium.[2]

---

[2]   In this regard, a CH equilibrium implicitly assumes that both parties commit to not renegotiate over the contract.

In the case of renegotiation, the long-term contracts should be designed to be robust to renegotiation, i.e., renegotiation-proof. This will require that the period 1 contract be pooling. Based on this observation, Dionne and Doherty (1994; henceforth DD) investigate the two-period model in which insurers should commit to the contracts and renegotiation is possible in (the beginning of) period 2. Except for the possibility of renegotiation, the structure is the same as in the previous subsection. The following analysis is based on DD.

Before proceeding to the analysis, it is important to note that the long-term contract needs to be carefully interpreted (Seog, 2008). Suppose that a long-term contract consists of a period 1 pooling contract and two sets of period 2 separating contracts (contingent on loss experiences) as discussed below. Even if the period 1 contract is pooling, it does not mean that the insurer cannot distinguish risk types in period 1. Note that the long-term contract is signed in period 1. By the definition of the long-term contract, the insured should select the period 2 contracts as well as the period 1 contract, when they sign the long-term contract in period 1. As a result, even if the period 1 contract is pooling, the insurer can observe the risk type of the insured from their choices of period 2 contracts, which will open up opportunities for renegotiation. Therefore, under a renegotiation-proof long-term contract, the contracts in each period should be pooling. However, we know that pooling cannot be an (RS) equilibrium outcome in period 2. In other words, no renegotiation-proof long-term contract may exist at an equilibrium, contrary to DD.

This problem may be resolved if some changes are made in the assumptions. First, the DD outcomes can be obtained if the insurer commits to not observe the choice of period 2 contracts in the long-term contract. Alternatively, we may interpret the long-term contract as a set of short-term contracts. In this case, it is important that insurers should still commit to offer the menu of period 2 contracts, since, without the commitment, insurers cannot offer the profitable period 1 contract (see the discussion in the previous section).[3] Even though neither change of assumptions is satisfactory, let us accept one of these changes, so that the following discussion is meaningful.

First of all, recall that the high-risk insured is offered C_H^{RS} in each period in the previous subsection. This result still holds in the semi-commitment with renegotiation case. However, one important difference from the no-renegotiation case is that, in period 1, the risk types should be pooled in the

---

[3] When the long-term contract is considered a set of short-term contracts, a cross-subsidy problem may arise. Under the RS (and DD) approach, each contract should break even. Therefore, the period 1 pooling contract should not be profitable, which is contradictory to DD. Under this interpretation of a long-term contract, the WMS approach seems to be more applicable than the RS approach.

long-term contract. This implies that some high-risk insureds should select the pooling period 1 contracts. This is possible only if high-risk insureds are indifferent between contracts for high risk and for low risk, which is also assumed in the previous subsection.

Let us denote the long-term contract by $C_P^T = \{C_P^1, C_{LN}^2, C_{HN}^2, C_{LA}^2, C_{HA}^2\}$, where superscripts 1 and 2 stand for periods; P for pooling; H and L for risk types; and A and N for loss experience and no experience, respectively. Now, assume that the pooling contract in period 1, C_P^1, is selected by all low-risk insureds and a proportion $1 - t$ of high-risk insureds. Now, let us focus on the period 2 contracts for insureds with no loss experience. Given the long-term contract and no loss experience, mutually beneficial optimal contracts K_{LN}^* and K_{HN}^* (in period 2 only) will solve the following program.

Program 8.3 (Renegotiation in period 2)

$$\max_{\{K_{LN}, K_{HN}\}} V_L(K_{LN}) \tag{8.6}$$

s.t.

$$V_H(K_{HN}) \geq V_H(K_{LN}),$$
$$\pi(K_{LN}) \geq M,$$
$$V_H(K_{HN}) \geq V_H(C_{HN}^2),$$

where M is the profit level allowed in period 2 as determined by the long-term contract. Note that M is not necessarily zero, since a subsidy is allowed between contracts in a long-term contract. If the solution to this program is different from the original long-term contract, then the contract is not renegotiation-proof. Therefore, C_{LN}^2 and C_{HN}^2 in the renegotiation-proof long-term contract should also solve this program. Note that the solution depends on t, since a subsidy between risks and time in a long-term contract depends on t. Now, let us denote the solution to the problem by $(K_{LN}(t), K_{HN}(t))$. Note that the rent M also depends on t: $M = M(t)$.

Note that the program resembles the RS program, except for the possibly nonzero profit condition and the minimum utility condition. When $M = 0$, and $C_{HN}^2 = 0$ (no insurance), then the program is no other than an RS program. In fact, the role of M is just to shift the profit line on the (W_0, W_1) plane, without changing the characteristics of RS contracts. Therefore, resulting contracts are two self-selecting contracts: full insurance for high risks and partial insurance for low risks, given the minimum utility condition.

A similar program is applied to the loss-experienced insureds, resulting in $(K_{LA}(t), K_{HA}(t))$. However, we may simplify the analysis by taking advantage of the intuition of the previous subsection. Recall that, in a

CH equilibrium, the possibility of switching insurers lowers the efficiency level because the loss-experienced insureds cannot be penalized severely ((8.5c) is binding). By the same intuition and the fact that we now have both risk types, the contracts for loss-experienced insureds are just RS equilibrium contracts: $C_{HA}^2 = C_H^{RS}$ and $C_{LA}^2 = C_L^{RS}$.

Let us consider the period 1 problem. As discussed above, high-risk insureds will be indifferent between the one-period contract for high risks, C_H^1, and the long-term contract, C_P^T. Since one-period contract for the high risk is the RS contract (see the discussion above), $C_H^1 = C_H^{RS}$. If the high-risk insured selects C_H^{RS} in period 1, then he will be offered $C_H^1 = C_H^{RS}$ in period 2.

Now, let us focus on the design of the long-term contract $C_P^T = \{C_P^1; C_{LN}^2, C_{HN}^2; C_{LA}^2, C_{HA}^2\}$. We suppose that a proportion t of high risks select C_H^1 and a proportion $1 - t$ of high risks select the pooling contract C_P^1. Note also that $t = 0$ is possible, in which case all insureds are pooled. Given t, the renegotiation-proof long-term contract will solve the following program in period 1. Let us first distinguish among contract choices of different risk types: $C_H^T = \{C_H^1, C_H^2\}$, $C_{PL}^T = \{C_P^1, C_{LN}^2, C_{LA}^2\}$, and $C_{PH}^T = \{C_P^1, C_{HN}^2, C_{HA}^2\}$.

Program 8.4 (Renegotiation-proof contract)

$$\max_{\{C_{PL}^T, C_{PH}^T\}} V_L(C_L^T) \tag{8.7}$$

s.t.

$$V_H(C_H^T) = V_H(C_{PH}^T), \tag{8.7a}$$

$$V_H(C_{PH}^T) \geq V_H(C_{PL}^T), \tag{8.7b}$$

$$V_L(C_{PL}^T) \geq \max[V_L(C_H^T), V_L(C_{PH}^T)], \tag{8.7c}$$

$$V_L(C_{LA}^2) \geq V_L(C_L^{RS}), \tag{8.7d}$$

$$V_H(C_{HA}^2) \geq V_H(C_H^{RS}), \tag{8.7e}$$

$$\begin{aligned}
\pi(C_P^T) = {} & (1-t)\theta(Q_P^1 - p_H I_P^1) + (1-\theta)(Q_P^1 - p_L I_P^1) \\
& + \rho[(1-t)\theta(1-p_H)(Q_{HN}^2 - p_H I_{HN}^2) \\
& + (1-\theta)(1-p_L)(Q_{LN}^2 - p_L I_{LN}^2)] \\
& + \rho[(1-t)\theta p_H (Q_{HA}^2 - p_H I_{HA}^2) \\
& + (1-\theta)p_L (Q_{LA}^2 - p_L I_{LA}^2)] = 0,
\end{aligned} \tag{8.7f}$$

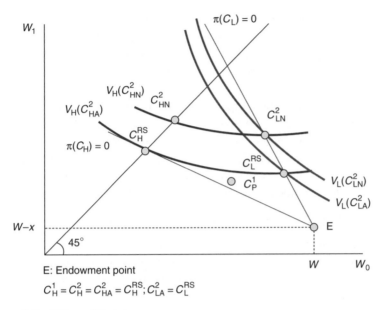

Figure 8.3 DD equilibrium.

$$V_H(C^2_{HN}) \geq V_H(K_{HN}(t)) \tag{8.7g}$$

Expressions (8.7a)–(8.7c) are ICs for period 1. Inequalities (8.7d) and (8.7e) are no switching conditions in period 2. Equation (8.7f) is the zero profit condition for the long-term contract where ρ represents the discount factor. Note that $\rho = 1$ for the CH equilibrium. Inequality (8.7g) is the renegotiation-proof condition. The ICs for C^2_{LN} and C^2_{HN} are implicit in (8.7g). Given that $C^2_H = C^{RS}_H, C^2_{HA} = C^{RS}_H$, and $C^2_{LA} = C^{RS}_L$, the ICs for period 2 are omitted, and (8.7d) and (8.7e) are binding. It is also clear that (8.7g) should be binding for a renegotiation-proof contract. As usual, (8.7c) is not binding. In sum, all constraints are binding, except for (8.7c). Then, the program will be solved by the usual optimization technique. The results of a DD equilibrium are depicted in Figure 8.3. The next proposition summarizes the results.

Proposition 8.3 (DD equilibrium: two-period model under semi-commitment and renegotiation).

(a) In period 1, a (short-term) RS contract for high-risk insureds and a long-term contract are offered.

(b) High-risk insureds are indifferent between the two contracts.

(c) For the long-term contract, the period 1 contract should be pooling and period 2 contracts are separating. The period 1 contract offers partial insurance. The period 2 contracts resemble RS contracts in that high risks are fully insured and low risks are partially insured.

(d) (Experience rating.) Insureds with no loss experience are offered more favorable contracts than insureds with loss experience. Insureds with loss experience are offered RS contracts.

(e) (Highballing.) The long-term contract exhibits a positive profit in period 1 and a negative profit in period 2. The negative profit in period 2 comes from the insureds with no loss experience.

Proof (Sketch.) (a) and (b) are discussed in the text.

For (c), note that period 2 is similar to the (one-period) RS case, given the information on loss experience. Thus, it is not surprising that period 2 contracts are separating as in RS. The result that the period 1 contract should be pooling is also discussed in the text above.

(d) is a common result for the two-period models as seen in the previous subsection. Since the loss experience produces important information regarding the risk types, it should be reflected in the period 2 contracts. The switching possibility prevents the insurers from severely penalizing the insureds with loss experience. As a result, RS contracts should be offered to them.

(e) is also common to the semi-commitment case. The positive profit in period 1 is offset by the negative profit in period 2. This implies that the resource transfer is made from period 1 to period 2. This resource transfer leads to a more efficient allocation since insurers have more information in period 2. □

8.2 Endogenous Information Acquisition

Standard adverse selection models conventionally start with the assumption that the insured initially has private information. Further, they assume that the information status of the insured is observed by the insurer, i.e., the insurer knows the fact that the insured has private information. Interesting cases can be found if we change these assumptions. For example, the insured initially may have no information. However, he can opt to be informed by acquiring information. That is, information status can be endogenously determined. Moreover, the insurer does not necessarily observe the information status of the insured.

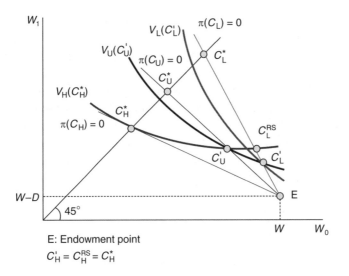

Figure 8.4   Information acquisition.

Let us briefly discuss the value of information acquisition. When a single decision maker is considered, more information will be always valuable. However, in the case of contracting, parties to a contract may interact with each other based on the additional information. Because of this interaction, the value of information acquisition can be negative or positive depending on the circumstances.

Suppose that an insured initially has no private information regarding his risk type. In this case, he will purchase full insurance which will expose him to no risk. Now, suppose that he can acquire, at no cost, perfect information regarding his risk type. If the information is public so that it can be observed by the insurer, then he will be offered full insurance by the insurer. However, the offer will depend on risk types (C_H^* and C_L^* in Figure 7.1 or Figure 8.4). Acquiring information exposes him to classification risk. As a result, the insured is worse off if he is informed. In this case, acquiring information can be undesirable socially as well as privately. If the information is private, then the situation is worse. Under the RS circumstance, the insured will be offered RS contracts ($C_H^{RS} = C_H^*$ and C_L^{RS}), where the low-risk insured is offered partial insurance. Thus, acquiring private information obviously has a negative value.

Note that the above result critically depends on the assumption that the insured initially has no private information. If the insured initially has private information regarding his risk type, then the insurer's acquisition of the information may enhance the efficiency, as seen in the previous chapter. For example, at an RS equilibrium under adverse selection, the low-risk insured selects C_L^{RS}. As the information becomes public, the low-risk insured will be offered C_L^*, instead of C_L^{RS}, which improves efficiency.

However, the situation becomes complicated if the initial private information is not perfect, i.e. the insured does not perfectly observe his risk type. At an RS equilibrium based on the imperfect private information, a low-risk insured will be offered partial insurance. Now, acquiring additional public information may have a negative or positive value depending on circumstances. On the negative side, better information exposes the insured to the classification risk. On the positive side, the low-risk insured will be offered full insurance. The net value of acquiring information is determined by balancing two countervailing forces (Crocker and Snow, 1992).

An important assumption of the above discussion is that the information status of an insured is public, i.e. the insurer can observe whether or not the insured has private information. When the information status is private, unlike in the above discussion, acquiring private information may have a positive value, even if the insured initially has no information. The rest of this section will discuss the effects of observability of information status on the value of information acquisition, based on Doherty and Thistle (1996).

Let us write θ_i for the population proportion of risk type i, where $i = H$, L, and $\theta_H + \theta_L = 1$. Information status depends on whether or not an insured knows his risk type. If the insured knows his risk type, then his information status is denoted by H or L, depending on his risk type. If he is not informed about his risk type, his information status is denoted by U. Define η_j as the population proportion of informational status, where $j = H$, L, U, and $\eta_H + \eta_L + \eta_U = 1$. Write ψ_i for the population proportion of risk types among uninformed insureds: $\psi_H + \psi_L = 1$. We have $\theta_i = \eta_i + \psi_i \eta_U$. The probability of loss is p_H, p_L, or p_U where $p_U = \psi_H p_H + \psi_L p_L$.

Suppose that insurers can observe the information status of insureds. Consider an uninformed insured. The insured will be offered C_U^* in Figure 8.4. His expected utility is $V_U(C_U^*) = U(W - p_U x)$. As the insured opts to become informed, he will be offered $\{C_H^*, C_L^*\}$ if insurers can observe risk types. The ex ante expected utility of the insured becomes $\psi_H V_H(C_H^*) + \psi_L V_L(C_L^*) = \psi_H U(W - p_H x) + \psi_L U(W - p_L x)$. Since $U(W - p_U x) \geq \psi_H U(W - p_H x) + \psi_L U(W - p_L x)$, for the risk averse insured, he is worse off as he becomes informed. Therefore, the insured prefers to be uninformed.

The value of information acquisition is still negative if the insurer cannot observe risk types, given that the insured opts to become informed. Recall that under an RS equilibrium, the insured will be offered $\{C_H^{RS} = C_H^*, C_L^{RS}\}$. Since $V_L(C_L^{RS}) < V_L(C_L^*)$, the ex ante expected utility of the insured becomes even lower. Thus, the insured prefers to be uninformed. By becoming informed, the insured's contract changes from C_U^* to the lottery of $\{C_H^*, C_L^*\}$ or $\{C_H^{RS} = C_H^*, C_L^{RS}\}$. In either case, the risk averse insured will be worse off.

The above observation, however, will be changed if the insurer cannot observe the information status of the insured. Let us first present the following proposition.

Proposition 8.4 Suppose that the insurer cannot observe the information status of the insured as well as risk types. Further assume that information acquisition cost is zero.

(a) Becoming informed has nonnegative (private) value to insureds at an equilibrium.

(b) The unique equilibrium contracts are $\{C_H^{RS}, C_L^{RS}\}$.

Proof Suppose that the insurer believes that the insured has become informed. Then RS contracts $\{C_H^{RS}, C_L^{RS}\}$ will be offered. If an initially uninformed insured remains uninformed, then he will select C_L^{RS}. If he opts to become informed, he will select C_H^{RS} or C_L^{RS}, given his risk types. Therefore, the value of information is

$$I = \psi_H V_H(C_H^{RS}) + \psi_L V_L(C_L^{RS}) - V_U(C_L^{RS}) = 0, \text{ noting that } V_H(C_H^{RS}) = V_H(C_L^{RS}).$$

Assuming that the insured becomes informed with $I = 0$, the belief of insurers is fulfilled. As a result, $\{C_H^{RS}, C_L^{RS}\}$ constitutes an equilibrium.

Now suppose that the insurer believes that the uninformed insured remains uninformed. Suppose that $\eta_H, \eta_L > 0$. Then, the situation is as if there are three types of risks: H, U, and L. In this case, the equilibrium contracts are $\{C_H' = C_H^*, C_U', C_L'\}$. The uninformed insured will select C_U'. Becoming informed, he will select C_H' or C_L' given that his risk type is revealed. The value of information is

$$I' = \psi_H V_H(C_H') + \psi_L V_L(C_L') - V_U(C_U').$$

Simultaneously adding and subtracting $\psi_H V_H(C_L')$ gives

$$I' = \psi_H V_H(C_H') - \psi_H V_H(C_L') + [\psi_H V_H(C_L') + \psi_L V_L(C_L') - V_U(C_U')]$$

$$= \psi_H V_H(C_H') - \psi_H V_H(C_L') > 0,$$

since $\psi_H V_H(C_L') + \psi_L V_L(C_L') = V_U(C_L') = V_U(C_U')$, where the former equality comes from $p_U = \psi_H p_H + \psi_L p_L$ and the latter equality comes from IC for the equilibrium in the three-type case. Therefore, the uninformed insured will become informed in the insurer's belief. The insurer's belief is not fulfilled. Similarly, we can show that information values are nonnegative when $\eta_H = 0$ or $\eta_L = 0$. In sum, the only possible equilibrium is the RS equilibrium in which all insureds are informed. □

When the insurer can observe the information status, the insureds remain uninformed and select C_U^*, a Pareto optimal contract. When the insurer cannot observe the information status, the insureds will become informed and select the lottery of $\{C_H^{RS}, C_L^{RS}\}$ depending on their type, which is worse than C_U^*. The unobservability of information status allows the insureds to behave opportunistically. Anticipating such opportunistic behavior, the insurer can only offer the RS contracts. As a result, the efficiency is lowered.

The following proposition reports the results when information acquisition cost is positive. Note that the positive cost will make the insureds' being informed worthless when the insurer believes he becomes informed, since the value of information is zero ($I = 0$) before netting the cost (see the proof of Proposition 8.4). On the other hand, the value of information is strictly positive when the insurer believes the insureds remain uninformed. In that case, if the cost is small enough, then the insureds will become informed. As a result, there will be no equilibrium. The following proposition summarizes this observation.

Proposition 8.5 Suppose that the insurer cannot observe the information status of the insured as well as risk types. Further assume that information acquisition disutility (cost) is separable from other utilities and is denoted by $K > 0$. Define $I' = \psi_H V_H(C_H') + \psi_L V_L(C_L') - V_U(C_U')$.

(a)   If $K > I'$, then $\{C_H', C_U', C_L'\}$ is at an equilibrium where $\eta_i > 0$ for all $i = H, L, U$. If all insureds are uninformed ($\eta_U = 1$), then C_U^* is at equilibrium.

(b)   If $K \leq I'$, then no equilibrium exists.

Proof When the insurer believes that the insureds will become informed, the insureds will not become informed, since the value of information net of cost is negative, $I - K = -K < 0$, where $I = \psi_H V_H(C_H^{RS}) + \psi_L V_L(C_L^{RS}) - V_U(C_L^{RS}) = 0$. When the insurer believes that the insureds will not become informed, the insureds are willing to be informed, if and only if the value of information net of cost is positive, $I' - K \geq 0$. Therefore, there is no equilibrium when $K \leq I'$. When $K > I'$, the insureds will remain uninformed and the insurer's belief is realized. In this case, $\{C_H', C_U', C_L'\}$ are equilibrium contracts if $\eta_i > 0$ for all i. If $\eta_U = 1$, then C_U^* is an equilibrium contract.   □

8.3   Classification of Risks

Given information asymmetry, insurers may find ways to classify or categorize risks based on available information. For example, a driver's risk

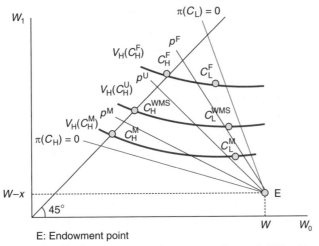

E: Endowment point

p^U, p^M, p^F: fair odds lines for corresponding probability of loss

Figure 8.5   Classification of risks.

may be related to his age or driving years. In this case, insurers may want to reflect this information which will lead to a more accurate risk classification. An interesting issue is how such a classification will affect the efficiency of insurance markets.

Given the standard RS setting, suppose further that there is classification technology available. We assume that the classification cost is zero, unless otherwise stated. The technology provides revised information about the population of each risk. The technology classifies insureds into two groups (G): M and F. Suppose that group M (F) includes a higher population proportion of high (low) risks than the average. In group G, the proportion of i-risk is revised to η_i^G, G = M, F and i = H, L, where $\eta_H^M > \theta_H$ and $\eta_L^F > \theta_L$. In group G, the average risk is $p^G = \eta_H^G p_H + \eta_L^G p_L$. Obviously, $p^M > p^U > p^F$, where p^U is the average risk of the whole population.

Now our question is whether or not this classification changes efficiency, or incentives of insureds or insurers. First, let us note that this classification in fact has no effect on the RS equilibrium contracts, assuming that they exist. This is apparent once we notice that RS contracts are the same regardless of the proportion of risks, as long as the equilibrium exists.

Now let us focus on the WMS equilibrium. Let us write $\{C_H^{WMS}, C_L^{WMS}\}$ for WMS contracts under no classification, and $\{C_H^G, C_L^G\}$ for the WMS contracts for group G under classification. Since these WMS contracts depend on the proportion of risks, contracts are different from those under no classification, unless they are equal to RS contracts. Figure 8.5 depicts the WMS equilibrium outcomes under no classification and under classification.

Compared with the no classification case, insureds in M are (weakly) worse off, while insureds in F are (weakly) better off (see Figure 8.5). It is interesting to see that insurers want to classify risks even if it makes insureds in M worse off. For this, suppose that all insurers do not classify risks. Then, an insurer will have an incentive to classify risks and offer WMS contracts to each group, since it will attract group F, while insureds in M will not select her offers. Note that the classification incentives survive the Wilson (1977) conjecture, since even if competitors withdraw their contracts, the contracts under classification are still (weakly) profitable. Therefore, insurers will use the classification technique, once it is available.

This observation also implies that the insurer will have an incentive to classify risks when the classification cost is positive but small enough. Moreover, the insurer is willing to classify risks even if the utility gain does not fully justify the classification cost, as long as the low-risk insured in F prefers C_L^F to C_L^{WMS}. This is because the insurer will make a profit as long as she can sell to the low-risk insured in F, while other non-classifying insurers will lose money.

Now, let us turn to the efficiency issue. Since the insureds in M become worse off under classification without a subsidy, we need some resource transfer from group F to group M to make insureds in M no worse off. A natural question is whether or not this classification will improve Pareto efficiency by proper transfer of resources.[4] The answer is that the efficiency level is never lowered and may be improved by classification in some cases. Instead of a formal proof, let us provide an intuitive explanation.

First, it is clear that the (second best) efficiency level never gets lowered by the classification technology, since insurers can still offer the same contracts as under no classification. The possibility of strict efficiency improvement can be easily observed by the following example. Consider the case in which WMS contracts under no classification coincide with RS contracts. Now further suppose that classification is accurate enough, so that group F includes a high proportion of low risks, making WMS contracts for group F different from RS contracts. Since WMS contracts are Pareto superior to RS contracts, we conclude that classification provides a strict efficiency improvement. It is also obvious that if the classification is not so accurate that WMS contracts for group F are still RS contracts, then there is no efficiency improvement. This observation shows that classification with higher accuracy is more likely to lead to an efficiency improvement and that locations of contracts under no classification are also important.

---

[4]   The market mechanism (competition and price) is ignored here.

The above discussion implies that classification may improve efficiency even when the classification cost is positive. Classification will improve efficiency if the cost is low enough that the positive effect of classification (along with resource transfer) is greater than the negative effects of the cost.

Finally, let us address the implementation of the efficiency improvement using a tax system. It is well known from welfare economics that a market can achieve Pareto efficiency with a proper resource transfer system or a tax system, when there is no information asymmetry. Crocker and Snow (1986) show that if the classification cost is zero, efficiency improvement can be achieved by a market mechanism (WMS equilibrium) under classification with a proper tax system (in which taxes depend on risks) forcing transfer from group F to M. However, if the classification cost is positive, there are cases in which a proper transfer cannot be made even if it will increase efficiency. For this, suppose that the classification cost exactly offsets the utility gain for the low-risk insureds in F. Then low-risk insureds in F cannot be taxed to subsidize the insured in M. On the other hand, tax cannot be levied only on the high-risk insureds in F, since then they will select C_L^F, not C_H^F. Even if such a resource transfer is desirable, it is not possible at an equilibrium.

Proposition 8.6 (Classification of risks).

(a) If the classification cost is zero, the classification of risks improves efficiency. A WMS equilibrium with a proper tax system can achieve the second best efficiency.

(b) If the classification cost is positive, insurers may have incentives to classify risks, even if it lowers the efficiency. It is possible that a WMS equilibrium with a tax system does not achieve the second best efficiency.

8.4   Multi-dimensional Adverse Selection

8.4.1   Insurer-sided adverse selection

In standard adverse selection models, insureds possess better information about risks than insurers. On the other hand, it is also true that insurers possess better information about some risks than insureds. For example, insureds have superior information about whether or not they are smokers, but health insurers may have superior information about how smoking affects the health condition of insureds, or better understanding of the results of a health examination. Insureds have superior information about their own driving habits, while insurers may have superior information about the mechanical problems and loss sizes of particular brands of automobile and the accident risks of various areas. This possibility leads to the concerns of insurer-sided and double-sided adverse selection problems, which are investigated in Villeneuve (2000, 2005) and Seog (2009a, 2009b).[5]

Suppose that the insured does not observe his own risk type (T = H or L) while the insurer can observe it. Since insurers with superior information offer contracts, this case can be described as a signaling game. We focus on the perfect Bayesian equilibrium (PBE) under competition.

A PBE is a set of contracts $\{C_H, C_L\}$ and beliefs such that (i) C_k is the insurer's profit-maximizing contract to type k, given contracts offered by other insurers and the beliefs of insureds, for k = H, L; (ii) beliefs about types of insureds are determined by Bayes' rule whenever applicable. In our case, Bayes' rule applies as follows. If an insured is offered a separating equilibrium contract, then he believes that his type is as dictated by the contract. If the contract is a pooling one, then the insured believes his type is the average one. If the insured is offered an off-the-equilibrium contract, or is offered different contracts from different insurers, then he is free to pick up any belief.

Villeneuve (2005) shows that diverse PBEs may exist. Such a multiplicity of equilibria is not desirable, when we are to obtain an intuition from the equilibrium. In order to focus our interests on a more robust equilibrium, let us require the PBE to be still optimal even if some insureds are allowed to visit one insurer among those announcing the same menus (for more details, see Seog, 2009a, 2009b).[6] This requirement can be justified by the possibility of positive search costs.

Now consider the following program in which an insurer offers separating PBE contracts $\{C_H^I, C_L^I\}$ that maximize expected utility of low risks, given ICs of the insurer and competition.

Program 8.5 (Insurer-sided adverse selection)

$$\max_{\{C_H, C_L\}} V_L(C_L) = p_L U(W - x - Q_L + I_L) + (1 - p_L)U(W - Q_L) \quad (8.8)$$

---

[5]   Seog (forthcoming) considers another double-sided adverse selection model in which insurance interacts with warranty in risk sharing.

[6]   Note that Villeneuve (2005) also provides refinements using Cho and Kreps (1987) and Bagwell and Ramey (1991), which lead to the efficient outcome. Our approach is different from Villeneuve's, since our focus is on the robustness of the equilibrium against the insured's search behavior.

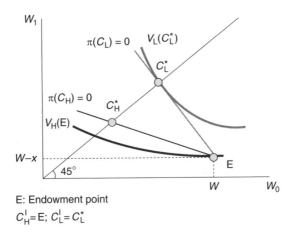

E: Endowment point
$C_H^I = E;\ C_L^I = C_L^*$

Figure 8.6 Insurer-sided adverse selection.

s.t. $\pi(C_k) = Q_k - p_k I_k \geq Q_m - p_k I_m$ for $k, m = H, L$, and $k \neq m$,[7]

$\pi(C_k) \geq 0$, for $k = H, L$,

$V_H(C_H) \geq V_H(E)$.

Note that E is the endowment point. $V_i(E)$ is the expected utility of the type i insured with no insurance. The first set of constraints describes the IC for the insurer. Note that these ICs distinguish the insurer-sided adverse selection from the standard adverse selection problem.[8] The second set of constraints describes the participation of insurers. The third set of constraints describes the participation of insureds. Solving the above program, we have the following result.

Proposition 8.7 (Insurer-sided adverse selection). At an equilibrium, low-risk insureds purchase actuarially fair full insurance, while high-risk insureds purchase no insurance.

Proof The equilibrium contracts are depicted as $\{C_H^I = E,\ C_L^I = C_L^*\}$ in Figure 8.6. Under competition, profits of insurers need to be zero at

---

[7] In detail, the constraints are $\alpha_H - p_H \beta_H \geq \alpha_L - p_H \beta_L$ and $\alpha_L - p_L \beta_L \geq \alpha_H - p_L \beta_H$.

[8] It is important to note that these constraints implicitly assume that the insurer can sell C_k to type m insureds, which, in turn, requires additional assumptions regarding the insurer's conjecture on the insured's purchase behavior. These constraints reflect our requirement that a PBE should be optimal even if some insureds are allowed to visit one insurer among those announcing the same menus. Seog (2009a, 2009b) suggests rationales for the validity of these constraints, such as the possibility of positive search costs.

equilibrium. Now let us show that, at an optimum, the IC for type L should be binding: $Q_L - p_L I_L = Q_H - p_L I_H$. Suppose otherwise. With $\pi(C_L^1) = 0$, the IC and the assumption that $p_H > p_L$ lead to the violation of nonnegative profits from the contract for the high risk since $0 = Q_L - p_L I_L > Q_H - p_L I_H \geq Q_H - p_H I_H$, a contradiction. Binding IC for type L and the zero profit together implies that high-risk insureds will be offered no insurance (E). The highest expected utility of low risks will be obtained by full insurance (C_L^*). For completeness, we need to specify the off-equilibrium beliefs to support this equilibrium. The following belief supports the equilibrium: Each insured conjectures that his risk type is low (T = L) if offered an off-the-equilibrium contract.[9]　　　□

The equilibrium results are in contrast to the standard case in which high risks are fully insured and low risks are partially insured. In the standard case in which insureds have superior information, the low-risk insureds bear the information cost. When the informed party is reversed, the result is also reversed. It is the high-risk insureds who bear the information cost, when insurers have superior information. This result may explain why some high risks are not insured in reality, unlike in the standard models. Notice that no pooling equilibrium can exist. For this, note that the expected profit should be zero under competition, implying that an insurer makes negative profits from high-risk insureds. Then, an insurer will prefer to offer no insurance to high-risk insureds.

More generally, it is natural to assume that each party to an insurance contract may have superior information about some part of risks to the other. This concern leads to a double-sided adverse selection model as follows. In its simplest model, the risk of an insured can be decomposed into a general risk and a specific risk. We assume that insurers have superior information about general risks (T_1) while insureds have superior information about specific risks (T_2). Each risk can be either high or low: T_i = H, L. An insured's risk type will be denoted by a combination of two risks: $T = T_1 T_2$ = HH, HL, LH, LL. We assume that the risks are additive in that the probability of a loss of T is $p_T = q_{T1} + r_{T2}$, where q and r represent the probabilities of loss of T_1 and T_2, respectively.

[9]　This belief passes the intuitive criterion of Cho and Kreps (1987). The intuitive criterion can be stated as follows. Suppose that when an off-the-equilibrium contract is offered, the beliefs of insureds should put a zero probability on type k, if the highest possible profit of the type k insurer generated by the contract is lower than the equilibrium profit. An equilibrium contract passes the intuitive criterion if the contract is optimal given such beliefs of insureds.

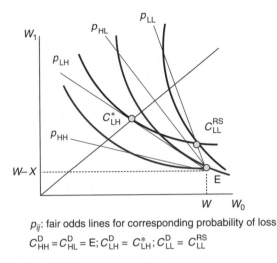

p_{ij}: fair odds lines for corresponding probability of loss

$C_{HH}^D = C_{HL}^D = E; C_{LH}^D = C_{LH}^*; C_{LL}^D = C_{LL}^{RS}$

Figure 8.7   Double-sided adverse selection.

In this case, the insurers will solve a program which is a combination of a screening game and a signaling game. Insurers need to screen insureds' private information T_2 (as in standard models) as well as signal their information T_1 (as in insurer-sided adverse selection models).

Program 8.6 (Double-sided adverse selection)

$$\max_{\{C_{LL}, C_{LH}, C_{HL}, C_{HH}\}} V_{LL}(C_{LL}) \tag{8.9}$$

s.t.

$$\pi(C_{ks}) \geq Q_{ks} - p_{ms}I_{ks}, \text{ for } k, m, s = H, L, \text{ and } m \neq k,$$

$$V_{ks}(C_{ks}) \geq V_{ks}(C_{km} : ks), \text{ for } k, m, s = H, L, \text{ and } m \neq k,$$

$$\pi(C_{km}) \geq 0 \text{ for } k, m = H, L,$$

$$V_{km}(C_{km}) \geq V_{km}(E) \text{ for } k, m = H, L.$$

The first set of constraints describes the IC for insurers regarding T_1, and the second set of constraints describes the self-selection for insureds regarding T_2. The third set of constraints describes the participation of insurers. The final set of constraints describes the participation of insureds.

As the model is a combination of the standard model and the insurer-sided adverse selection model, so is the equilibrium outcome. The results are summarized in the following proposition. Equilibrium contracts $\{C_{HH}^D, C_{HL}^D, C_{LH}^D, C_{LL}^D\}$ are depicted in Figure 8.7. Note that $C_{HH}^D = C_{HL}^D = E$, $C_{LH}^D = C_{LH}^*$ (full insurance), and $C_{LL}^D = C_{LL}^{RS}$.

Proposition 8.8 (Double-sided adverse selection). At an equilibrium:

(a)　Among low-general-risk insureds, low-specific-risk insureds purchase partial insurance, while high-specific-risk insureds purchase full insurance as in Rothschild and Stiglitz (1976). All contracts are actuarially fair.

(b)　High-general-risk insureds purchase no insurance.

Proof Omitted.　　　　　　　　　　　　　　　　　　　□

The results have several interesting implications. First, insurers are cream-skimming since they offer contracts only to low-general-risk insureds. Second, the relationship between insurance purchases and risk types is not in one direction, unlike one-sided adverse selection models. Where $p_{HL} \le p_{LH}$ as Figure 8.7, the highest risks (HH) are not insured, the second highest risks (LH) are fully insured, the third highest risks (HL) are not insured, and the lowest risks (LL) are partially insured.[10] That is, the relationship between insurance purchases and risk types is not in one direction under double-sided adverse selection.

8.4.2　Frequency risk and severity risk

Standard adverse selection models are focused on the loss probability, or frequency risk, assuming that the loss size, or severity, is fixed. In reality, it is possible that insureds are also faced with severity risks. There have been several attempts to understand the adverse selection problem when a severity risk exists. Doherty and Jung (1993) show that a severity risk may help resolve the adverse selection problem of frequency risk, when severity risks differ between different frequency risk types. For example, if a high frequency risk is associated with a high severity, then severity can be used as a categorization tool of the frequency risk. In an extreme case in which the supports of the severity distributions are not overlapping among frequency risk types, a first best outcome can be obtained, since severity fully reveals the frequency risk types of insureds.

Doherty and Schlesinger (1995) add a common severity risk to the frequency risk. In their model, severity risk itself cannot be used for categorization, since severity risk is the same across insureds. Instead, they investigate the effect of severity risk on the equilibrium outcome. They show that the introduction of severity risk increases the coverage for low risk, but decreases the social welfare in an RS equilibrium. Let us consider the RS setting, except for the random loss size. The loss size for insured *j*

---

[10]　If $p_{LH} < p_{HL}$, then the ranks of HL and LH will be reversed.

is determined as follows: $X_j = x + \varepsilon_j$, where $E(\varepsilon_j) = 0$, and the ε_j are independently and identically distributed across insureds. For simplicity, let us suppress the subscript j. Given the severity risk, the expected utility of risk type i becomes $V_i(Q_i, I_i) = (1 - p_i)U(W - Q_i) + p_i EU(W - x - \varepsilon + I_i - Q_i)$. Let us explicitly express indemnity as a coinsurance scheme: $I_i = \alpha X$.[11] Now let us find the indifference curve. Since the wealth level is random, it is convenient to describe the model in the (α, Q) plane instead of the (W_0, W_1) plane. The indifference curve in the (α, Q) plane can be obtained by totally differentiating $V_i(Q_i, I_i) = K$ with respect to α:

$$-(1 - p_i)U'(W_{i0})dQ/d\alpha + p_i EU(W_{i1})(-dQ/d\alpha + X) = 0,$$

where $W_{i0} = W - Q_i$, $W_{i1} = W - (1 - \alpha)(x + \varepsilon) - Q_i$. The slope of the indifference curve under severity risk (denoted by subscript S) becomes

$$
\begin{aligned}
dQ/d\alpha\,|_S &= \frac{p_i E\{U'(W_{i1})(x + \varepsilon)\}}{(1 - p_i)U'(W_{i0}) + p_i EU'(W_{i1})} \\
&= \frac{p_i[EU'(W_{i1})E(x + \varepsilon) + \mathrm{cov}(U'(W_{i1}), x + \varepsilon)]}{(1 - p_i)U'(W_{i0}) + p_i EU'(W_{i1})} \\
&= \frac{p_i EU'(W_{i1})x}{(1 - p_i)U'(W_{i0}) + p_i EU'(W_{i1})} \\
&\quad + \frac{p_i\,\mathrm{cov}(U'(W_{i1}), x + \varepsilon)}{(1 - p_i)U'(W_{i0}) + p_i EU/(W_{i1})}.
\end{aligned}
$$

(8.10)

Note that the first term is the slope of the indifference curve under no severity risk (denoted by subscript NS), which can be found by setting $\varepsilon \equiv 0$. Thus,

$$dQ/d\alpha\,|_S = dQ/d\alpha\,|_{NS} + \frac{p_i\,\mathrm{cov}(U'(W_{i1}), x + \varepsilon)}{(1 - p_i)U'(W_{i0}) + p_i EU'(W_{i1})}.$$

(8.11)

Note that $dQ/d\alpha|_{NS}$ is positive. Note also that at $\alpha = 1$, $dQ/d\alpha|_S = dQ/d\alpha|_{NS} = p_i x$. In both cases, the slope of the indifference curve meets the zero profit line tangentially. For $\alpha < 1$, however, $\mathrm{cov}(U'(W_{i1}), x + \varepsilon) > 0$, which implies that $dQ/d\alpha|_S > dQ/d\alpha|_{NS}$. Similarly for $\alpha > 1$, $\mathrm{cov}(U'(W_{i1}), x + \varepsilon) < 0$, which implies that $dQ/d\alpha|_S < dQ/d\alpha|_{NS}$. Therefore, the slope of the indifference curve under severity is steeper for $\alpha > 1$, but flatter for $\alpha > 1$ than that under no severity risk. Figure 8.8 depicts the zero profit line and indifference curves in (α, Q) plane.

[11]   In general, the insurance scheme can be more complicated. Ligon and Thistle (2008) consider a coinsurance with deductible, and Young and Browne (1997) consider a more general indemnity scheme.

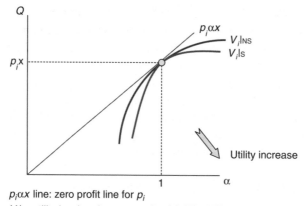

$p_i\alpha x$ line: zero profit line for p_i

$V_i|_T$: utility level under no severity risk (T = NS), or under severity risk (T = S)

Figure 8.8   Indifference curve under severity risk in the (coverage, premium) plane.

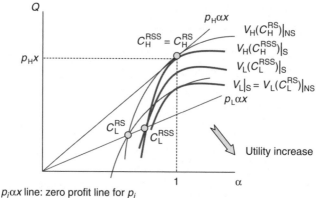

$p_i\alpha x$ line: zero profit line for p_i

$\{C_H^{RSS}, C_L^{RSS}\}$: RS equilibrium contracts under severity risk

$V_i|_T$: utility level under no severity risk (T=NS), or under severity risk (T=S)

Figure 8.9   RS equilibrium under severity risk in the (coverage, premium) plane.

Indifference curve under severity risk in the (coverage, premium) plane

The RS equilibrium under severity risk can be easily understood by incorporating the changed indifference curves. In Figure 8.9, the RS equilibrium contracts under no severity risk are denoted by $\{C_H^{RS}, C_L^{RS}\}$. Under severity risk, the RS equilibrium is denoted by $\{C_H^{RSS}, C_L^{RSS}\}$. The effect of the introduction of severity risk can be easily understood by considering the changed indifference curves.

RS equilibrium under severity risk in the (coverage, premium) plane

Proposition 8.9 For an RS equilibrium under severity risk, the following results hold:

(a) The high-risk insured is fully insured and the low-risk insured is partially insured. However, the low-risk insured obtains a higher level of coverage under severity risk than under no severity risk.

(b) Efficiency is lower under severity risk than under no severity risk, since the high-risk insured is no better off and the low-risk insured is strictly worse off.

(c) The likelihood of the existence of an RS equilibrium is lower under severity risk than under no severity risk.

Proof

(a) Since the indifference curves under severity risk are steeper where $\alpha < 1$, the RS contract for low risks should be located on the higher coverage level, denoted by C_L^{RSS} in Figure 8.9. Note that the RS contract for high risk is $C_H^{RSS} = C_H^{RS}$ which is the same as under no severity risk.

(b) Note that the high-risk insured is indifferent between C_L^{RS} under no severity risk and C_L^{RSS} under severity risk. Compared with C_L^{RS}, C_L^{RSS} is characterized by higher coverage and higher premium. Indifference for the high-risk insured implies:

$$(1 - p_H)U(W - Q_L^{RS}) + p_H U(W - x + I_L^{RS} - Q_L^{RS}) = (1 - p_H)U(W - Q_L^{RSS})$$
$$+ p_H EU(W - x - \varepsilon + I_L^{RSS} - Q_L^{RSS})$$

$$\Rightarrow (1 - p_H)[U(W - Q_L^{RS}) - U(W - Q_L^{RSS})] = p_H[EU(W - x - \varepsilon + I_L^{RSS} - Q_L^{RSS})$$
$$- U(W - x + I_L^{RS} - Q_L^{RS})]$$

$$\Rightarrow (1 - p_L)[U(W - Q_L^{RS}) - U(W - Q_L^{RSS})] > p_L[EU(W - x - \varepsilon$$
$$+ I_L^{RSS} - Q_L^{RSS}) - U(W - x + I_L^{RS} - Q_L^{RS})].$$

That is, the low-risk insured prefers C_L^{RS} under no severity risk to C_L^{RSS} under severity risk, since the low-risk insured has lower risk. Since the high-risk insured remains indifferent and the low-risk insured is worse off, the introduction of severity risk lowers efficiency.

(c) Since the utility level of the low-risk insured is lower under severity risk, the indifference curve under severity risk (denoted by $V_L(C_L^{RSS})|_S$ in Figure 8.9) is located above that under no severity risk (denoted by $V_L|_S = V_L(C_L^{RS})|_{NS}$). Thus, the threshold θ^{RSS} for the existence of an RS equilibrium should be higher than θ^{RS}. □

As in the frequency risk only, the high-risk insured is not hurt by severity risk. The cost should be borne by the low-risk insured. Although the low-risk insured is offered higher coverage under severity risk, he is worse off. As a result, social welfare is lower. In addition, an RS equilibrium is less likely to exist, because the lowered utility of the low-risk insured provides the low-risk insured with a stronger incentive to subsidize the high-risk insured.

8.4.3   Heterogeneity and the single crossing property

The above analyses are based on the assumption that the single crossing property holds. In general, however, insureds differ in diverse aspects including wealth, risk aversion, and background risks. These differences may make the indifference curves cross each other more than once (Smart, 2000; Wambach, 2000). The violation of the single crossing property can dramatically change the RS outcomes.

Let us consider the case in which high-risk insureds have higher initial wealth than low-risk insureds (see Wambach, 2000). We also assume that insureds exhibit decreasing absolute risk aversion. Except for the wealth levels, all others are the same as the RS cases. Let W_i be the initial wealth of risk type $i = H, L$. Then, $W_{i0} = W_i - Q_i$ in the no-loss state, $W_{i1} = W_i - x + I_i - Q_i$ in the loss state. The expected utility becomes

$$V_i(Q_i, I_i,) = (1 - p_i)U(W_i - Q_i) + p_i U(W_i - x + I_i - Q_i). \tag{8.12}$$

It is convenient to use (I, Q) plane instead of (W_0, W_1) plane, since the initial wealth positions are different across insureds. The slope of the indifferent curve in the (I, Q) plane is given by:

$$dQ/dI = \frac{p_i U'(W_{i1})}{(1 - p_i)U'(W_{i0}) + p_i U'(W_{i1})} = \left[1 + \frac{1 - p_i}{p_i} \frac{U'(W_{i0})}{U'(W_{i1})}\right]^{-1}. \tag{8.13}$$

Since the slope of the indifference curve increases in the probability of loss, the slope of the indifference curve of the high-risk insured is steeper than that of the low-risk insured, *ceteris paribus*.

Now the effect of the initial wealth on the slope can be found from the expression

$$\frac{d}{dW_i}\left(\frac{U'(W_{i0})}{U'(W_{i1})}\right) = \frac{U'(W_{i0})}{U'(W_{i1})}\{-ARA(W_{i0}) + ARA(W_{i1})\}, \tag{8.14}$$

where ARA(W) is the absolute risk aversion measure. Under DARA, an insured with lower wealth (thus with larger absolute risk aversion) will have a steeper (flatter) slope of the indifference curve where $W_{i0} > (<) W_{i1}$.

As a result, the slope of the indifference curve of the low-risk insured with low wealth can be steeper or flatter than that of the high-risk insured

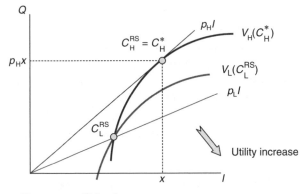

$p_i I$ line: zero profit line for p_i

Figure 8.10   RS equilibrium in the (indemnity, premium) plane.

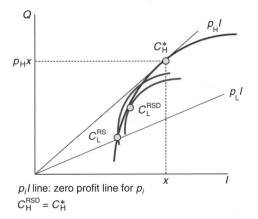

$p_i I$ line: zero profit line for p_i

$C_H^{RSD} = C_H^*$

Figure 8.11   Equilibrium when the single crossing property does not hold.

with high wealth. This result leads to the double crossing of indifference curves. In this case, insurers may make positive profits at an equilibrium, as shown in the next proposition.

In Figure 8.10, the standard RS equilibrium is depicted in the (I, Q) plane, where the initial wealth is not differentiated. Note that the indifference curves are upward sloping and concave. Full insurance is exhibited at $C_H^{RS} = C_H^*$. In Figure 8.11, the RS equilibrium is depicted when the initial wealth is differentiated. The equilibrium contracts are denoted by $\{C_H^{RSD}, C_L^{RSD}\}$.

Proposition 8.10 If the single crossing property does not hold, then a separating equilibrium may exist, in which insurers make positive profits.

Proof In Figure 8.11, C_H^{RSD} and C_L^{RSD} are equilibrium contracts. C_H^{RSD} offers full insurance for the high risk, which is C_H^{RS} of the RS equilibrium. C_L^{RS} is the standard RS contract for the low risk. Note, however, that C_L^{RS} cannot be an equilibrium contract for the low risk, since C_L^{RSD} provides the low-risk insured with a higher utility. Moreover, C_L^{RSD} is profitable, since it is located above the zero profit line for the low risk. A positive profit is possible since any contract on the zero profit line cannot solely attract the low-risk insured, or is less preferred to C_L^{RSD} by the low-risk insured. □

Readers may wonder how positive profits can be compatible with a competitive equilibrium. In general, positive profits will be removed by the entry of firms, or by the competition of firms. In our case, however, lowering the price of the contract for low risks will also attract the high risks. To prevent the high risks from selecting the contract for the low risk, the price of the contract for the high risk should also be lowered. By so doing, the positive profit from the low risk can be offset by the loss from the high risk. However, such a subsidy between contracts is not allowed at an RS equilibrium. Thus, the positive profit may persist under an RS equilibrium. If we use the WMS equilibrium which allows a subsidy between contracts, then the positive profit will disappear.

8.5   Conclusion

Basic adverse selection models are extended in this chapter. Here, we further study multi-period models, the information acquisition issue, the classification of risks, and the effects of multi-dimensional characteristics on the equilibrium outcomes. Each issue provides us with additional intuitions about the insurance contract and adverse selection issues. Diverse outcomes are observed as different issues are investigated. This implies that adverse selection interacts with diverse circumstances surrounding the contract. The results can be often complicated and multilateral.

BIBLIOGRAPHY

Bagwell, K. and G. Ramey (1991) Oligopoly limit pricing. *RAND Journal of Economics*, 22: 155–72.
Cho, I.-K. and D. M. Kreps (1987) Signaling games and stable equilibria. *Quarterly Journal of Economics*, 102: 179–221.

Cooper, R. and B. Hayes (1987) Multi-period insurance contracts. *International Journal of Industrial Organization*, 5: 211–31.

Crocker, K. J. and A. Snow (1985) The efficiency of competitive equilibria in insurance markets with adverse selection. *Journal of Public Economics*, 26: 207–19.

Crocker, K. J. and A. Snow (1986) The efficiency effects of categorical discrimination in the insurance industry. *Journal of Political Economy*, 94: 321–44.

Crocker, K. J. and A. Snow (1992) The social value of hidden information in adverse selection economics. *Journal of Public Economics*, 48: 317–47.

Crocker, K. J. and A. Snow (2000) The theory of risk classification. In G. Dionne (ed.), *Handbook of Insurance*. Boston: Kluwer Academic Publishers.

Dahlby, B. G. (1983) Adverse selection and statistical discrimination: an analysis of Canadian automobile insurance. *Journal of Public Economics*, 20: 121–30.

D'Arcy, S. P. and N. A. Doherty (1990) Adverse selection, private information and lowballing in insurance markets. *Journal of Business*, 63: 145–64.

Dionne, G. (1992) Adverse selection and repeated insurance contracts. In G. Dionne and S. Harrington (eds), *Foundation of Insurance Economics – Readings in Economics and Finance*. Boston: Kluwer Academic Publishers.

Dionne, G. and N. A. Doherty (1992) Adverse selection in insurance markets: a selective survey. In G. Dionne (ed.), *Contributions to Insurance Economics*. Boston: Kluwer Academic Publishers.

Dionne, G. and N. A. Doherty (1994) Adverse selection, commitment and renegotiation with application to insurance markets. *Journal of Political Economy*, 102: 209–35.

Dionne, G., N. A. Doherty, and N. Fombaron (2000) Adverse selection in insurance markets. In G. Dionne (ed.), *Handbook of Insurance*. Boston: Kluwer Academic Publishers.

Doherty, N. A. and H. J. Jung (1993) Adverse selection when loss severities differ: first-best and costly equilibria. *Geneva Papers on Risk and Insurance Theory*, 18: 173–82.

Doherty, N. A. and L. L. Posey (1998) On the value of a checkup: adverse selection, moral hazard and the value of information. *Journal of Risk and Insurance*, 65: 189–212.

Doherty, N. A. and H. Schlesinger (1995) Severity risk and the adverse selection of frequency risk. *Journal of Risk and Insurance*, 62: 649–65.

Doherty, N. A. and P. D. Thistle (1996) Adverse selection with endogenous information in insurance markets. *Journal of Public Economics*, 63: 83–102.

Hosios, A. J. and M. Peters (1989) Repeated insurance contracts with adverse selection and limited commitment. *Quarterly Journal of Economics*, 104: 229–53.

Hoy, M. (1982) Categorizing risks in the insurance industry. *Quarterly Journal of Economics*, 97: 321–36.

Laffont, J.-J. and J. Tirole (1990) Adverse selection and renegotiation in procurement. *Review of Economic Studies*, 57: 597–625.

Ligon, J. A. and P. D. Thistle (2008) Adverse selection with frequency and severity risk: alternative risk-sharing provisions. *Journal of Risk and Insurance*, 75: 825–46.

Nilssen, T. (2000) Consumer lock-in with asymmetric information. *International Journal of Industrial Organization*, 18: 641–66.

Puelz, R. and A. Snow (1994) Evidence on adverse selection: equilibrium signalling and cross-subsidization in the insurance market. *Journal of Political Economy*, 102: 236–57.

Rothschild, M. and J. E. Stiglitz (1976) Equilibrium in competitive insurance markets: an essay on the economics of imperfect information. *Quarterly Journal of Economics*, 90: 629–50.

Seog, S. H. (2008) A note on the renegotiation-proof contracts in the competitive insurance markets with information asymmetry. KAIST Business School Working Paper.

Seog, S. H. (2009a) Equilibrium refinement under the competition between insurers with superior information. Working Paper.

Seog, S. H. (2009b) Insurance markets with differential information. *Journal of Risk and Insurance*, 76: 279–94.

Seog, S. H. (forthcoming) Double-sided adverse selection in the product market and the role of the insurance market. *International Economic Review*.

Smart, M. (2000) Competitive insurance markets with two unobservables *International Economic Review*, 41: 153–69.

Spence, M. (1978) Product differentiation and performance in insurance markets. *Journal of Public Economics*, 10: 427–47.

Villeneuve, B. (2000) The consequences for a monopolistic insurance firm of evaluating risk better than customers: the adverse selection hypothesis reversed. *Geneva Papers on Risk and Insurance Theory*, 25: 65–79.

Villeneuve, B. (2005) Competition between insurers with superior information *European Economic Review*, 49: 321–40.

Wambach, A. (2000) Introducing heterogeneity in the Rothschild-Stiglitz model. *Journal of Risk and Insurance*, 67: 579–91.

Wilson, C. (1977) A model of insurance markets with incomplete information. *Journal of Economic Theory*, 16: 167–207.

Young, V. R. and M. J. Browne (1997) Explaining insurance policy provisions via adverse selection. *Geneva Papers on Risk and Insurance Theory*, 22: 121–34.

Chapter 9

Moral Hazard

Information asymmetry arises when one party to a contract cannot observe the other party's actions or characteristics. The difference between actions and characteristics is that actions can be changed and selected by one party, but characteristics cannot be altered. While the other party's characteristics are the issue in the adverse selection problem, actions are the issue in the moral hazard problem. When a person's action cannot be observed by others, he has incentives to select actions for his own interest, not as dictated by the contract. This problem is called a *moral hazard* problem.

In the insurance and economics literature, action often consists in efforts to prevent losses, managerial efforts, or investment decisions. While our exposition is focused on insurance contexts, our results can be applied to more general contracts with moral hazard problems.

In this and the next chapters, we investigate moral hazard problems. We distinguish two types of problem, ex ante and ex post. In the ex ante moral hazard problem, we consider a case in which insureds can select actions to lower risks or losses, where the actions are not directly observed by insurers. In the ex post moral hazard problem, we consider a case in which insureds may fraudulently claim losses, where the loss sizes are not directly observed by insurers. (In the literature, the ex post moral hazard often includes the case where the insured does not make efforts to reduce the loss size after an accident.) The ex post moral hazard is also commonly referred to as *fraud*. This chapter will be focused on the ex ante moral hazard problem, and the next chapter will discuss the ex post moral hazard problem. This chapter investigates the moral hazard problem with one action (Sections 9.1 and 9.2) and with multiple actions (Section 9.3). A moral hazard issue in health insurance is studied in Section 9.4. A binary case is investigated in the appendix to this chapter.

9.1   Moral Hazard with One Action

Consider the case in which two individuals 1 and 2 enter into a contract. Contract C dictates the levels of efforts (or actions) that individual 1 should select and the payment from individual 2 to individual 1. Let us denote e for effort levels. U^1 and U^2 are defined as utility functions of individuals 1 and 2, respectively. Under the assumption that the position for individual 2 is competitive, a (second-best) efficient outcome under the moral hazard problem can be obtained by solving the program

$$\max_{\{C, e\}} EU^1 \tag{9.1}$$

$$\text{s.t. } EU^2 \geq M,$$

$$e \text{ maximizes } EU^1, \text{ given } C.$$

The first constraint is a participation constraint. It requires that the contract should provide individual 2 with minimum utility M, where M is called a reservation utility. The second constraint reflects the moral hazard problem. Individual 1 selects effort e to maximize his own expected utility, given the contract term C. The second constraint is the incentive compatibility (IC) constraint for the insured. Note that in a typical principal–agent context, the second constraint is usually written as "e maximizes EU^2, given C," i.e., the moral hazard of individual 2. In our setting, however, we consider the moral hazard of individual 1, which is common in the competitive market.

In our insurance context, we adopt the following interpretations and assumptions. Individual 1 is an insured and individual 2 is an insurer. We focus on a competitive insurance market. We also assume that the insurer is risk neutral. In this setting, utility U^2 is the profit of the insurer. M is set to 0. Since insurance contracts dictate premium and indemnity, contract term C can be considered a set of a premium Q and the indemnity schedule contingent on realized states, $I(x)$. For notational simplicity, U will be used for U^1.

$$\max_{\{Q, I(x), e\}} EU$$

$$\text{s.t. } Q - EI \geq 0, \tag{9.2}$$

$$e \text{ maximizes } EU, \text{ given } \{Q, I(x)\}.$$

It is conventional to replace the second constraint with the first-order condition $\partial EU/\partial e = 0$. However, note that this convention is not without costs. It is well known that the FOC may not well describe the optimal

e (Mirrlees, 1974). For example, the optimal e may be obtained as a corner solution. This problem is commonly avoided by assuming that the effect of the effort on reducing loss is concavely increasing in the loss size.[1,2] Another technical problem is that the indifference curve of individual 1 is possibly not convex, which may result in a discontinuous demand function, leading to the nonexistence of a market equilibrium (see Arnott and Stiglitz, 1988a; Stiglitz, 1983; and also the appendix to this chapter). The nonexistence of the market equilibrium can often be avoided by assuming (as we do in this chapter) that each insured enters into an enforceable contract with only one insurer. We will also ignore the nonconvexity of indifference curves. As a result, our model is assumed to be free of the aforementioned technical problems, which will help focus on the intuitive explanation for moral hazard.

Notice that program (9.2) is the same as the program for Pareto efficiency in chapter 3, except for the second constraint. Therefore, program (9.2) can be understood as the program for Pareto efficiency under the moral hazard problem. Since moral hazard solutions solve program (9.2), they are second best efficient.

9.1.1   The case in which the action affects both loss prevention and loss reduction

For an intuitive exposition, we focus on a simple discrete model as follows. The insured has an initial wealth of W. He is facing a random loss x. With probability p_0, he does not experience a loss, $x = x_0 = 0$. With probability $1 - p_0$, a loss occurs. The loss size may have one of two values, $x = x_1$ with probability p_1 or $x = x_2$ with probability p_2, where $p_0 + p_1 + p_2 = 1$. The insurance contract is a set of the premium and the contingent indemnity schedule, $\{Q, I_1, I_2\}$, where I_i is the indemnity under state i (i.e., $x = x_i$). We assume that no indemnity is paid for no loss, $I_0 = 0$.

Given competition, an actuarially fair premium Q will satisfy $Q = p_1 I_1 + p_2 I_2$. The probability of loss occurrence is a function of the insured's effort

---

[1]   Two concepts, the monotone likelihood ratio condition (MLRC) and concavity of the distribution function condition (CDFC), are related here. See the text below for the definition of the MLRC. In the insurance context, the MLRC implies that the loss distribution function increases in effort level in the sense of first-order stochastic dominance (Rogerson, 1985b). The CDFC further requires that the loss distribution function increase at a decreasing rate in effort level. The MLRC and CDFC together are known to be sufficient conditions for the replacement of the IC with the first-order condition in the program under moral hazard when the utility of the insured is separable in wealth and effort.

[2]   In the binary case, this is satisfied with the assumption that $p'(e) < 0$, $p''(e) > 0$ and $p'(0) = -\infty$, where $p(e)$ is the probability of loss under effort level e.

level e for loss prevention. We assume that $p_0'(e) > 0$, and $p_0''(e) < 0$, and that $p_i'(e) < 0$ $p_i''(e) > 0$ for $i = 1, 2$. For simplicity, the disutility from the effort is assumed to be separable from other utility, and denoted by $v(e)$, where $v' > 0$ and $v'' > 0$. The effort exerted by the insured is not directly observable by the insurer. Under this moral hazard problem, the incentive compatibility constraint becomes

$$
\begin{aligned}
e = \arg\max_a \; & p_0 U(W - Q) + p_1 U(W - Q - x_1 + I_1) \\
& + p_2 U(W - Q - x_2 + I_2) - v(a)
\end{aligned}
\tag{9.3}
$$

This constraint will be replaced by the FOC

$$
\begin{aligned}
& p_0' U(W - Q) + p_1' U(W - Q - x_1 + I_1) \\
& + p_2' U(W - Q - x_2 + I_2) - v' = 0.
\end{aligned}
\tag{9.4}
$$

For notational simplicity, let us write U_i for $U(W_i)$, where W_i is the wealth at state i. Now the program is stated as follows.

$$
\begin{aligned}
\max_{\{e, Q, I_1, I_2\}} \; & p_0 U_0 + p_1 U_1 + p_2 U_2 - v \\
\text{s.t. } & Q - p_1 I_1 - p_2 I_2 = 0, \\
& p_0' U_0 + p_1' U_1 + p_2' U_2 - v' = 0.
\end{aligned}
\tag{9.5}
$$

The Lagrangian, with the multipliers γ and η, becomes

$$
\begin{aligned}
L = \; & p_0 U_0 + p_1 U_1 + p_2 U_2 - v + \gamma [Q - (p_1 I_1 + p_2 I_2)] \\
& + \eta [p_0' U_0 + p_1' U_1 + p_2' U_2 - v'].
\end{aligned}
\tag{9.6}
$$

Before solving this program, for reference, let us note the first best case in which the information asymmetry problem does not exist. The first best case can be obtained by removing the second constraint in the above program:

$$
\begin{aligned}
\max_{\{e, Q, I_1, I_2\}} \; & p_0 U_0 + p_1 U_1 + p_2 U_2 - v \\
\text{s.t. } & Q - p_1 I_1 - p_2 I_2 = 0.
\end{aligned}
\tag{9.7}
$$

We will solve first for program (9.5). The first best solutions can be obtained by letting $\eta = 0$.

For an interior solution to (9.5), we have the following FOCs:

$$L_e = p_0'U_0 + p_1'U_1 + p_2'U_2 - v' - \gamma(p_1'I_1 + p_2'I_2)$$
$$+ \eta[p_0'' U_0 + p_1'' U_1 + p_2'' U_2 - v''] = 0,$$
$$L_Q = -p_0U_0' - p_1U_1' - p_2U_2' + \gamma + \eta[-p_0'U_0' - p_1'U_1' - p_2'U_2'] = 0, \qquad (9.8)$$
$$L_{I_1} = p_1U_1' - \gamma p_1 + \eta p_1'U_1' = 0,$$
$$L_{I_2} = p_2p_2' - \gamma p_2 + \eta p_2'U_2' = 0.$$

The results of this program are summarized as follows:

Proposition 9.1

(a)   Under the moral hazard problem, the wealth level under no loss is higher than those under losses: $W_0 > W_1, W_2$.
(b)   The first best outcome dictates full insurance, $W_0 = W_1 = W_2$.

Proof First, noting the second constraint of program (9.5), $L_e = 0$ can be rewritten as

$$L_e = -\gamma(p_1'I_1 + p_2'I_2) + \eta[p_0''U_0 + p_1''U_1 + p_2''U_2 - v''] = 0. \qquad (9.9)$$

Note that $\gamma > 0$ is the usual outcome. It also follows that $\eta > 0$, since p_0', $p_2' < 0$ and $p_0''U_0 + p_1''U_1 + p_2''U_2 - v'' < 0$ from the optimality of e from the second constraint. Summing $L_{I_i} = 0$ over all i in the FOCs,

$$p_1U_1' + p_2U_2' - \gamma p_1 - \gamma p_2 + \eta[p_2'U_1' + p_2'U_2'] = 0$$

From this and $L_Q = 0$, we have

$$p_0U_0' - p_0\gamma + \eta p_0'U_0' = 0$$

$$\Rightarrow U_0' - \gamma + \eta U_0'(p_0' / p_0) = 0.$$

On the other hand, from the FOCs,

$$L_{I_i} = 0 \Rightarrow U_i' - \gamma + \eta U_i'(p_i'/p_i) = 0, \quad \text{for } i = 1, 2.$$

Thus, for any i, we have $U_i' - \gamma + \eta U_i'(p_i'/p_i) = 0$, or

$$\frac{1}{U_i'} = \frac{1}{\gamma} + \frac{\eta}{\gamma}\frac{p_i'}{p_i} \qquad (9.10)$$

Note that $p_0'/p_0 > 0 > p_i'/p_i$, for $i = 1, 2$. Since $\eta > 0$, we have $U_0' < U_i'$, or $W_0 > W_i$, for $i = 1, 2$.

(b)   No moral hazard problem implies $\eta = 0$. Then, from (10), $U_i' = \gamma$
for all i, implying full insurance.   □

The results are intuitive. The first best outcome minimizes the risk costs by imposing all risks on the risk neutral insurer (b), as seen in Chapter 3. Under the moral hazard problem, however, the insured has no incentive to make efforts under full insurance. Recall that the self-interested insured will select the effort level to maximize $p_0 U_0 + p_1 U_1 + p_2 U_2 - v$. Given full insurance, his utility becomes $(p_0 + p_1 + p_2)U_0 - v = U_0 - v$. Since U_0 is not a function of e, making efforts only lowers his utility. Therefore, he will select the effort level of zero. This outcome is not desirable, since the zero effort level eventually increases the premium (the first constraint). The incentive to make effort is provided by making the utility under losses lower than that under no loss, which explains (a).

It seems intuitive that the wealth level should be negatively related to the loss size: $W_0 \geq W_1 \geq W_2$. In general, however, this monotonic relation does not hold without further technical restriction. From (9.10), this relation can be obtained if the right-hand side is decreasing in the loss size. This, in turn, requires that p_i'/p_i be decreasing in the loss size, which holds under the so-called monotone likelihood ratio condition.

Monotone likelihood ratio condition (see Rogerson, 1985b). For $e' > e$, $p_i(e')/p_i(e)$ is decreasing in the loss size.

Note that p_i' is negative for $i = 1, 2$, and measures the marginal effect of the effort on loss prevention. The MLRC implies that the (normalized) marginal effect of the effort is increasing as the loss size increases. That is, the effort is more effective for higher losses. This implies that a high effort level is desired under MLRC. Such an effort level can be achieved by making the wealth under higher loss lower, which will provide the insured with a strong incentive to make efforts. As a result, the monotonic relation between the wealth level and the loss size is obtained.

Proposition 9.2 Under the MLRC, the wealth level is decreasing in loss size: $W_0 \geq W_1 \geq W_2$.[3]

Proof Obvious from (9.10).   □

When $W_0 > W_1 > W_2$, the insurance scheme can be interpreted as the combination of a deductible and coinsurance above the deductible. When

---

[3]   The inequality signs are strict when the decrease of p_i'/p_i is strict in the MLRC.

$W_0 = W_1 > W_2$, the insurance scheme can be interpreted as the combination of full insurance up to a limit and coinsurance above the limit.

9.1.2   The case of loss prevention only

Now suppose that the effort only affects the probability of loss occurrence without affecting the loss distribution given loss occurrence. In other words, $p_i(e) = q(e)r_i$ for $i = 1, 2$, where $q(e) = 1 - p_0(e)$, and r_i is a fixed probability of loss x_i, given loss occurrence. In this case, $p_i' = q'r_i$. Then (9.10) can be rewritten as

$$\frac{1}{U_I'} = \begin{cases} \dfrac{1}{\gamma} + \dfrac{\eta}{\gamma}\dfrac{p_0'}{p_0}, & \text{for } i = 0, \\[2ex] \dfrac{1}{\gamma} + \dfrac{\eta}{\gamma}\dfrac{q'}{q} = \dfrac{1}{\gamma} - \dfrac{\eta}{\gamma}\dfrac{p_0'}{1-p_0}, & \text{for } i = 1, 2. \end{cases} \qquad (9.11)$$

Now, inspection of (9.11) reveals that the wealth in a loss state does not depend on the loss sizes; and that the wealth level under no loss is higher than that under any loss. This observation implies that the insurance contract includes a strict deductible, $I(x) = x - D$. As a result, $W_0 = W - Q$, $W_1 = W_2 = W - Q - D$.

Proposition 9.3 Suppose that the effort affects only the probability of loss occurrence without affecting the loss distribution given loss occurrence. Then, an optimal insurance includes a strict deductible.

Proof See the text above.   □

Intuitively, when the effort affects the loss occurrence, it is desirable to provide incentives for efforts by lowering the wealth level under losses. However, since the effort does not affect the loss sizes, there is no need to penalize for the large loss sizes. As a result, a strict deductible is optimal since it removes risks given a loss occurrence, while it penalizes for a loss occurrence.

9.1.3   The case of loss reduction only

As a counter case, let us consider the case in which the effort only reduces loss sizes given loss occurrence without affecting the probability of loss occurrence. In other words, $p_i(e) = qr_i(e)$ for $i = 1, 2$, where $q = 1 - p_0$, and $r_i(e)$ is a probability of loss x_i under effort e, given loss occurrence. In this case, $p_i' = q' r_i$. It is reasonable to assume that a higher effort level increases the probability of the low loss size: $r_1' > 0$ and $r_2' < 0$. Then, (9.10) can be rewritten as

$$
\frac{1}{U_i'} =
\begin{cases}
\dfrac{1}{\gamma}, & \text{for } i = 0. \\[2ex]
\dfrac{1}{\gamma} + \dfrac{\eta}{\gamma} \dfrac{r_i'}{r_i}, & \text{for } i = 1, 2.
\end{cases}
\tag{9.12}
$$

Note that (9.12) will imply that $W_1 > W_0 > W_2$, since $r_1' > 0$ and $r_2' < 0$. However, this result requires overinsurance for x_1, or $I_1 > x_1$. Assuming that overinsurance is not allowed, the equation for x_1 in (9.12) cannot be satisfied. Instead, we have $I_1 = x_1$. As a result, we have that $W_0 = W_1 < W_2$, or equivalently that $I_1 = x_1$ and $I_2 < x_2$.

Proposition 9.4 Suppose that the effort affects only the loss distribution given loss occurrence without affecting the probability of loss occurrence. Then an optimal insurance includes full insurance up to a limit and coinsurance above the limit.

Proof See the text above. □

This result can be intuitively explained as follows. Since effort affects the loss sizes, the insured will be penalized for the large loss. This explains $W_1 > W_2$. On the other hand, the insured should not be penalized for a loss occurrence, since effort does not affect the occurrence of the loss. This implies that the utility under no loss should equal the (expected) utility under losses. For this, we should have that $W_1 > W_0 > W_2$, which explains (9.12). However, this will result in overinsurance. Avoiding overinsurance, W_1 can be increased only up to W_0.

9.2 Moral Hazard with One Action under a Continuous Loss Distribution

A continuous version of the moral hazard problem is often used in the literature. Define $f(x; e)$ as the probability density function of losses given effort e. We assume that $f(x; e)$ is continuous except at $x = 0$, where $f(0; e)$ is interpreted as a probability mass of no loss. Let us assume that $f_e(0; e) > 0$ and $f_e(x; e) < 0$, for $x > 0$, where the subscript implies partial derivatives. Now, program (9.2) can be stated as follows.

$$\max_{\{e,\,Q,\,I(x)\}} \int U(W-Q-x+I(x))f(x;e)dx - v(e) \tag{9.13}$$

$$\text{s.t. } Q - \int I(x)f(x;e)dx = 0,$$

$$\int U(W-Q-x+I(x))f_e(x;e)dx - v'(e) = 0.$$

The Lagrangian is

$$L = \int U(W-Q-x+I(x))f(x;e)dx - v(e)$$
$$+ \gamma[Q - \int I(x)f(x;e)dx] \tag{9.14}$$
$$+ \eta[\int U(W-Q-x+I(x))f_e(x;e)dx - v'(e)].$$

The FOCs are

$$L_e = \int U(W-Q-x+I(x))f_e(x;e)dx - v'(e)$$
$$- \gamma \int I(x)f_e(x;e)dx \tag{9.15}$$
$$+ \eta[\int U(W-Q-x+I(x))f_{ee}(x;e)dx - v''(e)] = 0,$$

$$L_{I(x)} = U'(W-Q-x+I(x))f(x;e) - \gamma f(x;e) + \eta U'(W-Q-x$$
$$+ I(x))f_e(x;e) = 0, \quad \text{for each } x.$$

$$L_Q = -\int U'(W-Q-x+I(x))f(x;e)dx + \gamma Q - \eta \int U'(W-Q-x$$
$$+ I(x))f_e(x;e)dx = 0.$$

Noting the second constraint, $L_e = 0$ can be arranged as

$$-\gamma \int I(x)f_e(x;e)dx$$
$$+ \eta[\int U(W-Q-x+I(x))f_{ee}(x;e)dx - v''(e)] = 0. \tag{9.16}$$

From $L_{I(x)} = 0$, we have

$$\frac{1}{U'(W-Q-x+I(x))} = \frac{1}{\gamma} + \frac{\eta}{\gamma}\frac{f_e(x;e)}{f(x;e)}. \tag{9.17}$$

Equations (9.16) and (9.17) are continuous versions of (9.9) and (9.10), respectively. Now, it is easy to see that the results of the discrete case still hold in the continuous case. As in the discrete version, the existence of the moral hazard problem implies $\eta > 0$. For, in (9.16), the first term is negative since $I(0) = 0$ and $f_e < 0$ for $x > 0$, and the bracket in the second term is negative from the optimality of e from the incentive constraint. From (9.17), the first best outcome dictates full insurance by setting $\eta = 0$. Under the moral hazard problem, it is easy to see that the wealth level under no loss is higher than that under losses. Now, let us define the continuous version of MLRC.

> Monotone likelihood ratio condition, continuous version (see Milgrom, 1981). For $e' > e$, $f(x; e')/f(x; e)$ is decreasing in the loss size.

Under the continuous version of MLRC, the wealth level is higher as the loss size is smaller. It is well known that MLRC holds for many familiar distributions including the normal distribution and the exponential distribution.

Now consider the case in which the effort affects only the loss occurrence. In other words, for $x > 0$, $f(x; e) = q(e)r(x)$, where $q(e) = 1 - f(0; e)$. Then (9.17) can be rewritten as

$$\frac{1}{U'(W - Q - x + I(x))} = \begin{cases} \dfrac{1}{\gamma} + \dfrac{\eta}{\gamma}\dfrac{f_e(0;e)}{f(0;e)}, & \text{for } x = 0. \\[2ex] \dfrac{1}{\gamma} - \dfrac{\eta}{\gamma}\dfrac{f_e(0;e)}{1 - f(0;e)}, & \text{for all } x > 0. \end{cases} \tag{9.18}$$

As a result, the wealth level under no loss is higher than that under a loss and the wealth levels under losses are equalized. This implies that a strict deductible is optimal.

Finally, let us consider the case in which the effort only reduces loss sizes given loss occurrence without affecting the probability of loss occurrence. In other words, for $x > 0$, $f(x; e) = qr(x; e)$, where $q = 1 - f(0)$ and $r(x; e)$ is a probability of loss x under effort e, given a loss occurrence. In this case, $f_e = qr_e$. Then (9.10) can be rewritten as

$$\frac{1}{U'(W - Q - x + I(x))} = \begin{cases} \dfrac{1}{\gamma}, & \text{for } x = 0. \\[2ex] \dfrac{1}{\gamma} + \dfrac{\eta}{\gamma}\dfrac{r_e(x;e)}{r(x;e)}, & \text{for all } x > 0. \end{cases} \tag{9.19}$$

Under the MLRC, (9.19) implies that $W_x \geq W_{x'}$ for $x \leq x'$. Analogous to the discrete case, (9.19) will imply that there is a loss X^L such that $W_x \geq W_0$ for $x \leq X^L$. However, given that no overinsurance is allowed, for $x \leq X^L$, (9.19) is not satisfied and we should have $I(x) = x$. For $x > X^L$, $I(x) < x$. As a result, we have that $W_0 = W_x \geq W_{x'}$, where $x \leq X^L \leq x'$. An optimal insurance contract entails full insurance up to a limit and coinsurance above the limit.

9.3   Moral Hazard with Multiple Actions

In this section, we consider the moral hazard problem in a slightly different setting from the previous section. First, we consider two actions, instead of one. One action is for the probability of a loss occurrence (loss prevention), and the other is for the loss distribution (loss reduction). Second, the disutility from each action is expressed as a monetary cost directly subtracted from wealth. As a result, effort is not separable from wealth. Our analysis shows that the results are basically the same as in the previous section, while we may also observe the interaction between two actions.

We keep the same discrete model as in the previous section, except for the following changes. Let us define p as the probability of a loss occurrence and r as the probability of a small loss ($x = x_1$), conditional on a loss occurrence. There are two distinctive efforts (i.e., actions), e and f. Effort e only affects p, while effort f only affects r. We assume that $p'(e) < 0$ and $p''(e) > 0$, and that $r'(f) > 0$ and $r''(f) < 0$. In other words, efforts have positive but decreasing marginal effects. We further make a technical assumption that $p'(0) = -\infty$ and $r'(0) = \infty$, which allows us to focus on the case in which positive efforts are optimal. The effort is expressed as its monetary cost. Recall that U_i denotes for $U(W_i)$ where W_i is the wealth at state i, $W_i = W - Q - e - f - x_i + I_i$, for $i = 0, 1, 2$. Now, the problem can be stated as follows.

$$\max_{\{e, f, Q, I_1, I_2\}} (1-p)U_0 + p[rU_1 + (1-r)U_2] \qquad (9.20)$$

$$\text{s.t. } Q = p[rI_1 + (1-r)I_2],$$

$$-p'U_0 + p'[rU_1 + (1-r)U_2] - (1-p)U_0' - p[rU_1' + (1-r)U_2'] = 0,$$

$$-(1-p)U_0' + p[r'U_1 - r'U_2 - rU_1' - (1-r)U_2'] = 0.$$

Note that the second and third constraints are the FOCs for efforts e and f, respectively. Notice that the nonseparation between effort and wealth makes the constraints more complicated than the separation case. Note also that overinsurance and negative indemnity are not allowed as usual: $0 \le I_i \le x_i$. The Lagrangian is

$$
\begin{aligned}
L = {} & (1-p)U_0 + p\{rU_1 + (1-r)U_2\} + \gamma[Q - p(rI_1 + (1-r)I_2)] \\
& + \eta\{-p'U_0 + p'[rU_1 + (1-r)U_2] - (1-p)U_0' \\
& - p[rU_1' + (1-r)U_2']\} + \phi[-(1-p)U_0' \\
& + p\{r'U_1 - r'U_2 - rU_1' - (1-r)U_2'\}].
\end{aligned}
\qquad (9.21)
$$

The five FOCs are as follows:

$$
\begin{aligned}
L_e =\ & -p'U_0 + p'[rU_1 + (1-r)U_2] - (1-p)U_0' - p[rU_1' \\
& + (1-r)U_2'] - \gamma p'(rI_1 + (1-r)I_2) \\
& + \eta\{-p''U_0 + p''[rU_1 + (1-r)U_2] \\
& + p'U_0' - p'[rU_1' + (1-r)U_2'] \\
& + p'U_0' - p'[rU_1' + (1-r)U_2'] \\
& + (1-p)U_0'' + p[rU_1'' + (1-r)U_2'']\} \\
& + \phi\{p'U_0' + p'[r'U_1 - r'U_2 - rU_1' \\
& - (1-r)U_2'] + (1-p)U_0'' \\
& - p[r'U_1' - r'U_2' - rU_1'' - (1-r)U_2'']\} = 0, \\
L_f =\ & -(1-p)U_0' + p\{r'U_1 - r'U_2 - rU_1' - (1-r) U_2'\} \\
& - \gamma p(r'I_1 - r'I_2) + \eta\{p'U_0' + p'[r'U_1 - r'U_2 - rU_1' \\
& - (1-r)U_2'] + (1-p)U_0'' - p[r'U_1' - r'U_2' - rU_1'' \\
& - (1-r)U_2'']\} + \phi\{(1-p)U_0'' + p[r''U_1 - r''U_2 - r'U_1' \\
& + r'U_2' - r'U_1' + r'U_2' + rU_1'' + (1-r)U_2'']\} = 0, \\
L_Q =\ & -(1-p)U_0' - p\{rU_1' + (1-r)U_2'\} + \gamma \\
& - \eta\{-p' U_0' + p'[rU_1' + (1-r)U_2'] \\
& - (1-p)U_0'' - p[rU_1'' + (1-r)U_2'']\} - \phi\{-(1-p)U_0'' \\
& + p[r'U_1' - r'U_2' - rU_1'' - (1-r)U_2'']\} = 0, \\
L_{I_1} =\ & prU_1' - \gamma pr + \eta[p'rU_1' - prU_1''] + \phi p\{r'U_1' - rU_1''\} = 0, \\
L_{I_2} =\ & p(1-r)U_2' - \gamma p(1-r) + \eta[p'(1-r)U_2' - p(1-r)U_2''] \\
& + \phi p\{-r'U_2' - (1-r)U_2''\} = 0.
\end{aligned}
$$

$$(9.22)$$

Note that I_i may be obtained as a corner solution. In such a case, $L_{I_i} \leq 0$ with $I_i = 0$, or $L_{I_i} \geq 0$ with $I_i = x_i$.

9.3.1 The case of loss prevention only

Let us first consider the case where the effort f is not relevant: $r' = 0$ for all f. In this case, we have $f = 0$ and $\phi = 0$. By simplifying the FOCs, we have

$$L_{I1} = prU_1' - \gamma pr + \eta[p'rU_1' - prU_1''] = 0 \tag{9.23}$$
$$\Rightarrow (p + \eta p')U_1' - \eta pU_1'' = \gamma p,$$

$$L_{I2} = p(1-r)U_2' - \gamma p(1-r) + \eta[p'(1-r)U_2' - p(1-r)U_2''] = 0 \tag{9.24}$$
$$\Rightarrow (p + \eta p')U_2' - \eta pU_2'' = \gamma p.$$

By comparing (9.23) and (9.24), we have that $W_1 = W_2$ or $W - Q - e - f - x_1 + I_1 = W - Q - e - f - x_2 + I_2$. In other words, $I_i = x_i - D$ for $i = 1, 2$, and for some $D \geq 0$. It is easy to see that $D > 0$, since if $D = 0$, the insured would select $e = 0$. However, $e = 0$ is not optimal from the assumption of $p'(0) = -\infty$. As a result, $W_0 > W_1 = W_2$. These results are summarized as follows.

Proposition 9.5 When the effort for loss reduction is not relevant, the optimal insurance contract includes a strict deductible.

9.3.2   The case of loss reduction only

We now consider the case in which effort e is not relevant: $p' = 0$ for all e. In this case, we have that $e = 0$ and $\eta = 0$. It is easy to see that $W_1 > W_2$, since, if not, the left-hand side of the third constraint becomes negative, implying that $f = 0$. However, $f = 0$ is not optimal, since $r'(0) = \infty$.

Let us show that $W_0 = W_1$, or $I_1 = x_1$. Suppose, for argument's sake, that $I_1 < x_1$. Note that $I_2 < x_2$ follows from $W_1 > W_2$. In this case, I_1 and I_2 are obtained as interior solutions satisfying the FOCs. By simplifying FOCs, we obtain the expressions

$$L_{I1} = prU_1' - \gamma pr + \phi p\{r'U_1' - rU_1''\} = 0$$
$$\Rightarrow (1 + \phi r'/r)U_1' - \phi U_1'' = \gamma \tag{9.25}$$
$$\Rightarrow (1 + \phi r'/r) - (\eta + \phi)U_1''/U_1' = \gamma/U_1',$$

$$L_{I2} = p(1-r)U_2' - \gamma p(1-r) + \phi p\{-r'U_2' - (1-r)U_2''\} = 0$$
$$\Rightarrow (1 - \phi r'/(1-r))U_2' - \phi U_2'' = \gamma \tag{9.26}$$
$$\Rightarrow (1 - \phi r'/(1-r)) - \phi U_2''/U_2' = \gamma/U_2'.$$

Summing (9.25) and (9.26) and multiplying by p gives

$$p\{rU_1' + (1-r)U_2'\} + \phi p[r'U_1' - r'U_2' - rU_1'' - (1-r)U_2''] - \gamma p = 0.$$

Plugging this expression into $L_Q = 0$, we have

$$-(1-p)U_0' + \phi(1-p)U_0'' + \gamma(1-p) = 0$$
$$\Rightarrow U_0' - \phi U_0'' = \gamma. \tag{9.27}$$

A comparison between (9.25) and (9.27) reveals that the left-hand side of (9.25) is greater than the left-hand side of (9.27) for a given wealth level. This result will imply that $W_1 > W_0$, or $I_1 > x_1$, under DARA. Recall, however, that overinsurance is not allowed. Therefore, we should have that $W_1 = W_0$. As a result, $W_0 = W_1 > W_2$, or $I_1 = x_1$ and $I_2 < x_2$. These results are summarized as follows.

> *Proposition 9.6* When the effort for loss prevention is not relevant, the optimal insurance contract, under DARA, includes full insurance up to a limit and coinsurance above the limit.

These results are basically the same as in the one-effort case. Refer to the discussion following Propositions 9.3 and 9.4 for intuitions.

9.3.3   The case of loss prevention and loss reduction

Now, let us consider the case in which $p' < 0$ and $r' > 0$. If both I_1 and I_2 are interior solutions, they should satisfy $L_{I_1} = 0$ and $L_{I_2} = 0$. Summing these equations, we have

$$L_{I_1} + L_{I_2} = p\{rU_1' + (1-r)\ U_2'\} + \eta\{p'[rU_1' + (1-r)\ U_2'] - p[rU_1''$$
$$+ (1-r)U_2'']\} + \phi p[r'U_1' - r'U_2' - rU_1'' - (1-r)U_2''] - \gamma p = 0.$$

Plugging this expression into $L_Q = 0$, we have

$$-(1-p)U_0' + \eta p'U_0' + \eta(1-p)U_0'' + \phi(1-p)U_0'' + \gamma(1-p) = 0$$
$$\Rightarrow [-(1-p) + \eta p']U_0' + (\eta+\phi)(1-p)U_0'' + \gamma(1-p) = 0 \tag{9.28}$$
$$[1 - \eta p'/(1-p)]U_0' - (\eta+\phi)U_0'' - \gamma = 0.$$

From $L_{I_1} = 0$, we have

$$(pr + \eta p'r + \phi pr')U_1' - pr(\eta+\phi)U_1'' - \gamma pr = 0$$
$$\Rightarrow (1 + \eta p'/p + \phi r'/r)U_1' - (\eta+\phi)U_1'' - \gamma = 0. \tag{9.29}$$

Similarly, from $L_{I_2} = 0$, we have

$$[p(1-r)+\eta p'(1-r)-\phi pr']U_2'-(\eta+\phi)p(1-r)U_2''-\gamma p(1-r)=0$$

$$\Rightarrow (1+\eta p'/p-\phi r'/(1-r))U_2'-(\eta+\phi)U_2''-\gamma=0. \tag{9.30}$$

Comparing (9.28) and (9.29), we have $W_0 > W_1$ under DARA if and only if

$$-\eta p'/p(1-p) > \phi r'/r. \tag{9.31}$$

If this inequality holds, interior solutions are obtained for both I_1 and I_2. If the inequality does not hold, then $W_0 = W_1$ and $I_1 = x_1$. Note that in (9.31), the left-hand side is related to e and the right-hand side to f. As $-p'$ is great relative to r', the left-hand side becomes larger than the right-hand side. As the efficiency of effort e overwhelms that of effort f, it is desirable to put a higher weight on effort e than on effort f. Therefore, the wealth difference between the no-loss state and the loss states becomes more significant than the wealth difference between the small-loss state and the large-loss state. This result leads to $W_0 > W_1$. On the other hand, as the effort f becomes more important, it is desirable to put a higher weight on effort f than on effort e. Therefore, the wealth difference between the small-loss state and the large-loss state becomes more significant than the wealth difference between the no-loss state and the loss states. As a result, W_1 becomes as large as W_0. Finally, from (9.29) and (9.30), we have $W_1 \geq W_2$. In sum, we have $W_0 \geq W_1 \geq W_2$ under (9.31). In this regard, (9.31) plays a similar role to MLRC in the one-action case.

Proposition 9.7 When both efforts for loss reduction and for loss prevention are relevant, we have, under DARA, that $W_0 \geq W_1 > W_2$, or $0 \leq x_1 - I_1 < x_2 - I_2$. $W_0 = W_1$ is obtained if (9.31) holds.

Proof See the text above.   □

This result implies that the optimal insurance contract includes either deductible or limit and coinsurance. This result is analogous to Proposition 9.2. In general, we find that the case of multiple actions is basically the same as the case of one action. One important lesson is that incentives should be provided to control moral hazard problems. In insurance contracts, deductibles, policy limits, and coinsurance can work as such incentive schemes.

9.4   Moral Hazard in Health Insurance

Moral hazard is also an important issue in health insurance (Pauly, 1968; Zeckhauser, 1970). Since the logic of the above sections is general, the results can be applied to the health insurance case. However, one interesting feature in health insurance is that the moral hazard problem also arises after the health loss occurs. Health insurance covers the treatment costs following a health loss. In this sense, the problem is often called an ex post moral hazard problem in the health insurance literature.[4] Unlike the models considered in the above sections, moral hazard is related to the treatment cost spent by the insured, not to loss probabilities. Another important issue is that the health status may not be fully recovered by treatment. These two features, among others, distinguish moral hazard in health insurance from those considered in the above sections.

We consider a simple model in which an insured faces a random health loss (Seog, 2009). The endowment wealth of the insured is W. The health risk is described by two states of nature, denoted by s: the no-loss state ($s = 0$) and the loss state ($s = 1$). The loss state can occur with probability p. The insured suffers a fixed health loss D in the loss state. In the loss state, the insured may select the medical treatment of cost x which enhances the health level by $H(x)$. We assume that $H'(x) > 0$ and $H''(x) < 0$. We assume that health level and health loss are expressed in monetary terms. The insured may purchase health insurance for treatment before the realization of health status. For simplicity, we consider a coinsurance contract, where coverage is denoted by α. The indemnity, I, is thus given by αx. The premium is actuarially fair: $Q = pI = \alpha px$.

When the insured purchases insurance contract (Q, I) and selects treatment x, his expected utility is expressed as

$$EU = (1 - p)U(W_0) + pU(W_1),$$

where $W_0 = W - Q$ and $W_1 = W - Q - D + H(x) - x + I$.

The moral hazard problem occurs because the insured selects treatment x to maximize the ex post utility after the health loss occurs. That is, an optimal x solves

$$\max_{x'} U(W - Q - D + H(x') - x' + \alpha x'), \text{ given } Q \text{ and } I.$$

Assuming an interior solution, this condition can be expressed as

$$pU'(W_1) \cdot (H' + \alpha - 1) = 0. \tag{9.32}$$

Under the assumption that $U' > 0$, the condition is equivalent to

$$H' + \alpha - 1 = 0.$$

Therefore, the problem can be stated as follows:[5]

---

[4] This moral hazard problem, however, is still classified as an ex ante one in this book, since moral hazard affects the future treatment cost.

[5] In principle, this problem statement is not correct, since the insurer can remove the moral hazard problem by penalizing any treatment level that is different from the first best. We are effectively assuming that the insurer cannot force the first best treatment. However, we adopt this setting since it is simple and captures the coinsurance feature in health insurance.

$$\max_{\alpha, \, Q, \, x} EU = (1-p)U(W_0) + pU(W_1) \tag{9.33}$$

s.t. $Q = p\alpha x$,

$H' + \alpha - 1 = 0$.

Now the Lagrangian can be expressed as

$$L = (1-p)U_0 + pU_1 + \gamma(Q - p\alpha x) + \eta(H' + \alpha - 1), \tag{9.34}$$

where $U_i = U(W_i)$, and γ and η are Lagrange multipliers. The FOCs are

$$L_x = pU_1'(H' + \alpha - 1) - \gamma p\alpha + \eta H'' = 0,$$
$$L\alpha = pU_1'x - \gamma px + \eta = 0,$$
$$L_Q = -(1-p)U_0' - pU_1' + \gamma = 0, \tag{9.35}$$
$$L_\lambda = Q - p\alpha x = 0,$$
$$L_\mu = H' + \alpha - 1 = 0.$$

For comparison, let us first find the first best outcome, assuming there is no moral hazard. The first best outcomes are obtained from FOCs (9.35) with $\eta = 0$.

Lemma 9.1 (First best outcome).

(a)   Treatment is determined to maximize the treatment efficiency.
(b)   Risk is fully hedged.
(c)   Overinsurance is optimal, if the health status is not fully recovered.

Proof With $\eta = 0$, the FOCs can be stated as follows:

$$L_x = pU_1'(H' + \alpha - 1) - \gamma p\alpha = 0,$$
$$L_\alpha = pU_1'x - \gamma px = 0,$$
$$L_Q = -(1-p)U_0' - pU_1' + \gamma = 0, \tag{9.36}$$
$$L_\lambda = Q - p\alpha x = 0.$$

From the FOCs, $\gamma = (1-p)U_0' + pU_1' = U_1'$, and $H' = 1$. That is, $U_0' = U_1'$, implying that $-D + H(x) - x + \alpha x = 0$. In sum, the first best solution (x^*, α^*) is characterized as follows:

(a) $H'(x^*) = 1$, implying the treatment efficiency since the marginal benefit of treatment equals the marginal cost;

(b) $U_0' = U_1'$, implying a full risk hedge; (c) $\alpha^* = [D - H(x^*)]/x^* + 1$, which is greater than 1 if $D > H(x^*)$.   □

Lemma 9.1 implies that the first best outcome achieves the cost efficiency in treatment and the complete risk hedge. On the other hand, α^* can be greater than 1, exhibiting overinsurance, if $D > H(x^*)$.[6] Given that a health loss is often not fully compensated, it may be the case that $D > H(x^*)$. Then, the first best coverage exhibits overinsurance. However, it is often the case that overinsurance is not allowed. To investigate such a case, let us define the *constrained first best outcome* as the first best outcome given that overinsurance is not allowed. If $D \leq H(x^*)$, then the constrained first best outcome is the same as the first best outcome. If $D > H(x^*)$, two solutions will differ from each other. Below, we will focus on the case of $D > H(x^*)$. Let us add superscript ** for the constrained first best solution. The solution exhibits the following properties.

Lemma 9.2 (Constrained first best outcome). Suppose that the health status is not fully recovered by the first best treatment. The constrained first best outcome has the following properties:

(a)   Insurance coverage is full.
(b)   The treatment is greater than the first-best treatment.

Proof

(a)   The optimal coverage α^{**} is 1, since the first best coverage α^* is greater than 1, when $D > H(x^*)$, from Lemma 9.1.
(b)   Suppose for argument's sake that $x^{**} \leq x^*$, which implies $H'(x^{**}) \geq 1$. Given $\alpha^{**} = 1$, we should have $\gamma^{**} = U_1' H'(x^{**})$ from $L_x = 0$ in (9.36). Plugging this expression into $L_Q = 0$, we have $U_0' \leq U_1'$, which implies that $H(x^*) \geq H(x^{**}) \geq D$, a contradiction.   □

With full coverage and $H(x^{**}) < D$, we have $U_0' > U_1'$.[7] From (9.36), $\gamma^{**} = (1 - p)U_0' + pU_1' \equiv EU' < U_1'$. In sum, the solution satisfies

$$H'(x^{**}) = \gamma^{**}/U_1' < 1, \text{ and } \alpha^{**} = 1. \tag{9.37}$$

It is important to note that the risk is not fully hedged, even if insurance coverage is full. This is because the health status is not fully recovered.

[6]   Technically, α^* can be negative if $H(x^*)$ is very high. We ignore this case, since it is not interesting.
[7]   Given $\alpha^{**} = 1$, $L\alpha = 0$ is ignored.

In order to compensate for the uncovered health loss, the insured selects a high level of treatment.

Now let us return to the moral hazard case. The solution will solve the first order conditions (9.35). The outcome is characterized as follows. Let us add superscript m for the solution.

Proposition 9.8 (Moral hazard in health insurance).

(a)   Insurance coverage is partial.

(b)   Insurance coverage is less than the first best coverage.

(c)   The treatment is greater than the first best treatment.

Proof From (9.35), we obtain

$$L_\mu = 0 \Rightarrow H' = 1 - \alpha,$$

$$L_Q = 0 \Rightarrow \gamma = EU' = (1-p)U_0' + pU_1' ,$$

$$L_\alpha = 0 \Rightarrow \eta = -p(1-p)x(U_1' - U_0'), \tag{9.38}$$

$$L_x = 0 \Rightarrow -\alpha\{(1-p)U_0' + pU_1' \} - (1-p)x(U_1' - U_0')H'' = 0,$$

$$L_\lambda = 0 \Rightarrow Q = p\alpha x.$$

(a)   First, full (or over)insurance is not optimal, because $\alpha^m \geq 1$ would imply $H' \leq 0$, an infinite treatment. Second, no insurance is not optimal, either. Suppose for argument's sake that $\alpha^m = 0$. In this case, $x^m = x^*$, since $H'(x^m) = 1$. This implies $U_1' > U_0'$, since $-D + H(x^*) - x^* = -\alpha^* x^* < 0$. On the other hand, for no insurance to be optimal, we should have $L_\alpha \leq 0$ at $\alpha = 0$. From $L_x = 0$ in (9.35), $\alpha^m = 0$ is followed by $\eta = 0$. Then $L_\alpha \leq 0$ implies $\gamma \geq U_1'$, which in turn implies $U_0' > U_1'$, since $\gamma = (1 - p)U_0' + pU_1'$ from $L_Q = 0$. We have a contradiction. Thus, $0 < \alpha^m < 1$.

(b)   Since $\alpha^m > 0$, the FOCs (9.35) fully characterize the solution. We also observe from (9.35) that $\gamma > 0$ and $\eta < 0$. If $\alpha^* \geq 1$, the result obviously holds. Now assume that $\alpha^* < 1$. Let us suppose for argument's sake that $\alpha^m \geq \alpha^*$. For any x, $H(x) - (1 - \alpha^m)x \geq H(x) - (1 - \alpha^*)x$. Since x^m maximizes $H(x) - (1 - \alpha^m)x$, we have $H(x^m) - (1 - \alpha^m)x^m \geq \max_x [H(x) - (1 - \alpha^*)x] \geq H(x^*) - (1 - \alpha^*)x^*$. Thus, $-D + H(x^m) - (1 - \alpha^m)x^m \geq -D + H(x^*) - (1 - \alpha^*)x^* = 0$. Then we have $U_0 < U_1$, implying $\eta > 0$, a contradiction.

(c)   The result that $x^m > x^*$ follows from $H'(x^m) = 1 - \alpha^m < 1$ with $\alpha^m > 0$. $\square$

The results are typical in the moral hazard literature. Let us provide intuitive explanations as follows. Full coverage is not desirable under moral hazard (part (a)). Positive insurance, however, is desirable, since, without insurance, the insured would assume too high a risk. The insurance coverage under moral hazard is less than the first best coverage (part (b)), since higher risk sharing lowers moral hazard costs. Part (c) states that moral hazard leads to higher treatment than the first best treatment. With a lower level of coverage than the first best, the insured is exposed to a high risk of a health loss. To compensate for the health loss, the insured will select a higher level of treatment than the first best.

There are several points to mention. First, the Lagrange multiplier μ is negative, unlike in the previous sections. This is because moral hazard leads to excess utilization of resources. The insurer wants the insured to reduce the treatment level. In the previous sections, the insurer wanted the insured to increase effort, resulting in positive Lagrange multiplier η.

Second, while $x^m > x^*$ from (c), the relative sizes between x^m and x^{**} are ambiguous when $x^{**} > x^*$. Let us define b by $H'(x^{**}) = 1 - b$. Note that $b > 0$ since $H'(x^{**}) < 1$, when $x^{**} > x^*$. Now, we have $x^m > x^{**}$ if and only if $\alpha^m > b$. From (9.37), $b = 1 - x^{**} / U^{**'}_1 = 1 - EU^{**'} / U^{**'}_1$, where U^{**} denotes the utility under the constrained first best outcome.

Under moral hazard, from (9.38), $\alpha^m = x^m H''(x^m)(1 - U^{m'}_1 / EU^{m'})$, where U^m denotes the utility under moral hazard. Thus, we have

$$x^m > x^{**} \text{ if and only if } x^m H''(x^m)(1 - 1/R^m) > 1 - R^{**}, \qquad (9.39)$$

where $R^m = EU^{m'} / U^{m'}_1$ and $R^{**} = EU^{**'} / U^{**'}_1$.

Expression (9.39) implies that x^m can be smaller than x^{**}. For example, as R^m becomes close to 1, x^m is likely to be smaller than x^{**}. Note that the treatment level is likely to be low and the risk hedge level is high (thus R^m is high) if the moral hazard problem is not severe. Thus, high R^m is likely to be associated with low x^m.

This observation may look contradictory to the conventional result that moral hazard leads to overutilization.[8] In the case of no moral hazard with the coverage constraint, risk is not fully hedged due to the coverage constraint. As a result, a higher level of treatment is needed to compensate for the incomplete risk hedge. If the risk hedge benefit is high enough, then the treatment level can be higher than that under moral hazard. Seog (2009) provides a CARA utility example for which x^m is smaller than x^{**}.

---

[8] However, recall that $x^m > x^*$.

9.5   Conclusion

Along with adverse selection, the moral hazard problem is an important issue in insurance and information economics. Moral hazard lowers the efficiency of the market. In the insurance context, the inefficiency comes from the fact that the insured does not make loss prevention and/or loss reduction efforts.

Like adverse selection, moral hazard considerations provide a rationale for partial insurance. Full insurance simply provides the insured with no incentive to make efforts, since all the loss will be borne by the insurer. Partial insurance makes the insured responsible for his actions. That is, partial insurance is a form of punishment for information problems. Note that the cost should be borne by the insured, not by the insurer. At the time of action selection, the insured seems to be in a superior position, since he can opportunistically select the action for his own interest. However, a rational insurer would reflect such opportunistic behavior in the contract in the first place. As a result, ex ante, the cost is imposed on the insured.

Note that we are focused on the contract design. Similar to the case of adverse selection, the insurer may try to directly monitor the action of the insured. To the extent that the insurer observes the action, she may want to use a direct method of penalizing the insured. In such a case, a full insurance contract may still be offered.

Moral hazard and adverse selection problems provide two important windows to understand diverse social institutions. Under the perfect market and zero transaction cost assumption, firms and organizations, laws, and rules would not have any meaning, since all individuals can interact with each other without incurring any costs. As the real world is not ideal and the transaction cost is positive, society has developed diverse social and economic institutions and laws. As information problems are main sources of transaction costs, it is not surprising to see that diverse economic and financial institutions are developed to cope with the information problems.

9.A   Appendix: Optimal Insurance in the Binary Loss Case

Let us investigate the optimal insurance contract in the binary loss case in which effort affects the probability of loss. We consider the case of two effort levels and the case of continuous effort levels, in turn.

9.A.1   The case of two effort levels

Suppose that there are two effort levels, e^H (high effort) and e^L (low effort), where $e^H > e^L$ and $p(e^H) < p(e^L)$. Let J be the net indemnity, $J = I - Q$. Then $W_0 = W - Q$, $W_1 = W - x + J$. The expected utility of the insured is expressed as

$$EU(J, Q: e) = (1 - p(e))U_0 + p(e)U_1 - e.$$

Now let us find the optimal insurance contract.

Let us first find the indifference curve given effort level. In the (J, Q) plane, the shape of the indifference curve given an effort level is obtained as follows. From $EU(J, Q: e) = \bar{U}$,

$$\frac{\partial EU}{\partial Q} \cdot dQ + \frac{\partial EU}{\partial J} dJ = 0.$$

$$\Rightarrow \frac{dQ}{dJ} = -\frac{\partial EU/\partial J}{\partial EU/\partial Q} = \frac{pU_1'}{(1-p)U_0'} > 0, \tag{9.A1}$$

$$\frac{d^2 Q}{dJ^2} = -\frac{dQ}{dJ}\left[ARA(W_1) + \frac{dQ}{dJ}ARA(W_0)\right] < 0, \tag{9.A2}$$

where $ARA(Wi) = -U_i''(W_i)/U_i'(W_i)$.

Thus, the indifference curve given an effort level is upward sloped and concave in the (J, Q) plane. It is easy to see that the slope under e^L is higher than the slope under e^H, since $p(e^L) > p(e^H)$ at each (J, Q) given. The indifference curves given effort levels are depicted in Figure 9A.1. Note, however, that the insured will select effort levels based on the insurance contract. Therefore, the indifference curves that we should consider are the ones that reflect this effort selection. Now, let us turn to the effort selection problem.

Given the insurance contract $\{Q, J\}$, the insured will prefer selecting high effort to low effort where

$$EU(J, Q: e^H) \geq EU(J, Q: e^L)$$

or

$$U_0 - U_1 \geq \frac{e^H - e^L}{p(e^L) - p(e^H)}.$$

In Figure 9A.1, LL' is depicted as the locus of (J, Q) to make the two effort levels indifferent. For example, at contract G, the insured is indifferent

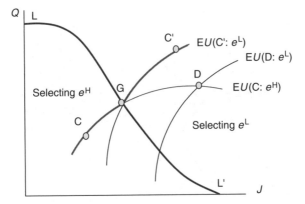

LL': the locus of (J, Q) where two effort levels are indifferent
CGC': the indifference curve after the effort selection

Figure 9A.1   Indifference curves and effort selection with two effort levels.

between the two effort levels. The high (low) effort is preferred inside (outside) LL'. Thus, the insured will select e^H for contract C, and e^L for contract D. An indifference curve after the effort selection is depicted as CGC' in Figure 9A.1. The indifference curves after considering the effort selection are never concave, even though indifference curves are concave given an effort level (Arnott and Stiglitz, 1988a).

The zero profit lines are depicted in Figure 9A.2. From $pQ - (1 - p)J = 0$, the slope of the zero profit line is $p/(1 - p)$. The slope is steeper for low effort than for high effort. Now, the optimal insurance contract will be determined where the expected utility is maximized on the zero profit line, corresponding to the effort levels. Contracts F^L and F^H denote full insurance contracts for the effort level e^L and e^H, respectively. With F^H, the insurer will lose money, since the insured will select the low effort. On the other hand, with F^L, the premium is so high that the insured is willing to purchase partial insurance. The partial insurance is optimal in our case. An optimal contract is depicted as C^* in Figure 9A.2. Figure 9A.3 redraws Figure 9A.2 in the (W_0, W_1) plane.

9.A.2   The case of continuous effort levels

A result similar to the case of two effort levels can be obtained when the effort levels are continuous. Noting that the effort level will solve $\max_a$ $EU(J, Q; a)$, given (J, Q), an interior solution (i.e., positive effort) will satisfy

$$\partial EU/\partial e = -p'U_0 + p'U_1 - 1 = 0. \tag{9.A3}$$

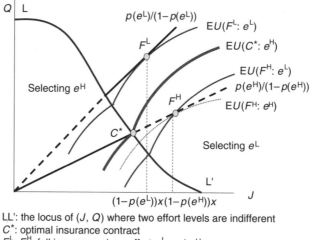

LL': the locus of (J, Q) where two effort levels are indifferent
C^*: optimal insurance contract
F^L, F^H: full insurance given effort e^L and e^H.

Figure 9A.2   Insurance contract with two effort levels.

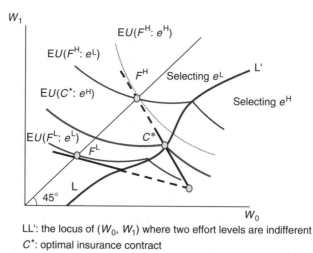

LL': the locus of (W_0, W_1) where two effort levels are indifferent
C^*: optimal insurance contract
F^L, F^H: full insurance given effort e^L and e^H.

Figure 9A.3   Insurance contract with two effort levels in (W_0, W_1) plane.

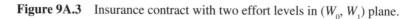

The solution e can be considered a function of (J, Q). Then, $EU(J, Q: e(J, Q))$ can be expressed as $V(J, Q)$, a function of (J, Q). Now let us find, the shape of the indifference curve after effort selection. From $V(J, Q) = \bar{V}$,

$$\frac{dQ}{dJ} = -\frac{\partial V / \partial J}{\partial V / \partial Q} = \frac{pU_1'}{(1-p)U_0'} > 0. \tag{9.A4}$$

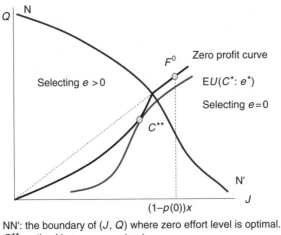

NN': the boundary of (J, Q) where zero effort level is optimal.
C^{**}: optimal insurance contract
F^0: full insurance given zero effort

Figure 9A.4   Insurance contract with continuous effort levels.

Note that we used $\partial EU/\partial e = 0$. Then

$$\frac{d^2Q}{dJ^2} = -\frac{dQ}{dJ}\left[\text{ARA}(W_1) + \frac{dQ}{dJ}\text{ARA}(W_0)\right] + \frac{U'_1}{U'_0}\frac{p'}{(1-p)^2}\frac{de}{dJ}. \qquad (9.A5)$$

Note that de/dJ is evaluated at $\overline{V}$. From the optimality condition (9A.3) for e,

$$\partial e/\partial J = -\frac{p'^2 U'_1}{p''} < 0 \quad \text{and} \quad \partial e/\partial Q = -\frac{p'^2 U'_0}{p''} < 0. \qquad (9.A6)$$

Thus,

$$de/dJ = \partial e/\partial J + (\partial e/\partial Q)(dQ/dJ) = -\frac{p'^2 U'_1}{p''} - \frac{p'^2 U'_0}{p''}\left(\frac{pU'}{(1-p)U'_0}\right)$$

$$= -\frac{p'^2 U'_1}{p''(1-p)} < 0.$$

As a result, the second term of (9.A5) is positive. The sign of d^2Q/dJ^2 can be negative or positive. That is, the indifference curve can be both concave and convex. Note that this result applies to the positive effort ($e > 0$), where the optimal effort is 0, $de/dJ = 0$, implying that the indifference curve is concave in the (J, Q) plane.

An optimal insurance contract is depicted in Figure 9A.4. The shape of the zero profit curve reflects the risk change following the effort change.

(A.6) implies that effort level is lowered by more insurance. Therefore, the slope of the curve is increasing over $p/(1 - p)$ insofar as the effort level is positive. As the effort level becomes 0, the zero profit curve becomes linear with slope $p(0)/(1 - p(0))$. The locus NN' represents the boundary of (J, Q) for which the zero effort is optimal. The optimal contract, C^{**} in the figure, is determined where the zero profit curve meets tangentially the indifference curve.

BIBLIOGRAPHY

Arnott, R. J. and J. E. Stiglitz (1988a) The basic analytics of moral hazard. *Scandinavian Journal of Economics*, 90: 383–413.

Arnott, R. J. and J. E. Stiglitz (1988b) Randomization with asymmetric information. *Rand Journal of Economics*, 19: 344–62.

Ehrlich, I. and G. S. Becker (1972) Market insurance, self-insurance and self-protection. *Journal of Political Economy*, 80: 623–48.

Fudenberg, D. and J. Tirole (1990) Moral hazard and renegotiation in agency contracts. *Econometrica*, 58: 1279–319.

Gjesdal, F. (1982) Information and incentives: the agency information problem. *Review of Economic Studies*, 49: 373–90.

Grossman, S. J. and O. D. Hart (1983) An analysis of the principal-agent problem. *Econometrica*, 51: 7–45.

Harris, M. and A. Raviv (1978) Some results on incentive contracts. *American Economic Review*, 68: 20–31.

Helpman, E. and J.-J. Laffont (1975) On moral hazard in general equilibrium. *Journal of Economic Theory*, 10: 8–23.

Holmström, B. (1979) Moral hazard and observability. *Bell Journal of Economics*, 10: 74–92.

Holmström, B. (1982) Moral hazard in teams. *Rand Journal of Economics*, 13: 324–40.

Holmström, B. and P. Milgrom (1991) Multitask principal-agent analyses: incentive contracts, asset ownership and job design. *Journal of Law, Economics and Organization*, 7: 24–52.

Hosios, A. J. and M. Peters (1989) Repeated insurance contracts with adverse selection and limited commitment. *Quarterly Journal of Economics* 104: 229–53.

Huberman, G., D. Mayers, and C. W. Smith Jr. (1983) Optimal insurance policy indemnity schedules. *Bell Journal of Economics*, 14: 415–26.

Jewitt, I. (1988) Justifying the first-order approach to principal-agent problems. *Econometrica*, 56: 1177–90.

Lambert, R. A. (1983) Long-term contracts and moral hazard. *Bell Journal of Economics*, 14: 441–52.

Milgrom, P. A. (1981) Good news and bad news: representation theorems and applications. *Bell Journal of Economics*, 12: 380–91.

Mirrlees, J. A. (1974) Notes on welfare economics, information, and uncertainty. In M. Balch, D. McFadden, and S. Wu (eds), *Essays on Economic Behavior under Uncertainty*. Amsterdam: North-Holland.

Mirrlees, J. A. (1999) The theory of moral hazard and unobservable behaviour: Part I. *Review of Economic Studies*, 66: 3–21.

Pauly, M. V. (1968) The economics of moral hazard: Comment. *American Economic Review*, 58: 531–7.

Pauly, M. V. (1974) Overinsurance and public provision of insurance: the roles of moral hazard and adverse selection. *Quarterly Journal of Economics*, 88: 44–62.

Rogerson, W. P. (1985a) Repeated moral hazard. *Econometrica*, 53: 69–76.

Rogerson, W. P. (1985b) The first-order approach to principal-agent problems. *Econometrica*, 53: 1357–67.

Rubinstein, A. and M. E. Yarri (1983) Repeated insurance contracts and moral hazard. *Journal of Economic Theory*, 30: 74–97.

Sappington, D. E. M. (1983) Limited liability contracts between principal and agent. *Journal of Economic Theory*, 29: 1–21.

Seog, S. H. (2009) Moral hazard and health insurance when treatment is preventive, KAIST Business School Working Paper.

Shavell, S. (1979a) Risk sharing and incentives in the principal and agent relationship. *Bell Journal of Economics*, 10: 55–73.

Shavell, S. (1979b) On moral hazard and insurance. *Quarterly Journal of Economics*, 93: 541–62.

Stiglitz, J. E. (1983) Risk, incentives and insurance: the pure theory of moral hazard. *Geneva Paper on Risk and Insurance*, 8: 4–33.

Winter, R. A. (2000) Optimal insurance under moral hazard. In G. Dionne (ed.), *Handbook of Insurance*. Boston: Kluwer Academic Publishers.

Zeckhauser, R. (1970) Medical insurance: a case study of the tradeoff between risk spreading and appropriate incentives. *Journal of Economic Theory*, 2: 10–26.

Chapter 10

Ex Post Moral Hazard and Fraud

In this chapter, we investigate the ex post moral hazard problem. By ex post moral hazard, we imply a situation in which insureds may make fraudulent claims about loss sizes. Since fraud may result in an increase in insurance benefit payments, fraud is the insureds' concern. Of course, this problem will disappear if insurers can observe the losses. Therefore, the main issue here is the observability of the loss sizes by insurers. In a costly state verification model, insurers are assumed to observe the loss sizes if they incur some audit costs. In this case, the tradeoff exists between the audit costs and the fraudulent claims. A higher level of audit will lower the level of fraud, but increase the audit costs. Equilibrium will be determined by comparing the audit costs with the saved insurance benefits from the reduction of fraud.

One special case will be found when the audit costs are extremely high. In a so-called costly state falsification model, insureds may spend their resources to mislead the insurers where insurers cannot observe the true loss sizes. In this case, the focus is on the tradeoff between the costs spent to mislead the insurers and the increased payments of insurance benefit.

Our discussion will be focused on the costly state verification case. In Section 10.1 we consider the deterministic audit case in which the insurer determines between audit and no audit. In Section 10.2 we allow the insurer to audit randomly. Random audit may lower the audit cost, which increases efficiency. In Section 10.3 we consider the case in which two types of insureds coexist. An opportunistic insured will file a fraudulent claim when the insurer does not audit, while an honest insured will never do so. Given that this type of information is private, this case corresponds to the adverse selection case. However, it is different from the standard adverse selection case in that types do not relate to risks, but to honesty. In Section 10.4 we discuss the importance of commitment in the ex post moral hazard context.

10.1   Deterministic Audit

The loss size, x, is private information of the insured, and cannot be directly observed by insurers. Let us define y_i as the announced loss size when the true loss size is x_i. In general, y_i can be different from x_i. The only way for an insurer to observe the loss sizes is through an audit of loss sizes. It is assumed that once the insurer audits, she can perfectly observe the loss size. Auditing incurs a cost of c. $I(y_i, x_i)$ is the insurance benefit payment when the claim is y_i and the true loss is x_i. For notational simplicity, $I(x_i)$ is taken to mean $I(x_i, x_i)$.

Potentially, it is possible that the insured files a fraudulent claim, $y_i \neq x_i$. Given loss x, the insured will file a claim y, and the insurer will determine whether or not she will audit. Let us define the audit set V as the set of losses on which an audit is rendered. The no-audit set V^c is the complement of the audit set. Let us first find the characteristics of the audit set and the no-audit set.

First, we may assume that the insurer will pay the same benefits for the claims of losses in V^c. This is because, if not, the insured can file a claim that provides the highest benefits on V^c. As a result, assuming the same benefit payment on V^c is without loss of generality. Let us call this payment I^N.

Second, for all losses in V, the insurer will have to pay more than I^N. To see this, suppose to the contrary that the insurance benefit payment for loss x in V is less than I^N. Then, the insured may get paid more if he files a claim of a loss in V^c. This implies that loss x should be in V^c, not in V, a contradiction.

Third, we can assume that the insured will tell the truth. Suppose that the insured suffers loss x in V. He will have no incentive to file a claim of another loss in V, since the insurer will audit and verify the true losses.[1] In addition, he will not file a claim of a loss in V^c, since he will receive a lower insurance benefit. As a result, he will not file a fraudulent claim. Now, suppose that the insured suffers loss x in V^c. He will not file a claim of a loss in V, since the insurer will audit. In addition, he will not file a claim of another loss in V^c, since he will receive the same insurance

---

[1]   If we impose some penalty for a detected fraud, then the insured will strictly prefer to tell the truth.

benefits. Therefore, for a loss in V^c, the insured will have no incentives to file a fraudulent claim. In sum, for any loss, the insured will not have any incentives to file a fraudulent claim.

Finally, suppose that x is in V and $x' > x$. Then, x' should be in V. If not, the insured will get paid more for a small loss, and less for a large loss. In this case, however, a risk averse insured will increase his utility by lowering the benefit for a small loss and increasing it for a large loss. These observations are summarized as follows.

Proposition 10.1 (Deterministic audit).

(a) The insurance benefit payment for all losses in the no-audit set is the same.
(b) The insurance benefit payment for a loss in the audit set is higher than that for a loss in the no-audit set.
(c) The insured will have no incentive to file fraudulent claims.
(d) The no-audit set has the form $[0, v]$, and the audit set has the form $(v, x_2]$, for some number v.

Proof See the text above. ☐

For an illustrative example, let us focus on a simple model in which there are two possible losses, x_1 and x_2, where $x_1 < x_2$. Let us write x_0 for no loss. Now the problem can be stated as follows.

$$\max\nolimits_{\{Q, I_0, I_1, I_2, v\}} p_0 U\left(W - Q + I_0\right) + p_1 U\left(W - Q - x_1 + I_1\right) \qquad (10.1)$$
$$+ \ p_2 U(W - Q - x_2 + I_2)$$
$$\text{s.t. } Q = p_0 I_0 + p_1 I_1 + p_2 I_2 + E(c)$$

where $I_i = I(x_i)$ and $E(c) = c \Pr(x > v)$, since the insurer will audit for losses in V. From Proposition 10.1, we also know that $I(x) > I^N$ for x in V and that $I(x) = I^N$ for x in V^c. It is clear from program (10.1) that the optimal contracts $\{Q, I_0, I_1, I_2\}$ are defined up to a constant. Adding a constant to all benefit payments and the price does not change the utility of the insured or the profit of the insurer.

The determination of the audit interval depends on the audit cost relative to the benefit of the audit. There are two extreme cases in which (i) the insurer audits all claims or (ii) the insurer never audits. The insurer may audit all claims if the audit cost is low enough. This case is not interesting for our purpose, since the insurer can always observe the true losses. This case corresponds to the standard case in which the insured will be fully insured, except that the premium includes fixed audit costs.[2] If the insurer never audits due to the expensive audit cost, then the insured will always file a fraudulent claim. This implies that the insurer will pay the insurance benefit of I^N ($I_i = I^N$ for all i) and the premium becomes I^N. This case also is not interesting since no risk is shared at all.

Now let us move on to our main case in which both the audit set and the non-audit set are not trivial. This case will be obtained when the audit cost is intermediate. Suppose that the insurer will audit only for the claim of x_2. No audit for x_0 and x_1 implies $I_0 = I_1 = I^N$, thus $W_0 > W_1$. The Lagrangian is

$$L = p_0 U \left(W - Q + I^N \right) + p_1 U \left(W - Q - x_1 + I^N \right)$$
$$+ p_2 U \left(W - Q - x_2 + I_2 \right) + \lambda \left(Q - p_0 I^N - p_1 I^N - p_2 I_2 - c p_2 \right). \tag{10.2}$$

The first-order conditions are

$$L_{I_2} = p_2 U_2' - \lambda p_2 = 0 \Rightarrow I_2 = x_2 - d,$$
$$L_{I^N} = p_0 U_0' + p_1 U_1' - \lambda (p_0 + p_1) = 0. \tag{10.3}$$

The premium becomes $Q = (1 - p_2)I^N + p_2(x_2 - d) + c p_2$.

Proposition 10.2 (Deterministic audit). The optimal insurance contract exhibits the following properties, where the optimal audit and the no-audit sets are non-trivial:

(a) The wealth level with a higher loss can be higher than the wealth level with a lower loss.
(b) The insurance benefit payment may include a positive deductible.

Proof For (a), note that, from the FOC, $U_2' = \lambda = [p_0 U_0' + p_1 U_1']/(p_0 + p_1)$. That is, U_2' is a weighted average of U_0' and U_1'. Since $U_0' < U_1'$, we have $U_0' < U_2' < U_1'$, or $W_0 > W_2 > W_1$. For (b), note that from $W_0 > W_2 > W_1$, we have that $I^N > - x_2 + I_2 > -x_1 + I^N$, which implies $I_2 > I^N$, confirming Proposition 10.1(b). If overinsurance is not allowed, then $I^N = 0$. In this case, the corresponding deductible level $d = d_0$ should satisfy that $0 < d_0 < x_1$. The premium becomes $Q = p_2(x_2 - d_0 + c)$. On the other hand, for full insurance for x_2 ($I_2 = x_2$, i.e., $d = 0$), we need to add d_0 to each benefit payment and the premium of the case of $I^N = 0$, implying that $I^N = d_0$, and $Q = (1 - p_2)d_0 + p_2(x_2 + c)$. $\qquad \square$

---

[2] Since the audit costs are reflected to the premium as a lump sum, it does not affect the optimality of full insurance.

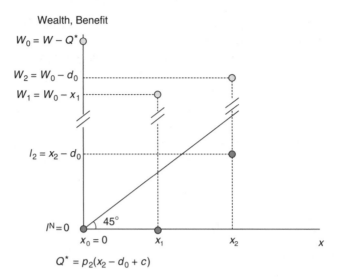

Figure 10.1   Deterministic audit: discrete losses.

The result for $I^N = 0$ is depicted in Figure 10.1.

Proposition 10.2(a) implies that a higher loss size may be associated with a higher wealth level. This finding contrasts with the standard results in which the wealth level is lower for a higher loss. This result comes from the fact that the insurer can observe high losses only. Since the insurance benefit payment for an audited loss is higher than that for a non-audited loss, the wealth level with a high loss can be higher than that with a low loss.

Proposition 10.2(b) points out that full insurance for an audited high loss may be accompanied with overinsurance for a non-audited low loss. Note that optimal levels of the benefit payment and the premium are not unique, since adding a constant to both the insurance premium and the payment does not change the result. Under the usual assumption that over-insurance is not allowed, we should have $I^N = 0$, since there is no loss in the no-audit set. In this case, full insurance for high loss x_2 is not optimal. For this, note that the insured is not paid for some positive loss (x_1). Full insurance for a high loss increases the gap between the utilities under audit and under no audit. This increased gap (i.e., risk) can be reduced by a partial coverage for the high loss, resulting in the increase of the utility. This explains why an optimal insurance scheme includes a deductible.

Note that Proposition 10.2 is obtained under the assumption that the optimal audit set is given. A fuller description of equilibrium outcomes should include the determination of the audit set. The equilibrium audit set will be determined by comparing the outcomes under different audit sets, which is not pursued here.

Finally, note that Proposition 10.2 also holds in the continuous loss case. To see this, suppose that the loss distribution $F(x)$ is defined on $[0, x^{max}]$. Given $F(x)$ and no-audit set $V^c = [0, v]$, an optimal insurance contract will solve the following program:

$$\max_{\{I^N, I(x), Q, v\}} \int_0^v U(W - Q - x + I^N) dF(x) \tag{10.4}$$

$$+ \int_v^{x^{max}} U(W - Q - x + I(x)) dF(x)$$

$$\text{s.t. } Q = F(v)I^N + \int_v^{x^{max}} (c + I(x)) dF(x).$$

Similarly to (10.3), the FOCs are obtained as follows:

$$U'\big(W - Q - x + I(x)\big)f(x) - \lambda f(x) = 0,$$
$$\int_0^v U'(W - Q - x + I^N) dF(x) - \lambda F(v) = 0. \tag{10.5}$$

From these FOCs, the benefit payment may include a deductible. $I(x) = x - d$, so that, for $x > v$, $U'(W - Q - x + I(x)) = U'(W - Q - d)$. We also have

$$U'(W - Q - d) = \frac{1}{F(v)} \int_0^v U'(W - Q - x + I^N) dF(x),$$

implying that the wealth level with a higher loss can be higher than the wealth level with a lower loss. If we set $I^N = 0$, the corresponding deductible level is between 0 and v: $0 < d_0 < v$.[3] This case is depicted in Figure 10.2.

10.2   Random Audit

It is often argued that a deterministic audit strategy may be excessively costly. Deterministic audit implies that the insurer will always audit for some losses (i.e., the probability of auditing is 1), and never for other losses (the probability of auditing is 0). Under random audit, the insurer may

---

[3]   We can show that the critical loss size v is positive, if the audit cost is positive. For the increase in v from zero will not have the first-order effect on the expected utility, while reducing the total audit cost.

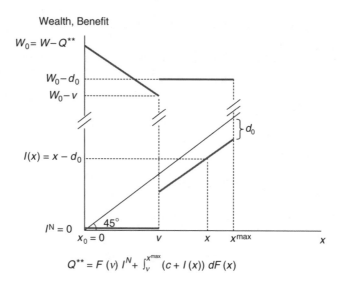

$$Q^{**} = F(v) I^N + \int_v^{x^{max}} (c + I(x)) \, dF(x)$$

Figure 10.2   Deterministic audit: continuous losses.

lower the probability of auditing even for the losses in the audit set (i.e., the probability of auditing can be less than 1). To the extent that the purpose of auditing is to induce the insured to tell the truth, random auditing can be more cost-efficient than deterministic auditing. This is because the insured may tell the truth, as long as auditing is frequent enough.

One important difference between this and the deterministic audit case is that the penalty for a detected fraud becomes important. For example, if the penalty is extremely high, then the insured will tell the truth even if the insurer audits very few times. In a more realistic case, the penalty may depend on the loss size and wealth levels.

From the revelation principle (Myerson, 1979) we can formulate the problem as a truth-telling one with a proper incentive constraint. Formally, let us define $a_i = a(x_i)$ as the probability of auditing when x_i is a claimed loss, where $x_0 = 0$ for no loss. We define $I_i^N = I^N(x_i)$ as the insurance benefit payment for claim x_i under no audit. Furthermore, we define $I_i = I(x_i)$ as the insurance benefit payment for loss x_i under audit, when no fraud is detected. Similarly, $I_i^P = I^P(x_i)$ is defined as the benefit payment for a false claim with true loss x_i, when a fraud is detected.[4] When $I_i^P < I_i$, the difference can be considered as a penalty for fraud. Note that the insurer will prefer as large a penalty as possible, since she can save the audit costs by lowering the audit probability. Now, our problem is of no interest if the

---

[4]   For expository simplicity, we are assuming that the benefit payment I_i^P does not depend on the claimed loss.

penalty can be arbitrarily large. Reflecting this observation, we assume that the maximum penalty is exogenously determined. Finally, note that optimal insurance contracts are determined up to a constant, since adding a constant to both the premium and the payment scheme does not change the outcome. We assume that overinsurance is not allowed, so that $I_0^N = I_0 = 0$.

Given a realized loss x_i, the expected utility of the insured under truth telling is

$$(1 - a_i)\, U\,(W - Q - x_i + I_i^N\,) + a_i U(W - Q - x_i + I_i). \tag{10.6}$$

If the insured files a fraudulent claim $x_j \neq x_i$, then his expected utility is

$$(1 - a_j)\, U\,(W - Q - x_i + I_j^N\,) + a_j U(W - Q - x_i + I_i^P\,). \tag{10.7}$$

Now, given x_i, the incentive compatibility (IC) constraint to make the insured tell the truth can be stated as

$$\begin{aligned} &(1 - a_i)\, U\,(W - Q - x_i + I_i^N) + a_i U(W - Q - x_i + I_i) \\ &\geq (1 - a_j)\ U(W - Q - x_i + I_j^N) \\ &+ a_j U(W - Q - x_i + I_i^P), \quad \text{for all } i, j. \end{aligned} \tag{10.8}$$

An equilibrium will be obtained by maximizing the insured's expected utility, subject to the zero profit condition and IC. Before analyzing further, we can derive from this IC several important facts regarding the benefit payment and the audit probability (see Mookherjee and P'ng, 1989). First, $I_i^N < I_i$ when $a_i > 0$. To see why, suppose, for argument's sake, that $I_i^N > I_i$. Let us slightly lower I_i^N and increase I_i simultaneously to keep the expected benefit $(1 - a_i)I_i^N + a_i I_i$ unchanged. This change increases the insured's utility (left-hand side of the IC) with x_i by reducing risk, thus does not violate the IC. Further, the insured with x_j will not report x_i, since the right-hand side of the IC, $(1 - a_i)U(W - Q - x_j + I_i^N) + a_i U(W - Q - x_j + I_i^P)$, will be lowered. Then, the insurer can save the audit costs by lowering a_i, a contradiction. Even though $I_i^N = I_i$, the same change does not have a first-order effect on the insured's utility, since it is at the full insurance position. However, it will save the total audit costs as in the case of $I_i^N > I_i$. In sum, we should have $I_i^N < I_i$.

Second, if $I_i^N < I_j^N$, then $a_i < a_j$. This result is intuitive, since a higher nonaudited payment with a lower audit probability would invite more fraud. Formally, suppose that $I_i^N < I_j^N$ and $a_i \geq a_j$. In this case, claiming x_j is strictly preferred to claiming x_i for a loss different from x_i. Then, slightly increasing

I_i^N and decreasing I_i, keeping the expected benefit payment unchanged, will increase the insured's utility by reducing risk without violating constraints.

Third, $a_0 = 0$ since there is no need to audit for no loss, when the insured cannot profit by claiming no loss.

Fourth, we can also show that if the expected utility under the truth telling is strictly higher than that under the detected fraud, then the audit probability should be strictly less than 1 for all i. That is, $a_i < 1$ for all i, if the following condition holds:

$$(1-a_i)U(W - Q - x_i + I_i^N) + a_iU(W - Q - x_i + I_i)$$
$$> U\left(W - Q - x_i + I_i^P\right), \quad \text{for all } i. \tag{10.9}$$

Suppose, for argument's sake, that $a_j = 1$ for some j. Given $x_i \neq x_j$, the right-hand side of the inequality condition (10.9) can be considered the expected utility under the fraudulent claim of x_j. The condition will still hold even if the insurer slightly lowers a_j and sets $I_j^N = I_j$. This change does not violate the IC given x_j, since it does not change the expected utility under truth telling given x_j. Since this change saves audit costs, it contradicts the optimality of $a_j = 1$. These observations are summarized as follows.

Proposition 10.3 (Random audit).

(a) Given that a loss has occurred, the insurance benefit payment under an audit is higher than that under no audit, if the audit probability for the loss is positive: $I_i^N < I_i$ when $a_i > 0$.

(b) Given two losses, the nonaudited payment is higher for a loss for which the audit probability is higher: if $I_i^N < I_j^N$, then $a_i < a_j$.

(c) The insurer will not audit for the lowest loss: $a_0 = 0$.

(d) If the expected utility under the truth telling is strictly higher than that under the detected fraud, then the audit probability should be strictly less than 1 for all i.

Proof See the text above.   □

For an illustrative example, let us consider a simple binary model. A loss x occurs with probability p. From the above discussion, it is clear that the insurer will not audit a claim of no loss, since no insured will profit by fraudulent claim of no loss. Preventing overinsurance leads to a zero benefit payment to the insured with the claim of no loss. Therefore, we only need the incentive constraint that the insured with no loss should not file the claim x. Let I^N and I be insurance benefit payments under no audit and audit, respectively, given truth telling. Given claim x, the insurer will audit with probability a. We assume that the penalty for a detected fraud is exogenously given, so that $I^P < 0$. Now the problem can be stated as

$$\max\nolimits_{\{Q,I^N,I,a\}} (1-p)U(W-Q) + p\{(1-a)U(W-Q-x+I^N)$$
$$+ aU(W-Q-x+I)\} \tag{10.10}$$
$$\text{s.t. } Q = p((1-a)I^N + aI) + pac,$$
$$U(W-Q) \geq (1-a)U(W-Q+I^N) + aU(W-Q+I^P),$$

$$L = (1-p)U(W-Q) + p\{(1-a)U(W-Q-x+I^N)$$
$$+ aU(W-Q-x+I)\} + \lambda[Q - p((1-a)I^N + aI) - pac]$$
$$+ \mu[U(W-Q) - (1-a)U(W-Q+I^N)$$
$$- aU(W-Q+I^P)]. \tag{10.11}$$

The FOCs are

$$L_a = p(-U_1 + U_2) - \lambda p(-I^N + I + c) + \mu[U_2 - U_3],$$
$$L_{I^N} = p(1-a)U'_1 - \lambda p(1-a) - \mu(1-a)U'_1,$$
$$L_I = paU'_2 - \lambda pa, \tag{10.12}$$
$$L_Q = -(1-p)U'_0 - p\{(1-a)U'_1 + aU'_2\} + \lambda$$
$$+ \mu[-U'_0 + (1-a)U'_1 + aU'_3],$$

where

$$U_0 = U(W-Q), \quad U_1 = U(W-Q-x+I^N),$$
$$U_2 = U(W-Q-x+I), \quad U_3 = U(W-Q+I^P).$$

From $L_I = 0$, $U'_2 = \lambda$,

$$L_{I^N} = 0 \Rightarrow (p-\mu)U'_1 = pU'_2 \Rightarrow U'_1 > U'_2 \Rightarrow W_1 < W_2 \Rightarrow I^N < I.$$

From $L_Q = 0$,

$$[-p\{(1-a)p/(p-\mu) + a\} + 1 + \mu\{(1-a)p/(p-\mu)\}] U'_2$$
$$= [(1-p) + \mu] U'_0$$
$$\Rightarrow (1-p)U'_2 + a\mu U'_3 = [(1-p) + \mu] U'_0.$$

Since $U_2' > U_0'$ and $U_3' > U_0'$, we should have $a < 1$. As the penalty increases, or equivalently as W_3 decreases, a becomes smaller, and

$$U_1' > U_2' > U_0' \Rightarrow W_1 < W_2 < W_0 \Rightarrow I^N < I < x.$$

The results are summarized as follows.

> *Proposition 10.4* (Random audit in a binary model). The insurance contract exhibits the following properties in an equilibrium:
>
> (a) The audited insurance benefit payment is higher than the nonaudited insurance benefit payment.
> (b) The loss is partially insured.
> (c) The audit probability is less than 1.
>
> *Proof* See the text above. ☐

Even though it seems natural that a higher loss is associated with a higher payment, such monotonicity is not obtained in general. To see this, note that increasing the audited payment for a high loss enhances efficiency by improving risk sharing. However, such risk sharing improvement can be achieved by increasing the nonaudited payment. As a result, a lower audited payment can be associated with a higher loss. In general, audit probabilities, nonaudited payment and audited payment should be considered simultaneously. Fagart and Picard (1999) show that monotonicity holds under a CARA utility. Note that risk attitude is separated from wealth level under CARA, simplifying the interactive effects.

10.3   Asymmetric Information and Fraud

The above approach implicitly assumes that all insureds are potential liars. However, in reality, not all insureds file fraudulent claims even if insurers do not audit. Some insureds may feel guilty if they claim fraudulently. In this section, we consider the case of the information asymmetry regarding honesty types, based on Picard (1996).

Suppose that there are two types of insureds: a proportion θ are opportunistic, and a proportion $1 - \theta$ are honest. Honest insureds always tell the truth, while opportunistic insureds may file fraudulent claims if doing so is profitable. The types are private information of the insureds.

In a simple binary model, we assume that loss x may occur with probability p. Once a loss occurs, both types of insureds will truthfully claim the loss. However, the difference between the two types of insureds can be found when no loss occurs. Given no loss, the opportunistic insureds may fraudulently file claims, while honest ones do not. Let us assume that the penalty $I^P < 0$ is exogenously given. We write a and b, respectively, for the audit probability of the insurer facing claim x, and for the fraud probability of the opportunistic insured given no loss. The audit cost is c.

Equilibrium contracts will be offered to the insured with which the insurer makes a zero expected profit. Denote by $r \in [0, 1]$ the proportion of the opportunistic insureds targeted by a contract.

Now let us first find a and b given a contract with r. Given no loss, the expected utility of the opportunistic insured under the fraud strategy b becomes

$$b\left[aU\left(W - Q + I^P\right) + (1 - a)U\left(W - Q + I\right)\right]$$
$$+ (1 - b)U\left(W - Q\right). \tag{10.13}$$

Given Q and I, let $a^e = a^e(Q, I)$ be the audit probability making the opportunistic insured indifferent between fraud and truth telling, given no loss. We have

$$U(W - Q) = a^e U(W - Q + I^P) + (1 - a^e)U(W - Q + I),$$

that is,

$$a^e = \frac{U(W - Q + I) - U(W - Q)}{U(W - Q + I) - U(W - Q + I^P)} \tag{10.14}$$

Thus, the optimal b will be

$$b = \begin{cases} 0, & \text{if } a \geq a^e, \\ 1, & \text{if } a < a^e. \end{cases} \tag{10.15}$$

Note that b can be any number in $[0, 1]$ for $a = a^e$; we assume that $b = 0$ is chosen in that case.

Now let us find the total cost of the contract per insured. The cost depends on whether or not a fraud is allowed. If the insurer wants to disallow a fraud, she can set the audit probability as $a = a^e$. In this case, the total cost becomes $pI + pa^e c$. If the insurer wants to allow a fraud with audit probability $a < a^e$, the total cost will be $pI + (1 - p)r(1 - a)I + (p + (1 - p)r)ac$.

If $c > (1 - p)rI/[p + (1 - p)r]$, then the total cost under a fraud allowed is increasing in a. Thus, $a = 0$ is the cost-minimizing audit probability, when a fraud is allowed. With $a = 0$, the total cost becomes $pI + (1 - p)rI$.

Comparing this with the total cost under no fraud, $pI + pa^e c$, we have that the total cost is minimized by choosing $a = 0$ if $c > (1 - p)rI/pa^e$, or $a = a^e$ if $(1 - p)rI/[p + (1 - p)r] < c \leq (1 - p)rI/pa^e$.

On the other hand, if $c \leq (1 - p)rI/[p+(1 - p)r]$, then the total cost under a fraud allowed is decreasing in a. Thus, the insurer will increase a if possible. When a hits a^e, the opportunistic insured will stop telling a lie. Comparing between two total costs, it is easy to see that $a = a^e$ minimizes the total cost. This observation is summarized as follows.

Lemma 10.1

(a)　If $c \leq (1 - p)rI/(pa^e)$, then the optimal solution is $a = a^e$ and $b = 0$. The total cost becomes $p(I + a^e c)$.

(b)　If $c > (1 - p)rI/(pa^e)$, then the optimal solution is $a = 0$ and $b = 1$. The total cost becomes $[p + (1 - p)r]I$.

(c)　In a competitive market, insurance premium $Q = \min[\{p + (1 - p) r\}I, p(I + a^e c)]$.

Proof See the text above. □

For a complete description of an equilibrium, we need to determine whether or not insured types are separated in an equilibrium. Note that a contract should make a zero profit in an equilibrium. For a contract to be an equilibrium one, there should not exist an alternative contract which provides a positive profit if offered.

What is important is the conjecture of insurers. Following Picard (1996), our analysis will be based on the Wilson (1977) conjecture. Under the Wilson conjecture, the profit of an alternative contract is calculated assuming that the existing contracts will be withdrawn, if their profits become negative after the alternative contract is offered.

First, we can show that no separating equilibrium can exist, in which honest insureds select contracts different from opportunistic insureds. To see this, suppose that a separating equilibrium exists. The optimal audit probability should be zero for the contract offered to the honest insureds. However, no audit will invite an opportunistic insured, since a fraudulent claim will provide the insured with a higher utility than telling the truth. This implies that an opportunistic insured will prefer the contract for the honest insureds to one for the opportunistic insureds, a contradiction.

Now, let us focus on a pooling equilibrium.[5] The proportion of the opportunistic insureds selecting the pooling contract is θ. The pooling

---

[5] Note that a contract attracting the opportunistic insureds only is not profitable. Then, another possible equilibrium candidate is that both the opportunistic insured and the honest insured are indifferent between two distinctive contracts, so that some select one contract

contract will maximize the expected utility of the honest insured, given the zero profit constraint, since otherwise there is another profitable contract which provides the honest insured with a higher utility.

Thus, the equilibrium will be obtained by solving the following program:[6]

$$\max_{Q, I} (1-p)U(W-Q) + pU(W-Q-x+I) \tag{10.16}$$

$$\text{s.t. } Q = \min[\{p+(1-p)\theta\}I, \, p(I+a^e c)]$$

where a and b are determined by Lemma 10.1.
The Lagrangian is

$$L = (1-p)U(W-Q) + pU(W-Q-x+I)$$
$$+ \lambda[\, Q - \min[\{p+(1-p)r\}I, p(I+a^e c)]\,].$$

The FOCs are

$$L_Q = -(1-p)U_0' - pU_1' + \lambda = 0, \tag{10.17}$$

$$L_I = pU_1' - \lambda\{p+(1-p)r\} = 0$$
$$\quad \text{if } \{p+(1-p)r\}I \leq p(I+a^e c), \quad \text{when } b=1,$$
$$= pU_1' - \lambda p[1+a^{e\prime}c] = 0$$
$$\quad \text{if } \{p+(1-p)r\}I > p(I+a^e c), \quad \text{when } b=0,$$

where $a^{e\prime}$ denotes $\partial a^e/\partial I$. Note that $a^{e\prime} > 0$.

Proposition 10.5 (Adverse selection model of fraud). The following hold in an equilibrium:

(a) The insureds should be pooled.
(b) The loss is partially insured.
(c) A fraud may be allowed.

Proof (a) See the text above.
(b), (c) From the FOCs, when $b = 1$,

$$U_1' = \lambda\{1 + (1-p)r/p\} \text{ and } L_Q = 0 \Rightarrow U_0' = \lambda(1-r).$$

---

and others select the other. However, it can be shown that such contracts cannot constitute an equilibrium, since the honest insured will prefer the contract solving (10.16) to the contract with higher r.

[6] We implicitly assume that the audit cost is not as high as for the honest insured to leave the market.

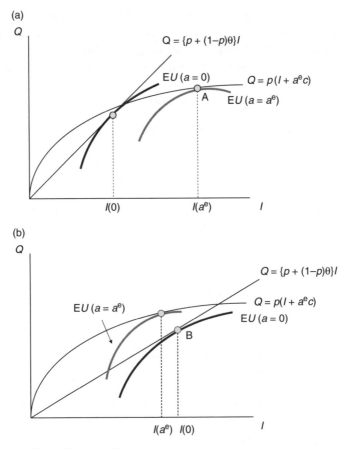

I(a): optimal benefit payment given a
EU(a = 0): expected utility of the honest insured with fraud allowed
EU(a = a^e): expected utility of the honest insured with fraud not allowed

Figure 10.3   Adverse selection model of fraud: (a) equilibrium in which fraud is not allowed; (b) equilibrium in which fraud is allowed.

When $b = 0$,

$$U_1' = \lambda(1 + a^{e\prime}c) \text{ and } L_Q = 0 \Rightarrow U_0' = \lambda(1 - p - a^{e\prime}c)/(1 - p).$$

In both cases, we have that $U_1' > U_0'$, or $I < x$, implying that partial insurance is optimal. From Lemma 10.1, we have that $a = 0$ for $b = 1$, and $a = a^e$ for $b = 0$. □

The equilibrium is depicted in Figure 10.3. $I(a)$ denotes the optimal insurance benefit payment given a. $EU(a)$ denotes the indifference curve of the honest insured with $I(a)$. In Figure 10.3(a), fraud is not allowed in an equilibrium (Proposition 10.5(a)), since $EU(a = a^e)$ is higher than $EU(a = 0)$. In Figure 10.3(b), fraud is allowed in an equilibrium (Proposition 10.5(b)), since $EU(a = 0)$ is higher than $EU(a = a^e)$. When fraud is allowed, the honest insured actually subsidizes the opportunistic insured. As the population proportion of the opportunistic insureds, θ, increases, the subsidy will also increase. Therefore, fraud is more likely to be allowed in an equilibrium, when θ is smaller.

For the contracts to be equilibrium ones, there should be no other contract which is profitable under the Wilson conjecture. A profitable contract will be the one attracting the honest insureds only. In such a case, however, the existing contract will earn a negative profit, which leads to its withdrawal under the Wilson conjecture. Once the existing contract is withdrawn, the new contract cannot be profitable. Thus, the new contract cannot be offered in the first place.

10.4   Caveat: Commitment

One interesting issue is the commitment problem. The above results hold only if the insurer commits not to opportunistically change the audit decision. Recall that the insured tells the truth in the deterministic audit or in the random audit cases. In the adverse selection case, with $a = a^e$, the opportunistic insured does not file a fraudulent claim. Knowing this fact, ex post, the insurer has an incentive to not audit at all, which will save the audit cost. However, if the insurer does not audit, the opportunistic insured will have an incentive to lie, which breaks the equilibrium.

In fact, such a commitment problem is typical in the information asymmetry setting. For example, consider the equilibrium in Rothschild and Stiglitz (1976). The only possible equilibrium is a separating equilibrium in which types of insureds are separated. Therefore, ex post, the insurer can tell the risk types of insureds given the contract choices. If the insurer can use that information to renegotiate with the insured, then the equilibrium will collapse, since high-risk insureds will purchase the contract for low-risk insureds. In other words, the separating equilibrium is possible only if the insurer commits not to use the information obtained from the separation.

Picard (1996) considers a no-commitment case in the adverse selection model of fraud. As discussed above, no commitment makes it impossible for the opportunistic insured to tell the truth in an equilibrium. A fraud should be allowed and partial insurance is offered in an equilibrium. However, the cost is increased (i.e., the efficiency is reduced) due to the lack of commitment, since the lack of commitment implies that the set of possible strategies of the insurer becomes smaller.

10.5   Conclusion

The ex post moral hazard is a significant problem in the insurance market. Since insurers often cannot directly observe the true loss size, opportunistic insureds have incentives to file fraudulent claims. Proper monitoring systems may help lower the moral hazard costs. However, it is not desirable to remove all the moral hazard problems when the monitoring cost is high.

BIBLIOGRAPHY

Bond, E. W. and K. J. Crocker (1997) Hardball and the soft touch: the economics of optimal insurance contracts with costly state verification and endogenous monitoring cost. *Journal of Public Economics*, 63: 239–64.

Crocker, K. J. and J. Morgan (1998) Is honesty the best policy? Curtailing insurance fraud through optimal incentive contracts. *Journal of Political Economy*, 106: 355–75.

Cummins, J. D. and S. Tennyson (1992) Controlling automobile insurance costs. *Journal of Economic Perspectives*, 6: 95–115.

Cummins, J. D. and S. Tennyson (1996) Moral hazard in insurance claiming: evidence from automobile insurance. *Journal of Risk and Uncertainty*, 12: 29–50.

Darby, M. R. and E. Karni (1973) Free competition and the optimal amount of fraud. *Journal of Law and Economics*, 16: 67–88.

Derrig, R. A., H. I. Weisberg, and X. Chen (1994) Behavioral factors and lotteries under no-fault with a monetary threshold: a study of Massachusetts automobile claims. *Journal of Risk and Insurance*, 61: 245–75.

Dionne, G. (1984) The effects of insurance on the possibilities of fraud. *Geneva Papers on Risk and Insurance*, 9: 304–21.

Dionne, G. and R. Gagné (2001) Deductible contracts against fraudulent claims: evidence from automobile insurance. *Review of Economics and Statistics*, 83: 290–301.

Fagart, M. and P. Picard (1999) Optimal insurance under random auditing. *Geneva Papers on Risk and Insurance Theory*, 29: 29–54.

Lacker, J. M. and J. A. Weinberg (1989) Optimal contracts under costly state falsification. *Journal of Political Economy*, 97: 1347–63.

Maggi, G. and A. Rodriguez-Clare (1995) Costly distortion of information in agency problems. *Rand Journal of Economics*, 26: 675–89.

Mookherjee, D. and I. P'ng (1989) Optimal auditing insurance and redistribution. *Quarterly Journal of Economics*, 104: 399–415.

Myerson, R. B. (1979) Incentive compatibility and the bargaining problem. *Econometrica*, 47: 61–74.

Picard, P. (1996) Auditing claims in insurance market with fraud: the credibility issue. *Journal of Public Economics*, 63: 27–56.

Picard, P. (2000a) Economic analysis of insurance fraud. In G. Dionne (ed.), *Handbook of Insurance*. Boston: Kluwer Academic Publishers.

Picard, P. (2000b) On the design of optimal insurance contracts under manipulation of audit cost. *International Economic Review*, 41: 1049–71.

Rothschild, M. and J. E. Stiglitz (1976) Equilibrium in competitive insurance markets: an essay on the economics of imperfect information. *Quarterly Journal of Economics*, 90: 629–50.

Stigler, G. J. (1970) The optimal enforcement of law. *Journal of Political Economy*, 78: 526–36.

Townsend, R. M. (1979) Optimal contracts and competitive markets with costly state verification. *Journal of Economics Theory*, 21: 265–93.

Wilson, C. (1977) A model of insurance markets with incomplete information. *Journal of Economic Theory*, 16: 167–207.

Part IV
Insurance Market

Chapter 11

Insurer Organization

In the insurance market, diverse insurer organizations are observed. Stock companies are a major type of organization in the insurance industry as well as in other industries. Mutual companies are another important type of organization in the insurance market. They are more common in financial sectors than in manufacturing sectors. No examination of the insurance market is complete unless it also considers Lloyd's. In this chapter, we investigate the characteristics of organizational forms and the rationales for the coexistence of such diverse organizational forms in the market.

The main functions of an organization are the owner, customer, and manager functions. The owners of an organization provide capital and bear the residual risks of the organization. The customers purchase the insurance product and will receive the indemnity/benefit payments from the organization. The managers operate the organization, and assume responsibility on behalf of the owners. Decision making is delegated to the managers from the owners. Different organizational forms have different characteristics in these functions. Such differences lead each organizational form to enjoy comparative advantages over others under different circumstances. Characteristics of organizational forms are presented first (Section 11.1). Then, we try to understand organizational forms in terms of risk sharing (Section 11.2), moral hazard (Section 11.3), and adverse selection (Section 11.4).[1]

---

[1] The coexistence of stocks and mutuals can be affected by other factors, including history and imperfect competition (Seog, 2006).

11.1   Characteristics of Organizational Forms

11.1.1   Stock companies

The stock company is a common organizational form among large corporations. A main characteristic of the stock company is the complete separability of the owner, customer, and manager functions (see Table 11.1). The owners can freely trade or alienate their ownerships (see Fama and Jensen, 1983a, 1983b; Mayers and Smith, 1981, 1986, 1988). While the owners bear the residual risks of the organization, their risk bearing is limited up to their invested amount (limited liability). The alienability of ownership and the limited liability create a strong incentive for the owners to provide capital to the firm. The alienability allows owners to diversify their portfolios with low costs. The limited liability also reduces the monitoring costs of the owners. In this respect, note that under unlimited liability, an owner's liability depends on other owners' wealth levels. In this case, the owner needs to monitor other owners' wealth positions to lower her liability. Limited liability lowers the need to monitor other owners, since an owner's liability is independent of another owner's wealth.

With the separability of functions, the firm can enjoy the benefit of specialization in each function. Owners can provide capital regardless of their managerial talents. Decision making can be delegated to the manager without considering his wealth. Customers make purchase decisions based on the cost of and benefit from products. Such specialization enhances the efficiency of the firm.

However, the separation may also create conflicts of interest among the stakeholders. Under information asymmetry, the manager may have an incentive to appropriate the firm's value or make a low effort, since the manager does not bear the full cost of his actions. Similarly, a conflict between owners and customers can exist. The owners may have an incentive to increase dividends to the owners or undertake a risky investment, which negatively affect the value to the customers.

In a stock company, diverse mechanisms are used to control the adverse incentives of the separation of functions. The monitoring of the manager

Table 11.1   Functional characteristics of organizations

Organization	Functional characteristics
Stocks	Customer = Owner ≠ Manager
Mutuals	Customer = Owner ≠ Manager
Lloyd's	Customer ≠ Owner = Manager

by external directors is an important internal control mechanism. Internal and external audits are another example. The distinctive control mechanism of the stock company is through the stock market. Institutional investors, large investors, and stock analysts constantly monitor the firm's operation. Stock price related compensation can align the manager's interest with the owners. A manager with bad performance can be fired by shareholders or by mergers and acquisitions (M&A). This explains the fact that, compared with the mutual companies, stock companies prevail in the nonlife insurance lines where the required level of managerial discretion is higher than in life insurance lines. When the managerial discretion level is high, a more efficient monitoring mechanism is needed.

Another important function of the stock market is raising capital. The existence of the stock market along with the alienability of ownership allows owners to provide capital more easily than in other organizational forms. The recent trend of demutualization can be explained by the fact that insurers prefer the stock forms for the ease of raising capital and M&A, as a response to globalization and intensifying competition.

11.1.2   Mutual companies

The mutual company is another important organizational form in the insurance market. Since the manager function is separated from the owner function in a mutual company, the conflict between owner and manager exists as in the case of the stock company. However, in a mutual company, the owner function is merged with the customer function. The customer becomes an owner of the firm. This implies that the conflict between owner and customer can be controlled more effectively in mutual forms than in stock forms. This point is supported by the evidence that stock organizations take higher risks than mutual organizations. For example, stock insurers purchase reinsurance more than mutual insurers (Mayers and Smith, 1990). It is also found that stock insurers, not mutual insurers, increase asset risks following the guaranty funds enactment (Lee, Mayers and Smith, 1997). The option theory application implies that higher asset risks increase the owner's value, by sacrificing the insured's value.

However, the benefit of controlling the conflict between the owner and the customer is offset by the relative difficulty in controlling the conflict between the manager and the owner, since there is no market for ownership trading like the stock market. Since the stock market provides an effective controlling mechanism, the nonexistence of such a market implies a less effective control of the manager.

The controlling mechanism of the manager in the mutual form is the redemption of the owner's claim (Fama and Jensen, 1983a, 1983b). The owner has the right to require the mutual company to redeem her ownership value, according to a predetermined pricing rule and procedure. Even though the redemption of the claim itself is a strong controlling mechanism, each owner does not have an incentive to monitor the manager, since she should bear the full monitoring cost, while she earns only the partial benefit of the monitoring. Thus, the controllability of the manager in the mutual company is weaker than in the stock company. This explains the fact that the mutual companies are more prevalent in life insurance which requires less managerial discretion. When the required managerial discretion level is low, the monitoring cost will be low too.

11.1.3   Lloyd's

In Lloyd's, the capital providers are called members. Members form syndicates through which they underwrite policies. Members' accounts are on a separate basis. That is, each member is responsible for her own portion of the risk. The members are classified into companies, individuals (known as "names"), and limited partnerships. Although managing agents are appointed to employ the underwriting staff and manage the syndicate on the members' behalf, the manager function is largely merged with the owner function in Lloyd's, thus minimizing the conflict between manager and owner. This explains why Lloyd's is involved with the less standardized reinsurance lines which require a high level of managerial discretion. However, to the extent that the members form a syndicate, there can be a conflict between members of the syndicate, which requires mutual monitoring among members as in a professional partnership. On the other hand, the merger between the manager and the owner functions may sacrifice the benefit from specialization, which explains why Lloyd's is confined to a few insurance lines.

11.2   Risk Sharing and the Organizational Form

The mutuality principle implies that a Pareto optimal allocation is obtained if the risks of a group of insureds are pooled and allocated to each insured based on the risk of the pool. The mutual form is the organization that takes advantage of the mutuality principle (see Doherty and Dionne, 1993). Thus, mutual insurers are potentially the optimal organizational form.

On the other hand, if the risk of a risk averse individual can be transferred to a risk neutral individual, the outcome is Pareto optimal. Under DARA, we may assume that individuals become less risk averse as their

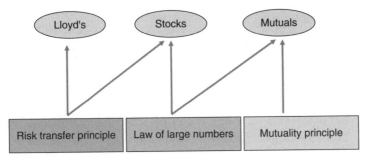

Figure 11.1   Organizations and the principles of insurance.

wealth level increases. This risk transfer principle is a feature of Lloyd's in that the individual members are rich enough to insure the risks. In addition, owners of the stock insurers can be considered less risk averse since they can diversify the risks in the stock market. Therefore, the risk transfer principle also justifies the existence of the stock insurers.

Both stock and mutual insurers may enjoy the diversification effect and the effect of the law of large numbers by making the pool size large. Both effects imply that the risk shared by each owner becomes small or ignorable as the risk pooling size becomes large enough. Both effects justify the importance of large insurers including both stock and mutual insurers.

On the other hand, it is important to note that the law of large numbers is applied to the case where risks are independent. Consider catastrophe risks such as floods, hurricanes and earthquakes. These catastrophe risks are not independent, so that the law of large numbers does not apply. Moreover, the size of a loss is very large, so that a few individuals cannot bear the full risks. As a result, the stock insurers and Lloyd's have disadvantages in insuring against catastrophe risks. While large stock insurers may take advantage of the large capital supply from the capital market, the full assumption of catastrophe risks may expose the insurers to excessively high risks.

One reaction to the lack of insurance is the formation of a risk sharing group, possibly including government. It is also easily observed that insurers often set limits of indemnity in catastrophe insurance, leading to risk sharing. As the mutuality principle implies, risk sharing between insurers and insureds is an efficient outcome, when all participants are risk averse. Therefore, these contracts can be interpreted as mutual-like forms exploiting the benefits of mutuality. The results of the foregoing discussion are summarized in the next proposition and are depicted in Figure 11.1.

Proposition 11.1

(a) The mutual organization can be efficient under the mutuality principle.
(b) The stock organization and Lloyd's can be efficient under the risk transfer principle.
(c) Large insurers including both stock and mutual organizations can be efficient under the diversification effect and the law of large numbers.

11.3 Moral Hazard and the Organizational Form

In this section, based on Mayers and Smith (1981, 1986, 1988, 1992, 1994), we formalize the discussion on the relationship between information problems and organizational forms under moral hazard. We focus on the stock and mutual organizations in this section. Notations and assumptions are summarized in Table 11.2.

The net value of the firm can be expressed as V minus moral hazard costs minus monitoring costs. For a mutual insurer, the owner/insured solves the following program for the optimal monitoring level:

$$\max_g V - T(g) - C_M(g),$$

with first-order condition (FOC)

$$-T' = C_M' \Rightarrow g^*.$$

The (net) firm value becomes

Table 11.2 Notation and assumptions

V: maximum value of the organization under no moral hazard
$V = E + P$
E: value to the owner
P: value to the insured
$T(g) = T_E(g) + T_P(g)$
T: moral hazard costs from the manager
T_i: cost share to the owner (E) or insured (P).
g: monitoring (or governance) level
$T_i'(g) \leq 0$ and $T_i''(g) \geq 0$.
$C_M(g)$: monitoring costs in mutual insurer
$C_S(g)$: monitoring costs in stock insurer
$C_i'(g) \geq 0$ and $C_i''(g) \geq 0$.
Assume that the monitoring of the manager is performed by owners.

$$W_M = V - [T_E(g^*) + T_P(g^*)] - C_M(g^*).$$

In the stock insurer, the owner solves the program

$$\max_g E - T_E(g) - C_S(g),$$

with FOC

$$-T_E' = C_S' \Rightarrow g^{**}.$$

The firm value becomes

$$W_S = V - [T_E(g^{**}) + T_P(g^{**})] - C_S(g^{**}).$$

A more efficient organization will have a higher firm value. If $W_M \geq W_S$, then mutual organizations are preferred to stock organizations, and vice versa. As discussed above, we may assume that the monitoring technology in stock insurers is more efficient than that in mutual insurers due to the access to capital markets. This difference in monitoring efficiency leads to the following assumption: C_S has a lower value and a flatter slope than C_M, $C_S(g) \leq C_M(g)$, and $C_S'(g) \leq C_M'(g)$.

On the other hand, owners in stock insurers may have a conflict with the insureds, since the two functions are separated. In our model, conflict costs can be incurred, because the stockholders ignore the effects of monitoring on the moral hazard cost share to insureds. Whether or not stock organization is preferred to mutual organization depends on the size of the monitoring efficiency relative to the conflict costs.

Now let us consider extreme cases. First, suppose that $T_P(g)$ is fixed. Then, we have the following FOCs: for a mutual,

$$-T_E' - C_M' = 0;$$

and for a stock,

$$-T_E' - C_S' = 0.$$

Since the monitoring by a stock is more efficient than a mutual, we have that $g^{**} \geq g^*$ and $W_S \geq W_M$.

Second, suppose that $C_M = C_S$. Then, we have the following FOCs: for a mutual,

$$-(T_E' + T_P') - C_M' = 0;$$

and for a stock,

$$-T_E' - C_M' = 0.$$

As long as $T_P' \leq 0$, then $g^* \geq g^{**}$. Since the mutual organization's solution maximizes the firm's value, we have $W_M \geq W_S$.

For a more general description, let us consider the following ideal organization program:

$$\max_g W_I\,(g) = V - T(g) - C_S(g).$$

Note that the owners take into account the total costs $T(g)$ with the efficient monitoring technology $C_S(g)$. The optimal solution g^{***} to this program is obtained with FOC

$$-T' - C_S' = 0.$$

Note that $W_I\,(g^{***}) \geq \max\,[W_M(g^*),\, W_S(g^{**})]$.

Now let us define the monitoring inefficiency (MI) costs of the mutual organization and the conflict costs (CC) as follows:

$$MI = W_I\,(g^{***}) - W_M(g^*) = T(g^*) + C_M(g^*) - [T(g^{***}) + C_S(g^{***})] \geq 0,$$

$$CC = W_I\,(g^{***}) - W_S(g^{**}) = T(g^{**}) + C_S(g^{**}) - [T(g^{***}) + C_S(g^{***})] \geq 0.$$

Now the stock organization is preferred to the mutual organization if and only if $W_S(g^{**}) - W_M(g^*) \geq 0$ or MI $\geq$ CC.

When the business activities of an insurer require a high level of managerial discretion, it also opens a high level of opportunity of appropriation of the firm's value by managers. In this case, monitoring efficiency is important, and MI becomes high. With high MI, stock organizations are more likely to be preferred to mutual organizations. Therefore, stock organizations are more prevalent in commercial lines with high underwriting risks or among geographically diversified insurers. On the other hand, mutual organizations are preferred where MI is low and/or CC is high. Therefore, mutual organizations are more prevalent in life insurance lines and among geographically concentrated insurers. Note that the insureds of life insurance are potentially exposed to a high risk of the owner's appropriation, since the contract period of life insurance is long. In addition, the mortality table is well developed, so that the discretion of the manager is not much needed compared to nonlife insurance. Thus, the mutual organization is a preferred form in life insurance.

Proposition 11.2 The mutual organization is preferred to the stock organization if its (relative) efficiency in controlling the conflicts between the owner and the customer is greater than its (relative) inefficiency in monitoring the manager.

11.4   Adverse Selection and the Organizational Form

Smith and Stutzer (1990) and Ligon and Thistle (2005) present adverse selection approaches to the organizational forms. It is argued that when insureds' risks are private information and insurers are exposed to an aggregate risk, high risks may be associated with stock insurers, and low risks with mutual insurers. A simple way of understanding this view is to reconsider Rothschild and Stiglitz (1976).

Recall that low-risk insureds purchase partial insurance, while high-risk insureds purchase full insurance in an equilibrium. Full insurance can be interpreted as a full risk transfer from insureds to insurers. Similarly, partial insurance can be interpreted as a risk sharing between insureds and insurers. In another interpretation, partial insurance can also be considered as a combination of the customer (insured) and the owner (insurer) functions. That is, partial insurance resembles the mutual organization. Let us decompose the merger between the customer and the owner functions in the mutual organization as follows. First, the insured, as a customer, transfers his risk fully to the insurer. The risk is pooled in the insurer. Then, as owners, the insureds collectively assume the risk of the pool. Due to the diversification effect, the risk per insured is less than the risk that he transfers to the insurer. In the extreme case in which the law of large numbers applies, each owner will not bear any risk. In other cases, an insured, as an owner, will bear some part of the risk he transfers.[2] This result is equivalent to the case where the insured purchases partial insurance.

From this viewpoint, partial insurance is interpreted as a contractual form allowing for sharing the insurer's risk. In that sense, participating insurance is one example of partial insurance, allowing insureds to participate in the insurer's profit sharing. As long as the merger of the customer and the owner functions is considered a main feature of the mutual organization, partial insurance is interpreted as a mutual form, while full insurance is interpreted as a stock form.

Proposition 11.3 If the insured's risk is private information and the insurer is exposed to an aggregate risk, then low-risk insureds are associated with the mutual organization while high-risk insureds are associated with the stock organization.

---

[2]   This result is similar to Ligon and Thistle's (2005) argument that the size of the mutual organization should be small to make the risk sharing significant.

11.5   Conclusion

Diverse organizational forms can be observed in the insurance market. The stock form, the mutual form, and Lloyd's are the main types. In a stock insurer, the owner function is separated from the customer function as well as from the manager function. In a mutual insurer, the owner function is merged with the customer function. In Lloyd's, the manager function is merged with the owner function. The coexistence of diverse organizations can be understood by the finding that different organizational forms can efficiently resolve the conflicts among stakeholders in different situations. Our focus is on the moral hazard and the adverse selection problems among owners, policyholders, and managers. In addition, different organizational forms exhibit different risk sharing features, which can be justified by the principles of insurance of Chapter 3.

BIBLIOGRAPHY

Doherty, N. A. and G. Dionne (1993) Insurance with undiversifiable risk: contract structure and organizational forms of insurance firms. *Journal of Risk and Uncertainty*, 6: 187–203.

Fagart, M.-C., N. Fombaron, and M. Jeleva (2002) Risk mutualization and competition in insurance markets. *Geneva Papers on Risk and Insurance Theory*, 27: 115–41.

Fama, E. F. and M. C. Jensen (1983a) Separation of ownership and control. *Journal of Law and Economics*, 26: 301–25.

Fama, E. F. and M. C. Jensen (1983b) Agency problems and residual claims. *Journal of Law and Economics*, 26: 327–49.

Garven, J. R. and S. W. Pottier (1995) Incentive contracting and the role of participation rights in stock insurers. *Journal of Risk and Insurance*, 62: 253–70.

Hansmann, H. (1985) The organization of insurance companies: mutual versus stock. *Journal of Law, Economics, and Organization*, 1: 125–54.

Kim, W. J., D. Mayers, and C. W. Smith, Jr. (1996) On the choice of insurance distribution systems. *Journal of Risk and Insurance*, 63: 207–27.

Lamm-Tennant, J. and L. T. Starks (1993) Stock versus mutual ownership structures: the risk implications. *Journal of Business*, 66: 29–46.

Lee, S. J., D. Mayers, and C. W. Smith, Jr. (1997) Guaranty finds and risk-taking behavior: evidence from the insurance industry, *Journal of Financial Economics*, 44: 3–24.

Ligon, J. A. and P. D. Thistle (2005) The formation of mutual insurers in markets with adverse selection. *Journal of Business*, 78: 529–55.

Mayers, D., A. Shivdasani, and C. W. Smith, Jr. (1997) Board composition in the life insurance industry. *Journal of Business*, 70: 33–63.

Mayers, D. and C. W. Smith, Jr. (1981) Contractual provisions, organizational structure, and conflict control in insurance markets. *Journal of Business*, 54: 407–34.

Mayers, D. and C. W. Smith, Jr. (1986) Ownership structure and control: the mutualization of stock life insurance companies. *Journal of Financial Economics*, 16: 73–98.

Mayers, D. and C. W. Smith, Jr. (1988) Ownership structure across lines of property casualty insurance. *Journal of Law and Economics*, 31: 351–78.

Mayers, D. and C. W. Smith, Jr. (1990) On the corporate demand for insurance: evidence from the reinsurance market. *Journal of Business*, 63: 19–40.

Mayers, D. and C. W. Smith, Jr. (1992) Executive compensation in the life insurance industry. *Journal of Business*, 65: 51–74.

Mayers, D. and C. W. Smith, Jr. (1994) Managerial discretion, regulation, and stock insurer ownership structure. *Journal of Risk and Insurance*, 61: 638–55.

Rothschild, M. and J. E. Stiglitz (1976) Equilibrium in competitive insurance markets: an essay on the economics of imperfect information. *Quarterly Journal of Economics*, 90: 629–50.

Seog, S. H. (2006) Limited competition, information asymmetry, and the organizational forms. *Asia-Pacific Journal of Risk and Insurance*, 2: 64–76.

Smith, B. D. and M. J. Stutzer (1990) Adverse selection, aggregate uncertainty, and the role for mutual insurance contracts. *Journal of Business*, 63: 493–510.

Wells, B. P., L. A. Cox, and K. M. Gaver (1995) Free cash flow in the life insurance industry. *Journal of Risk and Insurance*, 62: 50–64.

Chapter 12

Competition in the Insurance Market

Insurance goods are distinguished from conventional goods such as foods and manufactured goods in many aspects. First of all, insurance goods are individual, in that different individuals may pay different prices and receive different benefits even if they purchase the same insurance from one insurer. The individuality of insurance is related to several issues. For example, the different risks of individuals will be reflected in insurance contracts. Since the risks of individuals are often private information, insurers try to figure out the risks. This is the information asymmetry issue considered earlier. Individuality also implies that the information regarding one insured's insurance is not very helpful in understanding another insured's insurance. Therefore, insureds as well as insurers are exposed to the incomplete information problem.

Another distinguishing characteristic of insurance is that insurance is a so-called experience good, implying that the true quality cannot be known, or is difficult to know, at the time of purchase. As a matter of fact, it is probably difficult to know the quality of insurance even after purchase, unless insureds experience accidents or losses. In this sense, the insurance good has "credence" attributes defined as those which cannot be evaluated in normal use (Darby and Karni, 1973).

The third important characteristic of insurance is that sales precede production, which reverses the normal order for conventional goods. At the time of sale, the insurer makes a promise that she will pay for a loss that may occur in the future. In exchange for the promise, the insurer receives the premium from the insured. However, it is impossible to fully understand and describe future events. In the jargon of contract theory, the existence of diverse transaction costs makes the insurance contract incomplete.

This incompleteness, in turn, causes conflicts between insurer and insured to occur. Important sources of conflicts include the insurer's insolvency and the different interpretation of the contract terms.

All of the distinguishing characteristics of insurance point to incomplete information. Having extensively studied the incomplete information of insurers in the earlier chapters, this chapter is focused on the incomplete information of insureds. The incompleteness of information of insureds will affect the competition among insurers. Price competition may not be very aggressive, even if there are many insurers, since low price may imply low quality. We may observe differential prices in the market with the same quality, if insureds need to incur costs to get information regarding prices. As a result, the traditional perfect competition model of economics fails to apply to the insurance market. We may observe diverse prices and diverse qualities in the market. This chapter will investigate the features of price and quality distributions in the insurance market. We start with a simple linear model of duopoly to investigate the product differentiation (Section 12.1). Then we move on to more sophisticated search models where price and/or quality are not observable, ex ante (Sections 12.2 and 12.3). We consider both sequential and nonsequential searches. A multi-period model is studied in Section 12.4. A competitive model is also discussed in Section 12.5.

12.1   Linear Model

The simplest model for product differentiation is a linear city model (D'Aspremont, Gabszewicz, and Thisse, 1979).[1] In a line segment [0, 1], insureds are uniformly distributed. There are two competing ex ante homogeneous insurers, denoted by i or j, where $i, j = 1, 2$. Insurers are profit maximizers. Insurers produce homogeneous insurance goods with zero costs. Insurers should decide on their locations on the line and prices (premiums).

Given the insurers' locations and prices, an insured will travel to an insurer's location to purchase insurance. Suppose that the insured's utility is given by

$$U = v - Q - T, \tag{12.1}$$

where v is the expected utility from the insurance consumption, Q is the price (premium), and T is the transportation cost. The transportation cost T depends

[1]   See also the circular city model of Schlesinger and Schulenburg (1991).

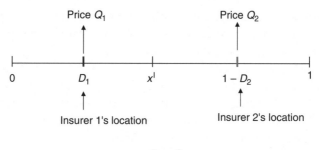

$$x^I = \frac{c[(1-D_2)^2 - D_1^2] + Q_2 - Q_1}{2c(1-D_2-D_1)}$$

Figure 12.1   Linear model.

on the distance of travel. For simplicity, we assume convex costs, $T(d) = cd^2$, where d is the distance that he travels and c is a positive constant. Suppose that an insurer is located at point x and offer price Q. When an insured purchases insurance from the insurer, his total costs are the sum of price Q and transportation costs T. Insureds will purchase insurance as long as its benefits are (weakly) greater than the total costs, which will be assumed in the model.

This problem can be stated as a two-stage game. Insurers find locations in stage 1 and prices in stage 2. In this setting, let us investigate a Nash equilibrium of the model. Let us tackle the stage 2 problem first. Suppose that insurers are located at points with distances D_1 and D_2 from the ends of the line, respectively ($D_1 + D_2 \le 1, D_1, D_2 \ge 0$), as depicted in Figure 12.1. Insurer i will determine an optimal price Q_i given insurer j's price Q_j.

Given locations, the profit function of insurer i is

$$\pi_i(Q_i, Q_j) = Q_i S_i(Q_i, Q_j), \text{ for } j \ne i,$$

where $S_i(., .)$ is the number of sales. Noting that insureds will select an insurer providing lower total costs, let us first find an insured who is indifferent between both insurers. If insured x (i.e., an insured who is located at point x) purchases from insurer 1, he will incur total costs of $c(x - D_1)^2 + Q_1$. If insured x purchases from insurer 2, he will incur total costs of $c(x - (1 - D_2))^2 + Q_2$. Therefore, insured x^I who is indifferent between two insurers will satisfy the equation

$$c(x - D_1)^2 + Q_1 = c(x - (1 - D_2))^2 + Q_2.$$

This gives

$$x^I = \frac{c[(1-D_2)^2 - D_1^2] + Q_2 - Q_1}{2c(1-D_2-D_1)}.$$

Assuming that all insureds purchase insurance, insurers' profits are

$$\pi_1(Q_1, Q_2) = Q_1 \frac{c[(1-D_2)^2 - D_1^2] + Q_2 - Q_1}{2c(1-D_2-D_1)},$$

$$\pi_2(Q_2, Q_1) = Q_2 \left\{ 1 - \frac{c[(1-D_2)^2 - D_1^2] + Q_2 - Q_1}{2c(1-D_2-D_1)} \right\}.$$

An optimal pricing will satisfy the first-order conditions (FOCs)

$$\partial\pi_1(Q_1, Q_2)/\partial Q_1 = 0 \quad \text{and} \quad \partial\pi_2(Q_2, Q_1)/\partial Q_2 = 0.$$

Solving these simultaneous equations for Q_1 and Q_2, we have

$$Q_1 = c(1-D_2-D_1)\left(1 + \frac{D_1-D_2}{3}\right),$$

$$Q_2 = c(1-D_2-D_1)\left(1 + \frac{D_2-D_1}{3}\right) \tag{12.2}$$

We assume that these prices are not high so that all insureds want to purchase insurance.

In stage 1, each insurer needs to find an optimal location, considering its effects on pricing in stage 2. Since (12.2) expresses prices as functions of locations, we plug them into the profit functions. Now profit functions can be expressed as functions of locations:

$$\pi_1^*(D_1, D_2) = \frac{1}{2}c\left(1 + \frac{D_1-D_2}{3}\right)^2 (1-D_2-D_1),$$

$$\pi_2^* (D_2, D_1) = \frac{1}{2}c\left(1 + \frac{D_2-D_1}{3}\right)^2 (1-D_2-D_1). \tag{12.3}$$

An optimal location can be found by calculating $\partial\pi_1^*(D_1, D_2)/\partial D_1$ and $\partial\pi_2^*(D_2, D_1)/\partial D_2$. A calculation shows that the derivatives have negative signs, $\partial\pi_i^*(D_i, D_j)/\partial D_i < 0$. As a result, the optimal locations are $D_1^* = D_2^* = 0$, implying that two insurers are located at the ends of the line, 0 and 1. Insurers want to be as far from each other as possible. In this case, prices become $c > 0$.

Proposition 12.1 In a linear model, insurers are located as far from each other as possible (i.e., at 0 and 1). Prices are above production costs.

Proof

$$\partial \pi_i^* (D_i, D_j) / \partial D_i = \frac{1}{2} c \left(1 + \frac{D_i - D_j}{3} \right) \frac{-1 - D_j - 3D_i}{3} < 0. \qquad \square$$

A crucial factor in the above result is the transportation costs. If no transportation costs are incurred, locations will not affect profits. In this case, prices will become zero, achieving a competitive level. Different locations are often interpreted as product differentiation such as different indemnity designs. Based on this interpretation, the result implies that insurance goods are differentiated as much as possible. The travel distance can be interpreted as the measure of mismatch between insured's preference and insurance goods. In sum, when insurance goods exhibit diverse characteristics over which insureds have different preferences, they are differentiated and prices are above competitive levels.

12.2   Price Search Model

The linear model does not take into account the quality of goods and search processes. Product differentiation in the linear model is horizontal in the sense that different insureds have different preferences (implied by different locations). Some characteristics of insurance may be vertical in the sense that all insureds have the same preference over them. For example, all insureds will prefer better services from insurers and lower insolvency probabilities. Such vertical characteristics will be referred to as qualities in this chapter. Moreover, qualities of insurance goods may be difficult to observe at time of purchase. The issues regarding quality differentiation will be studied in the next section.

In this section we investigate the case in which insureds do not know the precise price offers from insurers. Note that the linear model simply assumes that insureds already know all the prices that insurers offer. However, it may be difficult for an insured to get a right price, due to the individuality of insurance goods. Such incomplete information of insureds will lead to a less competitive market. Let us now formally consider the price search model.

In the price search model, it is assumed that insureds know of the price distribution, but do not know the prices offered by individual insurers. Insureds are identical except for their search costs. An insured is identified by his search cost. The search costs (and thus insureds) are uniformly distributed on $[0, C]$.

There are two insurers ($i = 1, 2$) that produce homogeneous insurance goods with possibly differential production costs. Suppose that insurer 1 is more efficient in production than insurer 2; $K_1 \leq K_2$, where K_i is the production cost of insure i. Assuming that $Q_1 \leq Q_2$, where Q_i is the price of insurer i, our focus is on the price distribution in an equilibrium. Write $S_i = S_i(Q_i, Q_j)$ for the number of sales of insurer i given prices Q_i and Q_j. Then, the profit of insurer i is

$$\pi_i = (Q_i - K_i)S_i.$$

The search pattern can be sequential or nonsequential. In a sequential search, the insured decides whether or not to search one more time after each search (Carlson and McAfee, 1983; MacMinn, 1980; Rob, 1985; Reinganum, 1979). His decision will depend on the marginal benefit from the additional search and the search costs. In general, there is a cutoff price that makes the insured indifferent between searching once more and stopping his search. The insured will keep searching until he finds a price lower than the cutoff price. In our simple model, the insured will search up to twice, since there are only two insurers.

In a nonsequential search, the insured decides how many times he will search, in the first step (Berger, Kleindorfer and Kunreuther, 1989; Burdett and Judd, 1983; MacMinn, 1980; Seog, 2002). The number of searches will be determined by comparing the marginal benefits of additional search and the search cost. In the second step, he searches as many times as determined in the first step. In the third and final step, he selects the lowest price among the prices that he obtained. In our simple model, the number of searches will be one or two, depending on the search cost. The general implications of the outcomes of both search models are similar as seen below. In both models, inefficient insurers can survive and prices are dispersed. In the following sections, we consider simplified versions of search models in a duopoly.

12.2.1   Sequential search

Insureds determine whether or not they make another search, given the price distribution. Since we are considering a duopoly, an insured will search once or twice. Suppose that the insured with search costs c searched once and has price quote Q_i. If he makes another search, then his benefit will be $\max[Q_i - Q_j, 0]$. Thus, he will search once more if $\max[Q_i - Q_j, 0] - c \geq 0$.

Price dispersion.   Let us first consider the case $Q_2 > Q_1$. In the first search, one half of insureds will visit insurer 1 offering lower price Q_1. They will not search again. The other half of insureds will visit first insurer 2 offering higher price, Q_2. Given Q_2, insureds with search costs lower than c^S will visit insurer 1 where $c^S = Q_2 - Q_1$.

The number of sales of each insurer becomes

$$S_1 = C/2 + (Q_2 - Q_1)/2, \quad S_2 = C/2 - (Q_2 - Q_1)/2. \quad [2] \tag{12.4}$$

Profits are

$$\pi_1 = (Q_1 - K_1)(C - Q_1 + Q_2)/2, \quad \pi_2 = (Q_2 - K_2)(C - Q_2 + Q_1)/2 \tag{12.5}$$

Assuming Cournot–Nash duopolistic competition, FOCs for optimal prices are

$$\begin{aligned}
\partial \pi_1 / \partial Q_1 &= (C - Q_1 + Q_2)/2 - (Q_1 - K_1)/2 = 0 \\
&\Rightarrow Q_1 = (C + Q_2 + K_1)/2, \\
\partial \pi_2 / \partial Q_2 &= (C - Q_2 + Q_1)/2 - (Q_2 - K_2)/2 = 0 \\
&\Rightarrow Q_2 = (C + Q_1 + K_2)/2
\end{aligned} \tag{12.6}$$

leading to

$$Q_1 = C + (2K_1 + K_2)/3, \quad Q_2 = C + (2K_2 + K_1)/3. \tag{12.7}$$

Note that $Q_2 - Q_1 = (K_2 - K_1)/3 > 0$. The average price is

$$EQ = (K_1 + K_2)/2 + C, \tag{12.8}$$

that is, the average production cost plus the largest search cost. Note also that $Q_i - K_i \geq 0$ as long as two insurers exist. In an equilibrium, the market shares are given by

$$S_1 = (3C + K_2 - K_1)/6, \quad S_2 = (3C + K_1 - K_2)/6. \tag{12.9}$$

The equilibrium profits are

$$\pi_1 = (3C + K_2 - K_1)^2/18, \quad \pi_2 = (3C + K_1 - K_2)^2/18 \tag{12.10}$$

From the analysis above, we find that prices are dispersed in an equilibrium, $Q_1 \leq Q_2$. Prices are above the production costs, $Q_i \geq K_i$. If insureds are perfectly informed (i.e., search costs are zero), then only efficient insurers will survive. Inefficient insurers can survive due to the incomplete information of insureds. The results of the analysis are summarized in the following proposition and in Table 12.1.

---

[2]   For simplicity, we assume that the reservation prices of insureds are high enough that all insureds will purchase insurance with prices that will be determined in the following analysis.

Table 12.1 Sequential price search model

	Production cost	Price	Profit	Market share
Insurer 1	K_1	$Q_1 = C$ $+(2K_1+K_2)/3$	$\pi_1 = (3C$ $+K_2-K_1)^2/18$	$S_1 = (3C$ $+K_2-K_1)/6$
Insurer 2	K_2	$Q_2 = C$ $+(2K_2+K_1)/3$	$\pi_2 = (3C$ $+K_1-K_2)^2/18$	$S_2 = (3C$ $+K_1-K_2)/6$

Proposition 12.2 (Sequential search).

(a) Price dispersion may be observed. In price dispersion, the average price is determined as the average production cost plus the largest search cost. The range of prices $(Q_2 - Q_1)$ increases, as the range of production costs $(K_2 - K_1)$ increases.

(b) Inefficient insurers can survive and profits are positive.

Proof See the text above. The average price is obtained from (12.8) and the range of prices is obtained from (12.7). □

The welfare losses of insureds can be clarified by comparing the above result with the case of complete information, when both insurers are efficient, $K_2 = K_1$. Our result implies that $Q_1 = Q_2 = C + K_1$. The profits of insurers are $\pi_1 = \pi_2 = C^2/2$. Under complete information, however, the price competition will lead to $Q_1 = Q_2 = K_1$. The profits of insurers are zero and a competitive outcome is achieved. Therefore, compared with the case of complete information, under incomplete information, prices are higher by C and profits are higher by $C^2/2$. Insureds have to incur higher costs to purchase insurance due to the higher prices, in addition to the search costs.

12.2.2 Nonsequential search

Now suppose that insureds perform nonsequential searches. In the non-sequential search, an insured first determines his number of searches by comparing the marginal benefits of additional searches and the search cost. Then, he makes that number of searches. Lastly, he selects the lowest price among the prices that he obtained. In our simple duopoly model, the number of searches will be one or two, depending on the search cost.

Price dispersion. Suppose that $Q_2 > Q_1$. When an insured searches once, the expected price is $EQ = (Q_1 + Q_2)/2$. If the insured searches twice, the price will be $\min[Q_1, Q_2] = Q_1$. Assuming that the insured's search cost is c, the optimal number of searches will be two if and only if the marginal benefit is higher than his search cost, that is, $c \leq c^N = (Q_2 - Q_1)/2$.

Given this search behavior, the number of sales of each insurer becomes

$$S_1 = c^N + (1/2)(C - c^N), \quad S_2 = (1/2)(C - c^N). \tag{12.11}$$

Profits are

$$\begin{aligned}
\pi_1 &= (Q_1 - K_1)\{c^N + (C - c^N)/2\} \\
&= \tfrac{1}{2}(Q_1 - K_1)\{C + (Q_2 - Q_1)/2\}, \\
\pi_2 &= (Q_2 - K_2)(C - c^N)/2 \\
&= \tfrac{1}{2}(Q_2 - K_2)\{C - (Q_2 - Q_1)/2\}.
\end{aligned} \tag{12.12}$$

The optimal price will be determined by the FOCs

$$\begin{aligned}
\partial \pi_1 / \partial Q_1 &= 0 \Rightarrow 2Q_1 = Q_2 + K_1 + 2C, \\
\partial \pi_2 / \partial Q_2 &= 0 \Rightarrow 2Q_2 = Q_1 + K_2 + 2C,
\end{aligned} \tag{12.13}$$

leading to

$$Q_1 = 2C + \tfrac{1}{3}(2K_1 + K_2), \quad Q_2 = 2C + \tfrac{1}{3}(2K_2 + K_1). \tag{12.14}$$

Note that $Q_2 - Q_1 = (K_2 - K_1)/3$, and the average price is $E(Q) = (K_1 + K_2)/2 + C$, as in the sequential search case. The average price is higher than the average production cost by the largest search cost.

Equilibrium profits are

$$\begin{aligned}
\pi_1 &= \tfrac{1}{2}(Q_1 - K_1)\{C + (Q_2 - Q_1)/2\} = (6C + K_2 - K_1)^2/36, \\
\pi_2 &= \tfrac{1}{2}(Q_2 - K_2)\{C - (Q_2 - Q_1)/2\} = (6C + K_1 - K_2)^2/36.
\end{aligned} \tag{12.15}$$

Similar to the sequential search case, inefficient insurers survive and earn positive profits. Prices are dispersed in an equilibrium. The results of the analysis are summarized in the following proposition and in Table 12.2.

Proposition 12.3 (Nonsequential search).

(a)   Price dispersion may be observed. In price dispersion, the average price is determined as the average production cost plus the largest search cost. The range of prices $(Q_2 - Q_1)$ increases as the range of production costs $(K_2 - K_1)$ increases.

(b)   Inefficient insurers can survive and profits are positive.

Table 12.2   Non-sequential price search model

	Production cost	Price	Profit	Market share
Insurer 1	K_1	$Q_1 = 2C$ $+ (2K_1 + K_2)/3$	$\pi_1 = (6C$ $+ K_2 - K_1)^2/36$	$S_1 = (6C$ $+ K_2 - K_1)/12$
Insurer 2	K_2	$Q_2 = 2C$ $+ (2K_2 + K_1)/3$	$\pi_2 = (6C$ $+ K_1 - K_2)^2/36$	$S_2 = (6C$ $+ K_1 - K_2)/12$

Proof See text above. The average price and the range of prices are obtained from (12.14). □

12.3   Price and Quality Search Model

Now let us consider the case in which insurance goods are differentiated by a vertical characteristic, that is, quality (MacMinn, 1986; MacMinn and Seog, 2008; Riordan, 1986; Shaked and Sutton, 1982). Qualities are distinguished from horizontal characteristics of the linear model in Section 12.1, in that all insureds have the same preferences over quality while they may have different preferences over horizontal characteristics. When the quality is observable at time of purchase, insureds make their purchase decision based on price and quality after search. Given price and quality, the insured can fully evaluate the good.

On the other hand, the quality of insurance is often not observable at time of purchase. In such a case, insureds may not fully evaluate the good at time of purchase, since price provides only partial information regarding the good. This information asymmetry may create an adverse selection problem, which causes costs in addition to the price search costs.

12.3.1   Observable quality

In the setting of the previous section, let us introduce the quality of insurer i, A_i, where $A_1 < A_2$. We may interpret the situation as saying that insurer 2 incurs a high cost to produce a high-quality insurance good. Now, unlike in the previous section, insurer 2 is not necessarily less efficient than insurer 1. The profit of insurer i is determined as before, $\pi_i = (Q_i - K_i)S_i$.

We also assume that insureds are willing to pay B more for high-quality goods than for low-quality goods. Before search, insureds know the price distribution, but do not know about the prices and the qualities of goods offered by individual insurers. Insureds are assumed to perform sequential searches. It is assumed that quality is observable at time of purchase.

Price and quality dispersion.   Our concern is with the existence of the price and quality dispersion in an equilibrium. Let us focus on the case of $Q_1 < Q_2$. Consider an insured with search cost c, given price distribution Q_1 and Q_2.

Suppose first that he visits insurer 1 quoting price Q_1. He will want to search once more if $Q_1 - (Q_2 - B) > c$. Let $c^* = Q_1 - Q_2 + B$. Then an insured with search cost $c < c^*$ will search twice if he happens to visit insurer 1 at the first search. Similarly, suppose that an insured visits insurer 2 quoting price Q_2. He will want to search once more if $(Q_2 - B) - Q_1 > c$, or $c < c^{**} = Q_2 - Q_1 - B$. Note that the signs of c^* and c^{**} are opposite. Thus, one of c^* and c^{**}, not both, is relevant in an equilibrium.

When $Q_2 - Q_1 \leq B$, c^* is relevant. In this case, the price difference is less than the additional benefit. Therefore, insureds with low search costs are willing to purchase the high-quality good despite spending more in search costs. When $Q_2 - Q_1 > B$, c^{**} is relevant. In this case, the price difference is greater than the additional benefit. Therefore, insureds with low search costs are willing to purchase the low-quality good despite spending more in search costs.

Case 1: $Q_2 - Q_1 \leq B$. The numbers of sales become

$$S_1 = (C - c^*)/2 = (C + Q_2 - Q_1 - B)/2,$$
$$S_2 = c^* + (C - c^*)/2 = (C + Q_1 - Q_2 + B)/2. \tag{12.16}$$

Note that $S_2 \geq S_1$. The profits are

$$\pi_1 = (Q_1 - K_1)(C + Q_2 - Q_1 - B)/2,$$
$$\pi_2 = (Q_2 - K_2)(C + Q_1 - Q_2 + B)/2. \tag{12.17}$$

The FOCs for optimal pricing are

$$\partial \pi_1/\partial Q_1 = (C + Q_2 - Q_1 - B)/2 - (Q_1 - K_1)/2 = 0,$$
$$\partial \pi_2/\partial Q_2 = (C + Q_1 - Q_2 + B)/2 - (Q_2 - K_2)/2 = 0, \tag{12.18}$$

leading to

$$Q_1 = (C + Q_2 + K_1 - B)/3, \quad Q_2 = (C + Q_1 + K_2 + B)/3. \tag{12.19}$$

By solving these simultaneous equations, we have equilibrium prices as follows:

$$Q_1 = C + (2K_1 + K_2 - B)/3, \quad Q_2 = C + (2K_2 + K_1 + B)/3. \tag{12.20}$$

Note that $Q_2 - Q_1 = (K_2 - K_1 + 2B)/3$. The average price $E(Q) = (K_1 + K_2)/2 + C$, as in the price search model of the previous section. Again, the average price is higher than the average production cost by the largest search cost.

The condition that $Q_2 - Q_1 \leq B$ reduces to that $K_2 - K_1 \leq B$ in the equilibrium. The production of insurer 2 is efficient in that the additional benefit B is greater than the increased production cost $K_2 - K_1$. Equilibrium numbers of sales are

$$S_1 = (3C + K_2 - K_1 - B)/6, \quad S_2 = (3C + K_1 - K_2 + B)/6. \tag{12.21}$$

Equilibrium profits are

$$\pi_1 = (3C + K_2 - K_1 - B)^2/18, \quad \pi_2 = (3C + K_1 - K_2 + B)^2/18. \tag{12.22}$$

Note that $\pi_1 \leq \pi_2$. For positive profits, we assume that $C \geq -(K_2 - K_1 - B)/3$.

Observe that prices are above production costs and profits are positive. The inefficient insurer (insurer 1 in this case) can survive. In sum, results are qualitatively similar to the same quality case ($B = 0$) of the previous section.

Case 2: $Q_2 - Q_1 > B$. The numbers of sales are

$$S_1 = c^{**} + (C - c^{**})/2 = (C + Q_2 - Q_1 - B)/2,$$
$$S_2 = (C - c^{**})/2 = (C + Q_1 - Q_2 + B)/2. \tag{12.23}$$

Note that $S_1 > S_2$. The equations have the same forms as in case 1. In fact, all other equations are also the same as those in case 1. Using the results of case 1, we have equilibrium prices.

$$Q_1 = C + (2K_1 + K_2 - B)/3, \quad Q_2 = C + (2K_2 + K_1 + B)/3. \tag{12.24}$$

Note that $Q_2 - Q_1 = (K_2 - K_1 + 2B)/3$. The average price is $E(Q) = (K_1 + K_2)/2 + C$, as in case 1.

Now the condition that $Q_2 - Q_1 > B$ reduces to that $K_2 - K_1 > B$. The production of insurer 2 is inefficient in that the additional benefit B is less than the increased production cost $K_2 - K_1$. The equilibrium numbers of sales and the profits are

$$S_1 = (3C + K_2 - K_1 - B)/6, \quad S_2 = (3C + K_1 - K_2 + B)/6. \tag{12.25}$$

The equilibrium profits are

$$\pi_1 = (3C + K_2 - K_1 - B)^2/18, \quad \pi_2 = (3C + K_1 - K_2 + B)^2/18. \tag{12.26}$$

Table 12.3   Price and quality search model

	Production cost and quality	Price	Profit	Market share
Insurer 1	K_1, A_1	$Q_1 = C + (2K_1 + K_2 - B)/3$	$\pi_1 = (3C + K_2 - K_1 - B)^2/18$	$S_1 = (3C + K_2 - K_1 - B)/6$
Insurer 2	K_2, A_2	$Q_2 = C + (2K_2 + K_1 + B)/3$	$\pi_2 = (3C + K_1 - K_2 + B)^2/18$	$S_2 = (3C + K_1 - K_2 + B)/6$

Note that $\pi_1 > \pi_2$. For positive profits, we assume that $C \geq (K_2 - K_1 - B)/3$. The results are qualitatively similar to case 1. Prices are above production costs and profits are positive. The inefficient insurer (insurer 2 in this case) can survive. The results of the analysis are summarized in the following proposition and in Table 12.3.

Proposition 12.4 (Observable quality).

(a)   Price and quality dispersion is observed. In such a case, the average price is determined as the average production cost plus the largest search cost. The range of prices $(Q_2 - Q_1)$ increases as the range of production costs $(K_2 - K_1)$ increases.
(b)   Inefficient insurers can survive and profits are positive.

Proof See text above. The average price and the range of prices are obtained from (12.20) and (12.24). □

12.3.2   Unobservable quality

If quality is not observable at time of purchase, an adverse selection problem arises, which leads to different results. For this, consider case 1 of the previous subsection. While insurer 2 has no incentive to offer Q_1, insurer 1 may have an incentive to mimic insurer 2 (i.e., offering Q_2), since it will produce a higher profit when insureds believe her to be a high-quality insurer. In such a case, insureds will not switch insurers, and the profit of insurer 1 becomes

$$\pi_1' = (Q_2 - K_1)(C/2) > \pi_1 = (Q_1 - K_1)(C - c^*)/2. \qquad (12.27)$$

Therefore, the equilibrium collapses. Since insureds cannot observe the quality, the low-quality insurer will announce that she produces high-quality goods.[3]

---

[3]   We do not seek an equilibrium in this case, since the next section will investigate this issue in a two-period model.

On the other hand, the results in case 2 of the previous subsection may still hold, since the high-quality insurer is less efficient than the low-quality insurer. By mimicking insurer 2, insurer 1 will earn a higher margin but lose market share. Thus, it is possible that insurer 1 does not mimic insurer 2. Similarly, insurer 2 may not want to mimic insurer 1, since it will lower the margin, although the market share will increase. In sum, it is possible that neither insurer may want to mimic the other insurer, leading to a separation.

In addition, if insurers can determine qualities, then no insurer will produce high-quality goods, since lowering quality will increase profits. The only possible result is that all insurers produce the low quality, so that a lemons market is obtained.

12.4   Multi-period Model with Unobservable Quality

Although the quality is not observable at time of purchase, it may be observable in the process of consumption. The effect of such quality revelation cannot be investigated in one-period models. On the other hand, it is also recognized that insurance has credence attributes, so that the qualities of insurance goods are not easy to observe even during normal consumption. For example, if an insured does not experience an accident, he may not know the true quality of his insurance. Reflecting these factors, we consider a simple two-period model as follows. Our discussion is based on MacMinn and Seog (2008).

To focus on the quality revelation issue, let us assume that insureds can fully observe prices, or, equivalently, the search cost is zero. The total number of insureds is normalized to be 1. There are two insurers as before. The quality of insurer i's good is denoted by A_i, with $A_1 < A_2$. Define $B = A_2 - A_1$. We assume that an insurer should incur production cost K_i to produce A_i-quality insurance, where $K_2 > K_1$. Each insurer determines prices in period 1, effective through period 2. In each period, insureds should make purchase decisions. Insureds cannot directly observe the quality at time of purchase. However, quality is revealed at the end of the period with probability r. Insureds are homogeneous and utilities in each period are denoted by

$$U = A - Q, \tag{12.28}$$

where A is the quality and Q is price.

As a reference, let us first consider the case of observable qualities. Note that the minimum $Q_i = K_i$. Since insureds also observe the prices, insurer 2 will set $Q_2 = Q_1 + B - \varepsilon$ as long as $Q_2 \geq K_2$, for arbitrarily small $\varepsilon > 0$. Likewise, insurer 1 will set $Q_1 = Q_2 - B - \varepsilon$ as long as $Q_1 \geq K_1$. Therefore, if $K_2 < K_1 + B$ (insurer 2 is more efficient), then only insurer 2 survives, and $Q_2 = K_1 + B$. If $K_2 > K_1 + B$ (insurer 1 is more efficient), then only insurer 1 survives, and $Q_1 = K_2 - B$. In summary:

$$\text{if } K_2 < K_1 + B, \text{ then } Q_2 = K_1 + B, \pi_2 = (K_1 + B - K_2)2;$$
$$\text{if } K_2 > K_1 + B, \text{ then } Q_1 = K_2 - B, \pi_1 = (K_2 - B - K_1)2; \qquad (12.29)$$
$$\text{if } K_2 = K_1 + B, \text{ then } Q_1 = K_1, Q_2 = K_2, \pi_1 = \pi_2 = 0.$$

When the quality is observable, only efficient insurers can survive in the market. Now, let us seek the equilibrium outcomes when qualities are not observable. It is easy to see that there is, generically, no separating equilibrium in which different quality insurers quote different prices.

When qualities are separated at time of purchase, the situation is equivalent to the case of observable qualities. As seen above, there is no separating equilibrium unless $K_2 = K_1 + B$. The outcome is described by (12.29). The nonexistence of a separating equilibrium is mainly due to the assumption that insureds can fully observe prices.

In a pooling equilibrium, different quality insurers quote the same price. Since qualities are not revealed in period 1, insureds will purchase randomly from either insurer. At the end of period 1, quality is revealed with probability r. Given that quality is revealed, the insureds who purchase from the low-quality insurer (i.e., insurer 1) will switch to insurer 2. Thus, the numbers of intertemporal sales are

$$S_1 = (2-r)/2, \quad S_2 = (2+r)/2. \qquad (12.30)$$

Insurers' profits are

$$\pi_1 = (Q - K_1)(2-r)/2, \quad \pi_2 = (Q - K_2)(2+r)/2 \qquad (12.31)$$

In this case, the expected utility of the insured in period 1 is

$EA - Q,$

and in period 2 is

$\frac{1}{2}\{rA_2 + (1-r)A_1 + A_2\} - Q.$

Therefore, the intertemporal expected utility is

$$EU(Q) = EA - Q + \tfrac{1}{2}\{rA_2 + (1-r)A_1 + A_2\} - Q$$
$$= 2A_1 + (2+r)B/2 - 2Q. \qquad (12.32)$$

This outcome can be an equilibrium if insurers do not have an incentive to deviate from offering price Q. To maximize the equilibrium possibility, let us assume that insureds believe that off-the-equilibrium prices are offered by a low-quality insurer. Now, let us check for the possibility of deviation. Suppose that insurer 1 wants to deviate to price Q'. Since insureds consider the deviator a low-quality insurer, the highest possible price Q' should be determined as follows:[4]

$$EU(Q) = EU(Q' : A_1), \tag{12.33}$$

where $EU(Q' : A_1) = 2A_1 - 2Q'$, the expected utility when the insured purchase from the low-quality insurer. Thus,

$$Q' = Q - (2+r)B/4. \tag{12.34}$$

For insurer 1 not to deviate, her profit from deviation should be lower than the equilibrium profit. Thus,

$$\pi_1' = (Q - (2+r)B/4 - K_1)2 \leq (Q - K_1)(2-r)/2. \tag{12.35}$$

leading to

$$Q \leq K_1 + B. \tag{12.36}$$

Once condition (12.36) holds, insurer 1 does not deviate from the equilibrium. By a similar logic, insurer 2 will not deviate if

$$Q \leq K_2 + \frac{2+r}{2-r}B. \tag{12.37}$$

Since the right-hand side of (12.37) is greater than the right-hand side of (12.36), no insurer will deviate if (12.36) holds. For a high-quality insurer to exist, $Q \geq K_2$, which, combined with (12.36), requires $K_2 - K_1 \leq B$. Thus, a high-quality insurer can survive only if she is efficient. However, a low-quality insurer can survive although she is inefficient. The results are summarized as follows.

---

[4]   There are two technical problems that we ignore in this treatment. First, we are ignoring the possibility that the insurer who does not sell in period 1 may wait until she can sell in period 2. We assume that the insurer who does not make any sale in period 1 should exit the market. Another technical problem arises, since beliefs regarding the deviator will also determine beliefs regarding the other insurer. This is mainly due to the duopoly setting. Since the duopoly setting is considered solely for expository simplicity, we ignore the change of beliefs regarding the nondeviator. However, incorporating those technical factors into the model does not substantially change our results.

Proposition 12.5 (Unobservable quality in a two-period model).

(a)   Generically, no separating equilibrium exists.

(b)   A pooling equilibrium may exist, in which insurers offer the same price. The pooling price is between the high-quality production cost (K_2) and the low-quality production cost plus the quality benefit ($K_1 + B$).

(c)   In a pooling equilibrium, quality dispersion is observed. The high-quality insurer can survive only if she is efficient. However, the low-quality insurer can survive even if she is inefficient.

(d)   In a pooling equilibrium, the profit and sales per period of the high-quality insurer increases, while the profit and sales per period of the low-quality insurer decreases.

Proof See the text above.   □

12.5   Competitive Model

We now consider a competitive case based on MacMinn (1980). The search costs of insureds are uniformly distributed on $[0, C]$, $c \sim U[0, C]$. The total number of insureds is normalized as one. Insureds are identified with their search costs. The cumulative distribution is c/C. Each insured purchases at most one good. The number of insurers is also normalized as one. Production costs are uniformly distributed on $[\underline{K}, \overline{K}]$, that is, $K \sim U[\underline{K}, \overline{K}]$. The distribution function and the density function of production costs are denoted by $H(K)$ and $h(K)$, respectively, where $h(K) = 1/(\overline{K} - \underline{K})$.

Each insured has a reservation (or critical) price that is defined as the price, such that he will buy the good, once he finds a price lower than or equal to the price. An insured's reservation price depends on his search cost.

Let us denote the price distribution and the density function by $F(Q)$ and $f(Q)$ with support $[\underline{Q}, \overline{Q}]$, with expected price μ, and standard deviation σ.

12.5.1   Reservation price

Consider an insured with search cost c. His reservation price, say R, is determined as follows. By definition, he will search once more if and only if the price Q that he obtained is higher than R. Thus, R should equalize between the search cost and the marginal benefit of one more search: $c = g(R)$, where $g(R)$ is the marginal benefit of search.

The marginal benefit is

$$g(R) = \int_{\underline{Q}}^{R} (R - Q)dF(Q) = \int_{\underline{Q}}^{R} F(Q)dQ,$$

where the second equality follows by integration by parts. Note that $g'(R) = F(R)$. The ex ante expected total search costs are $c/F(R)$, since $1/F(R)$ is the expected number of searches. Thus, the expected total price, which is the sum of price and the total search costs, becomes

$$\begin{aligned}
E(Q \mid Q \le R) + \frac{c}{F(R)} &= \frac{1}{F(R)} \left[\int_{\underline{Q}}^{R} QdF(Q) + c \right] \\
&\qquad\qquad\qquad\qquad\qquad\qquad\qquad (12.38)\\
&= \frac{1}{F(R)} \left[\int_{\underline{Q}}^{R} QdF(Q) + \int_{\underline{Q}}^{R} (R - Q)dF(Q) \right] = R
\end{aligned}$$

That is, reservation price R is none other than the expected total price that the insured expects to spend. Define $\bar{R}$ by $C = g(\bar{R})$. Since insurers who offer a price higher than $\bar{R}$ cannot make a sale, the highest price should be at most $\bar{R}$. Thus, for the insured with C,

$$C = g(\bar{R}) = \int_{\underline{Q}}^{\bar{R}} (\bar{R} - Q)dF(Q) = \bar{R} - \mu, \quad \text{or} \quad \bar{R} = C + \mu. \qquad (12.39)$$

12.5.2   Demand function

Now let us find the demand function for prices lower than (or equal to) Q. First of all, all insureds with reservation prices lower than Q will buy the good with price lower than Q. On the other hand, the insureds with reservation prices higher than Q may purchase goods with prices above Q, since they randomly select prices below the reservation prices. Consider an insured with reservation cost $R > Q$. The probability that he will end up with prices lower than Q is $F(Q \mid Q' \le R)$, where Q' represents the random variable of price. Given our assumption, the number (density) of insureds with each search cost is $1/C$. Thus, the expected demand from insureds with reservation price R $(> Q)$ is $(1/C)F(Q \mid Q' \le R)$. Note that

$$F(Q \mid Q' \le R) = \begin{cases} \dfrac{F(Q)}{F(R)}, & \text{for } R > Q \\ 1, & \text{for } R \le Q \end{cases}$$

Summation across all insureds will give the expected total demand at prices lower than Q,

$$\frac{1}{C}\left[\int_{g(\underline{R})}^{g(Q)} 1dc + \int_{g(Q)}^{g(\bar{R})} \frac{F(Q)}{F(g^{-1}(c))}dc\right]. \tag{12.40}$$

Differentiating this expression with respect to Q gives the expected demand at price Q,

$$D(Q)=\frac{1}{C}\int_{g(Q)}^{g(\bar{R})} \frac{f(Q)}{F(g^{-1}(c))}dc. \tag{12.41}$$

Now a change of variable and the fact that $g'(R) = F(R)$ leads to

$$\frac{1}{C}\int_{g(Q)}^{g(\bar{R})} \frac{f(Q)}{F(g^{-1}(c))}dc = \frac{1}{C}\int_{Q}^{\bar{R}} \frac{f(Q)}{F(R)}g'(R)dR$$

$$= \frac{1}{C}\int_{Q}^{\bar{R}} f(Q)dR = (1/C)f(Q)(\bar{R}-Q) \tag{12.42}$$

$$= \frac{1}{C}f(Q)(C+\mu-Q).$$

Since the number of insurers quoting price Q is $f(Q)$, the demand for an insurer quoting price Q becomes

$$S(Q)=\frac{1}{C}(C+\mu-Q). \tag{12.43}$$

12.5.3   Pricing

The profit function of an insurer with production cost K becomes

$$\pi(Q)=(Q-K)(1/C)(C+\mu-Q). \tag{12.44}$$

The profit maximizing price is determined by

$$Q=\phi(K)=(K+\mu+C)/2. \tag{12.45}$$

Taking expectations of both sides gives

$$\mu=E(K)+C. \tag{12.46}$$

That is, the average price is the sum of the average production costs and the highest search cost. As in the duopoly case, the average price is above the average costs. From (12.45),

$$K = \phi^{-1}(Q) = 2Q - (\mu + C), \tag{12.47}$$

$$\bar{K} = 2\bar{Q} - (\mu + C), \quad \text{and} \quad \underline{K} = 2\underline{Q} - (\mu + C). \tag{12.48}$$

From (12.46),

$$\phi^{-1}(Q) = 2Q - (E(K) + 2C). \tag{12.49}$$

Since $\bar{R} = C + \mu$ from (12.39), the highest price Q can make a positive sale if $\bar{K} \le 2C + E(K)$. We will assume that this is the case in the discussion below.

12.5.4   Price dispersion

Since different K leads to different price, we have

$$F(Q) = H(\phi^{-1}(Q)).$$

Thus,

$$f(Q) = h(\phi^{-1}(Q))\phi^{-1'}(Q) = 2h(2Q - [E(K) + 2C]).$$

Given that the cost distribution is also uniform, the resulting price distribution is also uniform, $U[\underline{Q}, \bar{Q}]$:

$$f(Q) = \frac{1}{\bar{Q} - \underline{Q}}, \quad F(Q) = \frac{Q - \underline{Q}}{\bar{Q} - \underline{Q}}.$$

The average price becomes

$$\mu = \frac{\underline{Q} + \bar{Q}}{2}.$$

Then, from (12.48), the boundary prices are

$$\bar{Q} = (3\bar{K} + \underline{K} + 4C)/4, \quad \underline{Q} = (3\underline{K} + \bar{K} + 4C)/4. \tag{12.50}$$

As a result, the average price can be expressed as

$$\mu = (\bar{K} + \underline{K})/2 + C. \tag{12.51}$$

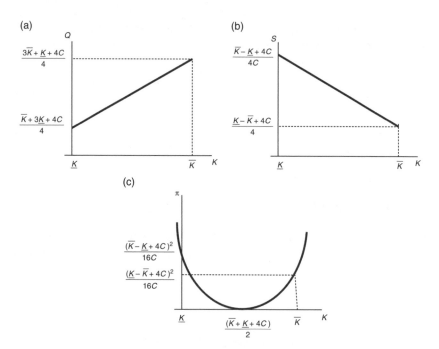

Figure 12.2   Competitive price search model: distribution of (a) price; (b) insurer demand; (c) profit.

Now,

$$Q = (K + \mu + C)/2 = \frac{(2K + \bar{K} + \underline{K} + 4C)}{4},$$ (12.52)

$$S(Q) = \frac{1}{C} \cdot \frac{(-2K + \bar{K} + \underline{K} + 4C)}{4},$$ (12.53)

$$\pi(Q) = \frac{1}{C} \cdot \frac{(-2K + \bar{K} + \underline{K} + 4C)^2}{16}.$$ (12.54)

The results of the analysis are summarized in the following proposition and in Figure 12.2.

Proposition 12.6 (Competitive model).

(a)   Price dispersion may be observed. In the price dispersion, the average price is determined as the average production cost plus the largest search cost. The range of prices $(\bar{Q} - \underline{Q})$ increases as the range of production costs $(\bar{K} - \underline{K})$ increases.

(b)   Inefficient insurers can survive and profits are positive.

Proof See the text above. The average price is obtained from (12.51) and the range of prices is obtained from (12.50).   □

The average price is the average production cost plus the largest search cost. This result is consistent with the duopoly models in Sections 12.2 and 12.3. Note also that most results are qualitatively the same as the duopoly case considered in earlier sections. That is, regardless of models, price dispersion may well be observed and inefficient insurers can survive. Profits are above the competitive levels. When qualities are differentiated, quality dispersion as well as price dispersion may be observed.

Our results above also show that price dispersion tends to disappear, as the difference between production costs goes to zero. That is, the production costs differential is a key element for the price dispersion. However, some researchers show that price dispersion may still exist even if production costs are the same (Burdett and Judd, 1983; Seog, 2002).

12.6   Conclusion

Incomplete information is one of the main characteristics of the insurance market. Incomplete information of insurers is often referred to as moral hazard and adverse selection, which is investigated in the earlier chapters. Incomplete information of insureds also arises, since insurance contracts are not easily understood and the solvency of insurers is uncertain. This incomplete information of insureds opens the possibility of less severe competition. As shown in this chapter, price dispersion is possible, inefficient insurers may survive, and profits are positive, even if the market can be described as competitive.

BIBLIOGRAPHY

Akerlof, G. A. (1970) The market for 'lemons': quality and the market mechanism. *Quarterly Journal of Economics*, 84: 488–500.

Bagwell, K. (1991) Optimal export policy for a new-product monopoly. *American Economic Review*, 81: 1156–69.

Berger, L. (1988) Word-of-mouth reputation in auto insurance markets. *Journal of Economic Behavior and Organization*, 10: 225–34.

Berger, L., P. Kleindorfer, and H. Kunreuther (1989) Dynamic model of the transmission of price information in auto insurance markets. *Journal of Risk and Insurance*, 56: 17–33.

Burdett, K. and K. Judd (1983) Equilibrium price dispersion. *Econometrica*, 51: 955–69.

Butters, G. R. (1977) Equilibrium distributions and the economics of information. *Review of Economic Studies*, 44: 465–91.

Carlson, J. and R. P. McAfee (1983) Discrete equilibrium price dispersion. *Journal of Political Economy*, 91: 480–93.

Dahlby, B. and D. West (1986) Price dispersion in an automobile insurance market. *Journal of Political Economy*, 94: 418–38.

Darby, M. R. and E. Karni (1973) Free competition and the optimal amount of fraud. *Journal of Law and Economics*, 16: 67–88.

D'Aspremont, C., J. J. Gabszewicz, and J.-F. Thisse (1979), On Hotelling's "Stability in competition." *Econometrica*, 47: 1145–50.

Lippman, S. A. and J. J. McCall (1979) *Studies in the Economics of Search.* Amsterdam: North-Holland.

MacMinn, R. D. (1980) Search and market equilibrium. *Journal of Political Economy*, 88: 308–27.

MacMinn, R. D. (1986) Search and the market for lemons. *Information Economics and Policy*, 2: 137–47.

MacMinn, R. D. and S. H. Seog (2008) Distribution of price and quality under information asymmetry. KAIST Business School Working Paper. http://ssrn.com/abstract=1182002.

Matthewson, G. (1983) Information, search and price variability of individual life insurance contracts. *Journal of Industrial Economics*, 32: 131–48.

Reinganum, J. (1979) A simple model of equilibrium price dispersion. *Journal of Political Economy*, 87: 851–8.

Riordan, M. H. (1986) Monopolistic competition with experience goods. *Quarterly Journal of Economics*, 101: 265–79.

Rob, R. (1985) Equilibrium price distributions. *Review of Economic Studies*, 52: 487–504.

Salop, S. and J. E. Stiglitz (1977) Bargains and ripoffs: a model of monopolistically competitive price dispersion. *Review of Economic Studies*, 44: 493–510.

Schlesinger, H. and J. Schulenburg (1991) Search costs, switching and product heterogeneity in an insurance market. *Journal of Risk and Insurance*, 58: 109–19.

Seog, S. H. (2002) Equilibrium price dispersion in the insurance market. *Journal of Risk and Insurance*, 69: 517–36.

Shaked, A. and J. Sutton (1982) Relaxing price competition through product differentiation. *Review of Economic Studies*, 49: 3–13.

Stigler, G. (1961) The economics of information. *Journal of Political Economy*, 69: 213–25.

Tirole, J. (1988) *The Theory of Industrial Organization.* Cambridge, MA: MIT Press.

Varian, H. R. (1980) A model of sales. *American Economic Review*, 70: 651–9.

Chapter 13

Insurance Cycle and Volatility

The insurance market has exhibited cycles between a soft market and a hard market. During a hard market period, prices increase and the level of coverage availability is lower. In contrast, during a soft market period, prices decrease and the level of coverage availability is higher. The underwriting profits of insurers also vary with the changes in market characteristics.

The insurance cycle (or underwriting cycle) refers to the cyclical behavior in which a hard market and a soft market follow each other. International insurance markets are known to exhibit insurance cycles (Chen, Wong, and Lee, 1999; Cummins and Outreville, 1987; Doherty and Kang, 1988; Lamm-Tennant and Weiss, 1997). The cycle periods are generally between 5 and 10 years, although the numbers vary across lines and countries.[1]

Given that the insurance premium is determined based on the discounted expected loss, price variation can be at least partially explained by the change in the discounted expected loss. However, it is also recognized that price may change more than is implied by the expected loss change.

The insurance literature has provided several other explanations for the insurance cycle and volatility. First, it is possible that prices may increase after a large loss, if prices are affected by past loss experiences. For example, if insurers set prices by extrapolating past claim costs, then a price increase will follow a large loss (Venezian, 1985). This approach, however, implies that the market is not rational, since a rational price should

---

[1] In the empirical literature, the insurance cycle is generally measured by the underwriting profit, loss ratio, or combined loss ratio among others.

reflect the expected future loss, not the past loss. Researchers have attempted to find more rational reasons for price changes.

Even if insurers and insured are rational, institutional and regulatory factors may result in the insurance cycle (Section 13.1). For example, data collection lags, regulatory lags, and accounting practice may well cause insurance cycles under rational expectations (Cummins and Outreville, 1987). When the expected loss is unchanged, prices may change due to changes in interest rates, since interest rates are used as discount rates (Doherty and Kang, 1988; Doherty and Garven 1995). When interest rates increase (decrease), prices will decrease (increase).

A main strand in the literature is formed by the so-called capital shock theories (Sections 13.2 and 13.3). Capital shock theories are focused on capital constraints after capital shocks such as catastrophes or unexpected increases in claims. Given capital constraints after capital shocks, insurers may want to raise capital from the capital market. If such external financing is costly, insurers may attempt to raise capital internally. For example, insurers may stop or reduce dividend payments. Raising insurance premiums is another form of internal capital raising. Capital shock theories explain hard markets in terms of capital shocks and costly external financing. They also provide an explanation for soft markets, since insurers may want to keep excess internal capital to avoid the external financing costs. Such excess internal capital allows insurers to lower prices and increase coverage, leading to soft markets.

The insurance literature connects diverse factors with costly external financing (Section 13.3). Insolvency regulations and the insurer's concern with insolvency risk may lead the insurer to increase prices, in order to avoid aggravating insolvency risks or to comply with regulatory requirements (Winter, 1991b, 1994; Gron, 1994a, 1994b). Interest rate changes may differently affect the assets and liabilities of the insurer, depending on their durations. A large change in interest rate leads to capital depletion, leading to a price increase (Doherty and Garven, 1995).

Since price is determined based on demand and supply, price changes should also be related to demand-side behavior. When insurance demand is elastic with respect to price, price increases will be tempered (Cagle and Harrington, 1995). A large loss may change the expectations of future losses of insureds as well as insurers. The change in expectations may lead to increased demand, which in turn increases prices (Lai et al., 2000; Seog, 2008). On the other hand, the insured's concern with insolvency risk may lead to a price decrease after a large loss, due to the increased insolvency risk (Cummins and Danzon, 1997).

In general, the capital shock theory is supported by empirical findings (Winter, 1991a, 1994; Gron, 1994a, 1994b; Doherty and Garven, 1995;

Lai et al., 2000; Doherty, Lamm-Tennant, and Starks, 2003). It is also reported that the price change is affected by the insured's concern the insolvency risk (Cummins and Danzon, 1997; Weiss and Chung, 2004).

13.1   Perfect Market Approaches

A market is called perfect if there are no transaction costs such as tax and information asymmetry costs. There are efforts to understand price changes under the perfect market.

13.1.1   Interest rates

When the market is perfect, premiums are determined based on the expected loss, and price variations can be explained by changes in expected loss and/ or discount rate. If we focus on the unit price, total price per expected loss, then the unit price will be affected only by the discount rate.

Let us consider the following simple one-period pricing model. Let us define Q as total price, x as the random loss, and $E(r)$ as the expected return. Then, the actuarially fair premium Q will be determined by the equation

$$(1 + E(r))Q = E(x),$$

that is,

$$Q = E(x)/(1 + E(r)). \tag{13.1}$$

Define the loss ratio as x/Q. Then the expected loss ratio is

$$E(x)/Q = 1 + E(r). \tag{13.2}$$

This formula implies that the loss ratio is positively related to the expected return of the investment. In this simple case, the underwriting return r_U can be defined by $(Q - x)/Q = 1 - x/Q$. Thus,

$$E(r_U) = -E(r). \tag{13.3}$$

Since insurers invest mainly in fixed income assets, the expected return is often regarded as an interest rate. Since the loss ratio is inversely related to the underwriting return, the expected returns or interest rates are inversely related to the underwriting return.

A similar result can be obtained by using the insurance capital asset pricing model (see Chapter 15). This incorporates the fair return to capital providers into pricing. In this model, the underwriting return is determined by

$$Er_U = -kr_f + \beta_U(Er_m - r_f), \tag{13.4}$$

where β_U is the underwriting beta and k is the liability to premium ratio (or funds generating factor). From this equation, it is clear that an increase in r_f will lead to lower Er_U.

> *Proposition 13.1* (Interest rate and underwriting profit). In a perfect market, the underwriting return is inversely related to the interest rate.

13.1.2   Institutional and regulatory intervention

While changes in interest rates affect the insurance price and the underwriting profit, they do not fully explain the patterns of price changes in the insurance market. Loss ratio changes often do not move in tandem with the interest changes. For example, the insurance cycles in the property casualty insurance lines of the USA are known to have cycle periods of about 6 years, which is not observed in the interest rate changes.

This observation implies that other factors may be important in understanding the price changes and the insurance cycle. Some researchers suggest that the cycle may be observed due to the institutional, regulatory, and accounting lags and interventions.

Let us write Π_t for the underwriting loss in period t, $\Pi_t = x_t - Q_t$, where x_t is the loss in period t and Q_t is the premium in period t.[2] In the literature, the existence of the insurance cycle is discussed in the context of the second-order autoregressive model as follows (see Venezian, 1985; Cummins and Outreville, 1987):

$$\Pi_t = a_0 + a_1\Pi_{t-1} + a_2\Pi_{t-2} + r_t \tag{13.5}$$

where r_t is the random error, with zero mean. A cycle is known to exist if $a_1 > 0$, $a_2 < 0$, and $a_1^2 + 4a_2 < 0$. The cycle period is calculated by $2\pi/\cos^{-1}(a_1/2\sqrt{-a_2})$.

Now, suppose that x_t is determined by

$$x_t = E(x_t) + e_t + w_t \tag{13.6}$$

where e_t is the systematic error term in period t with zero mean, and w_t is the nonsystematic error term in period t with a zero mean. The systematic error e_t represents a permanent change in loss sizes, thus becomes part of the expected losses in the future. The nonsystematic error w_t is not related to the permanent change in loss sizes. Neither error term is autocorrelated.

---

[2]   Underwriting losses, rather than profits, are used for notational convenience.

Given information available at the end of period $t - 1$, ϕ_{t-1},

$$E_{t-1}(x_t \mid \phi_{t-1}) = E_{t-1}(x_{t-1}) + e_{t-1}. \qquad (13.7)$$

Under rational expectations, a premium will be determined by

$$Q_t = E_{t-1}(x_t \mid \phi_{t-1}) = E_{t-1}(x_{t-1}) + e_{t-1}.^3 \qquad (13.8)$$

The underwriting loss thus becomes

$$\Pi_t = e_t + w_t. \qquad (13.9)$$

This equation implies that there is no cycle. That is, when the price is rationally determined under the perfect market, the insurance cycle should not exist.

Now let us investigate the effects of institutional interventions. The price in a given period may not fully reflect the information regarding the previous period, possibly due to data collection lag and regulatory lag. Suppose that the price in period t reflects the information in period $t - 2$, not $t - 1$. Then

$$\begin{aligned} Q_t &= E_{t-2}(x_t \mid \phi_{t-2}) = E_{t-2}(x_{t-2}) + E_{t-2}(e_{t-1}) + e_{t-2} \\ &= E_{t-2}(x_{t-2}) + e_{t-2}. \end{aligned} \qquad (13.10)$$

Underwriting loss becomes

$$\Pi_t = e_t + w_t + e_{t-1}. \qquad (13.11)$$

This result implies that $\{\Pi_t\}$ follows a first-order autoregressive process. In addition, under the renewal lag and the calendar-year reporting practice, the reported underwriting loss may partially reflect the past true underwriting losses. Let ρ denote the proportion of the current underwriting loss in the reported underwriting loss. The reported underwriting loss can be written as

$$\begin{aligned} \Pi_t^R &= \rho\Pi_t + (1-\rho)\Pi_{t-1} \\ &= \rho(e_t + w_t + e_{t-1}) + (1-\rho)(e_{t-1} + w_{t-1} + e_{t-2}). \end{aligned} \qquad (13.12)$$

This expression allows $\{\Pi_t^R\}$ to follow the desired second-order autoregressive process.

Proposition 13.2 (Institutional intervention and underwriting cycle). In a perfect market, institutional intervention may cause the reported underwriting profits to exhibit cyclical patterns.

---

[3]   To focus on the effects of institutional interventions, let us ignore the discount factors.

13.2   Costly External Financing and Market Imperfection

A large loss is often followed by a hard market. Although the perfect market approaches may partially help understand the changes in prices and underwriting profits, they fail to make a direct connection between a large loss and the subsequent price increase. If the market is perfect, prices should be determined based on the expected value of the future losses. However, a large loss experience in a given period does not necessarily imply an increase in the future risk. In such a case, a large loss in one period should not affect the price in the subsequent periods.

The price increase after a large loss may be understood once the imperfection of the market is introduced. When a large loss occurs, an insurer will have to use a lot of cash and assets to pay for the insureds' losses. Therefore, the insurer will need additional funds to make an investment for growth or to become solvent. If the capital market is perfect, then the investors will correctly value the insurer. Based on the correct valuation, the insurer will finance the fund with zero costs. However, if the financing is costly due to market imperfection, then the insurer may not want to raise funds in the capital market. In such a case, the insurer will try to stop paying dividends and/or increase the insurance premium. Thus, a price increase may follow a large loss. This approach is known as the capital shock (or capital constraint) theory.

The capital shock theory critically depends on the assumption of costly external financing, since without it the insurer will simply finance funds from the capital market. An important source of costly external financing is the debt overhang problem (see Section 5.1; and Myers, 1977). The main idea of the debt overhang problem is as follows. When the debt level of a firm is high, cash flows from projects will be used to pay for the debt. Knowing this fact, investors may refuse to provide new capital for projects, even if the projects have positive net present value (NPV). Thus, external financing becomes very costly or impossible, given the debt overhang problem. Since insurers assume large liabilities to pay for the losses after a large loss shock, the debt overhang problem may occur. As a result, after a large shock, insurers may find it difficult or impossible to raise capital externally.

Another source of costly external financing is adverse selection. Below, we present the basic model based on Seog and Lee (2008) which is a variant of Myers and Majluf (1984).

Suppose that there is negative capital shock including a loss shock. The capital shock weakens the insurer financially by increasing her liability. Facing capital depletion, she needs to raise capital in order to preserve the franchise value and to invest in new projects. Information asymmetry

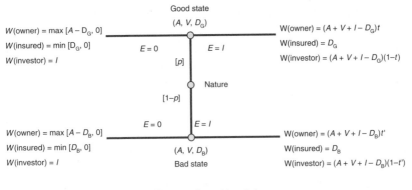

Good state
(A, V, D_G)

$W(\text{owner}) = \max [A - D_G, 0]$ $E = 0$ $E = I$ $W(\text{owner}) = (A + V + I - D_G)t$
$W(\text{insured}) = \min [D_G, 0]$ $W(\text{insured}) = D_G$
$W(\text{investor}) = I$ $[p]$ $W(\text{investor}) = (A + V + I - D_G)(1-t)$

Nature
$[1-p]$

$E = 0$ $E = I$
$W(\text{owner}) = \max [A - D_B, 0]$ $W(\text{owner}) = (A + V + I - D_B)t'$
$W(\text{insured}) = \min [D_B, 0]$ (A, V, D_B) $W(\text{insured}) = D_B$
$W(\text{investor}) = I$ Bad state $W(\text{investor}) = (A + V + I - D_B)(1-t')$

$W(k)$ = payoff to player k (k = owner, insured, investor).

$E = 0$ (no financing), I (financing)

t, t': the proportion of the insurer value net of liability distributed to the owner

Figure 13.1   External financing game under information asymmetry.

arises since at the time of financing, investors cannot directly observe the realized liability size of the insurer that the insurer observes.

The insurer has an asset A in place and an investment opportunity with NPV of $V > 0$. The investment opportunity requires the initial cost of I. For simplicity, the uncertainty is described by two states of nature regarding the size of the liability. The state (S) is good (G) with probability p, or bad (B) with probability $1 - p$. A good (bad) state implies low (high) liability, $D_B > D_G$, where D_S is the liability in state S.

We set up the model in a signaling game over two periods. In the first period, the (existing) owner of the insurer observes the realized state of nature and determines whether or not she seeks external financing through issuing stocks. The funding size is denoted by E. Let us focus on the binary case, $E = I$ or 0. Assume that the capital market is competitive and the fair return is zero, so that the investor will provide funds as long as he expects to earn nonnegative profit. The expected profit of the investor will be calculated based on his beliefs about the states which, in turn, depend on the interpretation of the funding behavior of the insurer, or signal. In an equilibrium, the beliefs should be fulfilled, and neither the owner of the insurer nor the investor should have an incentive to deviate from the equilibrium. The signaling game structure is depicted in Figure 13.1. At the end of each node, the payoffs to players are noted. When the insurer does not raise capital (at the left nodes), the payoff to the investor is simply noted as I. When the insurer raises capital (at the right nodes), the payoffs to the owner and the investor will depend on the stock price, which in turn depends on the investor's beliefs (see the analysis below).

In the second period, the information asymmetry problem resolves. The firm value is distributed to the insureds, the existing owner of the insurer, and the new owner (i.e., the investor) of the insurer (if the external financing is successful in the first period). The insurer becomes insolvent if the asset value is less than the liability value. In the insolvency case, the owners will receive nothing, since the insureds have the priority in the distribution of the firm value.

To incorporate the insolvency risk into the model, we focus on the case in which $A < D_B$ and $A + V + I - D_B > 0$. That is, in the bad state, the insurer's value is lower than the liability without investment, but is higher than the liability with investment. It turns out that the results of our model depend on the size of the capital shock (i.e., the size of the liability). For this, we separately consider the large capital shock case in which $A + V < D_B$ and the small capital shock case in which $A + V \geq D_B$. For simplicity, we assume that $A + V \geq D_G$.

Case 1: Large capital shock ($A + V < D_B$). If the investor provides funds I to the insurer in the bad state, the owners' value becomes $A + V + I - D_B$. Since this value is less than I, the investor will refuse to provide funding once the state is known to him. This is none other than the debt overhang problem (Myers, 1977). In this case, a separating equilibrium cannot exist in which the insurer in the bad state raises capital. In addition, there is no separating equilibrium in which the insurer in the good state raises capital, since the insurer in the bad state will have an incentive to raise capital, pretending to be the insurer in the good state. Therefore, only pooling equilibrium is possible. The next proposition characterizes the equilibrium outcomes.

Case 2: Small capital shock ($A + V \geq D_B$). In this case, the investor does not have to refuse to provide funds to the insurer in the bad state, as long as the stocks are fairly priced. This implies that the insurer in the bad state will raise capital in an equilibrium. There are two possible equilibrium outcomes: a pooling equilibrium in which the insurers in both states raise capital, and a separating equilibrium in which the insurer in the bad state raises capital. The next proposition characterizes the equilibrium outcomes.

Proposition 13.3 (Costly external financing).

(a)   In case 1 ($A + V < D_B$), two equilibria are possible.
      (a1) A pooling equilibrium in which the insurer in both states raises capital, if (i) $p \geq (D_B - A - V)/(D_B - D_G)$, and (ii) either (ii') $A - D_G \leq 0$ or (ii'') $A - D_G > 0$ and

$$V \geq V^* = \frac{-(A+I-E(D)) + \sqrt{(A+I-E(D))^2 + 4I(1-p)(D_B - D_G)}}{2},$$

where
$$E(D) = pD_G + (1-p)D_B.$$

(a2) A pooling equilibrium in which neither insurer raises capital and is supported by the off-the-equilibrium belief that the issuer is in the good state with probability $r \leq (D_B - A - V)/(D_B - D_G)$.

(b) In case 2 $(A + V \geq D_B)$, two equilibria are possible.

(b1) A pooling equilibrium in which the insurer in both states raises capital, if $A - D_G \leq 0$; or if $A - D_G > 0$ and

$$V \geq V^* = \frac{-(A+I-E(D)) + \sqrt{(A+I-E(D))^2 + 4I(1-p)(D_B - D_G)}}{2}.$$

(b2) A separating equilibrium in which the insurer in the bad state raises capital, if $A - D_G \geq 0$ and

$$V \leq V^{**} = \frac{-(A+I-D_B) + \sqrt{(A+I-D_B)^2 + 4I(D_B - D_G)}}{2}.$$

Proof Here, we provide intuitions only; see Seog and Lee (2008) for technical details.

(a1) Since the investor will invest only if he expects nonnegative profit, the probability of the good state should be high enough, leading to condition (i). On the other hand, the stock price of the insurer in the good (bad) state is undervalued (overvalued) in this pooling equilibrium. Thus, the insurer in the good state will raise capital only if the NPV of the investment is great enough to offset the loss in the undervaluation of the stock price. Condition (ii′) implies that the insurer in the good state will be insolvent without investment. In this case, the insurer will prefer to raise capital. Even if the insurer in the good state remains solvent without investment, the insurer will still raise capital if the NPV exceeds the loss due to the underpricing of stocks, which leads to condition (ii″).

(a2) Since the investor will not invest in the insurer in the bad state, he will refuse to invest if there is high belief that the issuer is in the bad state. Such an off-the-equilibrium belief is given in (a2). Given the belief, no insurer can raise capital.

(b1) The intuition is the same as in (a1). The difference is that the investor is willing to invest in the insurer in the bad state given a small capital shock. Therefore, we do not need the condition regarding the probability of the good state (p).

(b2)   In this equilibrium, the insurer in the good state should not have an incentives to raise capital. For this, NPV should be smaller than the loss due to the underpricing of stocks. Note that the critical NPV is different from (a1), since the market price is based on the bad state in this separating equilibrium.   □

The capital shock theory connects these results with the insurance price changes as follows. Due to the shock, insurers may have difficulties in raising the capital externally. Then they will attempt to raise capital internally by raising insurance premiums. This capital shock theory is based more on the large capital shock case (case 1) than on the small capital shock case (case 2). This is because, in case 1, the insurer in the bad state can always raise capital externally. On the other hand, in case 2, there is an equilibrium in which insurers cannot raise capital externally. In particular, if a shock is very large and affects many insurers, then the probability of the good state will be small so that $p < (D_B - A - V)/(D_B - D_G)$. In such a case, neither insurer can raise capital externally as described in (a2).

We note that the results also exhibit the debt overhang problem. In case 1, there is no equilibrium in which the insurer in the bad state alone raises capital, since the outside investor is afraid that she will not receive the fair value of the fund she invests. In fact, the adverse selection problem makes the debt overhang problem more serious, since the firm in the good state may not raise capital, if the investor thinks of the capital raising firm as a bad firm (a2). Therefore, the above results can be interpreted as the combined effects of the adverse selection and the debt overhang problems.

13.3   Capital Shock Approaches

In this section, we assume that the market is imperfect, that the capital of insurers is limited, and that external financing is costly as described in the previous section. The capital limit results in the capacity limits when insurers are concerned with the insolvency risk, or comply with the regulation requirements (Winter, 1991b, 1994; Gron, 1994a, 1994b). Given the capacity limit, the supply of insurers cannot be inelastic. The (short-run) supply curve is depicted in Figure 13.2 as curve S. The supply curve is horizontal for lower production levels, while it becomes positively sloped for the higher production levels. The market demand curve is denoted by curve D. The current equilibrium is E, at which the production level is below the capacity limit.

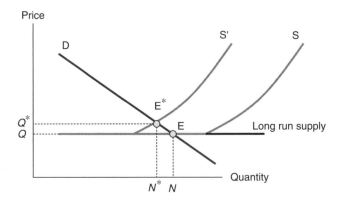

Figure 13.2   Equilibrium under capital constraints.

Now, suppose that a capital shock arrives. The capital shock will lower the capital limit of insurers. The supply curve then will move to the left as, for example, depicted by curve S'. As the shock is larger, the supply curve will move farther. Thus, it is more likely that the demand curve meets the supply curve where the supply curve is sloped upward. The new equilibrium is depicted as E^*. Obviously from this figure, a capital shock leads to higher prices and lower coverage. This exhibits a hard market. As the capital shortage is eventually resolved in the long run, the capital limit is enlarged so that the supply curve moves to the right. Then the price decreases and the coverage increases, resulting in a soft market.

In many cases, a capital shock results from a catastrophic loss. However, interest rate changes may also cause a capital shock. For this, let us define M_K as the duration of $K = A$ (asset), L (liability), and C (capital). Note that duration measures the sensitivity of the asset with respect to the change of interest rate:

$$M_K = -\frac{\partial K/\partial r}{K},$$

where r is the interest rate. From the identity $A = L + C$, we have

$$M_C = (M_A - M_L)\frac{A}{C} + M_L.$$

This implies that the duration of capital may be affected by the difference between the durations of the asset and the liability. If the interest rate goes up, the asset value and the liability value will decrease. However, if the duration of the asset is higher than the duration of the liability, then the duration of the capital is positive, implying that the capital value decreases. That is, an interest rate change with different sensitivities between the asset and the liability may cause capital depletion (Doherty and Garven, 1995).

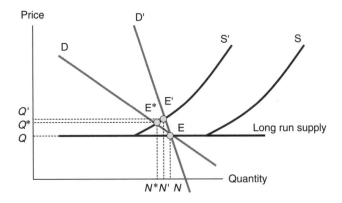

Figure 13.3   Demand elasticity and a capital shock.

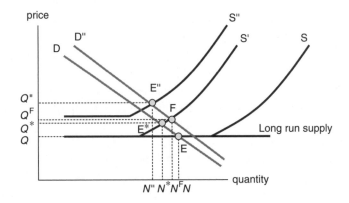

Figure 13.4   Change in the expectation of risk and a capital shock.

The effect of a capital shock on the price is also dependent on the demand. As depicted in Figure 13.3, D′ is the demand curve which exhibits a lower elasticity than D. With D′, the equilibrium is moved from E* to E′. The price increase is greater, but the coverage reduction is less severe (Cagle and Harrington, 1995).

On the other hand, a catastrophe may also change the expectation of risk. When insureds interpret a large loss shock as an increase in risk, then the demand curve will shift upward, since they are willing to pay higher prices. The resulting demand curve is denoted by D″ in Figure 13.4. The equilibrium is moved from E* to F. As a result, the price increase is greater, but the coverage reduction is less severe (Lai et al., 2000; Seog, 2008). If the insurers also perceive the shock as an increase in risk, then the supply curve will also shift upward. The resulting supply curve is denoted by S″ in Figure 13.4. The equilibrium is denoted by E″. Compared

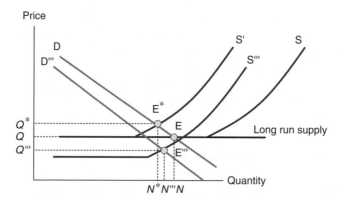

Figure 13.5   Price reflecting the insolvency risk and a capital shock.

with F, the price increase is higher and the coverage reduction is more severe. Compared with the original equilibrium E before the capital shock, the price increase is very large, and the coverage reduction is possibly very severe.

Up to now, we have ignored the fact that the insurance premium should reflect the insolvency risk of the insurer. Obviously, the risk of insolvency is important not only to insurers but also to insureds. The price that insureds are willing to pay will decrease as the insolvency risk increases, *ceteris paribus*. Assuming that all insurers' insolvency risks increase by the same magnitudes after a capital shock, both the demand and the supply curves will shift downward, as depicted in Figure 13.5. Now the demand and the supply curves are D''' and S'''. In the new equilibrium, E''', the price is decreased and the coverage is reduced, compared with the original equilibrium E (Cummins and Danzon, 1997; MacMinn and Seog, 2008).

In sum, the capacity constraints and the perception of the risk increase will tend to increase the price, while the insureds' concern with the increased insolvency risk will tend to lower the price. Furthermore, the capacity constraints and the insurers' perception of the risk increase will tend to reduce the coverage, while the insureds' concern with the increased insolvency risk and the insureds' perception of the risk increase will tend to increase the coverage.

13.4   Conclusion

The fluctuation of insurance premiums and underwriting profits may be a natural outcome of a risky business. The prices and profits will vary reflecting the market circumstances which, in turn, are affected by economic, financial and insurance variables. The insurance literature documents that prices and profits are affected by interest rates, catastrophic events, the perception of risks, and institutional intervention. Although costly external financing provides a basic rationale for the capital shock theory, it is important to note that costly external financing does not necessarily mean that insurers always fail to raise capital, since there is an equilibrium in which insurers can raise capital externally. Moreover, a capital shock itself does not have to cause the same information asymmetry problem for all insurers. For example, some insurers may be more transparent than others. A more transparent insurer will suffer less from the information asymmetry problem and can manage to raise capital with lower costs (Doherty et al., 2003).

BIBLIOGRAPHY

Angbazo, L. A. and R. Narayanan (1996) Catastrophic shocks in the property-liability insurance industry: evidence on regulatory and contagion effects. *Journal of Risk and Insurance*, 63: 619–37.

Berger, L. A. (1989) A model of the underwriting cycle in the property/liability insurance industry. *Journal of Risk and Insurance*, 50: 298–306.

Cagle, J. D. and S. E. Harrington (1995) Insurance supply with capacity constraints and endogenous insolvency risk. *Journal of Risk and Uncertainty*, 11: 219–32.

Chen, R., K. A. Wong, and H. C. Lee (1999) Underwriting cycles in Asia. *Journal of Risk and Insurance*, 66: 29–47.

Cummins, J. D. and P. M. Danzon (1997) Price, financial quality, and capital flows in insurance markets. *Journal of Financial Intermediation*, 6: 3–38.

Cummins, J. D. and S. E. Harrington (1985) Property-liability insurance rate regulation: estimation of underwriting betas using quarterly profit data. *Journal of Risk and Insurance*, 52: 16–43.

Cummins, J. D. and J. F. Outreville (1987) An international analysis of underwriting cycles in property-liability insurance. *Journal of Risk and Insurance*, 54: 246–62.

Cummins, J. D. and S. Tennyson (1992) Controlling automobile insurance costs. *Journal of Economic Perspectives*, 6: 95–115.

Doherty, N. A. and J. Garven (1995) Insurance cycles: interest rates and the capacity constraint model. *Journal of Business*, 68: 383–404.

Doherty, N. A. and H. B. Kang (1988) Price instability for a financial intermediary: interest rates and insurance price cycles. *Journal of Banking and Finance*, 12: 199–214.

Doherty, N. A., J. Lamm-Tennant, and L. S. Starks (2003), Insuring September 11th: market recovery and transparency. *Journal of Risk and Uncertainty*, 26: 179–99.

Doherty, N. A. and L. L. Posey (1997) Availability crises in insurance markets: optimal contracts with asymmetric information and capacity constraints. *Journal of Risk and Uncertainty*, 15: 55–80.

Fields, J. A. and E. Venezian (1989) Profit cycles in property-liability insurance: a disaggregated approach. *Journal of Risk and Insurance*, 56: 312-319.

Froot, K. A. (1999) The evolving market for catastrophic event risk. *Risk Management and Insurance Review*, 2: 1–28.

Froot, K. A., D. S. Scharfstein, and J. C. Stein (1993) Risk management: coordinating corporate investment and financing policies. *Journal of Finance*, 48: 1629–1658.

Froot, K. A. and J. C. Stein, (1998) Risk management, capital budgeting, and capital structure policy for financial institutions: an integrated approach. *Journal of Financial Economics*, 47: 55–82.

Fung, H.-G., G. Lai, G. A. Patterson, and R. C. Witt (1998) Underwriting cycles in property-liability insurance: an empirical analysis of industry and by-line data. *Journal of Risk and Insurance*, 65: 539–562.

Grace, M. F. and J. Hotchkiss (1995) External impacts on the property-liability insurance cycle. *Journal of Risk and Insurance*, 62: 738–754.

Gron, A. (1994a) Capacity constraints and cycles in property-casualty insurance markets. *RAND Journal of Economics*, 25: 110–127.

Gron, A. (1994b) Evidence of Capacity Constraints in Insurance Markets. *Journal of Law and Economics*, 37: 349–377.

Harrington, S. E. (1984) The Impact of Rate Regulation on Prices and Underwriting Results in the Property-Liability Insurance Industry: A Survey. *Journal of Risk and Insurance*, 51: 577–623.

Harrington, S. E. and P. M. Danzon (1994) Price Cutting in Liability Insurance Markets. *Journal of Business*, 67: 511–538.

Harrington, S. E. and P. M. Danzon (2000) The Economics of Liability Insurance. in Dionne, G. (ed), *Handbook of Insurance* (Boston, MA: Kluwer Academic Publishers).

Harrington, S. E. and G. Niehaus (1998) Race, Redlining, and Automobile Insurance Prices. *Journal of Business*, 71: 439–469.

Kleffner, A. E. and N. A. Doherty (1996) Costly risk and the supply of catastrophic insurance. *Journal of Risk and Insurance*, 63: 657–71.

Lai, G. C., R. C. Witt, H.-G. Fung, R. D. MacMinn, and P. L. Brockett (2000) Great (and not so great) expectations: an endogenous economic explication of insurance cycles and liability crises. *Journal of Risk and Insurance*, 67: 617–52.

Lamm-Tennant, J. and M. A. Weiss (1997) International insurance cycles: rational expectations/international intervention. *Journal of Risk and Insurance*, 64: 415–39.

MacMinn, R. D. and S. H. Seog (2008) Distribution of price and quality under information asymmetry. KAIST Business School Working Paper. http://ssrn.com/abstract=1182002.

Myers, S. C. (1977) Determinants of corporate borrowing. *Journal of Financial Economics*, 5: 147–75.

Myers, S. C. and N. C. Majluf (1984) Corporate financing and investment decisions when firms have information that investors do not. *Journal of Financial Economics*, 11: 187–221.

Niehaus, G. and A. Terry (1993) Evidence on the time series properties of insurance premiums and causes of the underwriting cycle: new support for the capital market imperfection hypothesis. *Journal of Risk and Insurance*, 60: 466–79.

Outreville, F. J. (1990) Underwriting cycles and rate regulation in automobile insurance markets. *Journal of Insurance Regulation*, 8: 274–86.

Seog, S. H. (2008) Informational cascade in the insurance market. *Journal of Risk and Insurance*, 75: 145–65.

Seog, S. H. and S. Lee (2008) Costly external financing and the capital shock theory of the insurance cycle. KAIST Business School Working Paper.

Sommer, D. W. (1996) The impact of firm risk on property-liability insurance prices. *Journal of Risk and Insurance*, 63: 501–14.

Tennyson, S. (1993) Regulatory lag in automobile insurance. *Journal of Risk and Insurance*, 60: 36–58.

Venezian, E. C. (1985) Ratemaking methods and profit cycles in property and liability insurance. *Journal of Risk and Insurance*, 52: 477–500.

Weiss, M. A. (2007) Underwriting cycles: a synthesis and further directions. *Journal of Insurance Issues*, 30: 31–45.

Weiss, M. A. and J. H. Chung (2004) U.S. reinsurance prices, financial quality, and global capacity. *Journal of Risk and Insurance*, 71: 437–67.

Winter, R. A. (1991a) The liability insurance market. *Journal of Economic Perspectives*, 5: 115–36.

Winter, R. A. (1991b) Solvency regulation and the insurance cycle. *Economic Inquiry*, 29: 458–71.

Winter, R. A. (1994) The dynamics of competitive insurance markets. *Journal of Financial Intermediation*, 3: 379–415.

Zanjani, G. (2002) Pricing and capital allocation in catastrophe insurance. *Journal of Financial Economics*, 65: 283–305.

Part V
Insurer Management

Chapter 14

Insurance Distribution Systems

Insurance markets are characterized by diverse distribution systems. Important distribution channels include direct writing, the exclusive agency, the independent agency, and the broker. The sales forces of the direct writing insurer are employees of the insurer. On the other hand, exclusive agents, independent agents, and brokers are not employees of insurers, and are independent business entities. The distinctions among them are made based on the contractual relationship with insurers.

The exclusive agent has an exclusive relationship with one insurer, so that the agent places the insured with the insurer that he represents. The independent agent has relationships with multiple insurers. Thus, the independent agent may potentially place the insured with any insurer with whom he has a relationship. In property casualty insurance lines in the USA, independent agents may possess the client lists, implying that the insured who purchases insurance through an independent agent is a client of the agent, not of the insurer. Ownership of the client list provides the independent agent with considerable negotiation power against insurers.

Unlike agents, brokers provide advice to insureds and help them pick the right insurers. Legally, brokers work for consumers, while agents work for insurers. Although brokers are legally differentiated from agents, the economic functions of the broker are often similar to those of the independent agents. Similarly, the economic functions of the sales forces of the direct writing insurers are often similar to those of the exclusive agents. Reflecting this observation, in this chapter, the independent agency includes the broker, and the exclusive agency includes direct writing, unless otherwise stated.

The two distribution systems have coexisted in the market for a long time. The exclusive agency is prevalent in personal property casualty insurance (such as personal auto insurance and homeowners' insurance) and the life insurance lines, while the independent agency is prevalent in the commercial property casualty insurance lines (such as commercial multiperil, workers' compensation, and general liability). The relative strengths and weaknesses of one distribution system compared with the other have been interesting research topics.

Moreover, Joskow (1973), Cummins and Vanderhei (1979), and Barrese and Nelson (1992) find that an exclusive agency is more cost efficient than an independent agency. Since the independent agency has coexisted with the exclusive agency in the market for a long time, the reason why such an inefficient distribution system can survive has also been an interesting academic question. Moreover, independent agencies are more prevalent than exclusive agencies in commercial lines. Researchers have found several rationales for the coexistence of distribution systems. We first discuss the regulation approach and the service difference approach in Section 14.1. Section 14.2 presents the transaction cost approach which is accepted widely in the literature. Section 14.3 discusses the search and match approach which focuses on the imperfect information of insureds and insurers. Section 14.4 discuses the effect of the operating leverage on the distribution systems. Section 14.5 investigates compensation schemes for agents, with the focus on commission and fee.

14.1   Regulation Approach and Service Difference Approach

Joskow (1973) attributes the survival of the independent agency to regulation. If regulation sets entry barriers or a price floor above a competitive level, then an inefficient insurer can survive, while an efficient insurer may enjoy above-normal profits. However, the coexistence of distribution systems has been observed even though insurance markets have been deregulated. Therefore, regulation does not seem to be a critical reason for the coexistence of the distribution systems.

Another possible rationale for the existence of the independent agency is it may provide better services or better product quality to insureds. Etgar (1976), Cummins and Weisbart (1977), Doerpinghaus (1991), and Barrese, Doerpinghaus and Nelson (1995) have investigated this issue. However, those empirical studies found mixed evidence. It is not clear if the independent agency provides better services to insureds than the exclusive agency.

14.2   Transaction Cost Approach

A main stream of this literature is transaction costs approaches. This approach emphasizes the interest conflicts among insurer, agent, and insureds. Since different distribution systems have different functions in controlling the conflicts, one agency can be preferred to the other agency, depending on the feature of the conflicts. Grossman and Hart (1986) provide a theoretical model for this approach. This addresses the organizational form focusing on vertical integration when the ownership affects the incentives to the owners. It shows that different organizational forms may be optimal under different circumstances. In the context of insurance distribution, exclusive agency is regarded as an integrated organizational form, while independent agency as a nonintegrated organizational form. The following discussion is based on Grossman and Hart (1986).

Suppose that there are two firms $i = 1, 2$. These firms may enter into a contract at time 0. The contract requires investments at times 0 and 1. Firm i needs to make an investment a_i at time 0. The investment is relationship-specific, which means the value of the investment is zero outside the contract. At time 1, firm i needs to make an investment b_i. Assume that b_1 and b_2 interact with each other to determine the time 1 value to firm i, $B_i(b_1, b_2)$. The total output value to i, V_i, is determined by $V_i = V_i(a_i, B_i(b_i, b_j))$. One important assumption is that a_i, b_i and B_i cannot be specified at time 0; they are ex ante noncontractible. We further assume that $\partial V_i / \partial B_i > 0$, $\partial^2 V_i / \partial a_i \partial B_i > 0$ and $\partial^2 V_i / \partial^2 a_i < 0$. That is, V_i is an increasing function of B_i, a_i and B_i are complementary, and an optimal a_i is uniquely determined.

Let us first find the first best outcome. At time 1, the first best investment b_i^F will be determined by

$$\partial[V_i(a_i, B_i(b_i, b_j)) + V_j(a_j, B_j(b_i, b_j))]/\partial b_i = 0, \quad \text{given } a_i, a_j. \tag{14.1}$$

Let $B_i^F = B_i(b_i^F, b_j^F)$. For simplicity, we assume that b_i^F is independent of a_i and a_j. Now the time 0 first best investment a_i^F is determined by

$$\partial[V_i(a_i, B_i^F) + V_j(a_j, B_j^F)]/\partial a_i = 0 \tag{14.2}$$

$$\Leftrightarrow \partial V_i(a_i, B_i^F)/\partial a_i = 0. \tag{14.3}$$

Let us define $V_i^F = V_i(a_i^F, B_i^F)$, the first best output value.

We investigate the two cases of decision making separately. In the first case, firms are not integrated. In the second case, firm 1 integrates firm 2, so that firm 1 controls firm 2.

Case 1: Non-integration. Since firms are independent, each firm i determines b_i simultaneously and noncooperatively at time 1. Given the a_i, let us denote the resulting investment by b_i^N, which satisfies

$$\partial V_i(a_i, B_i(b_i, b_j))/\partial b_i = 0 \Leftrightarrow \partial B_i(b_i, b_j)/\partial b_i = 0. \tag{14.4}$$

Note that b_i^N is independent of a_i under our assumption. The resulting time 1 value is $B_i^N = B_i(b_i^N, b_j^N)$, and the total output value is $V_i(a_i, B_i^N)$. Now, let us consider time 0 investment a_i^N, which will be determined by

$$\partial V_i(a_i, B_i^N)/\partial a_i = 0. \tag{14.5}$$

In general, $a_i^N \neq a_i^F$; and $b_i^N \neq b_i^F$.
Comparing (14.3) with (14.5),

$$a_i^N \geq a_i^F \Leftrightarrow B_i^N \geq B_i^F. \tag{14.6}$$

Case 2: Integration. Suppose that firm 1 controls firm 2. In this case, firm 1 determines b_1 and b_2 at time 1. The resulting time 1 investments, b_1^C and b_1^C are determined as follows:

$$\partial B_1(b_1, b_2)/\partial b_1 = 0 \Rightarrow b_1^C, \tag{14.7}$$

$$\partial B_1(b_1, b_2)/\partial b_2 = 0 \Rightarrow b_2^C. \tag{14.8}$$

Note that b_i^C is independent of a_i. Let us define $B_i^C = B_i(b_i^C, b_j^C)$. The time 0 investments a_i^C are determined by

$$\partial V_i(a_i, B_i^C)/\partial a_i = 0. \tag{14.9}$$

In general, $a_i^C \neq a_i^F$; and $b_i^C \neq b_i^F$. Comparing (14.3) with (14.9),

$$a_i^C \geq a_i^F \Leftrightarrow B_i^C \geq B_i^F. \tag{14.10}$$

In general, neither integration nor nonintegration yields a first best outcome. The following result exemplifies the optimality of integration/nonintegration under different circumstances.

Proposition 14.1 (Integration versus nonintegration).

(a)   Suppose that B_i depends mostly on b_i, for each i. Then, the nonintegration yields approximately the first best outcome.
(b)   Suppose that B_2 is not affected by b_1 and b_2. Then, the firm 1's control over firm 2 yields approximately the first best outcome.

Proof

(a)   The first-order condition (FOC) for the first best outcome (14.1) can be rewritten as

$$\partial[V_i(a_i, B_i(b_i, b_j)) + V_j(a_j, B_j(b_i, b_j))]/\partial b_i$$
$$\approx \partial V_i(a_i, B_i(b_i, b_j))/\partial b_i = 0 \Leftrightarrow \partial B_i(b_i, b_j))/\partial b_i = 0.$$

That is, (14.1) is approximately equal to (14.4). Thus, $b_i^N \approx b_i^F$ and $B_i^N \approx B_i^F$. We also have that $a_i^N \approx a_i^F$ since $B_i^N \approx B_i^F$.

(b)   The FOCs for the first best outcome (14.1) can be rewritten as

$$\partial[V_1(a_1, B_1(b_1, b_2)) + V_2(a_2, B_2(b_1, b_2))]/\partial b_1 \approx \partial V_1(a_1, B_1(b_1, b_2))/\partial b_1 = 0$$
$$\Leftrightarrow \partial B_1(b_1, b_2))/\partial b_1 = 0,$$

$$\partial[V_1(a_1, B_1(b_1, b_2)) + V_2(a_2, B_2(b_1, b_2))]/\partial b_2 \approx \partial V_1(a_1, B_1(b_1, b_2))/\partial b_2 = 0$$
$$\Leftrightarrow \partial B_1(b_1, b_2))/\partial b_2 = 0.$$

That is, (14.1) is approximately equal to (14.7) and (14.8). Thus, $b_i^C \approx b_i^F$ and $B_i^C \approx B_i^F$. We also have that $a_i^C \approx a_i^F$ since $B_i^C \approx B_i^F$.   □

This proposition is intuitive. When B_i depends primarily on b_i for each i, it must be approximately best to leave the investment decision b_i to firm i. This also leads to the best investment decision in time 0. On the other hand, if only B_1 depends on b_1 and b_2, then firm 2's investment decision is irrelevant to the outcome. In this case, it must be approximately best to leave both investment decisions b_1 and b_2 to firm 1. This result implies that, when one party's decision is critical to the outcome, she should be given control. On the other hand, nonintegration may be preferred to integration when separate decision making is important.

An interesting observation can be addressed as follows. Under firm 1 control, we have from (14.10) that $a_i^C \geq a_i^F$ if and only if $B_i^C \geq B_i^F$. Since firm 1 will select b_1 and b_2 to maximize B_1, $B_1^C \geq B_1^F$. Thus, $a_1^C \geq a_1^F$. In this case, $B_2^C \leq B_2^F$, since they are different from the first best. This implies that $a_2^C \leq a_2^F$. That is, firm 1 tends to overinvest and firm 2 tends to underinvest at time 0. The pairs of (B_1^F, B_2^F) and (B_1^C, B_2^C) are depicted in Figure 14.1. In Figure 14.1, $(B_1^{C'}, B_2^{C'})$ denotes the case of firm 2 control.

On the other hand, under nonintegration, we have from (14.6) that $a_i^N \geq a_i^F$ if and only if $B_i^N \geq B_i^F$. Now, each firm determines investment in a noncooperative manner. Since B_i^N is affected by b_j that is selected by firm j ($\neq i$), the outcome may well be that $B_i^N \leq B_i^F$ for $i = 1, 2$. In such a case, both firms will underinvest at time 0: $a_1^C \leq a_1^F$ and $a_2^C \leq a_2^F$. However, B_2^N may well be higher than B_2^C under firm 1 control, so that $a_2^N \geq a_2^C$ under firm 1 control. The pair of (B_1^F, B_2^F) is also depicted in Figure 14.1.

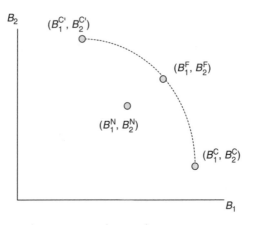

Figure 14.1   Integration versus nonintegration.

In sum, integration will increase the controlling firm's investment, while reducing the controlled firm's investment. If the benefit of the increased investment by the controlling firm is larger (smaller) than the cost following underinvestment by the controlled firm, then integration (nonintegration) is the preferred organizational structure. That is, integration is preferred when the controlling party's investment is significant for the output value.

We now apply the results to the selection of the insurance distribution systems. Let us consider firm 1 as an insurer, and firm 2 as an agent. The exclusive agency corresponds to the case of firm 1 control, and the independent agency to the nonintegration case. The results imply that under exclusive agency, the insurer tends to overinvest while the agent tends to underinvest. Under independence agency, both may underinvest, but the agent's investment will be greater than that under the exclusive agency and will be closer to the first best. Therefore, the exclusive agency is preferred to the independent agency if the insurer's investment is significant for the output value. On the other hand, the independent agency is preferred if the agent's investment is significant for the output value.

When does agent's investment become more important than insurer's? Ownership of the client list provides independent agents with bargaining power over insurers when insureds need to make decisions on maintaining or renewing the contracts. Therefore, when a persistent relationship between insureds and agents is important to the value, independent agency will be preferred (Grossman and Hart, 1986). Similarly, if the agent's efforts in risk selection and classification are important, then the independent agency is preferred (Regan and Tennyson, 1996). This observation implies that independent agency is more prevalent in lines where risks are complex and heterogeneous (Regan and Tennyson, 1996). On the other hand, if the renewal of contracts generally follows initial sales, then initial sales become more important. When the initial sales depend on the reputation of insurers, then insurer's investment in reputation building becomes important. For example, exclusive agency insurers will invest more in advertising than independent agency insurers (Marvel, 1982). This case also explains why the size of the exclusive agency insurer will be greater than that of the independent agency insurer (Sass and Gisser, 1989). Given that one of the important sources of value creation of the agent is to provide insureds with the monitoring service of insurers, independent agents can make greater efforts in monitoring insurers. Thus, when the monitoring of insurers is important, independent agency is preferred. For example, independent agency is more prevalent in long-term insurance and complex insurance lines. Since stock insurers are prevalent in these lines, stock insurers are more associated with the independent agency (Kim, Mayers and Smith, 1996).

14.3   Search and Match Approach

Insurance products are notorious for their complex structures. Insurance is a promise by the insurer which is a contingent claim associated with an uncertain future. Therefore, it is not easy to fully understand the characteristics of insurance products and the possibility of the fulfillment of the promises. Uninformedness is pervasive in the insurance market.

In this regard, agents and brokers may well be considered information providers. The search models focus on the information provision function of agents. Since independent agents deal with many insurers, independent agents can provide the insureds with more comprehensive information regarding insurers than exclusive agents. Based on this difference, the search models address how search costs may affect the coexistence of distribution systems. Let us investigate a simple search model.

14.3.1   Distribution of Insurers and Insureds

Insureds have different tastes in insurers' features such as services, product design, and financial strength. For simplicity, assume that insureds are evenly located on the $[0, 1] \times [0, S]$ rectangle, while insurers are located at the two end lines of the rectangle (i.e., $0 \times [0, S]$ and $1 \times [0, S]$) as shown in Figure 14.2. Insureds are identical except for their locations and search costs. The horizontal axis represents the preference and the vertical axis represents the search cost. The horizontal distance between an insured and an insurer determines the matching types. Insureds in $[0, \frac{1}{2}]$ on the horizontal axis prefer insurers at point 0 (i.e., insurers at $0 \times [0, S]$), and insureds in $(\frac{1}{2}, 1]$ on the horizontal axis prefers insurers at point 1 (i.e., insurers at $1 \times [0, S]$). However, each insured does not know his own location,

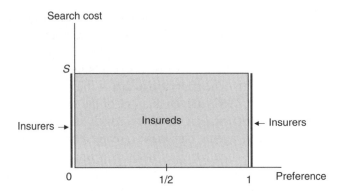

Figure 14.2   Search model: distribution of insurers and insureds.

or equivalently, he does not know which insurer is closer. To find out his matching insurer, an insured may opt to search directly or delegate search to an agent. Under direct search, the insured purchases insurance from insurers using the exclusive agency. We interpret the agent that is delegated the search as an independent agent. Thus, under delegated search, the insured purchases insurance from insurers using the independent agency.

When an insured directly searches, he randomly visits point 0 or 1. Once he visits one insurer, he can find out if the insurer is his matching type. If the insurer is his type, then he purchases insurance. If not, he visits the other location and purchases there. We assume that an insured will incur search cost s when he directly visits each location. The search costs are evenly distributed over $[0, S]$ as depicted in Figure 14.2.

14.3.2   Insurer's efficiency and price

Insurers are identical in production management, but may be different in their distribution management efficiency. For distribution systems, insurers may select the exclusive agency or the independent agency. If an insurer selects the exclusive agency, the direct marketing cost C is incurred. We suppose that there are two efficiency levels in direct marketing costs: $C = C^H, C^L, C^H > C^L$. On the other hand, if the insurer selects the independent agency, she can save direct marketing cost C, but should pay commission M to the agent. We suppose that M is fixed and competitively determined. Insurance markets are competitive. Thus, price is determined as the sum of the fair premium and the distribution costs (direct marketing costs or commission). Now consider an insurer with direct marketing cost C. If the insurer uses exclusive agency, her price becomes $Q + C$. If the insurer uses independent agency, her price becomes $Q + M$.

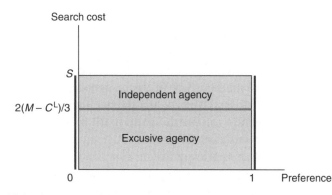

Figure 14.3   Search model: coexistence and market shares when $C_L < M < C_L + 3S/2$.

14.3.3   Equilibrium outcome

The outcome will be different based on the relative sizes of M and C. There are three possibilities to consider.

(i) $M \leq C^L$. In this case all insurers select the independent agency, and all insurers offer the same prices. This case occurs when the independent agency is very efficient.

(ii) $C^L < M < C^L + 3S/2$. This case is the main focus of our analysis. First, it is not possible that efficient insurers select the independent agency, while inefficient insurers select the exclusive agency. An efficient insurer would make a positive profit by selecting the exclusive agency. Let us focus on the case in which efficient insurers select the exclusive agency, while inefficient insurers select the independent agency. In this case, the price of the efficient insurer is $Q + C^L$ and the price of the inefficient insurer is $Q + M$.

Now let us consider an insured with search cost s. His problem is to choose between a direct search and a delegate search. To focus on distribution systems, let us separate risk reduction from distribution and search related costs. The risk reduction trade is the exchange of fair premium Q and contingent benefits. We suppose that this risk reduction trade results in the net utility U. In a direct search, the insured may search once or twice and will purchase from the exclusive agency insurer. Then the expected utility from the direct search becomes $U - C^L - 3s/2$. If the insured delegates search to an independent agent, then his utility becomes $U - M$. Therefore, an insured will purchase insurance through the exclusive agency if and only if $s \leq 2(M - C^L)/3$. Noting that the total market size is S, the market share of the exclusive agency is $2(M - C^L)/3S$; and the market share of the independent agency is $1 - 2(M - C^L)/3S$. The market shares are depicted in Figure 14.3.

As $M - C^L$ increases, the market share of exclusive agency becomes greater. That is, when the efficiency of the exclusive agency becomes large compared to the efficiency of the independent agency, the exclusive agency will prevail more in the market. On the other hand, as S increases, the market share of the independent agency becomes greater. That is, as search costs are smaller (larger), the exclusive (independent) agency will prevail more in the market.

(iii) $M \geq C^L + 3S/2$. In this case, the exclusive agency dominates the whole market. Note that an inefficient insurer cannot survive if both types of insurers select the exclusive agency. Only efficient insurers will survive in the market. The following proposition summarizes the discussion.

Proposition 14.2 (Search and match).

(a) If $M \leq C^L$, the independent agency dominates the whole market.
(b) If $C^L < M < C^L + 3S/2$, the exclusive agency and the independent agency coexist. The market share of the exclusive agency is $2(M - C^L)/3S$, while that of the independent agency is $1 - 2(M - C^L)/3S$.
(c) If $M \geq C^L + 3S/2$, the exclusive agency dominates the whole market. Only efficient insurers can survive.

Proof See the text above. □

An important implication of the proposition is that even if $M > C^L$, the independent agency survives, since it provides benefits to insureds with high search costs. On the other hand, no exclusive agency survives if $M \leq C^L$. Therefore, the coexistence of distribution systems is possible only if the independent agency is less efficient than the exclusive agency. This result may explain the cost differential observations in literature.

14.4   Operating Leverage Approach

A differential cost efficiency may result from a differential operating leverage (Seog, 2005). Different insurers may strategically select different operating leverage in competing with each other. From this viewpoint, the exclusive agency is identified with a high operating leverage, while the independent agency is identified with a low operating leverage. In an equilibrium, coexistence is possible, depending on the parameter values. Moreover, when two agencies coexist, the exclusive agency should exhibit higher cost efficiency. In this approach, the differential cost efficiency is a natural outcome of differential operating leverages.

Let us consider the following model based on Seog (2005). There are two potential insurers that should choose their distribution systems before production. There are two alternative distribution systems: exclusive agency and independent agency. The only difference between these two distribution systems is their "operating leverages." The exclusive agency is identified with a high operating leverage (low unit variable costs and high fixed costs), while the independent agency is identified with a low operating leverage (high unit variable costs and low fixed costs).

After determining their distribution systems, insurers produce insurance products. Competition is characterized by the Cournot–Nash duopoly. In the Cournot–Nash duopoly, each insurer determines its optimal quantities of products given price and the other insurer's behavior. The unit price of insurance is denoted by Q. For simplicity, we assume that the inverse demand function is linear, $Q = P_0 - bD$, where D is total insurance demand in the market, and P_0 and b are positive constants. On the cost side, the firm will incur variable and fixed costs for operation. We denote by c and c' the unit variable cost of an exclusive agency insurer and an independent agency insurer, respectively, and F and F' for total fixed cost of an exclusive agency insurer and an independent agency insurer, respectively. Our assumption on operating leverage implies that $c < c'$ and $F > F'$. The pairs (c, F) and (c', F') will be referred to as the operating leverages for an exclusive agency and an independent agency, respectively.

Let us first consider the case in which one insurer selects the exclusive agency, and the other selects the independent agency. With d insurance goods sold, an exclusive agency insurer's profit function is given by

$$\pi_{EA} = (Q-c)d - F - X(d), \qquad (14.11)$$

where $X(d)$ is the sum of random losses x that are incurred by the insurer's customers.

Note that $X(d)$ is also random, since the number of loss occurrences is random. By decomposing P_0 into $E(x) + e$, where $E(x)$ is the expected loss per unit, and $e \equiv P_0 - E(x)$, we have

$$\pi_{EA} = (E(x) + e - bD - c)d - F - X(d). \qquad (14.12)$$

Noting that $E(x)d = EX(d)$, the expected profit of an exclusive agency insurer becomes

$$E\pi_{EA} = (e - c - bD)d - F = (A - bD)d - F, \quad \text{where } A = e - c. \qquad (14.13)$$

Similarly, for an independent agency insurer, the expected profit with d' demand is given by

$$E\pi_{IA} = (A' - bD)d' - F', \quad \text{where } A' = e - c'. \qquad (14.14)$$

Note that $A > A'$. Now, let us consider the insurer's production decision. The exclusive agency insurer's problem is described and solved as follows:

$$\max_{\{d\}} E\pi_{EA} = (A - bD)d - F. \tag{14.15}$$

Note that $D = d + d_{IA}$, where d_{IA} is the product quantity of the independent agency insurer. The FOC is

$$E\pi_{EA'} = (A - bD) - bd = 0. \tag{14.16}$$

The solution is

$$d_{EA} = [A - bd_{IA}]/2b. \tag{14.17}$$

Similarly, an independent agency insurer's product quantity is given by

$$d_{IA} = [A' - bd_{EA}]/2b. \tag{14.18}$$

We now have the following result.

Lemma 14.1   (Operating leverage: production and profit).

(a)   The production quantities of the exclusive agency insurer and the independent agency insurer are respectively

$$d_{EA}^* = (2A - A')/3b;$$

$$d_{IA}^* = \begin{cases} (2A' - A)/3b, & \text{if } A'/[A - A'] > 1, \\ 0, & \text{otherwise.} \end{cases}$$

(b)   Total quantity (total market size) is $D^* = d_{EA}^* + d_{IA}^* = (A + A')/3$.

(c)   The expected profits of insurers are respectively

$$E\pi_{EA} = (2A - A')/9b - F;$$

$$E\pi_{IA} = \begin{cases} (2A' - A)^2/9b - F' & \text{if } A'/[A - A'] > 1, \\ -F', & \text{otherwise.} \end{cases}$$

(d)   If both insurers select the exclusive agency, then $d_{EA}^* = A/3b$ and $E\pi_{EA} = A^2/9b - F$.

(e)   If both insurers select the independent agency, then $d_{IA}^* = A'/3b$ and $E\pi_{IA} = A'^2/9b - F'$.

Parts (a)–(c) apply to the case in which two insurers select different distribution systems.

Proof Solving (14.17) and (14.18) simultaneously, we have (a)–(c). Parts (d) and (e) can also be obtained by similar logic.   □

If $A'/[A - A'] \leq 1$, then no insurer will select the independent agency. Thus, two distribution agencies may coexist only if $A'/[A - A'] > 1$. Note that d_{EA}^* increases and d_{IA}^* decreases in A. On the other hand, d_{EA}^* decreases and d_{IA}^* increases in A'.

In an equilibrium, insurers should make nonnegative expected profits given the optimal production decision described above; and have no incentive to change their marketing systems. For simplicity, let us simply assume that expected profits are nonnegative in any selection of distribution systems. Thus, we only need to check the incentives to change distribution systems.

If the exclusive agency insurer switches to the independent agency, her profit will become $A'^2/9b - F'$. Thus, the exclusive agency insurer will not change the distribution system if and only if

$$(2A - A')^2/9b - F \geq A'^2/9b - F' \text{ or } 4A(A - A') \geq 9b(F - F'). \qquad (14.19)$$

Likewise, the independent agency insurer will not change the distribution system if and only if

$$4A'(A - A') \leq 9b(F - F'). \qquad (14.20)$$

If both (14.19) and (14.20) hold, then the distribution systems coexist in an equilibrium. The following results report the equilibrium outcome.

Proposition 14.3 (Operating leverage: equilibrium outcome).

(a) When two distribution systems coexist, the profit of the exclusive agency insurer is strictly greater than the profit of the independent agency insurer.

(b) When two distribution systems coexist, the exclusive agency insurer produces higher quantities than the independent agency insurer.

Proof

(a) Assume, for argument's sake, that $E\pi_{EA} \leq E\pi_{IA}$, or
    $(2A - A')^2/9b - F \leq (2A' - A)^2/9b - F'$.
    This inequality can be rearranged into
    $3(A + A')(A - A') \leq 9b(F - F')$.
    Note that
    $3(A + A')(A - A') > \frac{9}{2}A(A - A')$,
    since $A' > A/2$ from $A'/[A - A'] > 1$. Thus, we have
    $\frac{9}{2}A(A - A') < 9b(F - F')$.
    However, this is contradictory to (14.19), so that the exclusive agency insurer will change the distribution system.

(b)   This result is easily obtained by comparing between $d^*_{EA} = (2A - A')/3b$ and $d^*_{IA} = (2A' - A)/3b$ of Lemma 14.1(a). □

Part (a) provides support for the empirical finding that the exclusive agency insurer is more efficient than the independent agency insurer, if the firm profit is used for efficiency measures.[1] Part (b) implies that the exclusive agency insurer is larger than the independent agency insurer (Sass and Gisser, 1989).

Even if the profit of the exclusive agency insurer is higher than that of the independent agency insurer, it does not imply that the independent agency insurer can do better by changing the distribution systems. Note that $E\pi_{EA} > E\pi_{IA}$ implies $3(A + A')(A - A') > 9b(F - F')$, while the independent agency insurer will not change the distribution system if and only if $4A'(A - A') \leq 9b (F - F')$ (see (14.20)). Both inequalities may well be satisfied simultaneously.

Unlike the independent agency insurer, the exclusive agency insurer is willing to change the distribution systems if $E\pi_{EA} \leq E\pi_{IA}$ as shown in the proof of (a). This asymmetric result comes from the differential operating leverages. The exclusive agency insurer has a high operating leverage, implying that a higher unit margin is earned as it produces. Thus, the exclusive agency insurer becomes aggressive in the market. When the independent agency insurer becomes an exclusive agency insurer, two exclusive agency insurers aggressively produce products, resulting in lower profits. However, when the exclusive agency insurer becomes an independent agency insurer, two independent agency insurers less aggressively produce products, resulting in higher profits. Therefore, the exclusive agency insurer is willing to change the marketing system if the independent agency insurer is more profitable than the exclusive agency insurer, while the independent agency insurer may not change even if the exclusive agency insurer is more profitable than the independent agency insurer.

Notice that the operating leverage may interact with diverse factors including transaction costs, services, and search costs which are considered above. Therefore, it is possible that the efficiency differences between distribution systems may be observed as a result of the interaction between such factors and the operating leverage.

14.5   Compensation Structure

In general, insurance agents are paid commissions based on the premium, while employee sales forces are paid salary. However, the details vary

---

[1]   When the unit profit is used for efficiency measures, the efficiency of the exclusive agency insurer can be higher or lower than that of the independent agency insurer.

across agency and insurance types. In property and casualty insurance in the USA, independent agents tend to be paid wholly by commission. The commission rates are not much different between new policy sales and policy renewals. While exclusive agents are also paid by commission, the commission rates are lower than those for the independent agents. In addition, the commission rates for policy renewals are much lower than those for new policy sales. In US life insurance, the commission rates for both agency types are high for new policy sales and low for policy renewals.

This difference can be explained based on the bargaining power derived from ownership of the client list (see Regan and Tennyson, 2000). In property and casualty insurance, the independent agents possess the ownership of the client lists. Therefore, if the commission rates are lower for policy renewal, the independent agents will have a strong incentive to place the insureds with another insurer instead of renewing the policy with the same insurer. However, independent agents in life insurance do not possess the client lists. Therefore, their commission patterns are similar to those for exclusive agents. On the other hand, the exclusive agency insurers tend to provide their agents with greater services of training and support and advertising than independent agency insurers. The high commission rates for new sales provide the agents with the incentive to make efforts to attract new sales.

Compensation schemes for brokers are an interesting case. Brokers are often paid by commission from the insurers. This convention may be problematic, since brokers legally represent insureds, not insurers, although the functions of brokers are similar to those of independent agents. It is often argued that the compensation for brokers should be based on fees from insureds, rather than on commission from insurers. Such commission may provide brokers with the incentives to place uninformed insureds with the insurers paying high commission, instead of placing them with right insurers. On the other hand, proponents for the commission scheme (including the contingent commission scheme) argue that commissions provide brokers with the incentives to match insureds with right insurers, so that insurers can maintain profits in the long run.[2] The relative efficiency between the fee scheme and the commission scheme may vary depending on circumstances. If the negative effect of exploiting uninformed insureds is high (low) relative to the positive effect of the incentive alignment between brokers and insurers, then the fee scheme is more (less) efficient than the commission scheme.

On the other hand, compensation schemes may differentially affect the competition among brokers, which leads to different efficiency levels

---

[2] Contingent commissions refer to the nonlinear commissions based on insurer's underwriting profits and volumes.

between two systems (Gravelle, 1994). We briefly review the model investigated in Gravelle (1994).

Consider a competitive insurance market in which insurers produce homogeneous insurance products with marginal cost C. The price quote is denoted by Q. There are potentially N homogeneous insureds who may purchase insurance. When an insured purchases the insurance, his utility becomes $B - m$, where B is the gross benefit from the insurance consumption and m denotes the mismatch disutility. We assume that m is uniformly distributed on $[0, M]$ and $C < B < C + M$. The insured, however, cannot directly observe the mismatch parameter m before purchase.

Insureds may purchase directly from the insurers or purchase via brokers. If an insured purchases via a broker, the broker provides perfect information about the mismatch parameter. We assume that each insurer is contacted by at most one broker, which provides the broker with the monopoly powers in their compensation.

The number of brokers in the market is denoted by n. Each broker should incur cost $K(n)$ to make contact with an insured, where $K'(n) \geq 0$. We assume that the reservation utility of the broker is 0. Let us write R for the broker's expected compensation per sale. R may have different forms and values depending on the compensation scheme. Now, the broker's expected profit is $R - K(n)$. We allow the free entry of brokers. Brokers will enter as long as the expected profit is positive.

An equilibrium is defined as the situation in which insurers make zero expected profits, brokers earn zero expected profits, and the insureds make purchase decisions to maximize their utilities. Now, let us consider two alternative compensation schemes: commission and fee.

14.5.1   Commission scheme

Let us consider an insured's purchase decision. Under direct purchase, the insured is uninformed about the mismatch parameter m. Then his decision is based on the expected utility. Given Q, the insured will purchase insurance if

$$EU(Q) = B - Q - E(m) \geq 0. \tag{14.21}$$

Noting that $E(m) = M/2$, the ex ante insured's surplus can be compactly expressed as

$$V_U^c(Q) = \max[0, B - Q - M/2]. \tag{14.22}$$

If the insured is informed via a broker, then his decision is based on the true mismatch parameter. He will purchase insurance if $B - Q - m \geq 0$, or $m \leq B - Q$. Thus, the ex ante insured's surplus can be expressed as

$$V_I^c(Q) = \int_0^{B-Q} (B - Q - m)\frac{1}{M}\,dm = \frac{(B-Q)^2}{2M}. \tag{14.23}$$

Now suppose that all insureds purchase insurance via brokers, which will be confirmed later. Under competition, the insurance price is set as the sum of the production cost C and the commission rate r per sale, so that the insurer's profit becomes zero. Moreover, the broker can set the commission rate to maximize her expected profit given that each insured is contacted by only one broker. Note that the expected revenue (commission) of the broker per sale depends on the price and the commission rate, r. We write

$$R = R(Q, r) = r \Pr(m \le B - Q) = r(B - Q)/M = r(B - C - r)/M.$$

The broker's expected profit becomes

$$r(B - C - r)/M - K(n). \tag{14.24}$$

The profit maximizing commission rate $r = (B - C)/2$, and the resulting expected commission

$$R = \frac{(B-C)^2}{4M}.$$

The insurance price Q becomes $(B + C)/2$. The insured's expected surplus under the commission scheme is

$$V_I^c(Q) = \frac{(B-Q)^2}{2M} = \frac{(B-C)^2}{8M}. \tag{14.25}$$

Note that the uninformed insured's expected surplus is

$$V_U^c(Q) \le B - Q - M/2 = (B - C - M)/2.$$

We have

$$V_I^c(Q) - V_U^c(Q) = \frac{(B-C-2M)^2}{8M} \ge 0.$$

Thus, all insureds will purchase via brokers, which confirms our assumption. The broker's expected profit per sale is $R - K(n)$. The brokers enter the market until $R - K(n) = 0$. The number of brokers is determined by

$$n^c = K^{-1}\frac{(B-C)^2}{4M}. \tag{14.26}$$

With $n = n^c$, the broker's expected profit is zero.

The ex ante social welfare is the sum of all expected utilities of insureds, insurers ($= 0$), and brokers ($= 0$):

$$S^c = NV_I^c = \frac{N(B-C)^2}{8M}. \tag{14.27}$$

14.5.2 Fee scheme

Now suppose that the brokers are paid fees by insureds. Competition leads the insurance price to be the production cost: $Q = C$. An uninformed insurer will directly purchase from an insurer if $EU(Q) = B - Q - M/2 \geq 0$. The ex ante insured's surplus can be expressed as

$$V_U^f(Q) = \max[0, B - Q - M/2] = \max[0, B - C - M/2]. \tag{14.28}$$

On the other hand, an insured may buy the information regarding m from the broker with fee s. Learning m, the insured will purchase insurance only if $B - Q - m \geq 0$, or $m \leq B - Q$. Thus, the ex ante insured's surplus is

$$V_I^f(Q) = (B-Q)^2/2M = (B-C)^2/2M. \tag{14.29}$$

An insured will buy the information from the broker if $J = V_I^f(Q) - V_U^f(Q) \geq s$. Noting that $Q = C$,

$$J = \begin{cases} \dfrac{(B-C)^2}{2M}, & \text{if } C < B < C + M/2, \\[2ex] \dfrac{(B-C-M)^2}{2M}, & \text{if } C + M/2 \leq B < C + M. \end{cases} \tag{14.30}$$

Note that $J > 0$. The broker will maximize her profit by setting the fee rate s to satisfy $s = J$. This will guarantee that all insureds purchase via brokers. In this case, $R = s$, and the expected profit of the broker per sales is $s - K(n)$.

The number of brokers is determined by $s - K(n) = 0$. That is,

$$n^f = \begin{cases} K^{-1}(s) \\[2ex] K^{-1}\left(\dfrac{(B-C)^2}{2M}\right), & \text{if } C < B < C + M/2, \\[3ex] K^{-1}\left(\dfrac{(B-C-M)^2}{2M}\right), & \text{if } C + M/2 \leq B < C + M \end{cases} \tag{14.31}$$

With $n = n^f$, the profits of brokers are zero.

The ex ante social welfare is

$$S^f = N(V_I^f - s) = NV_U^f$$

$$= \begin{cases} 0, & \text{if } C < B < C + M/2 \\ N[B - C - M/2], & \text{if } C + M/2 \leq B < C + M. \end{cases} \tag{14.32}$$

14.5.3   Comparison

The difference in social welfare is

$$S^c - S^f = \frac{N(B-C)^2}{8M} - N \max[0, B - C - M/2]$$

$$= \begin{cases} \dfrac{N(B-C)^2}{8M} & \text{if } C < B < C + M/2, \\[2ex] \dfrac{N[B - C - (4 - 2\sqrt{3})M][B - C - (4 + 2\sqrt{3})M]}{8M}, & \\[1ex] & \text{if } C + M/2 \leq B < C + M. \end{cases} \tag{14.33}$$

Figure 14.4 depicts the locus of $S^c - S^f$. $S^c - S^f \geq 0$ if and only if $C < B \leq C + (4 - 2\sqrt{3})M$, or $B \geq C + (4 + 2\sqrt{3})M$. Since we assume that $C < B < C + M$, the second range is not applicable. Thus,

$$S^c \geq S^f i \leftrightarrow B \leq B^S \equiv C + (4 - 2\sqrt{3})M. \tag{14.34}$$

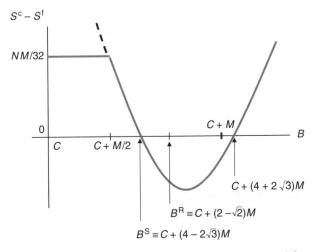

Figure 14.4   Social welfare difference between commission and fee.

Figure 14.5   Commission versus fee.

If the benefit from the insurance consumption is small, then the commission scheme is more efficient than the fee scheme. If the benefit is large, then the fee scheme is more efficient.

The broker's commission revenue is greater than the fee revenue if and only if

$$B > B^R \equiv C + (2 - \sqrt{2})M.$$

(14.35)

Note that $B^R > B^S$. It also follows that the number of brokers is greater under the commission scheme than under the fee scheme, if and only if $B > B^R$. The next proposition summarizes the discussion and Figure 14.5 depicts the comparison results.

Proposition 14.4 (Commission scheme and fee scheme compared).

(a)   Neither the commission scheme nor the fee scheme dominates the other in the sense of social welfare.
(b)   If the benefit of insurance consumption is small (large), the commission scheme is more (less) efficient than the fee scheme.
(c)   If the benefit of insurance consumption is large (small), the broker's revenue and the number of brokers are greater (smaller) under the commission scheme than under the fee scheme.

Under the fee scheme, brokers can receive fees regardless of the purchase decision. Under the commission scheme, however, brokers can receive commission only if the insured makes a purchase. When the gross benefit of insurance is low, the possibility of purchase is low. In such a case, the broker's revenue is greater under the fee scheme than under the commission scheme, as long as the insured is willing to pay the fees.

Due to the assumption of monopoly power of the brokers, the social welfare tends to be lower when the broker's revenue is higher. However, the relationship is not exact. For the middle range of B, $B^S \leq B \leq B^R$, the higher (fee) revenue of the broker is associated with higher social welfare.

If the compensation scheme is selected by the brokers based on the revenue, then the fee (commission) scheme is selected for $B \leq (>) B^R$. The broker's selection of the compensation scheme tends to be inefficient except for $B^S \leq B \leq B^R$. The compensation scheme is the fee scheme in such an efficient case. However, these results may be specific to the model, which makes it difficult to generalize the implications.

14.6   Conclusion

Insurance markets are characterized by diverse distribution systems including insurance agents, brokers and the employee sales forces. Distribution systems exist as middlemen between insurers and insureds. Due to the lack of perfect information, the middlemen play important roles in matching insureds with insurers. The middlemen may increase efficiency by resolving the information problems. Diverse distribution systems coexist since different systems exhibit strengths in different aspects. The literature focuses on service qualities, transaction costs, searches, and operation costs. Along with the selection of the distribution systems, the design of the compensation scheme seems to affect the efficiency of the insurance market.

BIBLIOGRAPHY

Alchian, A. A. and H. Demsetz (1972) Production, information costs, and economic organization. *American Economic Review*, 62: 777–95.

Anderson, E. (1985) The salesperson as outside agent or employee: a transaction cost analysis. *Marketing Science*, 4: 234–54.

Anderson, E., W. T. Ross, Jr. and B. Weitz (1998) Commitment and its consequences in the American agency system of selling insurance. *Journal of Risk and Insurance*, 65: 637–69.

Baranoff, E. and T. Sager (2003) The relations among organizational and distribution forms and capital and asset risk structures in the life insurance industry. *Journal of Risk and Insurance*, 70: 375–400.

Barrese, J., H. I. Doerpinghaus, and J. M. Nelson (1995) Do independent agent insurers provide superior service? The insurance marketing puzzle. *Journal of Risk and Insurance*, 62: 297–308.

Barrese, J. and J. M. Nelson (1992) Independent and exclusive agency insurers: a reexamination of the cost differential. *Journal of Risk and Insurance*, 59: 375–97.

Berger, A. N., J. D. Cummins, and M. A. Weiss (1997) The coexistence of multiple distribution systems for financial services: the case of property-liability insurance. *Journal of Business*, 70: 515–46.

Carr, R. A., J. D. Cummins, and L. Regan (1999) Efficiency and competitiveness in the U.S. life insurance industry: corporate, product, and distribution strategies. In J. D. Cummins and A. Santomero (eds), *Changes in the Life Insurance Industry: Efficiency, Technology, and Risk Management*. Boston: Kluwer Academic Publishers.

Cather, D. A., S. G. Gustavson and J. S. Trieschmann (1985) A profitability analysis of property-liability insurers using alternative distribution systems. *Journal of Risk and Insurance*, 52: 321–32.

Cummins, J. D., and J. VanDerhei (1979) A note on the relative efficiency of property-liability insurance distribution systems. *Bell Journal of Economics*, 10: 709–19.

Cummins, J. D. and S. N. Weisbart (1977) *The Impact of Consumer Services on Independent Insurance Agency Performance*. Glenmont, NY: IMA Education and Research Foundation.

Dahlby, B. and D. S. West (1986) Price dispersion in an automobile insurance market. *Journal of Political Economy*, 94: 418–38.

Darby, M. R. and E. Karni (1979) Free competition and the optimal amount of fraud. *Journal of Law and Economics*, 22: 67–88.

Doerpinghaus, H. I. (1991) An analysis of complaint data in the automobile insurance industry. *Journal of Risk and Insurance*, 58: 120–7.

Doherty, N. A. and S. H. Seog (2000) A dynamic model of the coexistence of distribution systems: an insurance example. *Singapore International Insurance and Actuarial Journal*, 4: 19–36.

Etgar, M. (1976) Service performance of insurance distribution. *Journal of Risk and Insurance*, 43: 487–99.

Gravell, H. (1993) Product price and advice quality: implications of the commission system in life assurance. *Geneva Papers on Risk and Insurance Theory*, 16: 3–19.

Gravell, H. (1994) Remunerating information providers: commissions versus fees in life insurance. *Journal of Risk and Insurance*, 61: 421–57.

Gron, A. (1995) Regulation and insurer competition: did insurers use rate regulation to reduce competition? *Journal of Risk and Uncertainty*, 11: 87–111.

Grossman, S. J. and O. D. Hart (1986) The costs and benefits of ownership: a theory of vertical and lateral integration. *Journal of Political Economy*, 94: 691–719.

Harrington, S. E. (1982) Operating expenses for agency and nonagency life insurers: further evidence. *Journal of Risk and Insurance*, 49: 229–55.

Joskow, P. L. (1973) Cartels, competition and regulation in the property-liability insurance industry. *Bell Journal of Economics and Management Science*, 4: 375–427.

Kim, W-J., D. Mayers, and C. W. Smith (1996) On the choice of insurance distribution systems. *Journal of Risk and Insurance*, 63: 207–27.

MacMinn, R. D. and S. H. Seog (2008) Distribution of price and quality under information asymmetry. KAIST Business School Working Paper. http://ssrn.com/abstract=1182002.

Martimort, D. (1996) Exclusive dealing, common agency, and multiprincipals incentive theory. *Rand Journal of Economics*, 27: 1–31.

Marvel, H. P. (1982) Exclusive dealing. *Journal of Law and Economics*, 25: 1–25.

Mathewson, G. F. (1983) Information, search and price variability of individual life insurance contracts. *Journal of Industrial Economics*, 32: 131–48.

Posey, L. L. and S. Tennyson (1998) The coexistence of distribution systems under price search: theory and some evidence from insurance. *Journal of Economics Behavior and Organization*, 35: 95–115.

Posey, L. L. and A. Yavas (1995) A search model of marketing systems in property-liability insurance. *Journal of Risk and Insurance*, 62: 666–89.

Pritchett, S. T. and B. Y. Brewster, Jr. (1979) Comparison of ordinary operating expense ratios for agency and non-agency insurers. *Journal of Risk and Insurance*, 46: 61–74.

Puelz, R. and A. Snow (1991) Efficient contracting in a market for life insurance agents with asymmetric information. *Journal of Risk and Insurance*, 58: 729–36.

Regan, L. (1997) Vertical integration in the property-liability insurance industry: a transactions cost approach. *Journal of Risk and Insurance*, 64: 41–62.

Regan, L. and S. Tennyson (1996) Agent discretion and the choice of insurance distribution system. *Journal of Law and Economics*, 39: 637–66.

Regan, L. and S. Tennyson (2000) Insurance distribution systems. In G. Dionne (ed.), *Handbook of Insurance*. Boston: Kluwer Academic Publishers.

Regan, L. and L. Tzeng (1999) Vertical integration and ownership form in the property-liability insurance industry. *Journal of Risk and Insurance*, 66: 253–274.

Sass, T. R. and M. Gisser (1989) Agency costs, firm size and exclusive dealing. *Journal of Law and Economics*, 32: 381–400.

Seog, S. H. (1999) The coexistence of distribution systems when consumers are not informed. *Geneva Papers on Risk and Insurance Theory*, 24: 173–92.

Seog, S. H. (2005) Distribution systems and operating leverage. *Asia-Pacific Journal of Risk and Insurance*, 1(1): 45–61.

Venezia, I., D. Galai and Z. Shapira (1999) Exclusive vs. independent agents: a separating equilibrium approach. *Journal of Economic Behavior & Organization*, 40: 443–56.

Williamson, O. E. (1979) Transaction-cost economics: the governance of contractual relations. *Journal of Law and Economics*, 22: 233–61.

Chapter 15

Insurance Pricing

Insurance pricing is traditionally an area of actuarial science. As financial pricing techniques have been developed in finance, they have also found applications in insurance. In both actuarial science and finance, sophisticated pricing techniques have been developed. It is beyond our scope to cover all the details of such pricing techniques in this chapter. Instead, our intention is to briefly introduce a few prominent pricing techniques and discuss their implications.

An insurance premium is composed of two parts: the pure premium and the loaded premium. The pure premium is the discounted expected loss. Since insurance is an exchange between the premium and the payment for the loss, accurate estimation of the loss distribution is essential in insurance pricing. The loaded premium represents the insurer's costs and profits. As the insurer has to incur sales and administration costs, such costs should be included in the price. In addition, the owners of the insurer need to earn some returns on their invested capital. If the capital and insurance markets are competitive, the owners expect to earn fair returns. These returns are included in the price.

Traditional actuarial pricing puts its emphasis on the estimation of the loss distribution. Without knowledge of the loss distribution, the insurer cannot set the right price and manage the risk. On the other hand, the financial pricing is more focused on the concept of fair return. The fair return should be determined in the financial market based on the tradeoff relationship between risk and return. Since the fair return is used as a discount rate, it can be an important ingredient in calculating the pure premium, especially when the contract period is long. Actuarial pricing is briefly introduced in Section 15.1. Economic asset pricing theories including state pricing and consumption-based pricing are introduced in Section 15.2. Section 15.3 investigates financial pricing approaches which apply the capital asset pricing model, prevent value, and the option pricing theory to insurance pricing.

15.1   Actuarial Pricing of Insurance

15.1.1   Individual risk theory

Let us consider the loss distribution of an individual exposure unit, n. Denote by x^n the discrete random loss of n. The loss distribution is described by

$$x^n = x_1^n, \ldots, x_{I(n)}^n; \; p_1^n, \ldots, p_{I(n)}^n,$$

where x_i^n is a realized loss, and p_i^n is a probability of loss x_i^n. The expected loss and the variance of the loss distribution are:

$$\mu_n = E_n(x^n) = \sum p_i^n x_i^n$$
$$\sigma_n^2 = E_n((x^n - E_n(x^n))^2 = \sum_{i=1}^{I(n)} p_i^n (x_i^n - E_n(x^n))^2. \tag{15.1}$$

When there are N units in a pool, with $1 \leq n \leq N$, the expected loss and the variance of the loss of the pool are

$$\mu(N) = \sum \mu_i = \mu_1 + \ldots + \mu_N. \tag{15.2}$$

$$\sigma^2(N) = \sum_n \sigma_n^2 + \sum_n \sum_{m \neq n} \sigma_{nm}, \quad \text{where } \sigma_{nm} = \text{cov}(x^n, x^m). \tag{15.3}$$

For a homogenous group, $\mu_n = \mu$, $\sigma_n^2 = \sigma^2$, $\sigma_{nm} = \rho\sigma^2$. Thus,

$\mu(N) = N\mu.$

$\sigma^2(N) = N\sigma^2 + N(N-1)\rho\sigma^2.$

Given these values, the pure premium (ignoring discounting) for the pool becomes $\mu(N)/N$. In the case of a homogenous pool, the pure premium is simply μ.

As discussed in Chapter 3, the law of large numbers allows the insurer to reduce the risk per unit by enlarging the pool size. In the homogenous case, the unit variance is

$$\frac{\sigma^2(N)}{N} = \frac{\sigma^2}{N} + \frac{(N-1)}{N}\rho\sigma^2.$$

In addition, when the distributions are independent, $\rho = 0$. Thus, the unit variance is σ^2/N, which tends to zero as N goes to infinity. The understanding of the loss distribution and the risk pattern under pooling is crucial in risk management as well as pricing. For example, when the law of large numbers holds, the buffer fund per unit becomes ignorable.

15.1.2   Collective risk theory

Instead of considering the individual exposure unit, we may consider the pool collectively. In this approach, the loss distribution from a pool specifically takes into account the risks of frequency as well as severity. The loss of the pool is denoted by $x = \sum_{i=1}^{N} x_i$, where x_i is the ith loss severity and N is the total number of loss occurrences (frequency). Both frequency and severity are exposed to risks. Unlike in the individual risk approach, the number of exposure units is not included.

Let $S^n(x)$ be the cumulative probability that severity is less than or equal to x given frequency n (nth convolution of severity distribution). Let $p(n)$ be the probability that the frequency is n. The loss distribution is expressed as the cumulative distribution

$$F(x) = \sum_{n=1}^{N} p(n)S^n(x),$$

where $F(x)$ is the cumulative probability that total loss of the pool is less than or equal to x. In actuarial science, mathematical approaches have been developed to incorporate diverse distributions to study both individual and collective risk theories (see Panjer and Willmot, 1992).

15.1.3   Pricing

Once the loss distribution is known, the insurance premium in one period setting can be obtained by:

$$Q = \delta\mu + C + \pi, \tag{15.4}$$

where μ is the expected value of benefit payment per the exposure unit, δ is the discount factor, C is the expenses and costs per unit, and π is fair profit per unit to the insurer. Assuming $C = cQ$, $\pi = fQ$, then

$$Q = \delta\mu + cQ + fQ \Rightarrow Q = \mu\delta / (1 - c - f). \tag{15.5}$$

That is, the price is obtained from the expected value of benefit payment discounted by the discount rate $(1 - c - f)/\delta - 1$. Obviously, the discount rate needs to be properly determined for correct pricing. The discount rate becomes more important if insurance is a long-term contract. Asset pricing theories say that a proper discount rate needs to be determined based on the risk which is, in turn, affected by economic agent's risk attitudes and market structures. Let us now turn to asset pricing theories that provide some useful techniques for determining asset values and discount rates.

15.2   Asset Pricing: No Arbitrage and the Complete Market

We consider a one-period setting. The current time and beginning of the period is denoted by $t = 0$, and the end of the period is denoted by $t = 1$. Let us assume that the uncertainty of $t = 1$ can be described by the set of discrete states of nature $SN = \{S_1, \ldots, S_E\}$. There are K tradable securities (or, assets, or contracts): $X_1, \ldots, X_K$. A security is identified by the set of payoffs that the owner receives in each state. The payoffs of security X_i at $t = 1$ are denoted by $(X_i(S_1), \ldots, X_i(S_E))'$. Let A, which will be called the payoff matrix, be a $K \times E$ matrix in which each row represents the payoffs of a security.

$$A = \begin{pmatrix} X_1(S_1), \ldots, X_1(S_E) \\ X_2(S_1), \ldots, X_2(S_E) \\ \vdots \quad \vdots \quad \vdots \\ X_K(S_1), \ldots, X_K(S_E) \end{pmatrix}. \tag{15.6}$$

A portfolio is a combination of securities, which is identified by the numbers of securities held in the portfolio. Portfolio $Z = (z_1, \ldots, z_K)'$, where z_k is the number of security X_k held in Z. The payoffs of Z at $t = 1$ are denoted by $(Z(S_1), \ldots, Z(S_E))'$, where $Z(S_i) = z_1 X_1(S_i) + \ldots + z_K X_K(S_i)$. That is, the payoff of Z can be expressed as AZ'.

A security is called redundant if its payoffs can be replicated by a portfolio composed of other securities. That is, X_i is redundant if there is a portfolio Z such that $X_i(S) = Z(S)$ for all S.

Now, define Q_i as the price of a security X_i at $t = 0$. The price vector $Q = (Q_1, \ldots, Q_K)'$. Note that the price of portfolio Z is given by $z_1 Q_1 + \ldots + z_K Q_K$, or simply $Z'Q$ in matrix form. Suppose that there exists a vector $q = (q(S_1), \ldots, q(S_E))'$ with all elements $q(S_i)$ strictly positive, such that prices of securities can be expressed as

$$Q_i = q(S_1)X_i(S_1) + q(S_2)X_i(S_2) + \ldots + q(S_E)X_i(S_E), \quad \text{for all } X_i. \tag{15.7}$$

Then we call $q(S)$ the state price for state S, and q the state price vector.

An Arrow–Debreu security contingent on S, X^S, is a security that yields $1 in state S, and $0 in all other states: $X^S(S) = 1$, $X^S(S') = 0$, where $S' \neq S$. Given state prices, the prices of the Arrow–Debreu securities should be equal to the state prices. This is because the price of X^S is

$$q(S_1) \cdot 0 + \dots + q(S) \cdot 1 + \dots + q(S_E) \cdot 0 = q(S).$$

15.2.1   No arbitrage

An arbitrage opportunity is a portfolio Z that produces nonnegative payoffs, while its price is nonpositive, excluding the case of all zero. That is,

$Z'Q = 0$, and $Z(S) \geq 0$ for all S, and $Z(S') > 0$ for some S';
or $Z'Q < 0$, and $Z(S) \geq 0$, for all S.

The existence of an arbitrage opportunity implies that individuals can make money without incurring costs. An individual can make an infinite profit by trading the opportunity infinitely. No arbitrage refers to the case in which there is no arbitrage opportunity. No arbitrage implies the "law of one price." If a security has two prices, then it opens an arbitrage opportunity by selling it at a high price and buying it at a low price.

Proposition 15.1 No arbitrage is equivalent to the existence of a state price vector with strictly positive elements.

Proof Let us first state the Farkas lemma.

Farkas lemma Let B be a real $K \times E$ matrix, and b a real $K \times 1$ vector. Only one, not both, of the following should hold.

(i)   There exists a solution $x \geq 0$ to $Bx = b$, where x is an $E \times 1$ vector.
(ii) There exists y such that $y'B \geq 0$, and $y'b < 0$, where y is a $K \times 1$ vector.   □
      ($\Rightarrow$) Let us replace B and b in the Farkas lemma with A and Q. If (ii) holds, then there exists a portfolio Z such that $Z'A \geq 0$, and $Z'Q < 0$. This is contradictory to no arbitrage. If (i) holds, there exists a vector $q \geq 0$ such that $Aq = Q$, where $q = (q_1, \dots, q_E)$. Then $Q = Aq$, or $Q_i = q_1 X_i(S_1) + q_2 X_i(S_2) + \dots + q_E X_i(S_E)$, for all X_i. Now set $q(S_j) = q_j$. Strict positivity of q_j follows, since if $q_i = 0$ for some i, then $z_i > 0$ with $z_j = 0$, $j \neq i$, would make an arbitrage opportunity.
      ($\Leftarrow$) The converse is easily obtained by noting that $Z'Q = \Sigma_i Z(S_i) q_i(S_i) \leq 0$ should imply that $Z(S_i) = 0$, for all S_i; or $Z(S_i) < 0$, for some S_i, since $q(S_i) > 0$ for all S_i.   □

15.2.2   Complete market

A market is complete if, for any payoff vector $(c(S_1), \ldots, c(S_E))$, there is a portfolio Z such that payoffs $Z(S_i) = c(S_i)$ for all S_i. In a complete market, any payoff structure can be generated by a portfolio of existing securities. From linear algebra, a market is complete if and only if matrix A has rank E, that is, there should be E independent rows (securities). With rank E, matrix A can be transformed to a matrix with a diagonal submatrix $E \times E$ with 1s in diagonal. This observation leads to the following result: A market is complete if Arrow–Debreu securities for all states of nature can be constructed from the traded assets. A complete market does not require all Arrow-Debreu securities to actuarially exist. Even if no Arrow–Debreu securities are directly traded, the market is complete as long as they can be made by combining existing securities.

> *Proposition 15.2* In a complete market, the state price vector is uniquely determined under no arbitrage.

> *Proof* This is easily obtained by noting that state prices are uniquely determined in a complete market.   □

Assume, for example, that at $t = 1$ there are two states of nature $SN = \{U, D\}$, with probabilities $p(U), p(D) = 1 - p(U)$. Suppose there are two securities B and X. B is a risk-free security with interest rate r_f, and X is called a stock. Let prices be $Q_B = 1$, and $Q_X = P$. The payoffs of the securities are denoted by

$$\text{Payoff}(B) = (1 + r_f, 1 + r_f),\tag{15.8}$$

$$\text{Payoff}(X) = (uP, dP), u > 1 > d.\tag{15.9}$$

These are combined into a payoff matrix

$$A = \begin{pmatrix} 1 + r_f & 1 + r_f \\ uP & dP \end{pmatrix}.\tag{15.10}$$

State prices $\{q(U), q(D)\}$ at $t = 0$ can be found from the simultaneous equations

$$\begin{aligned} 1 &= (q(U) + q(D))(1 + r_f), \\ P &= q(U)uP + q(D)dP, \end{aligned}\tag{15.11}$$

leading to

$$q(U) = \frac{(1+r_f)-d}{(1+r_f)(u-d)}, \quad q(D) = \frac{u-(1+r_f)}{(1+r_f)(u-d)} \tag{15.12}$$

If $u \le 1 + r_f$, an arbitrage opportunity exists. To see this, let $Z = (P, -1)$. The cost (price) of Z is $Z'Q = P \cdot 1 - 1 \cdot P = 0$.

The payoffs of Z are

$$Z(U) = (1+r_f)P - uP \ge 0,$$

$$Z(D) = (1+r_f)P - dP > 0.$$

No arbitrage implies $u > 1 + r_f$.

Given state prices, we can price any new securities. For a security $Y = (Y(U), Y(D))$,

$$Q_Y = q(U)Y(U) + q(D)Y(D)$$

$$= \frac{(1+r_f)-d}{(1+r_f)(u-d)}Y(U) + \frac{u-(1+r_f)}{(1+r_f)(u-d)}Y(D). \tag{15.13}$$

Risk neutral pricing.   From the risk-free security B,

$$1 = (q(U) + q(D))(1+ r_f),$$

that is,

$$q(U) + q(D) = 1/(1+ r_f).$$

Define

$$q'(U) = (1+ r_f)q(U) = \frac{(1+r_f)-d}{u-d}, \quad q'(D) = (1+ r_f)q(D) = \frac{(1+r_f)-d}{u-d}.$$

Then

$$q'(U) + q'(D) = 1.$$

Also

$$Q_Y = q(U)Y(U) + q(D)Y(D)$$

$$= \frac{1}{1+r_f}\left[q'(U)Y(U) + q'(D)Y(D)\right] \tag{15.14}$$

$$= \frac{1}{1+r_f}E_{q'}(Y),$$

where $E_{q'}(Y) = q'(U)Y(U) + q'(D)Y(D)$, the expected value of the $Y(S)$ with the probabilities $q'(U)$ and $q'(D)$.

Note that $q'(U)$ and $q'(D)$ are not the true probabilities of states $p(U)$, $p(D)$. (Given state prices, the probabilities are not important in pricing.)

However, for pricing purposes, we may consider them *pseudo* probabilities of states to find the pseudo expected value of the payoffs. Then, the price of Y can be obtained by discounting the pseudo expected value with the risk-free rate (15.14). Since the price of the security is calculated as if the expected value is discounted by the risk-free rate, this pricing is often called risk-neutral pricing. It should be noted that it does not mean that individuals are risk neutral. The pseudo probabilities $\{q'(U), q'(D)\}$ are also called risk-neutral probabilities, or equivalent martingale measure in the literature.

Consider again the price of Y, $Q_Y = q(U)Y(U) + q(D)Y(D)$. By multiplying each term on the right-hand side by $p(S)/p(S)$, the price can be expressed as f

$$Q_Y = q(U)Y(U) + q(D)Y(D)$$

$$= p(U)\left[\frac{q(U)}{p(U)}Y(U)\right] + p(D)\left[\frac{q(D)}{p(D)}Y(D)\right]$$

Let us define $m(S) = q(S)/p(S)$. Then,

$$Q_Y = p(U)[m(U)Y(U)] + p(D)[m(D)Y(D)]$$
$$= E[mY].$$
(15.15)

In comparison with (15.14), the price is expressed by the true expected value across true probabilities p. The term $m(S) = q(S)/p(S)$ is the ratio of state price to the probability of the state. This term is incorporated into pricing as if it is a discount factor. Since $\{m(S)\}$ is affected by the realized states of nature, it is called a *stochastic discount* factor or pricing kernel. Note that

$$E(m) = q(U) + q(D) = 1/(1+r_f).$$
(15.16)

Let us define the gross rate of return of Y by $R_Y(S) = Y(S)/Q_Y$. From $Q_Y = E(mY)$, we have

$$1 = E(mR_Y).$$
(15.17)

Insurance pricing.   Suppose that a random loss distribution is as follows: no loss in state U, and loss L in state D at $t = 1$. Consider an insurance contract I, paying for a coverage α of loss L in state D: $I(U) = 0$, $I(D) = \alpha L$. Then, the price of the insurance contract at $t = 0$ is

$$Q_I = q(U)0 + q(D)\alpha L = q(D)L$$

$$= \frac{1}{1+r_f}q'(D)\alpha L = \frac{1}{1+r_f}E_{q'}(I).$$
(15.18)

Using the stochastic discount factor, we can express the price as

$$
\begin{aligned}
Q_I &= q(U)0 + q(D)\alpha L = p(U)[m(U) \cdot 0] \\
&+ p(U)[m(D) \cdot \alpha L] = E(mI).
\end{aligned}
\tag{15.19}
$$

Consumption-based pricing.   In the above discussion, we assumed that the prices of B and S are already given. In general, however, those prices should be endogenously determined by economic agents. Below, let us focus on how the prices are determined as a result of optimal consumption selections.

While a right price should be determined as an equilibrium outcome, an equilibrium model may be too complicated to analyze. Instead, it is often assumed in the literature that a market can be represented by one agent, implying that there is only one agent in the market. While this representative agent approach is far from complete, it greatly simplifies the analysis without losing important intuitions (see Cochrane, 2005; Lengwiler, 2006). Following this convention, we will focus on one individual's optimal selection.

At $t = 0$ individual i consumes some portion of his endowment wealth and invests the remaining wealth in a portfolio. At $t = 1$, he consumes the portfolio payoffs. We write δ for the discount factor. Let us assume that there are two securities B and X and that there are two states of nature at time 1. The endowment is W_i^0 at time 0. The individual's utility is denoted by U_i.

Let us denote individual i's portfolio as $Z_i = (z_{iB}, z_{iX})$. The wealth in state S at time 1 is denoted by $W_i(S) = z_{iB}B(S) + z_{iX}X(S)$. Then, the utility can be expressed as

$$
U_i(W_i(S)) = U_i(z_{iB}B(S) + z_{iX}X(S)).
$$

Our concern is the portfolio selection at $t = 0$. Given the budget constraint, $z_{iB}Q_B + z_{iX}Q_X = W_i^0$, individual i will solve the following portfolio selection problem

$$
\max\nolimits_{Zi,C_i^0} U_i(C_i^0) + \delta E U_i(W_i(S))
\tag{15.20}
$$

$$
\text{s.t. } z_{iB}Q_B + z_{iX}Q_X + C_i^0 = W_i^0,
$$

with first-order conditions (FOCs)

$$
\begin{aligned}
Lz_{iB} &= \delta E[U_i'(W_i(S))B(S)] - \lambda_i Q_B = 0, \\
Lz_{iX} &= \delta E[U_i'(W_i(S))X(S)] - \lambda_i Q_X = 0, \\
L_{C_i^0} &= U_i'(C_i^0) - \lambda_i = 0,
\end{aligned}
\tag{15.21}
$$

where λ_i is the Lagrange multiplier, leading to

$$\lambda_i Q_B = \delta[p(U)U_i'(W_i(U))B(U) + p(D)U_i'(W_i(D))B(D)],$$
$$\lambda_i Q_X = \delta[p(U)U_i'(W_i(U))X(U) + p(D)U_i'(W_i(D))X(D)].^1 \tag{15.22}$$

The state price can be expressed as follows. Recall that the price of any asset (or a portfolio) Y can be obtained by $Q_Y = q(U)Y(U) + q(D)Y(D)$. By comparing this with (15.22) we have

$$q(U) = \delta p(U)U_i'(W_i(U)) / \lambda_i, \quad q(D) = \delta p(D)U_i'(W_i(D)) / \lambda_i. \tag{15.23}$$

The stochastic discount factor is

$$m(U) = q(U)/p(U) = \delta U_i'(W_i(U)) / \lambda_i,$$
$$m(D) = \delta U_i'(W_i(D)) / \lambda_i. \tag{15.24}$$

Since $\lambda_i = U_i'(C_i^0)$ from the FOCs, we have
$m(U) = q(U)/p(U) = \delta U_i'(W_i(U))/U_i'(C_i^0), m(D) = \delta U_i'(W_i(D))/U_i'(C_i^0)$, for all i.
Succinctly,

$$m(S) = \delta U_i'(W_i(S)) / U_i'(C_i^0). \tag{15.25}$$

Recall that $1 = E(mR_Y)$. From this, we can derive an interesting pricing rule as follows:

$$1 = E(m)E(R_Y) + \text{cov}(m, R_Y), \quad \text{since cov}(m, R_Y) = E(mR_Y) - E(m)E(R_Y)$$

$$\Rightarrow E(R_Y) - 1/E(m) = -\text{cov}(m, R_Y)/E(m)$$
$$\Rightarrow E(R_Y) - R_f = -\text{cov}(m, R_Y)/E(m). \tag{15.26}$$

Using (15.25) and $E(m) = 1/R_f$, where $R_f \equiv 1 + r_f$,

$$E(R_Y) - R_f = -R_f \delta \text{cov}(U_i'(W_i), R_Y) / U_i'(C_i^0). \tag{15.27}$$

Or, using (15.25) and $E(m) = \delta E U_i'(W_i)/U_i'(C_i^0)$,

$$E(R_Y) - R_f = -\text{cov}(U_i'(W_i), R_Y) / EU_i'(W_i). \tag{15.28}$$

---

[1]   Although we are focused on one individual, this relationship should hold for any individual in the market if there is more than one individual. Thus, for $j \neq i$,

$$U_i'(W_i(U))/\lambda_i = U_j'(W_j(U))/\lambda_j,$$

$$U_i'(W_i(D))/\lambda_i = U_j'(W_j(D))/\lambda_j.$$

That is, the marginal utility from the additional payoff from a security normalized by the shadow price of the budget constraint should be equalized across individuals. In an equilibrium, the price levels will be adjusted to clear the market.

This relation, called the *consumption-based capital asset pricing model* (Breeden, 1979), implies that the risk premium of an asset (or a portfolio) is negatively related to the covariance between the marginal utility at $t = 1$ and the return of the asset. Note that higher wealth is associated with lower marginal utility under risk aversion. Therefore, the covariance becomes negative if the return of the asset is high when the wealth level is high. In such a case, the risk premium should be high, implying that the asset price should be low. For this, note that the asset contributes to the risk of total wealth. Such a risk increasing asset should pay a high risk premium in order for a risk averse individual to purchase the asset.

Now suppose that (W_i) can be expressed as $aR_M + b$, for some portfolio M, where a and b are constants. Then

$$E(R_Y) - R_f = -R_f \delta a \frac{\text{cov}(R_M, R_Y)}{U_i'(C_i^0)}.$$

For $Y = M$,

$$E(R_M) - R_f = -R_f \delta a \frac{\sigma_M^2}{U_i'(C_i^0)}, \quad \text{where } \sigma_M^2 = \text{var}(R_M).$$

Thus,

$$E(R_Y) - R_f = \beta_Y (E(R_M) - R_f), \quad \text{where } \beta_Y = \frac{\text{cov}(R_M, R_Y)}{\sigma_M^2}. \tag{15.29}$$

In terms of net return,

$$E(r_Y) - r_f = \beta_Y (E(r_M) - r_f). \tag{15.30}$$

This relation is called the *capital asset pricing model* (CAPM; Sharpe, 1964). In the CAPM, portfolio M, called the market portfolio, should include all assets with weights based on their market values in order to clear the market.

15.3   Financial Pricing of Insurance

15.3.1   Insurance CAPM

Insurance CAPM (ICAPM) can be derived using financial CAPM (15.30). Consider a one-period model in which the insurer receives the premium at the beginning of the period ($t = 0$) and pays for losses at the end of the period ($t = 1$). Let us decompose the net income of an insurer (π) into net investment income (I) and the net underwriting income (U).

$$\pi = I + U. \tag{15.31}$$

Here, the underwriting income U is the premium income net of losses and expenses, $U = Q - X$, where Q is the premium and X is the losses and expenses. An asset (A) is the sum of liabilities (or loss reserves, R) and equity (E):

$$A = R + E. \tag{15.32}$$

Let us define the rates of return r_A on the asset, r_E on the equity, and r_U on underwriting, where $r_U = (Q - X)/Q$. Since the investment income is earned on investment of the asset, $I = r_A A$. The underwriting income is $U = r_U Q$. Finally, the net income is $\pi = r_E E$.
Thus, (15.31) can be rewritten as

$$r_E E = r_A A + r_U Q. \tag{15.33}$$

Rearranging this equation leads to

$$r_E = r_A (A/E) + r_U (Q/E) = r_A (ks + 1) + r_U s, \tag{15.34}$$

where $k = R/Q$ is the liability to premium ratio (or funds generating factor) and

$s = Q/E$ is the premium to equity ratio.

Now let us take the expectation of (15.34) and replace Er_E and Er_A with the CAPM formulas

$$Er_E = r_f + \beta_E (Er_M - r_f),$$
$$Er_A = r_f + \beta_A (Er_M - r_f).$$

We have the following result.

Proposition 15.3 (ICAPM). The expected rate of return on underwriting is given by

$$Er_U = -kr_f + \beta_U (Er_M - r_f), \tag{15.35}$$

where $\beta_U = (1/s)\beta_E - \beta_A (k + 1/s)$.
    The ICAPM expresses the expected underwriting return as the sum of $-kr_f$ and $\beta_U (Er_M - r_f)$. The main difference between this and the usual CAPM is that the constant term is $-kr_f$, instead of r_f. For this, note first that the return r_U is defined in a different way from the usual portfolio returns, reflecting the fact that insurers receive premiums first and incur costs later. From the viewpoint of insureds, the rate of return is $r_{IN} = (X - Q)/Q$. Then

$r_{IN} = -r_U$. Thus, the insurance premium as present value of the insurance is $Q = E(X)/(1 + Er_{IN}) = E(X)/(1 - Er_U)$.

Second, why should the first term be $-kr_f$, instead of r_f? Suppose that the loss has no systematic risk, $\beta_U = 0$. Then $Er_U = -kr_f$. Note that insurers receive premiums at time 0 and pay the loss at time 1. Then, the insurers can invest the funds generated from premiums in the risk-free projects. The funds generated from premiums are measured by k. As a result, insurers will accept the loss of kr_f per dollar of earned premium, since they can make it up from fund investments.

The second term in the ICAPM is the usual CAPM term. Insurers should be compensated for bearing the systematic risk (β) of insurance. An increase in β_U will increase prices. For example, when the loss occurrence is negatively related to the market return, insurers assume higher risks when insuring the losses. As a result, the premium will go up.

While the ICAPM provides a simple intuitive model, it shares the same problems with the CAPM. First, the ICAPM is a one-period model, while many insurance products are long-term contracts. Second, the ICAPM ignores the insolvency risk. Third, insurance is not a traded asset, while the CAPM assumes that assets are tradable.

15.3.2   Present value model of insurance

A fundamental financial pricing model includes the present value (PV) model. The PV model is applied to insurance pricing by Myers and Cohn (1987) and Taylor (1994). From this approach, the price of an asset should reflect the present values of the cash flows that the asset generates. In a competitive market, the price should be determined such that the PV of cash outflows by owning the asset should be equal to PV of cash inflows from the asset. Unlike the ICAPM, the PV method can be applied to a multi-period case.

$$\text{PV(cash inflows)} - \text{PV(cash outflows)} = 0. \tag{15.36}$$

In the insurance case, cash inflows include premium and investment incomes, whereas cash outflows include the loss and expenses, and taxes. Specifically, the premium will satisfy

$$\text{PV(premiums)} = \text{PV(losses \& expenses)} + \text{PV(taxes)}. \tag{15.37}$$

The following discussion is based on Taylor (1994). We assume that premiums are received at the beginning of each period. Investment is also made at the beginnings of periods. Costs are incurred at the ends of periods. The time subscript t denotes the end of period t (or the beginning of period $t + 1$). Before we state our assumption, we require some notation. Let X_t be the losses and expenses at time t; Q_t the premium for period $t+1$; S_t the surplus (equity) at time t; R_t the liability (for loss payment) at time t; τ the tax rate both on the investment income and on the underwriting income; r_f the risk free rate or discount rate for premium; r_I the fair rate of return for losses and expenses; and r_A the fair rate of return for asset investment.

In this notation,

$$PV(\text{premiums}) = \sum_{t=1}^{T} \frac{Q_{t-1}}{(1+r_f)^{t-1}}, \tag{15.38}$$

$$PV(\text{losses and expenses}) = \sum_{t=1}^{T} \frac{E(X_t)}{(1+E(r_I))^t}. \tag{15.39}$$

For the PV of taxes, we need to first find the investment income and the underwriting income. Note that R_t can be written as

$$\begin{aligned} R_t &= \sum_{s=t}^{T} \frac{E(X_{s+1})}{(1+E(r_I))^{s+1-t}} - \sum_{s=t}^{T} \frac{Q_s}{(1+r_f)^{s-t}} \\ &= R_t^X - R_t^Q \end{aligned} \tag{15.40}$$

Note that

$$(1+r_I)R_t^X = X_{t+1} + R_{t+1}^X, \tag{15.41}$$

$$(1+r_f)R_t^Q = (1+r_f)Q_t + R_{t+1}^Q. \tag{15.42}$$

The gross investment income in period t is

$$(1+r_A)A_{t-1} \text{ where } A_{t-1} = S_{t-1} + R_{t-1} + Q_{t-1}.^2 \tag{15.43}$$

The underwriting income in period t can be written as

$$U_t = Q_{t-1} - X_t + R_{t-1} - R_t, \tag{15.44}$$

Using (15.41) and (15.42), we have

$$U_t = -r_I R_{t-1}^X + r_f(R_{t-1}^Q - Q_{t-1}) \tag{15.45}$$

Now, the tax costs at time t is the tax at time t, $\tau(r_A A_{t-1} + U_t)$. Thus,

$$PV(\text{tax at time } t) = PV[\tau(r_A A_{t-1} + U_t)]. \tag{15.46}$$

---

² Note that Q_{t-1} is the premium for period t, which is received at the beginning of period t.

Now our next question is how to calculate PV of tax. Let us first state the following useful result which is often called the Myers theorem.

Lemma 15.1 (Myers theorem). The PV of tax on the risky investment return is equal to the PV of tax on the risk-free investment.

Proof

$$PV(\text{tax on investment income on } \$1) = \tau PV(1 + r_A - 1) = \tau[PV(1 + r_A) - PV(1)]$$
$$= \tau(1 - 1/(1 + r_f)) = \tau r_f/(1 + r_f). \qquad \Box$$

The Myers theorem implies that, for the purpose of PV of tax, we can consider the investment as the risk-free investment. Using the Myers theorem and (15.43),

$$PV(\text{tax at } t) = \tau \left[\frac{r_f(S_{t-1} + R^X_{t-1})}{(1 + r_f)^t} - \frac{E(r_I)R^X_{t-1}}{(1 + E(r_I))^t} \right]. \tag{15.47}$$

We then have the following result.

Proposition 15.4 (Insurance premium by PV). The PV of premiums should be determined by

$$\sum_{t=1}^{T} \frac{Q_{t-1}}{(1 + r_f)^{t-1}} = \sum_{t=1}^{T} \frac{E(X_t)}{(1 + E(r_I))^t} + \tau \sum_{t=1}^{T} \left[\frac{r_f(S_{t-1} + R^X_{t-1})}{(1 + r_f)^t} - \frac{E(r_I)R^X_{t-1}}{(1 + E(r_I))^t} \right],$$

where S_{t-1}, R^X_{t-1} and R^Q_{t-1} are evaluated at time 0.

The PV method overcomes the criticism of the one-period ICAPM. The PV method can incorporate diverse cash flows as needed. However, unlike the ICAPM, the PV methods do not say what the fair return on underwriting $E(r_I)$ should be. In this case, the ICAPM can be used to find $E(r_I)$. One important weakness of both the ICAPM and the PV method is that the insolvency risk is not properly considered in the model.

15.3.3 Option pricing model of insurance

Consider the following one-period setting. Insurance, I, is traded at time 0. As an exchange of premium, insurance I will cover the random loss that occurs at time 1. At time 1, the random loss and the random asset value of the insurer are realized. At time 1, the random loss X_1 can be either 0 or X;

and the random asset value V_1 can be V or L, where $V > X > L$. That is, there are four states of nature at time 1:

S_1: $X_1 = 0$ and $V_1 = V$;
S_2: $X_1 = 0$ and $V_1 = L$;
S_3: $X_1 = X$ and $V_1 = V$;
S_4: $X_1 = X$ and $V_1 = L$.

Note that in state S_4, the insurer becomes insolvent. The insured receives L which is less than X. The insurance contract, I, provides payoffs 0, 0, X, and L in each state. From the state pricing theory in Section 15.2, given state prices $\{q_i\}$, the insurance price can be written as

$$Q(I) = q_1 0 + q_2 0 + q_3 X + q_4 L = q_3 X + q_4 L. \tag{15.48}$$

By the risk-neutral pricing of Section 15.2, we have that

$$Q(I) = E_q(I)/(1 + r_f),$$

where $q_1 + q_2 + q_3 + q_4 = 1/(1 + r_f)$, $q_i' = (1 + r_f)q_i$.

This state pricing method can incorporate insurer's insolvency risk into pricing. To see this more clearly, let us decompose insurance payoffs as follows:

$$\text{Payoff}(I) = X_1 - \max [X_1 - V_1, 0], \tag{15.49}$$

where $X_1 = 0$ or X, $V_1 = V$ or L. The first term on the right-hand side, X_1, denotes the loss amount assuming that there is no insolvency. The second term, $\max [X_1 - V_1, 0]$, is the payoff of a put option such that X_1 is the exercise price and V_1 is the underlying asset price. This put option is often called an insolvency put option (or a default put option) from the viewpoint of owners of the insurer. That this put option is subtracted implies that insureds short the put option. In case of insolvency, the insureds will lose as much as the payoff of the insolvency put option.

The price of the insurance is thus

$$Q(I) = PV(X_1) - PV(\max[X_1 - V_1, 0])$$
$$= (q_3 + q_4)X - q_4(X - L) = q_3 X + q_4 L. \tag{15.50}$$

Thus, we retrieve (15.48).

In this approach, the insurance premium can be expressed as the value under no insolvency risk net of the insolvency put option value. Intuitively, the premium that insureds are willing to pay should be reduced as much as the costs due to the insolvency risk.

Modern finance provides the option pricing model in a continuous time setting, using a set of mathematical techniques of stochastic calculus. Once we find the insolvency put option value, the insurance premium can be obtained by subtracting the put option value from the value under no insolvency risk. Since the technical details of the option pricing are beyond our scope, let us simply report a basic result of the option pricing approach. The following result is from Cummins (1988).

At time t, insurance is traded. A random loss will occur at time T. Both the loss development and the insurer's asset value follow geometric Brownian motion processes. The instantaneous correlation between two Brownian motions is ρ. That is,

$$\frac{dX_t}{X_t} = \mu_X dt + \sigma_X dW_t^1,$$

$$\frac{dA_t}{A_t} = \mu_A dt + \sigma_A dW_t^2, \tag{15.51}$$

$$dW_t^1 \cdot dW_t^2 = \rho dt.$$

Proposition 15.5 (Insurance premium by option pricing). Under the assumptions in the text above, the insurance premium at time t is obtained as follows:

$$Q_t(I) = X_t e^{-(r_f - r_X)(T-t)} - [-A_t N(-d_1) + X_t e^{-r_f(T-t)} N(-d_2)], \tag{15.52}$$

where

$$d_1 = \frac{\log(A_t / X_t) + \frac{1}{2}\sigma^2(T-t)}{\sigma\sqrt{T-t}},$$

$$d_2 = d_1 - \sigma\sqrt{T-t},$$

$$\sigma = \sigma_A^2 + \sigma_X^2 - 2\sigma_A\sigma_X\rho,$$

$$r_X = \mu_X - \pi,$$

where π is the risk premium for bearing insurance risk (which can be negative).

Proof Omitted.   □

Although the option approach considers the insolvency risk, there are several problems with this approach. First, the standard (European) option approach assumes that the loss occurs at a fixed time. However, a loss can occur at any time, in which case the American option approach is more appropriate. The option approach assumes the return is lognormally distributed, which is not necessarily true for a loss development. Moreover, the option pricing is not accurate for a long-term contract like insurance. Insurance may also exhibit very complicated features, such as surrender and lapses. Like other financial pricing approaches, the option pricing approach suffers from the fact that insurance is not tradable in the secondary market. In addition, it is not clear how the insolvency put option value should be allocated to insurance lines, where the insurer operates in multiple lines. The option pricing approach seems more suitable to the total insureds' value, rather than to individual insurance pricing. Recently, insolvency risk allocation methods have been developed in the literature (see Cummins 2000; Denault, 2001; Merton and Perold, 1993; Myers and Read, 2001; Powers, 2007; Seog and Shin, 2008).

15.4   Conclusion

The development of actuarial science and financial pricing models has provided useful techniques and intuitions for determining insurance pricing. Traditionally, the focus of insurance pricing has been on the characterization of the loss distribution. While knowledge of the loss distribution is important, insurance pricing is also affected by the financial market. Therefore, it is a natural outcome that the actuarial science approach is combined with the financial pricing approach. However, the complexity of the insurance contract remains a challenge in achieving accurate pricing.

BIBLIOGRAPHY

Biger, N. and Y. Kahane (1978) Risk considerations in insurance ratemaking. *Journal of Risk and Insurance*, 45: 121–32.
Breeden, D. T. (1979) An intertemporal asset pricing model with stochastic consumption and investment opportunities. *Journal of Financial Economics*, 7: 265–96.
Cochrane, J. H. (2005) *Asset Pricing*, revised edition. Princeton, NJ: Princeton University Press.
Cummins, J. D. (1988) Risk-based premiums for insurance guaranty funds. *Journal of Finance*, 43: 823–39.
Cummins, J. D. (1990) Multi-period discounted cash flow ratemaking models in property-liability insurance. *Journal of Risk and Insurance* 57: 79–109.

Cummins, J. D. (2000) Allocation of capital in the insurance industry. *Risk Management and Insurance Review*, 3: 7–27.

Cummins, J. D. and H. Geman (1995) Pricing catastrophe insurance futures and call spreads: an arbitrage approach. *Journal of Fixed Income*, 4: 46–57.

Cummins, J. D. and S. E. Harrington (1987) *Fair Rate of Return in Property-Liability Insurance*. Boston: Kluwer Academic Publishers.

Cummins, J. D. and R. D. Phillips (2000) Applications of financial pricing models in property-liability insurance. In G. Dionne (ed.), *Handbook of Insurance*. Boston: Kluwer Academic Publishers.

D'Arcy, S. P. and N. A. Doherty (1990) Adverse selection, private information, and lowballing in insurance markets. *Journal of Business*, 63: 145–61.

D'Arcy, S. P. and J. R. Garven (1990) Property-liability insurance pricing models: an empirical evaluation. *Journal of Risk and Insurance*, 57: 391–430.

Demange, G. and G. Laroque (2006) *Finance and the Economics of Uncertainty*. Oxford: Blackwell Publishing Co.

Denault, M. (2001) Coherent allocation of risk capital. *Journal of Risk*, 4: 1–34.

Derrig, R. A. (1994) Theoretical considerations of the effect of federal income taxes on investment income in property-liability ratemaking. *Journal of Risk and Insurance*, 61: 691–709.

Doherty, N. A and J. Garven (1986) Price regulation in property/liability insurance: a contingent claims approach. *Journal of Finance*, 41: 1031–50.

Fairley, W. (1979) Investment income and profit margins in property-liability insurance: theory and empirical tests. *Bell Journal of Economics*, 10: 192–210.

Geske, R. (1977) The valuation of corporate liabilities as compound options. *Journal of Financial and Quantitative Analysis*, 12: 541–52.

Geske, R. (1979) The valuation of compound options. *Journal of Financial Economics*, 7: 63–81.

Hill, R. (1979) Profit regulation in property-liability insurance. *Bell Journal of Economics*, 10: 172–91.

Kraus, A. and S. Ross (1982) The determination of fair profits for the property-liability insurance firm. *Journal of Finance*, 33: 1015–28.

Lengwiler, Y. (2006) *Microfoundations of Financial Economics*. Princeton, NJ: Princeton University Press.

Merton, R. C. and A. F. Perold (1993) Theory of risk capital in financial firms. *Journal of Applied Corporate Finance*, 6: 16–32.

Myers, S. and R. Cohn (1987) Insurance rate regulation and the capital asset pricing model. In J. D. Cummins and S. E. Harrington (eds), *Fair Rate of Return in Property-Liability Insurance*. Boston: Kluwer Academic Publishers.

Myers, S. C. and J. A. Read, Jr. (2001) Capital allocation for insurance companies. *Journal of Risk and Insurance*, 68: 545–80.

Panjer, H. H. and G. E. Willmot (1992) *Insurance Risk Models*. Schaumburg, IL: Society of Actuaries.

Phillips, R. D., J. D. Cummins, and F. Allen (1998) Financial pricing of insurance in the multiple line insurance company. *Journal of Risk and Insurance*, 65: 597–636.

Powers, M. R. (2007) Using Aumann-Shapley values to allocate insurance risk: the case of inhomogeneous losses. *North American Actuarial Journal*, 11(3): 113–27.

Seog, S. H. and S. Shin (2008) Comparison between the financial theory and the cooperative game theory in risk capital allocation. KAIST Business School Working Paper.

Sharpe, W. F. (1964) Capital asset prices: a theory of market equilibrium under conditions of risk. *Journal of Finance*, 19: 425–42.

Shimko, D. C. (1992) The valuation of multiple claim insurance contracts. *Journal of Financial and Quantitative Analysis*, 27: 229–46.

Sommer, D. W. (1996) The impact of firm risk on property-liability insurance prices. *Journal of Risk and Insurance*, 63: 501–14.

Taylor, G. (1994) Fair premium rating methods and the relations between them. *Journal of Risk and Insurance*, 61: 592–615.

Appendix

Optimization of Real Valued Function with Constraints

A.1 General Optimization Technique

Many economic problems are expressed as optimization problems with constraints. In this appendix, we briefly review the techniques for solving such optimization problems. This problem can be stated as follows:

Program 1 (Maximization with inequality constraints)

$$\max_{\{x\}} \quad f(x)$$

s.t. $\quad g_i(x) \leq 0, i = 1, \ldots, m$

where x is a vector in R^n, and $f(x)$ and $g_i(x)$ are differentiable functions from R^n to R. The $g_i(x)$ represent constraints, such as budget constraints, resource constraints, and information constraints. The solution to the program should maximize $f(x)$, while satisfying constraints $g_i(x) \leq 0$, for all i. To solve the program, define the Lagrangian as

$$L = f(x) - \Sigma \lambda_i g_i(x),$$

where λ_i is a constant attached to each constraint, which is called a Lagrange multiplier.

Theorem 1 (Necessary conditions: Kuhn–Tucker conditions). Suppose that all binding constraints are independent.[1] If x^* solves Program A.1,

---

[1] Binding constraints are independent if gradient vectors, $\nabla g_i = [\partial g_i(x^*)/\partial x_1, \ldots, \partial g_i(x^*)/\partial x_n]'$, of binding constraints are linearly independent. If not, at least one of the binding constraints is redundant.

then there exist nonnegative Lagrange multipliers ($\lambda_i \geq 0$) for all i, which satisfy the following conditions:

First-order condition (FOC)

$\partial L/\partial x_j = \partial f(x^*)/\partial x_j - \Sigma\, \lambda_i(\partial g_i(x^*)/\, \partial x_j) = 0$,
  for each variable x_j, $j = 1, \ldots, n$.

Complementary-slackness condition (CSC): $\lambda_i g_i(x^*) = 0$, $g_i(x^*) \leq 0$, $i = 1, \ldots, m$.

Proof See Kuhn and Tucker (1951) and Luenberger (1973). □

Theorem 1 presents the first-order conditions for a local maximum. To guarantee that $f(x^*)$ is a local maximum, the second-order condition should also be satisfied. Let B the set of independent binding constraints. Now, define the Hessian matrix of L as

$$D^2 L(x) = \begin{pmatrix} \dfrac{\partial^2 f(x)}{\partial x_1^2} - \displaystyle\sum_{i \in B} \lambda_i \dfrac{\partial^2 g_i(x)}{\partial x_1^2}, & \cdots & \dfrac{\partial^2 f(x)}{\partial x_1 \partial x_j} - \displaystyle\sum_{i \in B} \lambda_i \dfrac{\partial^2 g_i(x)}{\partial x_1 \partial x_j}, & \cdots & \dfrac{\partial^2 f(x)}{\partial x_1 \partial x_n} - \displaystyle\sum_{i \in B} \lambda_i \dfrac{\partial^2 g_i(x)}{\partial x_1 \partial x_n} \\[2ex] \vdots & \ddots & \vdots & \ddots & \vdots \\[1ex] \dfrac{\partial^2 f(x)}{\partial x_j \partial x_1} - \displaystyle\sum_{i \in B} \lambda_i \dfrac{\partial^2 g_i(x)}{\partial x_j \partial x_1}, & \cdots & \dfrac{\partial^2 f(x)}{\partial x_j^2} - \displaystyle\sum_{i \in B} \lambda_i \dfrac{\partial^2 g_i(x)}{\partial x_j^2}, & \cdots & \dfrac{\partial^2 f(x)}{\partial x_j \partial x_n} - \displaystyle\sum_{i \in B} \lambda_i \dfrac{\partial^2 g_i(x)}{\partial x_j \partial x_n} \\[2ex] \vdots & \ddots & \vdots & \ddots & \vdots \\[1ex] \dfrac{\partial^2 f(x)}{\partial x_n \partial x_1} - \displaystyle\sum_{i \in B} \lambda_i \dfrac{\partial^2 g_i(x)}{\partial x_n \partial x_1}, & \cdots & \dfrac{\partial^2 f(x)}{\partial x_n \partial x_j} - \displaystyle\sum_{i \in B} \lambda_i \dfrac{\partial^2 g_i(x)}{\partial x_n \partial x_j}, & \cdots & \dfrac{\partial^2 f(x)}{\partial x_n^2} - \displaystyle\sum_{i \in B} \lambda_i \dfrac{\partial^2 g_i(x)}{\partial x_n^2} \end{pmatrix}$$

or more compactly,

$$D^2 L(x) = D^2 f(x) - \sum_{i \in B} \lambda_i D^2 g_i(x).$$

If $f(x^*)$ is to be a local maximum, $D^2 L(x^*)$ should be negative semidefinite on the constraint surface $\{h \in R^n: \nabla g_i(x^*) \cdot h = 0\}$.[2] If $D^2(x^*)$ is negative definite on the constraint surface, $f(x^*)$ is a strictly local maximum.

We present steps that help to find a solution that satisfies the Kuhn–Tucker conditions as follows.

Step 1: Construct an optimization program

$\max_{\{x\}} f(x)$
s.t. $g_i(x) \leq 0$, $i = 1, \ldots, m$.

---

[2] A symmetric matrix H is *negative semidefinite*, when $x'Hx \leq 0$ holds for all vectors x. A symmetric matrix H is *negative definite*, when $x'Hx < 0$ holds for all nonzero vectors x.

Step 2: Define the Lagrangian with Lagrange multipliers attached to constraints:

$$L = f(x) - \Sigma \lambda_i g_i(x).$$

Step 3: Write down the FOC for each variable x_j, $j = 1, \ldots, n$:

$$\partial L / \partial x_j = \partial f(x) / \partial x_j - \Sigma \lambda_i (\partial g_i(x) / \partial x_j) = 0.$$

Step 4: Write down the CSC for each Lagrange multiplier:

$$\lambda_i g_i(x) = 0, \ i = 1, \ldots, m.$$

Step 5: Identify all possible combinations of CSCs. There are two possibilities for each Lagrange multiplier:

(i) $\lambda_i > 0$, $g_i(x) = 0$;
(ii) $\lambda_i = 0$, $g_i(x) \le 0$.

Case (ii) is considered a non-binding case.[3] Therefore, we have 2^m possible cases, for there are m constraints.

Step 6: For each case of CSC combinations, solve the FOC. Repeat the process for all cases. This is a trial-and-error procedure. A case should be eliminated when any inconsistency is found. You may save time and effort by excluding some cases based on intuition and available information.

Example 1 (Illustration of steps). Suppose that we need to maximize $f(x_1, x_2) = 2x_2 - x_1$, given constraint $x_1 + x_2 \le 4$. Each variable x_i is also required to be nonnegative.

Step 1: Construct an optimization program:

$$\text{Max}_{\{x_1, x_2\}} \ f(x_1, x_2) = 2x_2 - x_1$$
$$\text{s.t.} \quad x_1 + x_2 \le 4$$
$$x_1 \ge 0$$
$$x_2 \ge 0.$$

Step 1′: Rewrite the program in the standard form:

$$\text{Max}_{\{x_1, x_2\}} \ 2x_2 - x_1$$
$$\text{s.t.} \quad x_1 + x_2 - 4 \le 0$$
$$-x_1 \le 0$$
$$-x_2 \le 0.$$

Step 2: Define the Lagrangian:

$$L = 2x_2 - x_1 - \lambda_1 (x_1 + x_2 - 4) + \lambda_2 x_1 + \lambda_3 x_2.$$

---

[3]   Case (ii) includes the case in which $\lambda_i = 0$ and $g_i(x) = 0$ at the edge.

Step 3: Write down the FOC for each variable:

$$L_1 = -1 - \lambda_1 + \lambda_2 = 0$$
$$L_2 = 2 - \lambda_1 + \lambda_3 = 0.$$

Step 4: Write down the CSC for each Lagrange multiplier:

$$\lambda_1 (x_1 + x_2 - 4) = 0$$
$$\lambda_2 x_1 = 0$$
$$\lambda_3 x_2 = 0.$$

Step 5: Identify all possible combinations of CSCs:

C1: $\lambda_1 = 0, \lambda_2 = 0, \lambda_3 = 0$
C2: $\lambda_1 = 0, \lambda_2 = 0, \lambda_3 > 0$
C3: $\lambda_1 = 0, \lambda_2 > 0, \lambda_3 = 0$
C4: $\lambda_1 = 0, \lambda_2 > 0, \lambda_3 > 0$
C5: $\lambda_1 > 0, \lambda_2 = 0, \lambda_3 = 0$
C6: $\lambda_1 > 0, \lambda_2 = 0, \lambda_3 > 0$
C7: $\lambda_1 > 0, \lambda_2 > 0, \lambda_3 = 0$
C8: $\lambda_1 > 0, \lambda_2 > 0, \lambda_3 > 0.$

Step 6: For each CSC combination, solve the FOC.

First, we can exclude C1, C2, C3 and C5 by FOCs in step 3, which requires that at least two Lagrange multipliers be positive.

Second, let us solve the FOCs for each remaining case.

C4: From FOCs in step 3, $\lambda_2 = 1$, $\lambda_3 = -3 < 0$. A contradiction.
C6: From FOCs in step 3, $\lambda_1 = -1 < 0$. A contradiction.
C8: From CSCs in step 4, we should have $x_1 + x_2 = 4$, $x_1 = 0$, and $x_2 = 0$. A contradiction.

C7: From FOCs in step 3, $\lambda_1 = 2$, $\lambda_2 = 3$. From CSCs, we have a unique solution: $x_1^* = 0$, $x_2^* = 4$. The objective function becomes $f(x_1^*, x_2^*) = 8$.

If a solution is obtained at the boundary of the feasible set, then it is called a corner solution. Otherwise, it is called an interior solution. In Example 1, $x_1^* (= 0)$ is a corner solution, and $x_2^* (= 4)$ is an interior solution.

Example 2 (Optimization with bound constraints).

$$\max_{\{x\}} f(x)$$
s.t $\quad x_{min} \leq x \leq x_{max}$, where $x_{min} < x_{max}$.

The constraint can be rearranged into two constraints as follows.

$$x - x_{max} \leq 0$$
$$x_{min} - x \leq 0.$$

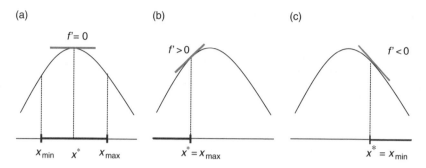

Figure A.1   Optimization with bound constraints: (a) case 1; (b) case 2; (c) case 3

The Lagrangian and FOCs are as follows:

$$L(x) = f(x) - \lambda_{max}(x - x_{max}) - \lambda_{min}(x_{min} - x)$$
$$\text{FOC: } dL/dx = df/dx - \lambda_{max} + \lambda_{min} = 0$$
$$\text{CSC: } \lambda_{max}(x - x_{max}) = 0, \lambda_{min}(x_{min} - x) = 0.$$

Combining the FOC and CSCs, three cases are possible (see Figure A.1).

Case 1: $\lambda_{max} = 0, \lambda_{min} = 0$.
   We have $x_{min} \leq x^* \leq x_{max}$; and $df(x^*)/dx = 0$.

Case 2: $\lambda_{max} > 0, \lambda_{min} = 0$.
   We have $x^* = x_{max}$; and $df(x^*)/dx > 0$.

Case 3: $\lambda_{max} = 0, \lambda_{min} > 0$.
   We have $x^* = x_{min}$; and $df(x^*)/dx < 0$.

Note that the case of $\lambda_{max} > 0$ and $\lambda_{min} > 0$ is not possible, since $x_{min} < x_{max}$.

A.2   Optimization with Nonnegativity Constraints

In many economic applications, it is often required that the variables be nonnegative: $x_j \geq 0, j = 1, \ldots, n$. We may solve the problem as in Program A.1. That is, the Lagrangian, FOCs and CSCs are as follows.

$$L = f(x) - \Sigma \lambda_i g_i(x) + \Sigma \delta_j x_j$$
$$\text{FOC: } \partial L(x^*)/\partial x_j = 0, j = 1, \ldots, n$$
$$\text{CSC: } \lambda_i g_i(x^*) = 0, i = 1, \ldots, m$$
$$\delta_j x_j^* = 0, j = 1, \ldots, n.$$

Here, the number of Lagrange multipliers is $m + n$. Now, using the idea of Example 2, we can simplify the procedure to solve the problem.

Program A.2 (Maximization with nonnegativity constraints)

$\max_{\{x\}} f(x)$
s.t $g_i(x) \le 0, i = 1,\ldots, m$
      $x_j \ge 0, j = 1,\ldots, n.$

First, construct the Lagrangian, ignoring the nonnegativity constraints:
$L = f(x) - \Sigma \lambda_i g_i(x).$

Second, write down the CSCs regarding constraints $g_i(x) \le 0$:

$\lambda_i g_i(x^*) = 0, i = 1, \ldots, m.$

Third, write down the modified FOCs for each x_j, which take into account the nonnegativity constraints:

$[\partial L(x^*)/\partial x_j] x_j^* = 0, j = 1,\ldots, n$
$\partial L(x^*)/\partial x_j \le 0$
$x_j^* \ge 0.$

The modified FOCs can be classified into two cases:

Case 1: $x_j^* > 0, \partial L(x^*)/\partial x_j = 0.$

Case 2: $x_j^* = 0, \partial L(x^*)/\partial x_j \le 0.$

The idea of these modified FOCs is similar to that of the CSCs for Lagrange multipliers. By comparing Program A.2 with Program A.1, the two cases correspond to the following cases from Program A.1.

Case 1′: $\partial[f(x^*) - \Sigma \lambda_i g_i(x^*)]/\partial x_j + \delta_j = 0,$
        $x_j^* > 0, \delta_j = 0.$
Case 2′: $\partial[f(x^*) - \Sigma \lambda_i g_i(x^*)]/\partial x_j + \delta_j = 0,$
        $x_j^* = 0, \delta_j \ge 0.$

A.3   Optimization with Equality Constraints

Now let us consider the program including equality constraints.

Program A.3 (Maximization with equality constraints)

$\max_{\{x\}} f(x)$
s.t $g_i(x) = 0, i = 1,\ldots, e$
      $g_i(x) \le 0, i = e+1, \ldots, m.$

We can solve this program using the Kuhn–Tucker method described in Section A.1. The procedure becomes simpler, since we do not need to check for the non-binding constraint cases for $i = 1,\ldots, e$ in step 5. On the other hand, the Lagrange multipliers for the equality constraints may be either nonnegative or negative.

A.4   Interpretation of Lagrange Multiplier

Let us consider the maximization problem with a constraint as follows:

max $f(x)$
s.t $G_i(x) = B_i, i = 1, \ldots, m$

where B_i is a constant.[4] In economics, B_i is often interpreted as a budget (resource) limit. Given this interpretation, the program seeks optimal consumption (resource allocation) given the budget (resource) limits. Note that B_i is exogenously given, and is not a decision variable.

This program can be rewritten in the standard form as

max $f(x)$
s.t $g_i(x; B_i) = 0,$

where $g_i(x; B_i) = G_i(x) - B_i$.

From the FOC,

$$\partial f(x)/\partial x_j - \Sigma_i \lambda_i \partial G_i(x)/\partial x_j = 0.$$

Now, let $F(B)$ be the maximized $f(x)$ of the above program: that is, $F(B) = f(x^*(B))$, where $B = (B_1, \ldots, B_m)'$. Now, let us slightly increase B_k, for some k:

$$\partial F(B)/\partial B_k = \Sigma_j \{\partial f(x^*(B))/\partial x_j\} \partial x_j(B)/\partial B_k.$$

From the FOC,

$$\partial F(B)/\partial B_k = \Sigma_j \Sigma_i \{\lambda_i \partial G_i(x^*(B))/\partial x_j\} \partial x_j(B)/\partial B_k.$$

Since $G_i(x^*(B)) = B_i$, where the B_i are fixed except for B_k,

$$\Sigma_j \{\partial G_i(x^*(B))/\partial x_j\} \partial x_j(B)/\partial B_k = 0, \quad \text{for } i \neq k,$$
$$\Sigma_j \{\partial G_k(x^*(B))/\partial x_j\} \partial x_j(B)/\partial B_k = 1.$$

---

[4]   Note that we do not assume that the problem should be with all equality constraints. We simply focus on the binding constraints.

Thus,

$$\partial F(B)/\partial B_k = \lambda_k.$$

This result implies that a Lagrange multiplier can be interpreted as the marginal contribution of the corresponding resource to the objective function. In this sense, a Lagrange multiplier is often called a shadow price.

BIBLIOGRAPHY

Kuhn, H. and Tucker, A. W. (1951) Nonlinear programming. In J. Neyman (ed.), *Proceedings of the Second Berkeley Symposium on Mathematical Statistics and Probability* (pp. 481–92). Berkeley: University of California Press

Luenberger, D. G. (1973) *Introduction to Linear and Nonlinear Programming.* New York: John Wiley & Sons, Inc.

Index